Chełmno

and the

Holocaust

Chełmno

and the

Holocaust

The History of Hitler's
First Death Camp

Patrick Montague

Foreword by Christopher R. Browning

The University of North Carolina Press
Chapel Hill

First published by I.B.Tauris & Co Ltd in the United Kingdom

ISBN: 978-0-8078-3527-2

A full CIP record for this book is available from the Library of Congress.

Typeset in Palatino by MPS Limited, a Macmillan Company
Printed and bound in Great Britain by CPI Group (UK) Ltd, Croydon, CR0 4YY

16 15 14 13 12   5 4 3 2 1

This book is dedicated to all the men, women and children who labored and who died in the Chełmno death camp; may they never be forgotten.

Contents

List of Illustrations

List of Maps

Acknowledgments

This book is the result of a project that eventually stretched over a 20 year period. So many people intersected with this work over the years that it is truly impossible to name them all. A sincere thank you seems less than adequate. Others who cannot go unnamed and whom I want to acknowledge and thank here are as follows:

The University of Kansas and specifically Professor Anna Cienciala for her professionalism, wisdom and encouragement. The Fulbright Program for acknowledging the importance of pursuing this topic and its generous support. The staffs of all of the institutions and archives cited within the pages of this book. I was always treated professionally and courteously. I am especially grateful to the Institute of National Remembrance (IPN) in Warsaw and Poznań (Agata Gut), the Jewish Historical Institute in Warsaw (Ruta Sakowska, Jan Jagielski), the Central Office of the State Justice Administration for the Investigation of National Socialist Crimes in Ludwigsburg (Willi Dressen) as well as the United States Holocaust Memorial Museum in Washington, D.C. (Benton Arnovitz).

Anna Wiszniewska for her generosity in unselfishly devoting her time to the laborious task of assisting in the translation and verification of numerous documents. Przemysław Nowicki for his knowledge of local Polish history and pointing me in directions I wouldn't have gone without his assistance. Łucja Pawlicka-Nowak and Zdzisław Lorek from the Chełmno branch of the District Museum in Konin, Poland, for their professional and personal devotion to the topic of this book and willingness to share their knowledge of the intricacies of the camp. Christopher Browning from the University of North Carolina at Chapel Hill for agreeing to read and share his thoughts on the manuscript and for his encouragement to see the project through to its completion. Naphtali Lau-Lavie for sharing his recollections of the war and his personal knowledge and involvement in saving the lives of two men who desperately needed a friend. Szymon and Hava Srebrnik for their gracious hospitality, remarkable patience and fortitude while recounting horrific events. The Widawski family in Belgium and Israel for responding so openly to a stranger with so many personal questions. Sara Roy for sharing so much of her time and family history, for her encouragement and belief in the value of this project and for her efforts in ensuring the results of my endeavor will be available to future generations.

While many individuals contributed in various ways to this book, I bear sole responsibility for any shortcomings and deficiencies that remain within these pages.

Patrick Montague

Foreword

The small Polish village of Chełmno was the site of the first Nazi death camp, which unlike the larger and better known death camps that followed—Bełżec, Sobibór, Treblinka, Auschwitz-Birkenau and Majdanek—used mobile gas vans rather than stationary gas chambers. What has been known about the Chełmno camp until now in mainstream Western and Israeli Holocaust scholarship stems mostly from the investigation and trial of 12 defendants in Bonn in 1962–63. Invaluable as that investigation and trial were as a source of historical knowledge by virtue of the numerous judicial interrogations and interviews that it produced and preserved, its main purpose was to provide evidence and reach judgment concerning the actions of specific defendants, not to write a comprehensive history of the camp. But for historians without knowledge of the Polish language or access to Polish archives at the height of the Cold War, the trial records were the best source with which they had to work. What we now know, thanks to the meticulous and exhaustive research conducted by Patrick Montague, is that great quantities of vital evidence concerning Chełmno were also stored in Polish archives but had never been sufficiently accessed, examined and incorporated into Holocaust scholarship. The full incorporation of this vital evidence from Polish archives into our historical knowledge of the Chełmno death camp is one of the major achievements of Patrick Montague's book.

Equally important, Patrick Montague has written a book that allows the reader to hear the multiple voices of witnesses who experienced the camp in one way or another. In addition to the chilling testimonies of perpetrators taken for postwar trials, the reader encounters the vivid accounts of others: Heinz May, the German forester who supervised the land that became the site of the death camp's mass graves and crematoria; various Polish villagers, as well as Henryk Mania and Henryk Maliczak, Polish prisoners of the Germans who temporarily ascended to a position of privileged collaborators at Chełmno before descending to the position of victim prisoners at Mauthausen; and above all the harrowing accounts of four escapees, Szlama Winer, Mordechai Żurawski, Michał Podchlebnik and Szymon Srebrnik—the latter two now known to those who have seen Claude Lanzmann's film *Shoah*.

Historical scholarship is a collective endeavor that builds on past achievements and grows as each historian adds his or her own contribution to the pool of knowledge. Thanks to Patrick Montague, what we now know about the Chełmno death camp is significantly greater than before.

Christopher R. Browning
Frank Porter Graham Professor of History
University of North Carolina at Chapel Hill

Map 1. Reichsgau Wartheland

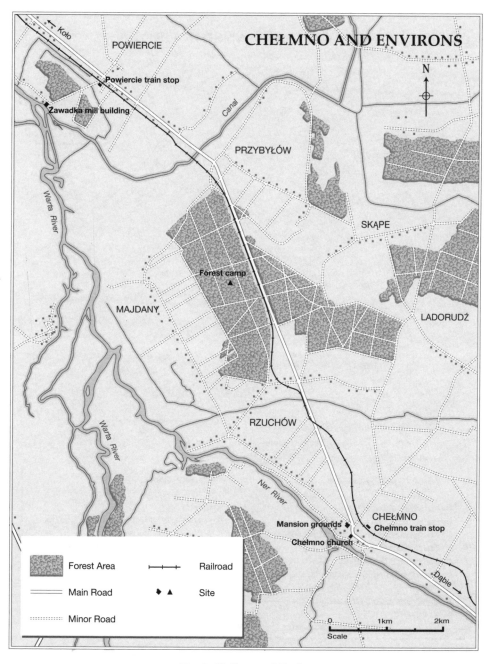

Map 2. Chełmno and Environs

CHEŁMNO VILLAGE AND MANSION GROUNDS

N

0   50m   100m
Scale

Forest Camp and Koło

Rzuchów and Majdany

Koło

Ladorudz

Narrow gauge train tracks

Dąbie

Perimeter fence

CHEŁMNO

Ner River

Dąbie and Łódź

Based on Zdzisław Lorek map

INSIDE CAMP PERIMETER	OUTSIDE CAMP PERIMETER
1 Mansion (1st period)	A Church
1a Ramp to gas van (1st period)	B Headquarters (local government building)
2 Courtyard wooden fence* (1st period)	C Administration (church rectory)
3 Grainary building	D Police quarters (volunteer fire department)
4 Sorting tent* (2nd period)	E Canteen (Banaszewski house)
5 Storage building/Burmeister office* (2nd period)	F Mess hall (Krzyżanowski house)
6 Garage	G School house
7 Shredding station* (2nd period)	H Train stop
8 Well	

* Location approximate   --- Fence   o Pits for burning victims' belongings

Map 3. Chełmno Village and Mansion Grounds

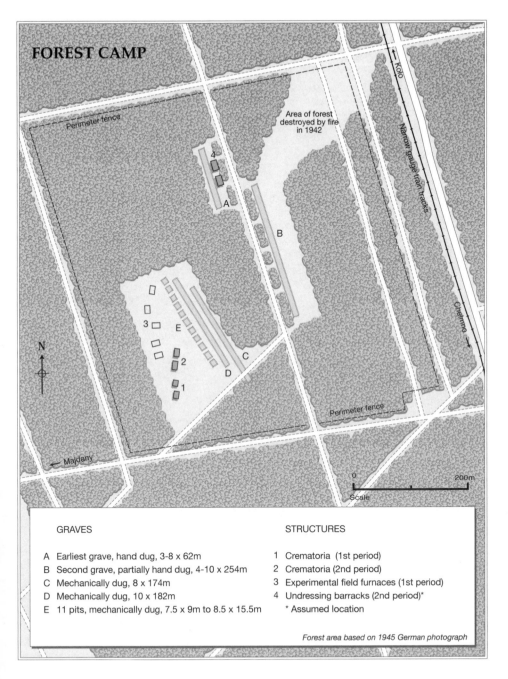

FOREST CAMP

Area of forest destroyed by fire in 1942

Perimeter fence

Koło

Narrow gauge train tracks

Chełmno

Perimeter fence

← Majdany

N

4

A

B

3

E

C

D

2

1

0   200m
Scale

GRAVES

A Earliest grave, hand dug, 3-8 x 62m
B Second grave, partially hand dug, 4-10 x 254m
C Mechanically dug, 8 x 174m
D Mechanically dug, 10 x 182m
E 11 pits, mechanically dug, 7.5 x 9m to 8.5 x 15.5m

STRUCTURES

1 Crematoria (1st period)
2 Crematoria (2nd period)
3 Experimental field furnaces (1st period)
4 Undressing barracks (2nd period)*
   * Assumed location

Forest area based on 1945 German photograph

Map 4. Forest Camp

Introduction

The literature on the extermination of the Jews during the Second World War is vast. It is common knowledge that millions of people perished in the Holocaust, yet research concerning the extermination centers, where many of the victims actually died, is limited at best. The purpose of the present work is to fill this major gap in knowledge with respect to one of these camps. While the literature is extensive regarding the Auschwitz-Birkenau concentration camp complex, it is extremely limited with respect to the four sole-purpose extermination centers of Treblinka, Sobibór, Bełżec and Chełmno.[1] Of these, Chełmno—the first extermination center established by the National Socialist regime—and its unique history, which served as the bureaucratic catalyst and operational prototype for the other camps and what ultimately has become known as the Final Solution, remains a relative enigma. The purpose of this work is to shed light on this little known but crucial chapter of the Holocaust and to clarify lingering misconceptions that surround the history of the camp. Chełmno broke a psychological barrier by actually establishing an extermination camp and provided a structural template on which the other camps could build.

The literature on the Chełmno camp is meager. During the postwar period, the primary sources of information on Chełmno were two books, both published in Polish. The first of these works, *Obóz Straceń w Chełmnie nad Nerem* [The Death Camp in Chełmno-on-Ner] by Judge Władysław Bednarz,[2] outlined the results of the Polish government's postwar investigation of the camp which was conducted by the author of the work. The second book, *Obóz zagłady w Chełmnie nad Nerem* [The Extermination Camp in Chełmno-on-Ner] by Professor Edward Serwański,[3] appeared in the mid-1960s after the trial in Bonn, West Germany, of 12 former members of the camp staff, but offered little new in substantive terms to the subject. Furthermore, a synopsis of the Bednarz investigation, translated into English and published in 1947, was included in the first volume of the *Bulletin of the Main Commission for the Investigation of German Crimes in Poland*. While the print run and distribution of this volume were limited, the journal article became a key source for the English-language reader.

It was not until the mid-1980s that the District Museum in Konin, Poland, began conducting archeological work and publishing information devoted to the Chełmno death camp. During the past two decades three additional books were published, one in Polish by Janusz Gulczyński,

Obóz Śmierci w Chełmnie nad Nerem[4] [The Death Camp in Chełmno-on-Ner], and two in German; the first by Manfred Struck, *Chełmno/Kulmhof, Ein Vergessener Ort des Holocaust?*[5] [Chełmno/Kulmhof, A Forgotten Place of the Holocaust?] and the second by Shmuel Krakowski, *Das Todeslager Chełmno/Kulmhof, Der Beginn der Endlösung*[6] [The Chełmno/Kulmhof Death Camp, The Beginning of the Final Solution]. However, these three works present merely a broad overview of the subject, far from a comprehensive history of the camp. The main contribution of these books is raising awareness of the camp for readers of the language in which the works were written.

There are several reasons for the dearth of published research on the Chełmno death camp. First, the camp was systematically liquidated over a period of some four months prior to the arrival of the Red Army in January 1945, leaving little physical evidence behind to investigate. Second, of the more than 150,000 people murdered at Chełmno[7] only six of the camp's prisoners survived the war and, of these six men, only three were located for questioning immediately after the war. Other contributing factors include the absence of the camp's records and other relevant Nazi documents. While postwar trials of individual members of the camp staff (Bruno Israel, Walter Piller, Herman Gielow) were held in Poland soon after the war, the material contained within the court records has been largely ignored by researchers. In addition, although camp personnel took numerous photographs of Chełmno's operations, these photographs tragically remain lost to history and therefore the substantive content (documentation) of the photographs as well as the impact of the visual image are also lost.

Given the scarcity of known resources, the Chełmno camp has consistently presented the researcher with a formidable challenge. The two main types of information needed to assemble a history of the Chełmno death camp are eyewitness testimonies and documents. With respect to eyewitnesses, the Chełmno camp provides three different types, the camp staff, the Jewish prisoners forced to labor in the camp and the residents of the village and surrounding area, referred to respectively as the perpetrators, victims and bystanders. The Germans who served as members of the camp staff, and in the case of Chełmno the Poles who served as laborers, would be an excellent source of information; after all, they were the ones who carried out the extermination. Their testimonies are in fact very useful as they do provide a substantial quantity of information. However, these testimonies are for the most part lacking, as they were given primarily in connection with pre-trial investigations and therefore information is rarely volunteered. Testimonies given in this type of situation tend to be self-incriminating and so responses to questions are bereft of the kind of detail so valuable to the researcher.

The Jewish victims are the second type of eyewitness in Chełmno. Unfortunately, of the thousands of people sent to the camp, only seven men successfully escaped and, of these seven, only six survived the war. Amazingly, these six key witnesses were never properly questioned, particularly just after the war when the events they had experienced were still fresh in their minds. Many questions remain unanswered in spite of the testimony given by three of the Jewish survivors to Polish authorities and their testimony given in connection with the Bonn trial.

As eyewitnesses to the daily events happening around the camp, the local residents are the source of a significant amount of valuable information. However, the scope of this information is limited as they did not have direct access to the camp or the extermination procedure. Nor were they privy to the decision-making process of the camp staff. Most of the local villagers were simple peasant families who tried to go about their lives with as little interaction with the soldiers as possible. Many were generally afraid of these officials, particularly the SS officials. This is understandable. Therefore, the researcher is often left with a single testimony or statement upon which to reconstruct a particular event, or indeed to patch together an entire history.

There are few documents relating directly to Chełmno. The camp's own records, the most important primary source, have not been found and according to at least one account were destroyed at the end of the war. Despite the issues mentioned above, there are three key primary sources for any serious examination of Chełmno. The first is the Polish government's investigation of the Chełmno extermination camp conducted immediately after the war in 1945. Colloquially referred to as the Bednarz investigation, this crucial work is currently housed in the archives of the Institute of National Remembrance in Warsaw, Poland. The investigation includes, among other findings, invaluable testimonies by three of the camp's survivors as well as by local villagers who were employed in the camp as cooks and cleaners, and others who witnessed the killing process as it occurred outside their homes. Much of the information contained in these testimonies is published here for the first time. The second key source is the prosecutor's pre-trial inquiry into the activities of the former camp staff conducted in Germany during the late 1950s and early 1960s. These materials, located at the Federal Archives in Ludwigsburg, Germany, include testimonies from individuals who worked in the camp, collected as part of an effort to bring criminal charges against camp officials. The third indispensable source of information is the uniquely detailed testimony of Szlama Winer, the second person to escape from Chełmno. After fleeing the camp in January 1942, Winer made his way to the Warsaw ghetto and filed an extensive report on the time he spent in the camp. Winer died a few months later in the extermination camp at Bełżec, but his testimony miraculously survived the war and is part of the Ringelblum Archive, currently housed in the Jewish Historical Institute in Warsaw, Poland. Winer's testimony stands alone, providing an incredibly in-depth eyewitness account of the camp's operations as seen through the eyes of a Jewish prisoner. Winer's report is reproduced in this volume in its entirety. Collectively, these testimonies by camp staff (perpetrators), local villagers (bystanders) and Jewish prisoners (victims) provide critical insight into the extermination process by some of those who witnessed and participated in it. Without these three sources no meaningful history of the Chełmno death camp can be written.

Three other important sources that provide a fuller understanding of Chełmno are the postwar testimonies of two key figures, Henryk Mania and Henryk Maliczak, prisoners who worked for Hauptsturmführer Herbert Lange's Sonderkommando during both the mobile killing operations conducted as part of the Euthanasia Program and the later stationary extermination program of the Chełmno period. These testimonies have not been previously cited in the literature. The interviews of these men, conducted in the 1960s, provide a greater understanding of the mobile and static operations, critically tie the two periods together and are vital as they offer the only eyewitness testimony to the events leading up to and including the mass murder perpetrated inside the Chełmno camp. Additional facts, also absent from the literature, are contained in the records of the pre-trial investigation of Henryk Mania, who in 2001 was convicted of complicity in genocide for his activities in Chełmno. The third source originates from a chapter of the postwar memoir of Heinz May, the German government official in charge of the forest where the camp's victims—first gassed to death in vans—were initially buried and their bodies later exhumed and burned. This document provides invaluable information concerning the camp's early and later operations from one of a handful of individuals with direct access to those operations.

Secondary sources include both general and specialized works (academic and scholarly studies, research projects, personal memoirs as well as a work of fiction based on a meeting with a survivor of Chełmno) in English, Polish and German on the Second World War in general and the Holocaust in particular. Primary and secondary sources are quoted extensively throughout the text, thereby allowing the participants in these horrible events to speak directly. The importance of the testimonies by the eyewitnesses—victims, perpetrators and bystanders—cannot be overemphasized. Their words form the backbone of the camp's history. They must be allowed to speak for themselves.

Of course a critical eye is required with respect to these firsthand accounts. Is the testimony of a traumatized survivor accurate? Is the testimony authentic? What about the perpetrators and the content of their testimonies? They certainly have reason to deflect and minimize their own participation, yet they do not deny their employment in the death camp; the camp existed and they witnessed the murders (if not participated in them). Even the bystanders are not neccessarily neutral observers. To one degree or another each category of eyewitness is prejudiced. Complete accuracy in these testimonies should not be expected, even discounting intentional distortions particularly originating from perpetrators. While individual "facts" may vary from witness to witness, what emerges from the universe of testimonies cannot be denied: No less than 152,000 people were murdered in Chełmno, despite the efforts of the killers to cover up the crime.

Notwithstanding the above-mentioned difficulties, a history of the camp does emerge from the documentary evidence that has survived. The history of the Chełmno death camp is the story of how a portion of the population residing in today's western Poland, and others deported to it, were murdered in a cold-blooded, calculated and deceptive manner as a matter of government policy. Broader issues surrounding Chełmno, such as government policy toward the Jews of occupied Poland in general and the history of the Łódź ghetto in particular, which provided so many of the camp's victims, are well covered in the literature and are therefore kept to a minimum in this work. However, for purposes of context, some attention is focused on the Euthanasia Program and the activities of Sonderkommando Lange, critical events leading to the establishment of the death camp.

The Chełmno death camp was unique in several respects, the first of which is the fact that no death camp by this name ever officially existed. Chełmno is the Polish name of the village where the camp was established. The German civil administration changed the name of this village in 1940 to Kulmhof, prior to the establishment of the camp. The villages of Treblinka, Sobibór and Bełżec were not renamed and therefore no issue exists regarding the names of the death camps established in these villages. Moreover, historical accuracy has been maintained in the case of Auschwitz, the German name of the town of Oświęcim. Poles, if no one else, would certainly be outraged if the Auschwitz camp was referred to as the Oświęcim camp. However, the term "Chełmno death camp" has raised few objections, from either the Polish community or Holocaust scholars. This situation may originate from the aforementioned English-language translation and publication of the first volume of the *Bulletin of the Main Commission for the Investigation of German Crimes in Poland* in 1947, in which the name "Chełmno" was used, usually in regard to the location of the extermination camp, but not exclusively. This article was a primary source of information about the camp for the English-speaking reader. Whatever the reason for this inaccuracy in name, the Kulmhof death camp is generally known and referred to in English as the "Chełmno death camp" and, while not historically accurate, the term is used throughout this work.[8]

The Chełmno camp is also unique in that it was the first camp established by the Nazi regime for the sole purpose of committing mass murder. The camp began operating before the infamous Wannsee Conference during which the organization and implementation of the Final Solution of the Jewish Question was discussed. Chełmno was also the only extermination camp liquidated and later reactivated. Its use of gas vans as opposed to static gas chambers, even after the other extermination camps had proven the efficacy of the chambers, was another unique feature of the camp. The other single purpose killing centers—the Operation Reinhard [Aktion Reinard] camps of Treblinka, Bełżec and Sobibór—were located to the east of Chełmno in the General Government [Generalgouvernement] and were administered collectively. Chełmno was located in the newly created Warthegau, a portion of western Poland that was incorporated into the German Reich and fell under an administrative bureaucracy completely separate from the Aktion Reinhard camps.

The use of gas to kill thousands of people in the Wartheland occurred in two stages. The first was within the framework of the so-called Euthanasia Program, which largely involved the gassing of mentally and physically disabled patients in psychiatric hospitals and other facilities. This operation was mobile in nature and did not specifically target Jews; the criterion for selection was a supposed mental or physical deficiency. The second stage, implemented based on the experience gained from the first stage, involved establishing a stationary facility to which the victims were transported for the sole purpose of gassing them. These victims, primarily Jews and to a lesser degree Roma, were selected on the basis of a supposed "racial deficiency." The static facility, the first of its kind, was the Chełmno extermination center.

Chełmno served as the template for establishing the subsequent killing centers but, in comparison, the prototype was primitive but effective. The camp lacked elements commonly associated with concentration or extermination camps. The characteristic barbed wire fencing, rows of barracks and guard towers were not present in Chełmno. Other than purpose, logistics was the thread common to the later Aktion Reinhard camps. The locations were isolated yet accessible. Due to the large number of targeted victims, rail lines were key. Once at the camps, victims were deceptively put at ease. People in the transports arriving at Treblinka believed they were at a normal train station. Many remained ignorant even during the processing stage, when heads were shaved (a step absent at Chełmno) and clothing removed. By the time victims stood before a gas van or gas chamber, it was too late; their fate was sealed. Treblinka, Bełżec and Sobibór were built on these fundamentals. They were also built, literally, from the ground up (while Chełmno utilized pre-existing structures) and so were specifically constructed to meet the requirements of an extermination center. Rail lines were brought directly into the camps. Workshops for various purposes were constructed, as were storage facilities. (Treblinka even had a small zoo.) Gas chambers were constructed and located a short walk from the reception area and the sector for body disposal placed next to the gassing facilities. At Chełmno, a drive of four kilometers, one way, was required to dispose of the bodies. Chełmno was established on the authority of Arthur Greiser, the Provincial Governor, to solve a "local problem," while the Aktion Reinhard camps were instituted by Adolf Hitler to solve a "European problem." Chełmno, with its limited killing capacity, was adequate to achieve its initial objective of murdering 100,000 people. The Aktion Reinhard camps adopted the model and "improved" on it in order to meet their much more ambitious goal of murdering millions of people.

The road to Chełmno was a long one and part of a complex process that began even before 1925, when Adolf Hitler set his twisted philosophy to paper in his book *Mein Kampf*. Just one year after the First World War, Hitler wrote that the Jews were the cause of "racial tuberculosis among nations" and the "final aim" of this problem must be the "removal of the Jews altogether."[9] Milestones along this road include Hitler's appointment as Chancellor in January 1933, the takeover of government institutions and indoctrination of the German public, the establishment of concentration camps, adoption of the Nuremburg Laws, forced sterilization, "mercy killing," the outbreak of the Second World War, the grisly work of the Einsatzgruppen in the Soviet Union and, of course, the progressively restrictive measures taken against the Jewish population as a whole.

In order to understand how this progression brought a small detachment of SS men to a pastoral village in rural Poland to launch a campaign of mass murder, it is vital to take a step back to before the outbreak of the Second World War. The covertly conducted Euthanasia Program and its expansion into the newly incorporated territory of the Warthegau leads to the very doorstep of Chełmno. By September 1941, all of the elements had come together, making the great leap from concentration camp to extermination camp in fact only a small step.

CHAPTER 1

Prologue

The Euthanasia Program

"Euthanasia" is a word derived from the Greek language meaning "helping to die." The modern concept of "physician-assisted suicide" has nothing in common with what has become known as the Euthanasia Program conducted by the National Socialist regime. This program was based on racial theory and eugenics. The health of the victim was secondary or played no role at all. Neither the patient nor the family had any say in the process and, in fact, were completely unaware of what was happening.

Euthanasia remains a controversial subject today, as it was when it was debated during the Weimar Republic. This debate, part of psychiatric reform in general, was an element of a much larger discussion of the welfare state and the lack of financial resources to maintain the system during the ongoing economic depression. At the core of this dialogue was the concept of the collective versus the individual. When the National Socialists came to power in Germany in January 1933, the debate was over. The first legal step toward involuntary euthanasia was the Law for the Prevention of Offspring with Hereditary Diseases, signed in July 1933. This law mandated the compulsory sterilization of the disabled. The Marriage Health Law followed the next year, which prohibited a marriage if either of the partners suffered from a disability covered by the sterilization law. More laws followed. As a result of these laws, between 1934 and 1945, some 400,000 people were subjected to the procedures, tubal ligation, and later the use of radium and X rays for females and vasectomy for males.[1] Cases for sterilization were brought before a panel of experts for deliberation, a perfunctory point as the patients were considered defective.

As part of the overall propaganda campaign of indoctrinating the population to the ideals of National Socialism, the German government immediately launched a campaign aimed at convincing the population of the "benefits" of euthanasia. However, Hitler believed it more practical not to implement a euthanasia policy during peacetime, fearing negative public reaction. He also believed that in time of war (which he was planning in the second half of the 1930s) "when the attention of the entire world is turned on military operations and when the value of human life in any case counts for less, it would be easier to free the people from the burden of the mentally ill."[2]

In May 1939, Hitler ordered bureaucrats within his Chancellery of the Führer [Kanzlei des Führers, KdF] to establish an organization, the Reich Committee for the Scientific Registering of Severe Hereditary and Congenital Diseases, to oversee a program of providing "mercy deaths" for children. Midwives and physicians were required to register children born with deformities. Candidates for the program were vetted by a panel of experts. These children were sent to so-called special child groups and killed either by administering a lethal injection or by starvation. Dr. Hermann Pfannmüller, the director of one such institution where children were euthanized, preferred the method of slow starvation. One visitor recalled that during a tour of the facility in late 1939, Dr. Pfannmüller picked up one of the children from its bed and

> [...] exhibited the child like a dead rabbit, he asserted with a knowing expression and a cynical grin: For this one it will take two to three more days. The picture of this fat grinning man, in his fleshy hands the whimpering skeleton, surrounded by other starving children, is still vivid in my mind. [... Asked] whether a quicker death with injections, etc., would not at least be more merciful, [the doctor] then praised his methods again as more practical in view of the foreign press. [...] Pfannmüller also did not hide the fact that among the children to be murdered ... were also children who were not mentally ill, namely children of Jewish parents.[3]

Some 6,000 children perished in the so-called children's euthanasia program, which continued throughout the war despite Hitler issuing a halt order in August 1941.

In the summer of 1939, Hitler ordered Reichleiter Philipp Bouhler of the Führer's Chancellery and Professor Karl Brandt, an inner-circle physician, both of whom were already overseeing the children's Euthanasia Program, to establish the bureaucratic structures necessary to carry out a clandestine adult euthanasia program as hospital beds and medical personnel would soon be required for the war effort. Physicians were selected, meetings were held and plans drawn up. Hitler received periodic briefings and, in October 1939, put his official seal of approval on the program by signing a document, backdated to September 1, 1939 (the outbreak of the war).

> Reichleiter Bouhler and the physician Dr. Brandt are charged with the responsibility of extending the authority of certain physicians, to be designated by name. These latter will be able to grant a mercy death to patients considered incurable according to the best of human judgment.
>
> Adolf Hitler[4]

This was not a public document and it was not published while Hitler was in power. Hitler issued the order, or authorization, which was illegal under existing German law, as the head of the Nazi party, on his personal stationary of the Chancellery of the Führer, and not as the Chancellor of Germany. The purpose of the document was to provide the program with an air of legitimacy in persuading physicians to participate in it. Karl Brandt and Philipp Bouhler assigned Viktor Brack, the head of the Chancellery's Department II, State and Party Affairs, to administer the program, whose staff eventually occupied a building rented by the Führer's Chancellery located in Berlin at 4 Tiergartenstrasse from which the program took its code name, Operation T4 [Aktion T4]. Each person brought into the program was told the nature of the operation, asked if they agreed to participate (no one was forced) and, if so, was subsequently sworn to secrecy. By the outbreak of the war in 1939, Hitler had the bureaucracy in place to begin secretly murdering the mentally ill.[5]

A total of six euthanasia centers were established: Grafeneck in Württemberg, Brandenburg near Berlin, Hartheim near Linz in Austria, Sonnenstein in Pirna, Saxony, Bernburg in Saxony, and Hadamar in Hessen. Each facility was equipped with a gas chamber. In mid-1940, a Stuttgart police official, Christian Wirth, was appointed head of administration at the Hartheim facility. Wirth has been described as a gross, crude and florid individual. In regard to the necessity of conducting the Euthanasia Program, Wirth spoke of "doing away with useless mouths" and said that "sentimental slobber" about such people made him "puke."[6]

Grafeneck Castle, a hospice for invalids, was taken over by T4 personnel in October 1939, and designated Facility A. Operations began the following month. The geographical area of responsibility of this center covered Austria and even south into northern Italy. (Cooperation was established with the Italian government with respect to patients of German origin living in this region of Italy.)

The center in Brandenburg, code named Facility B, was established in an old prison. Its area of responsibility covered patients in Saxony, Schleswig-Holstein, Brandenburg, Brunswick, Mecklenburg and Anhalt, as well as the cities of Hamburg and Berlin. This facility was closed in November 1940, and the personnel transferred to the "Facility for Care and Nursing" located in Bernburg, which had better technical capabilities.

Hartheim Castle, located near Linz, Austria, was code named Facility C. The victims sent to this center came from Austria, part of Saxony, southern Germany and even Yugoslavia and Bohemia-Moravia. One of the officials assigned to this institution later described Hartheim as an "undisciplined pigsty."[7]

Facility D was the code name for the Facility for Care and Nursing at Sonnenstein. T4 personnel took up residence here in April 1940. The geographic area of responsibility covered Thuringia, parts of Saxony and Silesia, as well as parts of southern Germany.

The Grafeneck facility ceased operations in December 1940. The personnel were transferred to Facility E, Hadamar, located near Limburg. Patients arriving to Hadamar originated from Rhineland-Palatinate, North Rhine-Westphalia and Lower Saxony.

All hospices and asylums in Germany were sent patient registration forms. Patients were to be classified into three groups. Among others, Group One included people with epilepsy and therapy-resistant paralysis, while Group Two included all patients who had been continuously hospitalized for at least five years. It has been stated that most of the patients classified in these groups were not terminally ill. "They were suffering no pain, and the majority of them were not on the point of dying and did not wish to die."[8] Institutions that were uncooperative in filling out the questionnaires, filled them out incorrectly or incompletely, received visits from a T4 commission. When required, the commission filled out the forms itself, even without examining the patients.

These questionnaires were transferred to the T4 central office where they were reviewed by a panel of three experts. Each case was decided by either a plus sign (extermination), minus sign (postponement) or a question mark (further consideration) inked on the patient's medical record. Lists were then drawn up for individual asylums and nursing homes of those patients designated for euthanasia. The lists were transferred to the relevant euthanasia center for processing. Each facility had buses and drivers at its disposal for picking up and transporting the victims to the centers.

The role played by the SS in the Euthanasia Program in Germany was limited but important. The Chancellery of the Führer required technical experts and materials (drugs and gas) for the T4 killing centers to function and, in regard to maintaining secrecy, the SS was the logical source to provide them. For rendering these technical services, close cooperation was established between Viktor Brack from the Chancellery of the Führer and Reinhard Heydrich's Reich Security Main Office [Reichssicherheitshauptamt–RSHA], and specifically the Section for Chemical Analysis [Referat Chemie] within the Technical Institute for the Detection of Crime [Kriminaltechnisches Institut, KTI]. This section was headed by a chemical engineer and SS officer Albert Widmann.

KTI was tasked with experimenting and determining the best way to terminate the lives of those subject to the program. At a subsequent demonstration conducted at the euthanasia facility in Brandenburg—attended by many high ranking functionaries including Karl Brandt, Philipp Bouhler and Dr. Leonardo Conti (the Reich health leader), as well as by Viktor Brack, Albert Widmann and the notorious Christian Wirth—one group of patients received injections of drugs, while a second group was escorted into a gas chamber to which carbon monoxide gas was introduced. The drugs were deemed to be less effective than the carbon monoxide and those given drugs were eventually gassed in the chamber as well. Dr. Brandt chose gas as the program's killing agent.[9]

One of Widmann's technical experts, Untersturmführer August Becker, who was also in attendance at the Brandenburg demonstration, procured steel cylinders for the carbon monoxide gas from a factory owned by Mannesmann Rohrenwerke, a tube and pipe manufacturer. These cylinders, with a capacity of some 40 liters, were subsequently filled with the deadly gas at the IG Farben factory in Ludwigshafen and delivered to the euthanasia institutes.[10] Becker was a hands-on expert, not only delivering the gas, but attending, advising and supervising the gassing process.

As instituted, the actual killing procedure was simple and deceptive. Patients were brought to a room where they undressed. They were then photographed and subject to a cursory examination, the purpose of which was not medical in nature but to ensure that administrative formalities were met. A number was subsequently marked on the backs of the victims for later identification. These unfortunate people were then assembled in a waiting room where soap and towels were distributed. Finally, the patients were led into a gas chamber, cleverly disguised as a shower or inhalation room. Once inside, the door was closed and the gas turned on. Some patients simply collapsed, others began screaming and beating on the walls and door. When the physician deemed all inside were dead, usually after some 20 minutes, the gas was turned off and fresh air was pumped into the chamber expelling the carbon monoxide. The corpses were then taken to the crematory and burned.[11] The Chełmno death camp would be the first to adopt this model for the "assembly line" extermination of Jews in the Wartheland. Months later the model was also employed, along with T4 personnel, in the Aktion Reinhard extermination centers of Bełżec, Sobibór and Treblinka.

Hitler issued an order on August 24, 1941, to halt the gassings within the framework of Aktion T4 due to increasing public knowledge about the killings and, just as the Führer predicted, subsequent popular disquiet. According to a T4 statistician, 70,273 disabled persons from Austrian and German psychiatric institutions were murdered in the T4 euthanasia institutes between January 1940 and August 1941, some 35,000 each year.[12] In fact, the killing continued until the end of the war in what is now referred to as "wild" euthanasia. Thousands of patients were killed all across Germany and Austria by doctors and nurses administering lethal injections or by starvation.

The SS became increasingly involved in the Euthanasia Program in the spring of 1941, when it launched Operation 14f13, which involved the killing of concentration camp inmates. Camp doctors singled out prisoners for special treatment with the final selection being made by visiting T4 physicians. The victims were transported to T4 facilities and gassed. It is estimated that up to 20,000 inmates were killed under the auspices of this program, which was officially terminated in 1943.

According to Viktor Brack, the reason Hitler ordered the establishment of the Euthanasia Program in Germany was "to eliminate those people confined to insane asylums and similar institutions who could no longer be of any use to the Reich. They were considered useless eaters and Hitler felt that by exterminating these so-called useless eaters, it would be possible to relieve more doctors, male and female nurses, and other personnel, hospital beds and other facilities for the use of the armed forces."[13] According to the above-mentioned T4 statistician, getting rid of these "useless eaters" saved the German state RM (*Reich Mark*) 885,439,980 over a ten-year period and, in terms of food, the state saved 13,492,440 kilograms of meat and sausage. If this absurdity is taken further, the savings breaks down to about 192 kilograms per person or some 0.053 kilograms per person per day over the ten-year period. Perhaps more importantly than a savings in sausage, the Euthanasia Program not only provided trained personnel for subsequent employment in the camps of the Aktion Reinhard program, but also served as a psychological stepping stone for the program's administrators and technicians.

Mobile Killing Operations

The establishment of a killing unit to conduct limited mobile operations at health care facilities throughout the Warthegau was the penultimate step before the establishment of a static facility to kill a second, larger group of victims. The mobile operations were part of the centrally planned Euthanasia Program, but administered and conducted locally.

The Euthanasia Program expanded with Germany's invasion of Poland on September 1, 1939, and the subsequent dismemberment of this country. Like all other institutions in Poland, facilities for the mentally and physically disabled throughout the country were taken over and administered by the newly established German administration. The method of so-called euthanasia employed in these newly acquired facilities varied from hospital to hospital, but generally consisted in administering lethal injections (for example, in Lubiniec), starvation (Kobierzyn) and/or shooting (Chełm Lubelski).[1]

Only in the Warthegau was gassing added to the above list. Brack's expansion of the Euthanasia Program into the western portion of the former Polish state did not require building a separate bureaucracy; he simply established another euthanasia institute. However, this facility differed fundamentally from the others in Germany in that it was essentially a mobile institute. The facility—Sonderkommando Lange, a special SS detachment with a gas chamber on wheels—traveled to the "patients."

With the outbreak of the war and Germany's subsequent incorporation of this territory into the newly created Warthegau, six psychiatric facilities, located in Owińska (outside Poznań), Gniezno (Dziekanka), Kościan, Warta, Łódź (Kochanówka) and Gostynin, fell under the control of the Provincial Administration [Gauselbstverwaltung, GSV] in Poznań. The Central Office for Patient Transfers [Zentrale für Krankenverlegung], tasked with preparing and providing the families of the patients with fictitious data about their fates, fell under the GSV. The Central Office also maintained a register containing the fictitious place of the alleged burial of the patients' bodies at the Dziekanka facility's cemetery. A special Office of Vital Statistics, within the Central Office, prepared the death certificates with fictitious dates and causes of death. As in Germany, all hospices and asylums in those areas of Poland incorporated into the Reich were sent patient registration forms. Lists of patients were prepared in the psychiatric hospitals being the basis for their later evacuation, although there were exceptions to this rule. Some of the medical and nursing staffs were fired, the use of medicines was limited and an order was issued that no patients were to be released.

The first step toward the mass murder of patients was the preparation of patient lists by the newly appointed facility directors. In order to hide the actual purpose of the operations from the Polish personnel in the facilities the so-called transfer of patients to other facilities was referred to as an "evacuation," a term associated with the resettlement of Poles to the General Government also being conducted at the time. Internal correspondence, however, described the transfers as the purging of the mentally ill from institutions. The lists of special patient transfers to other institutions, containing the names of the patients to be "purged," were then sent to HSSPF [Higher SS and Police Leader] Wilhelm Koppe who was responsible for conducting the evacuation.[2]

The gassing of the mentally handicapped in the Warthegau would be overseen operationally, but not administratively, primarily by the SS. The convoluted nature of Nazi bureaucracy is notorious and is no different in this case. Chains of command and areas of responsibility overlapped. Heinrich Himmler, the head of the SS, had a representative in each province, the HSSPF, who reported directly to him as well as to the senior state official, the Provincial Governor [Reichsstatthalter]. In the Warthegau, the HSSPF was Gruppenführer Wilhelm Koppe whose office was located in Poznań. Koppe was operationally responsible for the killing operations conducted by Sonderkommando Lange in his area. While Koppe claimed Sonderkommando Lange was under his command[3] and Lange was officially assigned to the Poznań Gestapo Office, he also stated that the gassing operation in the Wartheland was under the supervision of Viktor Brack of the Führer's Chancellery.[4] Shortly after his posting to the Poznań Gestapo office, while filing a routine report for Berlin, deputy director Sturmbannführer Dr. Alfred Trenker asked for verification that Lange headed a Sonderkommando. The response from Gruppenführer Heinrich Müller, chief of the Gestapo, was designated "top secret" and stated that Sonderkommando Lange was subordinated to the chief of the Security Police (Heydrich) and the relevant chain of command ran from Sonderkommando Lange through the Reich Security Main Office (RSHA) to the chief of the Security Police. With this, Trenker figuratively washed his hands of this unit.[5] Lange frequently traveled to Berlin for consultations to work out the details of his assignment. These meetings at RSHA led to the decision that Lange would experiment with cylinders of carbon monoxide gas as the killing agent. The unique nature of his assignment ties him directly to the central authorities of the Euthanasia Program.

These consultations occurred in the October–November 1939 timeframe. The decision to experiment with cylinders of gas predated the previously mentioned Brandenburg demonstration, following which Brandt chose gas over drugs as the preferred killing agent for use in the Old Reich. The precise date of the Brandenburg test demonstration is not known; participants stated the two-day event took place in the December 1939–January 1940 period.[6] Therefore, in making his decision, Brandt must have also considered the results Lange had already obtained.

Very little has been written about the man who eventually established the Chełmno extermination camp. Herbert Lange was born in Menzlin, West Pomerania (north of Berlin) in September 1909, joined the Nazi party in May 1932, before it came to power, and the SS almost a year later in March 1933. In 1938, he joined the Criminal Police [Kriminalpolizei, Kripo] and the SS Security Service [Sicherheitsdienst, SD]. Lange married in 1935 and had two children, in 1936 and 1938. Herbert Lange was a no-nonsense, fanatical Nazi. His superiors were apparently pleased with his work. Lange received promotions from Second Lieutenant [Untersturmführer] to First Lieutenant [Obersturmführer] on April 20, 1940, after murdering patients in psychiatric hospitals, to Captain [Hauptsturmführer] on September 1, 1941, which could well be associated with his assignment to Chełmno, from Criminal Commissar [Kriminalkommissar] to Criminal Counselor [Kriminalrat] in July 1942, after gassing men, women and children in Chełmno and his subsequent transfer to Berlin, and from Hauptsturmführer to Major [Sturmbannführer] on October 1, 1944, following his contributions associated with reprisals against conspirators and alleged conspirators connected with the assassination attempt on Hitler's life in July 1944.[7]

The 30-year-old Lange entered Poland attached to Standartenführer Erich Naumann's Einsatzgruppe VI. The Einsatzgruppen followed the German army into Poland rooting out and eliminating those elements of Polish society deemed hostile and a potential threat to German interests. Einsatzgruppe VI was disbanded in November 1939, and Lange, together with other members of the unit, was officially assigned to the newly formed Gestapo office in Poznań. According to Dr. Alfred Trenker, who was transferred to Poznań in March 1940 and eventually became close to Lange and his family, Lange headed the Gestapo office's Department IIG, which dealt with the illegal possession of weapons and explosives, sabotage and assaults against Germans.[8] It is known that Lange participated in the execution of Polish civilians sentenced by German courts. The victims were taken to the forest in Zakrzewo and other locations outside Poznań and shot.[9] According to a district forester, some 30,000 Poles lost their lives in this way.[10] Trenker also stated that Lange headed Department IIE (employment of forced laborers and transfers to educational labor camps) at the same time or possibly later. At the beginning of 1941, Rottenführer Walter Burmeister was assigned to the Poznań Gestapo office as the driver for Department IIE. According to Burmeister, Lange was in charge of this department.[11] It has also been stated he headed the guard unit assigned to protect the provincial governor, Arthur Greiser.[12]

In addition Lange is said to have been the first commandant of Fort VII (Fort Colomb), part of the complex of defensive fortifications built around Poznań in the nineteenth century, and to have been responsible for organizing the prison, staffing it and receiving the first prisoners.[13] Fort VII was briefly designated a concentration camp, but following the reorganization of the police in Poland it became a Gestapo prison in November 1939. In mid-1941, the prison was again reorganized and officially bore the name Prison of the Security Police and Educational Labor Camp [Polizeigefängnis der Sicherheitspolizei und Arbeitserziehungslager].[14] Regardless of the name, this installation was a chamber of horrors; the prisoners were subjected to unspeakable torture while waiting to be tried before a court, sent to a concentration camp or simply executed. Whether or not Lange served briefly as the first commandant of Fort VII, he was certainly no stranger to this Gestapo prison.

The special unit Lange assembled was known as Sonderkommando Lange. The detachment consisted of some 15 men from the security services. (Neither the exact number nor all the names of the members of this unit are known with certainty.) Lange had an assistant, an SS officer and two non-commissioned officers serving in leadership positions. His black Mercedes was driven by a specially assigned chauffeur.[15] Based on subsequent events it can only be concluded that Lange was ordered to establish a simple method of terminating the lives of patients included in the Euthanasia Program, within the area of the Warthegau, and to conduct the program.

Lange began working on this program weeks after the German invasion of Poland, frequently traveling to Berlin for consultations, one result of which was the decision to send the SS chemist and self-described gassing expert, Dr. August Becker, to Poznań to provide technical assistance.[16] As noted previously, Becker would later also procure the gas cylinders for the Brandenburg demonstration. Fort VII provided Becker and Lange with the accommodations required to experiment with the killing method. One of the bunkers in the prison was selected and converted into a gas chamber by sealing the door with clay—a primitive but effective solution. Very little is known about the details surrounding the experiments at Fort VII. What little information is known primarily originates from prisoners in Fort VII who witnessed specific events and managed to survive the war.

One of these prisoners later recalled the following event, which may have been the first transport of victims to the prison:

> One day the sound of a truck motor electrified everybody. We were certain that the truck drove into the underground corridor, that a new transport was being prepared. But when the truck pulled up to our cell and the guards closed the peepholes, we were surprised. Strange voices could be heard over the sound of the truck's engine. Unnatural laughter, wailing, crying, gay and somber singing, random words, the voices of women—swearing, laughing, children screaming—all of this made a terrible impression on us. We instinctively felt that something horrible was happening behind that iron door. Finally, we very cautiously half opened the peephole to see what was happening. It is difficult to describe the macabre scene we saw. People were pulled or carried from the truck who were abnormal or who we assumed were incurably ill, as some behaved quite normally and, by all appearances, were prostitutes. There were senile old women as well as small children and teenagers. All of them were driven into one of the cells while being beaten and verbally abused. Their voices could be heard for some time; later there was only silence.[17]

The State Psychiatric Hospital in Owińska was one of three psychiatric institutions in the Poznań Voivodship and one of the oldest in the country, celebrating its centenary in 1938. The murder of the patients in this facility is frequently attributed to Sonderkommando Lange. In a report prepared in October 1945, Dr. Zdzisław Jaroszewski, who worked at the facility, described how the 1,100 hospital patients, including 78 children, were killed six years earlier in November 1939. According to this report, Hauptsturmführer Sachs [Sacks?], a former police official in Gdańsk, commanded the SS detachment that carried out the evacuation of the patients. Two canvass covered trucks and a detachment of SS men arrived, occupied the hospital, and subsequently began loading patients, hands tied behind their backs, into the trucks. The SS men accompanying the trucks wore pistols and shovels on their belts. As the days passed, hospital staff and patients became increasingly suspicious and anxious when different locations were given each time they asked the destination of the transports. No news reached them from the evacuated patients and traces of blood were seen on the uniforms of the SS men following their return to the hospital. Eventually, patients would beg for mercy when forced into the trucks. Finally, they were given an injection of 2 cubic centimeters of somnifen to calm nerves an hour before being evacuated. Nevertheless, one patient called out from a truck: *Jeszcze Polska nie zginęła* [Poland has not yet perished], a line from the Polish national anthem. One of the SS men, angered by this, yelled back at her: *Warte mal, du verfluchtes Ast, du kriegst bald eure "Polska nie zginęła."* [Just wait you damn ass, I'll show you your "Poland is not yet dead."] The last to leave the hospital were the children. By the beginning of December, the hospital had no more patients.[18]

According to Dr. Jaroszewski, the evacuation began around November 1. The men were the first to be taken away. Only then were the women and children evacuated. The report also states that the women and final transports were sent to Fort VII and gassed. Based on this report, Lange did participate in murdering patients from this hospital, but it is not clear if he had overall organizational responsibility of the operation. The timeframe provided by Dr. Jaroszewski (there were no patients left in the hospital by the beginning of December) would indicate that Lange was not prepared to carry out mobile operations at the beginning of November. However, the women and children from the Owińska facility did provide Lange with the guinea pigs he required for his experiments as confirmed by eyewitnesses.

Henryk Mania was a teenager studying metalworking in September 1939 when Germany attacked Poland. Within two weeks, he was arrested for allegedly trying to poison a German. After working on a chain gang for a few weeks repairing roads and rail lines, he was among a group of prisoners transferred from a jail in the town of Wolsztyn to a cell in Fort VII. After a short period of time, only a few of his fellow prisoners were still alive. Mania, Marian Libelt and Wacław Świtała from Rakoniewice were transferred to a new cell, designated with the initials "SK" [Sonderkommando], in which four other Polish prisoners were being held: Henryk Maliczak, Stanisław Polubiński, Stanisław Szymański and Kajetan Skrzypczyński.

> The same day that we were moved to the "SK" cell, we were called out by an SS man, but not the one who normally guarded the corridor. Two trucks, loaded with people, were parked in the courtyard of Fort VII and surrounded by SS men. These people were mentally ill, you could tell by looking at them. We were ordered to take these people from the trucks to a separate bunker. The SS men supervised us, yelling and pushing. We also carried steel cylinders, like those used for oxygen, from the truck and put them near the bunker. After leading the people into the bunker and closing the iron door, the SS men ordered us to seal the door with clay, after which they took us back to our cell. After a short period of time, we were again taken to the courtyard. We were ordered to remove the clay, open the door and remove the corpses of the gassed mental patients. I found out later that the prisoners in whose cell we were placed had done this previously; they themselves told me. I carried the corpses from the bunker to the truck. After loading the truck with the corpses of the patients, we were returned to our cell. The gassing of the mental patients

described above was repeated several more times [...] However, I do know that they were patients brought to Fort VII from the psychiatric hospital in Owińska near Poznań.[19]

Mania didn't know it at the time, but he had just become a laborer in the Fort VII Sonderkommando. The 16-year-old also didn't know that there was a second "SK" cell. Mania's group was detailed to escort the victims from the trucks in which they arrived to the bunker used for gassing. Afterwards, the group carried the corpses to trucks waiting to take them for burial in a secluded wooded area. A second group of prisoners was taken to the forest to dig the mass graves and bury the victims. Members of this second group included Leszek Jaskólski and a forester by profession, Franciszek Piekarski, the most senior member of the group at age 55 who served as the leader of these prisoners and who Mania and the others feared. The two groups of prisoners were later held together in a single cell (number 62) and isolated from the other prisoners.[20]

Henryk Maliczak, a gardener by profession, was 36 years old when he was arrested in November 1939, and imprisoned by the Gestapo in the town of Kościan.[21] After some three weeks, Maliczak, who would later be referred to as Heinrich the Elder (to distinguish him from the younger Henryk Mania), was transferred to Fort VII in Poznań and found himself sitting in a cell designated with the letters "SK."

> We were initially employed in transporting and burying the corpses of the mentally ill. The first victims came from the psychiatric hospital in [Owińska]. They were transported by truck to Fort VII and gassed in a bunker the door and window of which had been hermetically sealed. I saw how members of the camp staff and others, dressed in SS uniforms, observed the gassing through a window in the [door of the] bunker. A special group of approximately ten SS men, not Fort VII personnel, transported the mentally ill from the hospital in [Owińska] and gassed them. This group was commanded by an SS man named Lange [...]. The gassing occurred in this way two or three times over a period of several days. [...] The victims were calm; I suppose they had been tranquillized with injections. Our role in this activity consisted in carrying the corpses of the victims to trucks which transported them to forests near the town of Oborniki. Here we threw the corpses into previously dug pits. [...] We learned from members of Lange's kommando that the victims came from [Owińska] and were mentally ill. They tried to put us at ease, saying that such people had to be eliminated.[22]

These mass graves were discovered after the war in section 163 of the Różnowo Forest under the administration of the Oborniki Forest Inspectorate.[23]

The testimonies of these eyewitnesses show that while Lange may have actually traveled to the hospital to pick up patients, something not mentioned in Dr. Jaroszewski's report, this would have involved only the latter group of patients. On November 28, 1939, 27 patients from the

Neurological and Psychiatric Clinic of Poznań University were discharged and "evacuated" in an unknown direction. It is assumed that they also were killed as part of Lange's gassing experiments.[24] According to Mania, these experiments at Fort VII lasted about one month.

Other than mass graves in forests, Lange also disposed of corpses at the Institute of Forensic Medicine of Poznań University. According to Michał Woroch, who worked at the institute, Lange appeared one day and asked to speak to his boss. A few minutes later, Woroch and a colleague were summoned to the office and told to show Lange the crematorium. After examining the installation Lange announced that corpses would be brought to the facility to be cremated. The two employees were sworn to secrecy and told that if they did not cooperate, it would be considered sabotage and they would be thrown into the oven. Bodies began arriving the next day, eventually as many as 70 per day, and continued to arrive throughout the war. These corpses came from the prison on Młyńska Street, Fort VII, and later the camp in Żabikowo (Poggenburg).[25]

As Lange had orders to kill the mentally disabled over a wide area, it must have been obvious that it would be much more efficient to go to the victims rather than bringing the victims to Fort VII and then transporting the corpses to some outlaying forest for burial. After establishing that carbon monoxide gas was an effective killing agent, what Lange needed was a mobile gas chamber. There are no surviving documents about the development of this vehicle and it is not known who came up with the idea of putting a gas chamber on wheels. The only information concerning the development of this gas van are two sentences contained in the post-war testimony of Henryk Maliczak, the Fort VII prisoner and gravedigger for Sonderkommando Lange: "This vehicle was converted for this purpose in the courtyard of the Soldier's Home, the Gestapo headquarters in Poznań. Four prisoners from our group, including myself and the carpenter Józef Szymański, had to line the interior of the vehicle with plywood."[26] This vehicle became known as the infamous Kaiser's Kaffee van as for a period of time the sides of the vehicle featured the logo of the "Kaiser's Kaffee Geschäft" [Kaiser's Coffee Company], a well-known German firm, founded in 1880. Sonderkommando Lange was the only unit to have operated such a vehicle. In fact, there are no cases of operations employing a gas van being conducted simultaneously in two different locations during this period.

Physical descriptions of this van vary among the witnesses who were present at the hospitals during the evacuations. In their testimonies from 1964 and 1967, Mania and Maliczak never mention there being more than one van in operation. However, in an interview granted to a Czech journalist in 1962, Mania stated that two vehicles were used for gassing. There is no transcript of this interview, only a police report filed after the interview was given.[27] Various eyewitness testimonies of hospital personnel refer to the gassing vehicle in the plural, but often within the same testimony the singular is also used. There is no testimony describing two gas vans operating in conjunction with one another. In analyzing testimonies as a whole, within a given operation, it is clear that only one gassing van was used. It cannot be concluded from Mania's one-time assertion of there being two gas vans that both were used at the same time. If indeed there were two such vans, a second vehicle may have been employed temporarily, perhaps due to some technical problem with the Kaiser's Kaffee van. The best evidence of a second gassing vehicle is the description of the contraption used during the operation conducted at the Hospital for the Indigent in Śrem (see below).

Having established the Sonderkommando, conducted gassing experiments and converting what was described as a furniture truck into a gas chamber on wheels, Lange was ready to begin the Euthanasia Program in the Warthegau, with its mobile killing operations. When the bureaucrats in the Gauselbstverwaltung prepared the paperwork for an evacuation, the order was transferred to HSSPF Koppe, and Lange was dispatched.

Two years before the Chełmno camp became operational, Lange began mobile gassing operations on December 7, 1939, at the Dziekanka Psychiatric Hospital in Gniezno, some 50 kilometers east of Poznań. This facility housed 1,172 patients on September 11, 1939, when the Germans arrived and took over the hospital. The director of the facility, Dr. Wiktor Ratka, assumed his position following the death of the previous director, Dr. Aleksander Piotrowski, in 1933. The staff was terrorized; some of the personnel were transferred and others fired. Dr. Ratka, however, stayed on and willingly adopted the new German procedures. The victims were transported almost daily until December 19, when the holiday season apparently interrupted the operation. A total of 595 patients were gassed during this initial phase. Sonderkommando Lange returned after the New Year and evacuated 110 patients on January 8, 110 on each of the next two days and 118 on January 12.[28]

Sonderkommando Lange gassed 1,043 mentally disabled patients during this operation leaving behind just over one dozen German and one dozen Polish patients in the facility. The hospital continued to function during the war as new patients of various nationalities arrived from numerous other institutions. The hospital's director, Dr. Ratka, later joined other T4 physicians traveling to concentration camps as expert evaluators and selecting victims for the 14f13 program.

While Lange and his Sonderkommando were gassing the patients from the Dziekanka facility, Heinrich Himmler flew from Łódź to Poznań as part of a tour inspecting housing prepared for Baltic Germans being settled in the Warthegau in conjunction with the Germanization program. During his stay in Poznań, Himmler may have also attended a demonstration gassing at Fort VII on December 13. The gassing involved a small number of victims, probably the 31 patients transported from Dziekanka that very day. They entered the bunker singing and laughing. The doors were closed, and as the gas filled the chamber, the victims inside sat down on the straw scattered around the floor and expired. The purpose was to demonstrate to Himmler that the deaths were painless.[29] Himmler's thoughts concerning the gassing are not known but it can be assumed that he was satisfied with what he witnessed, thereby providing Lange with the Reichsführer's official seal of approval to continue mobile gassing operations.

Just three days after the operation at the Dziekanka hospital in Gniezno, the Sonderkommando drove some 40 kilometers south of Poznań to the State Psychiatric Hospital located in the town of Kościan. In September 1939, the hospital's Polish administration was replaced by Fritz Lemberger as hospital director, Hans Meding as inspector and Wilhelm Haydn as chief nurse.

The hospital had a patient population of approximately 600 in January 1940. Sonderkommando Lange arrived at the hospital with four vehicles: a passenger car, two trucks and a large, black, hermetically sealed van with the inscription "Kaiser's Kaffee Geschäft."[30] On January 15, 1940, despite the cold weather, patients were lightly dressed when loaded into the vehicles by the SS men. It was noted that the trucks left in the direction of Poznań and that spruce branches were stuck to the vehicles upon their return, indicating that the patients had been taken directly to some forest. The evacuation continued in a similar manner on January 22, 1940. At this time, the Jarogniewice Forest outside Kościan was guarded by SS sentries. The Sonderkommando vehicles were seen entering this forest. When the operation had concluded, the tracks of the vehicles led to three mass graves. Women's and men's clothing, rosaries, darning thread and other items were found at the gravesite.[31]

Sonderkommando Lange murdered 236 male and 298 female psychiatric patients from the Kościan hospital on January 15 and 22, 1940. However, this was only the first "evacuation" of patients from the facility. In February, some 1,200 patients from German hospitals in Obrzyce, Lebork and Ukermunder were brought to the hospital in Kościan where they met a similar fate.[32]

Henryk Mania recalled the operation in Kościan where he and twelve other prisoners, along with shovels, pickaxes and cylinders of gas, were taken to a forest to dig the graves for the patients. The Polish prisoners also carried the steel cylinders to the gas van, which were connected to a valve, and then operated by a member of the Sonderkommando. After the victims suffocated to death, the Poles emptied the van and buried the patients in the pits.[33]

Henryk Maliczak added that the patients from this hospital were buried not only in the forest near Stęszew but in the Jarogniewice Forest as well, both of which are located north of Kościan on the road to Poznań.[34] The T4 functionaries simultaneously tried to remove any traces of the crime, among others, by setting up fictitious graves on the hospital grounds that were later shown to family members of the murdered patients as the resting places of their loved ones who died of natural causes.[35] At the actual burial sites, efforts were made to camouflage the crime scene. In February and March 1944, Sonderkommando Legath, a special unit that was assembled and assigned the task of eliminating this and other burial sites, dug up the corpses and burned them. Again, the sites were camouflaged by planting trees around the area.[36]

Mania, Maliczak and the other Polish prisoners were returned to Fort VII in Poznań. Lange had assembled a detail of 13 Polish gravediggers. However, not all of these men were employed in every operation. The core group comprised eight men: Jaskólski, Libelt, Maliczak, Mania, Piekarski, Polubiński, Skrzypczyński and Szymański. The size of the detail varied depending on the particular needs of an individual operation.

The Voivodship Hospital for Mental and Nervous Disorders in Gostynin was a relatively new facility, built between 1929 and 1933. On September 1, 1939, the hospital had 459 patients and admitted many refugees and wounded as a result of the ensuing military campaign. The facility's director, Dr. Eugeniusz Wilczkowski, was called up for military service but returned to the hospital in October following the cessation of military operations.

At the beginning of February 1940, Gestapo officials arrived at the Psychiatric Hospital in Gostynin, located north of Kutno, with orders to evacuate 18 patients. Shovels and a machine gun were seen inside the truck. The patients were quickly and brutally loaded into the truck, which drove off in the direction of a nearby forest. Soon afterwards, the sounds of a machine gun were heard coming from the forest. Later, hospital personnel found the grave which had been camouflaged with small seedlings.[37] Germans took over the administration of the hospital shortly afterwards. Jewish patients began to be fed separately from the Polish and Germans patients. In the spring of 1940 the hospital received a directive stating that all Jewish patients were to be evacuated. Canvass covered trucks arrived, the patients were loaded into them, and the trucks drove off in an unknown direction.

It is not clear if Lange and his unit was involved in shooting the 18 patients. There are no documented cases of a Sonderkommando Lange operation being conducted exclusively by shooting. However, Henryk Maliczak remembered digging graves in a forest outside the town during a one-day operation.[38] Eventually, the hospital began receiving new patients brought in from other facilities, setting the stage for the next evacuation.

This operation occurred in the usual manner except the patients were actually taken to another facility located in the town of Pleszów. Nurses accompanied one of the final transports leaving Gostynin and were extremely depressed when they returned. They eventually recounted that the patients had been given an injection of scopolamine and then loaded into hermetically sealed vans. Those inside were killed and, after reaching the forest, the corpses were placed in prepared pits.[39]

The facility in Gostynin continued to function until mid-1944 when the patients were transferred to other hospitals to make room for wounded German soldiers. As the front moved west, many of these German patients died during their own evacuation when the train they were traveling in was bombed from the air. At the end of the war, the hospital was nothing more than an empty shell; all of the equipment had been plundered.

The State Psychiatric Hospital near Łódź, known as Kochanówka, was established in 1902. By the outbreak of the Second World War, the hospital had undergone dramatic expansion and comprised seven pavilions with approximately 700 patients. Initially, the German administration did not interfere with the hospital's management but civilian and military officials did make periodic inspections. The situation at the hospital changed on February 1, 1940, when it received an order from the Public Health Department [Gesundheitsamt], which forbid discharging patients and warned of severe penalties if any patients escaped. However, admitting new patients was not forbidden. At the beginning of March, the Gesundheitsamt sent a commission to the hospital, led by the SS anthropologist Dr. Herbert Grohmann, a specialist on racial affairs and the director of Aktion T4 in the Łódź District. The commission, comprising military men armed with pistols and riding crops, ordered a list to be prepared with the personal details, diagnosis and nationality of the patients. An air of catastrophe hung over the hospital. The first "evacuation" of patients occurred on March 13–15. Jewish patients were the first to be taken away.

Under the command of an SS official named Budnik,[40] more than a dozen SS men arrived at the hospital and took up residence on the ground floor of ward 6. The operation was now standard procedure: Employing three canvass covered trucks and the "Kaiser's Kaffee" van, the Sonderkommando escorted the patients to a forest outside Zgierz, just north of Łódź. Over the course of three days, approximately 500 patients were killed. The Sonderkommando returned to Kochanówka almost two weeks later and transported the remaining patients between March 27 and March 28, 1940. When asked what address should be given to the family members of the evacuated patients, Dr. Grohmann said they should direct enquiries to the county administration office [Landratura] in Poznań.

Following these operations, the Polish staff was dismissed (some doctors and nurses were eventually rehired), German medical personnel hired, and a subsequent evacuation of patients occurred in mid-1941.[41]

Wacław Berłowski was employed at the Kochanówka hospital from 1933 to 1941 as a metalworker/locksmith and witnessed members of the Sonderkommando beating and pushing the patients, wearing only their robes and underwear, as they were packed into the trucks. He also pointed out that the SS men carried pistols with them around the hospital, but when escorting the trucks as they departed with the patients onboard, they took automatic weapons, extra belts of ammunition and shovels. However, it is the method of killing the patients that stands out here. Berłowski also stated that the Sonderkommando employed several vehicles to transport the patients.

> They were regular trucks with canvass coverings. Only one of them was a completely closed, metal vehicle, the interior of which was hermetically pan-eled with wood. This van had no windows. I repaired the van together with Antoni Buła. The inscription "Cafe Kaiser" was written on the side on the van. During the repair work we noticed that a pipe lead out from the motor. This pipe was flexible; it lead out from the middle of the motor, from un-derneath and was connected to the body of the rear compartment. We also noticed that there was a grated opening in the floor of the vehicle. The pipe running from the motor led to this opening. This pipe was attached to an adaptor. Antoni Buła can provide additional details as he is a professional driver. When we saw this pipe Buła said that it was for gassing people. This vehicle was never washed by personnel from the hospital, but occasion-ally Jews were brought from the city to do it. This vehicle was gone from the hospital for three to four hours at a time after transporting a group of patients.[42]

Taken on its own, this rather detailed description of the exhaust system on the gas van is a fairly convincing piece of testimony. However, when the man mentioned in the testimony, Antoni Buła, was asked about this issue he stated he never repaired the vehicle.[43] As a result the description given by Berłowski is suspect. This could be a case of mistaken identity, the event may have occurred at a later date with a different individual, or Berłowski simply made up the story, repeating particulars he heard immediately after the war. It was also reported that the Sonderkommando transported cases and cylinders in the trucks as the unit deported to the forest. Taps or valves were also seen on the Kaiser's Kaffee van.[44] The cylinders were obviously the containers for the carbon monoxide gas and the taps on the vehicle were for connecting the hose running from the gas cylinder. Therefore, it is apparent the killing method involved the use of bottled carbon monoxide and not exhaust gas.

The two gravediggers had little to say about the part they played in the murder of the mental patients from the hospital in Łódź. Mania did confirm that during the operation the Polish gravediggers stayed at the hospital.

> We were quartered on the grounds of the facility during the operation. The gassing of the patients here occurred in the following way: They were loaded onto trucks which transported them under armed SS escort to the forest. [...] I remember that there was a structure in the forest, something like an earthen bunker or dugout. We were ordered to take the patients from the truck to the dugout in which they were gassed. I believe gas from a cylinder was used but I can't remember how it was introduced into the interior. The patients were passive; they had apparently been given a sedative beforehand.[45]

Just days following the operation at Kochanówka, Lange and his Sonderkommando arrived in the small town of Warta, located some 15 kilometers north of Sieradz and less than 40 kilometers east of Kalisz. The state hospital for mental and neurological disorders, which opened in 1908, was taken over by the Gauselbstverwaltung in November 1939. The director of the hospital, Dr. Karol Szymański, had been called up for military service in August 1939 (and was murdered by the Russians in the Katyń forest in April 1940).[46] Employees were subjected to a thorough vetting process, but it was not until March 1940 that the first German doctors arrived, including the new director, Dr. Hans Renfranz, to the newly renamed hospital (Gauheilanstaht in Warta bei Schieratz). Hospital regulations were tightened, visiting hours shortened and everyone was put on notice that things would soon change.

Toward the end of March, things did change. A list of patients was drawn up by Dr. Lemberger (who had been transferred from the hospital in Kościan) and Dr. Renfranz. On March 30, a commission, comprising two civilians and four SS men, arrived at the hospital and spoke with the director. Shortly thereafter, the two civilians left, while the SS men ordered accommodations be arranged for approximately 28 people. These four men remained on the grounds of the facility, spending the night in the administration building. The following day Sonderkommando Lange drove up to the hospital. Lange arrived in his Mercedes, accompanied by the two canvass covered military trucks and the Kaiser's Kaffee van. The unit was accommodated on the first floor of the administration building.

The 13 Polish gravediggers that accompanied the Sonderkommando were quartered in the city jail. Hospital employees took food to them under an armed escort of Volksdeutsche [ethnic Germans]. The prisoners and hospital employees were not allowed to speak to each other. During the day the Polish gravediggers were transported, with shovels and under escort, in the direction of Rossoszyca, a small village located about 11 kilometers east of Warta. Approximately 400 meters off the main road, they dug three parallel pits measuring some nine by three and a half meters.[47]

On Tuesday, April 2, the Sonderkommando's trucks assembled in the courtyard of the hospital. Injections were ordered. Orderlies and nurses then led the patients to the trucks waiting outside. Accompanied by verbal and physical abuse, the Kaiser's Kaffee van was loaded first, then the trucks. The engines were started and the vehicles drove off from the hospital in the direction of Rossoszyca to meet Mania, Maliczak and the others, waiting for them in the forest. Only the canvass covered trucks returned to the facility to pick up a new load of patients.

Over the course of the three-day operation, from April 2–4, 1940, Sonderkommando Lange transported 499 patients from the psychiatric facility in Warta to the forest across the river in the vicinity of the villages of Włyn and Rossoszyca. The gassed patients included Jews, Poles, Germans and patients of other nationalities. A single Jewish patient, Chawe Markuze, is said to have survived Lange's handiwork, allegedly because of her unusual charm. She was later transported to the General Government. The Sonderkommando remained at the hospital on April 5; eating, drinking and resting. The next day a farewell celebration was hosted by the director at which the party-goers drank until they passed out in the early morning hours. In conversations the following day the Sonderkommando let it be known they were headed to the county hospital in Turek; also mentioned were Konin and Włocławek.[48] After witnessing this operation, Dr. Renfranz and his wife referred to Lange and his men as the "psychopath's club".[49] This is the last operation in which the logo "Kaiser's Kaffee Geschäft" was reportedly seen on the sides of the gas van.

Sonderkommando Lange received orders to conduct one operation outside the Warthegau. At a meeting held in Poznań, HSSPF Wilhelm Koppe informed his counterpart from Kaliningrad (Konigsberg), Wilhelm Rediess, about Sonderkommando Lange and its use of a gas van to kill mental patients in the Warthegau. Rediess had already reached an agreement with the Gauleiter of the area, Erich Koch, to kill the mental patients in his area in exchange for the use of a hospital for the needs of the SS and asked Koppe if he could borrow Lange and his Sonderkommando to carry out the task. After consulting with Himmler, a deal was struck and the inspectors of the Sipo and SD in Poznań and Kaliningrad, Ernst Damzog and Otto Rasch, worked out the details.[50]

The operation took place in the town of Działdowo (Soldau), which at the time was located in East Prussia. Hospitals in the area were ordered to vacate patients as occurred earlier in Pomerania. The Soldau transit camp was established in 1939 by Dr. Otto Rasch, who later commanded Einsatzgruppe C, which murdered thousands of civilians in the Ukraine. Polish political prisoners were secretly and routinely executed in the camp on orders of the commandant Hauptsturmführer Hans Krause. The issuance of the new evacuation order exceeded Krause's ability to carry it out.

Testimony regarding the killing originates from the gravedigger Henryk Mania.

> We were quartered in a camp located at a former military barracks. Several vehicles, that is the entire Sonderkommando and the entire group of 13 prisoners, had traveled from Poznań. It was summer. We dug pits in the forest that could be reached by crossing a small river near Działdowo. Once we were even allowed to bathe in it, under guard of course. Digging the pits was very difficult work as we were ordered to dig them as quickly as possible. We worked from morning to night. Later, a group of prisoners from the camp in Działdowo were brought in to help. The forest was probably secured by guards from the camp. If I remember correctly, the mental patients were transported from the hospital to the forest in trucks. They were patients from a hospital or hospitals probably located in East Prussia. Therefore, they must have been Germans, although I cannot rule out that patients from around Działdowo were also involved, that is Poles. I believe the patients had been taken from the hospitals to the camp in Działdowo, from where they were transported the next day to the execution site in the forest. Here the patients were led to the special vehicle and gassed. If I remember correctly, gas cylinders were also used in this instance. The special vehicle was probably brought from Poznań. I cannot say how long the operation lasted or how many victims were involved. I remember that after the pits had been dug, the SS men from the Sonderkommando ordered the prisoners from the Działdowo camp employed in digging the pits to line up and then run. Shots were then fired from a machine gun and a large part of the prisoners were killed. Several of them managed to escape, but the camp personnel were notified and conducted a hunt for them. These prisoners were caught and shot for "trying to escape."[51]

Henryk Maliczak seconds the details related by his companion Mania, adding that the Gauleiter of East Prussia, Erich Koch, appeared at dawn one day to visit the site and examine the pits.[52]

Mania may not have remembered how many victims he buried in the forest between May 21 and June 8, 1940, but HSSPF Wilhelm Koppe did: 1,558. Koppe's deal with Rediess, made through RSHA, involved Rediess paying Koppe RM 10 for every person killed. After arriving in Działdowo, Lange personally received RM 2,000 from Dr. Otto Rasch as a down payment to cover his operating expenses. However, following the operation the balance remained unpaid. Koppe was not amused and thus began a series of correspondence in an effort to collect, even bringing the matter to the attention of Himmler's office. It is not clear if he ever did collect but, more importantly, this correspondence makes it clear that Koppe was operationally responsible for Sonderkommando Lange.[53]

Following the operation in Działdowo and a farewell party, Sonderkommando Lange went back to Poznań and the Polish prisoners were returned to their cell in Fort VII. They did not see Lange again for about a year. Gauleiter Koch was apparently quite pleased with Lange's work in Działdowo as he presented Lange with an inscribed amber box as a token of his appreciation.[54] Himmler was so appreciative of the efforts of Lange and his Sonderkommando he ordered them to take a vacation. According to one source, they chose the Netherlands.[55]

There is no evidence Sonderkommando Lange operated as a unit for the next 12 months. It is believed Lange spent this time working at the Poznań Gestapo office. In June 1941, the unit was reactivated and conducted a two-stage operation at the Dziekanka facility in Gniezno on June 3–4 and July 3–5, 1941. Based on the number of patients included in the transports (June 3: 40 patients; June 4: 18 patients; July 3: 41 patients; July 4: 33 patients; July 5: 26 patients), Lange loaded the gas van once a day.[56]

On June 4, 1941, an SS official named Fischer from GSV in Poznań arrived at the Hospital for the Indigent [Zakład dla Ubogich] in Śrem, located south of Poznań, and informed the administration that a transport of psychiatric patients from Gostynin would arrive in the next couple of days for a brief stay. This transport of 70 patients arrived by train on June 9. Several weeks prior, Dr. Ratka from the Psychiatric Hospital in Dziekanka came to Śrem and examined the patients. A name list was drawn up. Fischer informed the personnel that the patients on the list would be leaving the facility together with the patients brought in from Gostynin. At 10:45 on the morning of June 10, a car with five Gestapo officials arrived. Following behind the car was what can be described as a flatbed truck carrying a large tank and pulling a hermetically sealed metal trailer with hoses running from the tank to the trailer. Several men got out of the cab. A third vehicle also arrived: a canvass covered truck carrying 13 civilians. One of these civilians, outside earshot of the Gestapo officials, said in Polish, "We're with these criminals." The officials were served a generous breakfast of bread, ham, scrambled eggs and tea. The civilians in the truck were given bread and pork fat. After breakfast, patients were led outside and packed into the van. The Gestapo officials urged the nurses to be careful because "they are also people, and they're ill." The rear doors were then closed and bolted with three locks on the top, middle and bottom. The convoy of three vehicles then drove away in an unknown direction. This procedure was repeated during the next two days. Over the three-day period, a total of 70 patients from Gostynin and 56 patients from the Śrem facility were loaded into the vehicle.[57]

Following the operation in Śrem, Sonderkommando Lange proceeded to Łódź and revisited the Kochanówka facility. A list of names of mainly outpatients was drawn up and certified by Dr. Grohmann, the T4 specialist. Lange and his unit were housed on the grounds of the hospital, in villa number six.[58] One employee stated the gas van was similar to the gas van used a year earlier, but the Kaiser's Kaffee logo was absent during the later operation. He also noticed several rubber hoses running from the motor to the trailer.[59] Another member of the hospital staff stated a man named Lange always accompanied the transports as they departed from the hospital. She also recalled the group of Poles that accompanied the SS men. They were under German guard and taken from the hospital with shovels on the same days the patients were evacuated. She also overheard one of these Poles tell another "You know, I'll never forget the look of that woman who convulsively grabbed my hand and begged for help."[60] During this operation, which began on June 16, 150 patients were evacuated from the hospital.

In addition to the operations by Sonderkommando Lange described above, the unit was also responsible for the murder of patients in other facilities. Lange and his mobile killing squad are also believed to have played a role in the murder of patients in a nursing home in Bojanowo near the town of Leszno;[61] the Jewish hospital on Wesoła Street in the Łódź ghetto;[62] nursing homes and hospices in Łódź;[63] a home for the elderly in Stawiszyn;[64] unknown victims, probably German patients transported from the Old Reich, buried in a forest near Międzychód;[65] as well as a group of Jewish men the Sonderkommando picked up in Frankfurt-am-Oder and drove to a forest outside Nowy Tomyśl. The cylinders of gas they brought with them were not needed as the victims suffocated in the back of the van during the trip. The bodies were buried in the forest.[66]

Maliczak remembered being in Międzychód, saying it was in the spring or summer, and that there were four mass graves with about 50 corpses buried in each one. He heard from members of the SK that the victims were German mental patients. During this operation both Mania and Maliczak recalled that a Nazi dignitary, wearing a gray uniform with wide, white facings, arrived on the scene while they were carrying the corpses of the gassed victims over to the pits. Maliczak believed it was some kind of an inspection. During the official's brief visit, the gravediggers and corpse carriers were ordered to treat the bodies with respect, as according to the dignitary "they are people too." After the official departed, things returned to normal; the corpses were thrown out and dragged to the pits accompanied by the yelling and shoving of the SS men. Wilhelm Schmerse, a member of Sonderkommando Legath, the special unit assigned the task of eliminating this and other burial sites, also remembers being in Międzychód in connection with his duties. He estimated that approximately 500 corpses were buried in the graves.[67]

Hitler officially stopped the Euthanasia Program in August 1941. Bouhler and Brandt hoped to continue the program following the war. In order to preserve the trained personnel in Germany as an intact unit, and after consulting with Himmler, Viktor Brack was ordered to transfer the personnel to Lublin, Poland, where they were placed at the disposal of Brigadeführer Odilo Globocnik, the SS and Police Leader of the Lublin District. These men would eventually staff the extermination camps of Treblinka, Sobibór and Bełżec. Sonderkommando Lange was not sent to Lublin. One month after Hitler issued his stop order, Lange and his unit appeared in the town of Konin to begin a new assignment.

The Turning Point

The Governor of the Warthegau, Arthur Greiser, had a problem—a Jewish problem. Despite repeated efforts he had failed to achieve his dream of a province free of Jews. Unable to push his problem onto others, he decided to take matters into his own hands and acquired the approval to do so from his superior, Adolf Hitler.

Reichsgau Posen, later designated Reichsgau Wartheland, and also known as the Warthegau, was created from sections of Poland's western territory on the basis of a Führer order, dated October 8, 1939. This province was divided into three administrative districts: Inowrocław (Hohensalza); Kalisz (Kalisch), later changed to Łódź (Litzmannstadt); and Poznań (Posen). Each district was subdivided into counties. The Warthegau was administered from Poznań by Arthur Greiser, a decorated veteran of the First World War. In September 1918, just before the armistice, he sustained serious injuries when his plane was shot down. After release from the hospital Greiser was transfered to the area of Danzig, where he settled in the 1920s. During this time, he dabbled in the volatile sphere of politics in the free city and joined a Masonic lodge. He focused on making money in the business world, starting his own company dealing in fats and oils in 1923. However, by 1929 the company collapsed, a pivotal point in Greiser's life. It was at this time that the future governor became emersed in politics, joining the Nazi party in December 1929 and quickly rising in its ranks, becoming a member of the Danzig Senate and eventually President of the Senate at the end of 1934.[1] Greiser became a fanatical Nazi and anti-Semite. On September 12, 1939, following the outbreak of the war with Poland, he was appointed head of the civil administration in Poznań and, on October 26, Governor [Reichstatthalter] and Provincial Party Leader [Gauleiter] of Reichsgau Wartheland, thereby controlling the organs of both the state and Nazi party respectively.

With the establishment of the Warthegau, Greiser found himself ruling over a population of some five million people, comprising Poles, Jews and Germans. Poles made up the vast bulk of the population, approximately 4.2 million people, followed by some 400,000 Jews and about 325,000 Germans. This demographic reality posed a major problem for Greiser as he envisoned creating "a model Gau of the Great German Reich," an impossibility with more than 90 percent of the inhabitants considered subhumans. Nevertheless, he simultaneously viewed the situation as an opportunity to build a National-Socialist province from the ground up.[2]

The solution to this problem was to involve massive population transfers. German settlers were to be brought into the province from lands in the East to populate the area. Poles and Jews, meanwhile, were to be deported to the East. Today this is called "ethnic cleansing." This migration envisoned millions of people moving in both directions. Greiser's dream met reality head on when the goals of expelling the bulk of the population while simultaneously building a model Gau proved mutually exclusive. Greiser needed the Poles to keep the economy from completely collapsing, but without expelling them the incoming Germans had no place to settle.

Over the course of the next two years, a number of plans involving population transfers were drawn up, but efforts to exert authority and practical issues (diplomatic considerations, the ongoing war, mismanagement, lack of available trains, etc.) led to results falling far short of the original goals. One such example is the second short-range plan [*Nahplan*]. On November 12, 1940, Obergruppenführer Wilhelm Koppe announced that 200,000 Poles and 100,000 Jews would be deported to the General Government as a step in making the Warthegau a province for Germans only.[3] This resettlement plan eventually bogged down due to bureaucratic bickering with Greiser pushing for the removal of these people from his area of administration and Hans Frank, Greiser's counterpart in the General Government, having second thoughts about accepting them. In the end, this idea was dropped when it was decided not to create a Jewish reservation in the Lublin district of the General Government. Despite the difficulties, by March 1941, some 272,000 Poles had been deported to the General Government.[4] The continual failure of the resettlement plans led to increased frustration among local leaders.[5]

At the outbreak of the war approximately 400,000 Jews lived in the area that was to become the Warthegau. The vast majority, about 326,000, lived in the district of Łódź, of which 233,000 Jews resided within the city of Łódź. The district of Inowrocław had a Jewish population of approximately 54,000, while Poznań had the smallest Jewish population with only some 4,500 inhabitants.[6] As a result of the German deportation policy, by March 1940, the Jewish populations of the Poznań District and western counties of the Inowrocław District had been expelled.

In 1940, ghettos were established across the Warthegau in areas still inhabited by Jews. The purpose of the ghettos was to concentrate and subordinate the Jewish population until the issue of their removal was settled. Crowding the Jewish population into concentrated areas also made housing available for the ethnic Germans being resettled into the area, though this actually had limited impact as the incoming Germans needed the apartments of middle-class Poles in the towns and cities and the relatively larger farms of rural Poles. It has been estimated that by the early months of 1940 the Jewish population of the Warthegau had declined—due in part to the deportation program, the flight of many civilians and to outright murder—to approximately 260,000.[7] By May 1, 1940, the Jewish population of the city of Łódź, now sealed inside the ghetto, had decreased to 163,177.[8]

It must have been obvious to Arthur Greiser that the best solution to his "Jewish problem" was to take matters into his own hands. This is precisely what he did, turning to Hitler with a request that he be granted permission to solve the Jewish problem in his province. While there are no minutes of this meeting, it is inconceivable that Greiser, Himmler and Heydrich would have moved forward with such a plan without Hitler's approval. The initiative is referred to in Greiser's letter to Himmler, dated May 1, 1942, the subject of which is a subsequent proposal to Himmler to provide "special treatment" to Poles with tuberculosis. In the letter Greiser informed Himmler that "the special treatment of about 100,000 Jews in the territory of my district, approved by you in agreement with the Chief of the Reich Security Main Office, Obergruppenführer Heydrich, can be completed within the next two to three months."[9]

Both Heydrich, who received a copy of the letter from Koppe, and Himmler agreed to the proposal without reservation, only noting that individual measures be discussed with the Security Police "in order to ensure inconspicuous accomplishment of the task."[10] However, Greiser's proposal was opposed by the Deputy Chief of the Public Health Office, Dr. Blome, who in a letter to Greiser demanded Hitler agree to the proposal due to the importance of the issue.[11] Greiser again turned to Himmler querying him whether the issue actually required a presentation to the Führer, adding "I personally don't think we have to consult the Führer again in this matter, all the more since he told me at the last meeting concerning the Jews that I should act according to my best judgment."[12]

The content of the above correspondence clearly illustrates the criminal initiative and leading role played by Greiser. The correspondence not only shows that Greiser was the instigator of the campaign to exterminate Jews in his territory, but also shows him attempting to launch a second campaign to exterminate thousands of Poles with tuberculosis using Sonderkommando Kulmhof to do so.[13] Equally important, Hitler granted Greiser the authority to proceed with his plan. Adolf Eichmann testified at his trial that "Greiser [arranged] for those from Litzmannstadt who were unable to work to be killed. Section IVB4 [which Eichmann headed] had nothing to do with that." He later went on to say that there was a special arrangement in regard to the Warthegau and that "Greiser then managed to establish for himself a special position there as regards the Litzmannstadt ghetto."[14] Eichmann's point was not to minimize the role his office played in the extermination, only that it was Greiser who initiated it and had the authority to so act.

Based on surviving documents, it cannot be determined precisely when Greiser obtained his special authorization from Hitler and more specifically when he issued the order to murder the Jews in the Wartheland. However, the timeframe would begin in mid-July 1941, when Sturmbannführer Rolf-Heinz Höppner, the head of the Emigration Central Office [Umwandererzentralstelle] in Poznań, sent a memorandum to Eichmann in Berlin. This memorandum and accompanying note spells out that a plan is under consideration by Greiser. The cut-off date for establishing the period in which Greiser issued his order would be mid-September 1941, the date of the first mass execution of Jews in the Wartheland.

Within this two-month window a conference of county commissioners of the Łódź District was held on July 24, 1941. At the meeting District President Übelhör informed the commissioners that, in liquidating the provincial ghettos, sick Jews were not to be resettled in Łódź. On Greiser's orders, they were to be left where they were. Übelhör repeated this in a letter dated August 16, 1941.[15] This order is confirmed in a later Łódź Gestapo report to Inspector Ernst Damzog in Poznań, dated May 9, 1942, stating that in liquidating the provincial ghettos those Jews who were unable to work were not to be resettled to the Łódź ghetto, but were to be left where they were (left at the disposal of the Sonderkommando) according to Greiser's order.[16] On September 20, 1941, Greiser ordered Oberführer Dr. Georg Herbert Mehlhorn, director of Department I (General, Domestic and Financial Matters) in the Governor's Office in Poznań, "to work out all the issues necessary connected with accommodating and employing the Jews and Gypsies of the Wartheland."[17]

Based on the above-mentioned dates and the activities surrounding them, Greiser obtained Hitler's permission to exterminate the Jews in his province sometime between mid-July and mid-September 1941, probably closer to the former than the latter date. It is also within this timeframe that Greiser issued the extermination order, an order that was executed not only by the SS and Gestapo, but by a wide range of government officials.

Conducting the extermination plan involved not only physical liquidation, but also roundups and selections in the smaller ghettos; coordination with local police; transports to Chełmno; transports to the Łódź ghetto; the confiscation, processing and sale of property; and the administration of the Łódź ghetto. Dr. Mehlhorn coordinated the activities of the district presidents in Łódź (Friedrich Übelhör and, from December 15, 1942, Dr. Hermann Riediger) and Inowrocław (Dr. Hans Burckhardt) as well as the commissioners in those counties where ghettos had been established. The director of the Financial and Budget Department of the Governor's Office, Dr. Friedrich Hausler, in cooperation with the Oberbürgermeister of Łódź, Werner Ventzki and the Łódź Ghetto Administration, under Hans

Biebow, was responsible for economic and financial affairs. Operational responsibility involving the selection, dispatch and transport of Jews from the ghettos to Chełmno fell under the jurisdiction of the security police, and in particular the Jewish affairs office, initially section IIB4, of the Łódź Gestapo, headed by Günter Fuchs. The Schutzpolizei (or Schupo) was assigned the task of guarding the camp in Chełmno.[18]

The degree of Dr. Mehlhorn's involvement with the Chełmno death camp is not fully understood but appears to be much greater than has appeared in the literature. One of the Polish workers employed in the camp stated that Polizeimeister Willi Lenz and "Melhorn from the SS," supervised the Jewish Waldkommando.[19] Although Mehlhorn was not a supervisor of the Waldkommando, a position far below his station, the fact that he was so labeled by someone on the scene suggests the official asserted significant direct authority with respect to the forest camp for a certain period of time. The duties entrusted to Dr. Mehlhorn included such details as covering up the mass graves of the victims in the forest outside Chełmno. Mehlhorn ordered Heinz May, the state forestry official directly responsible for the forest in which the graves were located, to report to him in Poznań where he personally discussed the issue with the forester. May was told to provide the SS Sonderkommando with the materials necessary to meticulously camouflage the graves and added that "if worst comes to worst [if the existence of the graves became public], we will have to pretend that these too are murdered German nationals."[20]

The Jewish population in the Warthegau had been stripped of all rights and concentrated into confined areas, ghettos, to restrict their movements and exploit them in the form of slave labor. These ghettos were a transitional measure, a kind of holding pen until the inhabitants could be transported "to the east" at some later date. The term "to the east" would become a euphemism for extermination but its original meaning was literal. The change in policy on the local level was proposed due to the recognition that the Jews would remain in the Warthegau for an indefinite period and the most favorable course of action would be their total exploitation. The policy was developed on the local level in Poznań and subsequently approved on the central level in Berlin. It was a major step "forward" toward total extermination. The eventual establishment of the Chełmno death camp was a local matter, albeit approved at the highest level due to its very nature, developed to solve a local "problem."

The policy is outlined in the aforementioned document originating from the Emigration Central Office in Poznań. A note written by the head of this office, Sturmbannführer Rolf-Heinz Höppner, accompanied the memorandum, dated July 16, 1941, and was sent to his colleague in Berlin, Obersturmbannführer Adolf Eichmann.

Dear Comrade Eichmann,

Enclosed is a memorandum on the results of various discussions held locally in the office of the Reich Governor. I would be grateful to have your reactions sometime. These things sound in part fantastic, but in my view are thoroughly feasible.

Memorandum

Subject: Solution of the Jewish Question

During discussions in the office of the Reich Governor various groups broached the solution of the Jewish question in Warthe province. The following solution is being proposed:

1. All the Jews of Warthe Province will be taken to a camp for 300,000 Jews which will be erected in barracks form as close as possible to the coal precincts and which will contain barracks-like installations for economic enterprises, tailor shops, shoe manufacturing plants, etc.
2. All Jews of Warthe Province will be brought into this camp. Jews capable of labor may be constituted into labor columns as needed and drawn from the camp.
3. In my view, a camp of this type may be guarded by SS Brig. Gen. Albert with substantially fewer police forces than are required now. Furthermore, the danger of epidemics, which always exists in the Łódź and other ghettos for the surrounding population, will be minimized.
4. This winter there is a danger that not all the Jews can be fed anymore. One should weigh honestly, if the most humane solution might not be to finish off those of the Jews who are not employable by means of some quick-working device. At any rate, that would be more pleasant than to let them starve to death.
5. For the rest, the proposal was made that in this camp all the Jewish women, from whom one could still expect children, should be sterilized so that the Jewish problem may actually be solved completely with this generation.
6. The Reich Governor has not yet expressed an opinion in this matter. There is an impression that District President Übelhör does not wish to see the ghetto in Łódź disappear since he [his office] seems to profit quite well with it. As an example of how one can profit from the Jews, I was told that the Reich Labor Ministry pays 6 Reichmark from a special fund for each employed Jew, but that the Jew costs only 80 Pfennige.[21]

This plan may have sounded fantastic to Höppner, but can the same be said for Greiser? During 1939 and 1940, Greiser oversaw Sonderkommando Lange as it traveled around his province murdering mental patients. With the invasion of the Soviet Union in June 1941, on Hitler's orders the mobile killing squads of the Einsatzgruppen began shooting Jewish men. Following a number of discussions in July between Hitler and Himmler, this order was expanded in August to include women and children.[22] Greiser was certainly aware of this and his proposal was merely a "humane plan that only called for a quick-working device for the unproductive." Who could object to this? No new threshold would be crossed; no great leap had to be taken.

While no direct connection, in the form of an official approval document, has been established between the Höppner memorandum and the establishment of the Chełmno death camp, it was essentially this plan that was subsequently adopted. All of the Jews living in the Warthegau were eventually concentrated in one big "camp": the Łódź ghetto. The camp was to be profitable and those unfit for work were finished off by some "quick-working device": Chełmno. Mordechai Chaim Rumkowski, the head of the Łódź ghetto Council of Elders (the local Jewish Council or Judenrat), believed that the Jews had value to the Nazis only so long as they were productive. Rumkowski focused his efforts on trying to make the ghetto so productive that the Nazis would view the Jews as indispensable. In fact, he had no other options. Of course this strategy only went so far, since the fate of the Jews was ultimately based on ideological and not economic grounds.

The involvement of the highest levels of government in establishing the Chełmno camp is also illustrated by the testimony of HSSPF Wilhelm Koppe. His postwar testimony is typical for higher level perpetrators, disavowing knowledge and shifting blame, but it also contains elements of truth.

> It was in 1940, or may have been 1941, that I learned that a commissar from Berlin was to arrive in the Warthegau with an SS kommando that would carry out the evacuation of the Jews in this province. At the time I did not for one moment imagine that all the Jews were to be exterminated. Greiser also believed that Jews fit for work would be kept for production. I thought that the special Kommando from Berlin and its Commissar, whose name I later discovered was Lange, would be employed only on an experimental basis to begin with. This idea was based on the fact that a certain Dr. Brack, of Hitler's private Chancellery, had already done some preparatory work with poison gases, and that these were to be tried out by the Sonderkommando Lange.
>
> I am certain that I heard about the employment of Sonderkommando Lange from Damzog [Inspector of the Security Police in Reichsgau Wartheland]. Furthermore, Dr. Brandt [Obersturmbannführer Rudolf Brandt, head of Himmler's personal staff] informed me by telephone that an operation against the Jews was being prepared. The conversation went something like this:
>
> Dr. Brandt told me that Dr. Brack had already carried out experiments with gas in Berlin, that these experiments had almost been completed, and that it was planned that he, Dr. Brack, would be put in charge of testing these gases in the Warthegau. Sonderkommando Lange was the obvious choice for carrying out the gassings. [. . .] As a result of this conversation it became absolutely clear to me what kind of operation was intended against the Jews in the Warthegau. As it was an operation that concerned my province, I found myself confronted with a moral dilemma. As head of the SS and police leader, I was directly

involved on a moral and ethical level. Day and night I considered possibilities of averting the planned operation by some clever tactic or other. I telephoned for an appointment to see Gauleiter Greiser. During this meeting I didn't have to explain the purpose of my visit. I realized immediately that Greiser knew about the planned operation. I told him that it seemed that the Warthegau was to become the scene of certain experiments that, as a human being, one could not accept. I asked whose responsibility it would be should the experiments go ahead. Greiser intimated that it was an order from the Führer and that it could not be sabotaged.[23]

In addition to the Hitler–Himmler discussions of July to expand the authority of the Einsatzgruppen to kill women and children, it was also at this time that the central level of government launched an initiative to establish a policy concerning the fate of the Jewish population living under German rule. On July 31, 1941, Hermann Göring authorized Reinhard Heydrich to prepare a "total solution" regarding the Jewish question. This initiative came two weeks after the Höppner memorandum and may have been a reaction to Greiser's plan of putting his own house in order, not to mention the changing state of affairs on the eastern front. In the months that followed a number of new measures were taken that sealed the fate of European Jewry.

In mid-September 1941, Hitler was presented with a number of new, independent initiatives to deport Jews living in the Reich. These initiatives urged him to reconsider his policy of waiting until military victory was achieved in the Soviet Union before deporting all Jews from the Old Reich. For reasons unknown, but with the smell of military victory in the air, Hitler relented. On September 17, the decision was taken to deport German, Austrian and Czech Jews to the Łódź ghetto.

On the local level, Himmler informed Greiser and Koppe on September 18, that it was the Führer's wish the Old Reich and the Protectorate be cleared of Jews as soon as possible. The first step would involve deporting some 60,000 Jews from the Old Reich to the Łódź ghetto. This was a temporary measure to be taken until they could be transported further eastward in the spring. Łódź may have been chosen as a destination for these western deportees aware that Greiser was launching his campaign to kill 100,000 Jews in his territory thereby "making room" for the new arrivals in the Warthegau.

By mid-1940 rural ghettos had been established in the central area of the Wartheland. These were so-called open ghettos that did not have walls enclosing the inhabitants. The communities were self-administered through the establishment of Jewish Councils. Contacts between the Jews and local Poles were not encouraged by the German authorities, but completely separating the two communities was impossible under the circumstances. Labor camps for Jews were also established throughout the region, such as Czarków in Konin County and Borek in Gostyń County[24] that provided a work force to perform menial labor for local and state authorities. At least 160 such camps were functioning in 1942–43, with the slave laborers building roads, railroad lines, and toiling on various water, construction and forestry projects. Some of those unable to work any longer were transported to Chełmno and killed.[25]

In Konin County rural ghettos for the Jewish population were set up in the towns of Grodziec, Rzgów and Zagórów. The 2,000 inhabitants of the Grodziec ghetto mainly originated from Konin. Some 1,000 Jews were settled in the Rzgów ghetto, largely from Słupca, while Zagórów concentrated some 2,500–3,000 Jews from Golina, Kleczew, Kazimierz Biskupi and other localities.[26] It is not known why these specific locations were selected to concentrate the Jews; they were not areas with significant pre-war Jewish communities. However, the purpose of moving the Jewish population into rural areas was to make housing available for the German families being settled in the area. Conditions were harsh. These people had to find shelter wherever they could. Most moved in with Polish families.[27] Some were able to ply their trade, some were employed in forced labor projects and others were murdered outright but, by and large and relatively speaking, the Jews were left to their own devices.

This state of affairs continued until the critical month of September 1941 when Greiser's extermination plan was set in motion with the order to liquidate these ghettos. The Jews in Konin County were killed, not resettled, in a two-phase operation and were the first victims of Arthur Greiser's solution to the Jewish Question in the Wartheland. This opening salvo on the Jewish population is considered by some to be experimental, just as Lange's activities at Fort VII had been prior to implementing the mobile killing operations of the disabled. The Sonderkommando's victims had been the mentally ill, mainly confined in institutions. Lange's new victims were not debilitated in this way and there must have been some concern as to how they would react to the situation in which they found themselves. Moreover, given the planned number of victims (100,000), there must have been some concern if the killing method employed to date was up to the task. These operations are important as they are the first killings associated with Sonderkommando Lange in which the victims were victims only because they were Jewish and therefore a manifestation of the change in policy on the highest levels of the Nazi administration. In addition they show that the Nazi regime was experimenting with the killing method in order to meet the challenge of the task ahead.

The first phase of this operation began in mid-September with the liquidation of the Grodziec and Rzgów ghettos. Officials appeared at the local police station and arrangements were made with the commandant. The Jewish inhabitants were subsequently informed that they were to be evacuated to the east, to either Bessarabia or the Black Sea, to work on farms. In Rzgów the Jews were then ordered to assemble at the fire station with their belongings and ordered to pay a fee of RM 4 to cover the cost of a medical examination to determine each person's ability to work. Luggage was set to one side as it would travel separately and the owners would pick it up later at their destination. The Jews were treated with relative respect so as not to arouse any suspicions. The men, women and children were loaded into horse-drawn wagons, driven by local Poles, and taken to the old synagogue in Konin.[28] From Konin, the Jews were taken to the Niesłusz-Rudzica forest where they were murdered and buried in three mass graves during the last ten days of September and the first ten days of October. The entire operation proceeded at a pace set by the capacity of the machinery of death in the forest.

Details concerning the murder of the people from these ghettos are vague at best. German documents do not exist and Polish postwar documentation is incomplete and secondary in nature. No eyewitnesses have come forward with an account of what happened in the forest. Piotr Zalas was the forester for the Niesłusz-Rudzica forest during the war and lived near the area where the victims were killed. He reported that a passenger car and two canvass covered trucks arrived one day and a Gestapo official (probably Lange) told him to clear everyone out of the forest; that it was off limits until further notice. The forester complied.[29] Thereafter, numerous witnesses from the area reported seeing a parade of vehicles, a passenger car with SS officers followed by a truck full of soldiers and then a black van that looked like a refrigerator, traveling along the road from Konin to the Niesłusz-Rudzica forest. These vehicles entered the forest in the morning and did not leave until the evening. Throughout the day trucks loaded with Jews drove into the forest and shortly afterwards left the scene, their cargo bays empty.

The above-mentioned forester stated that the operation occurred on September 24, 25, 26 and October 3, 1941. Other local residents generally concurred that the killings were carried out over a two-week period during this time. Zalas saw the men, women and children taken into the forest and repeatedly heard the sound of machine guns firing in the forest during the first day, but only individual shots thereafter. On September 28, two days after the first round of killings, Zalas went to the site of the mass graves and noted that it was camouflaged with branches and that some "stinking liquid that smelled of chemicals" was leaking out of the graves. He also went to the location, just meters away, where the victims disembarked from the trucks that brought them to the forest. There, he saw various items including men's, women's, and children's clothing, combs, stockings, shoes, soap, sponges, gingerbread, and lemonade bottles. The next day, military police officials returned to the site, buried some of the items and took the remainder with them.[30]

Another local forest worker entered that section of the forest known as Długa Łąka [Long Meadow] with two of his colleagues and saw two graves about 50 meters long. The graves were covered only with tree branches as a temporary means of camouflage. The corpses appeared to have been thrown inside the graves and not placed there. While standing at the gravesite, they heard the sound of trucks approaching. Scared, they began to run from the area. The soldiers arriving in the trucks spotted the men and gave chase. Shots were fired, but they managed to escape due to their intimate knowledge of the area.[31]

The testimonies of Henryk Maliczak and Henryk Mania confirm that Sonderkommando Lange was responsible for murdering the victims. From Mania's perspective, the operation in Konin occurred in the following way.

> ... [F]irst we had to dig pits in the forest. Jews, I believe from Konin and surrounding towns, were transported to the forest in trucks. First, they completely undressed and entered the gas van, which then drove to a pit we had dug. I did not witness the loading and gassing of the Jews; I just assume this is what occurred based on previous experience. Our job was to unload the naked corpses and throw them into the pit. Entire families were gassed, as among the bodies were men, women and children. Following our work each day, we loaded the clothing into the gas van, which was driven to the Gestapo office in Konin. We then had to search the clothing for valuables. I am unable to say how long this operation lasted or how many victims there were, but it continued for several days. This was the beginning of the campaign of exterminating the Jews.[32]

Mania does not mention experimenting with a new killing method. It may well be that he simply failed to mention it or perhaps he did not witness one. The only novelty for the gravedigger, in regard to the killing process, was the fact that the victims were exclusively Jewish and not mental patients. Stanisław Polubiński, another member of Lange's Polish labor kommando, later told Józef Grabowski, who lived in the village of Chełmno during the war, that Sonderkommando Lange murdered Jews from Konin prior to establishing the Chełmno camp.[33]

Following the operation in the Niesłusz-Rudzica forest, Sonderkommando Lange was sent to Kalisz to evacuate patients from yet another facility. In October 1939, the Jewish Council in Kalisz registered some 20,000 Jews in the city. The vast majority of these people were deported to the General Government as part of the resettlement program. By the end of 1941, the population of the ghetto was less than 500.[34] On October 26, 1941, the local Jewish Council was informed that patients in the old folks home were to be transferred in order to reduce the danger of epidemics breaking out. The patient transfer was to begin at ten o'clock the next morning. Patients were to be washed and provided fresh underwear. All other arrangements had been taken care of. The same day mechanics returning from work at the Gestapo headquarters reported seeing a large number of unknown Gestapo officials and a large black van that appeared to be hermetically sealed (no windows or other means of ventilation). Many people in the ghetto connected these two events. Most were apprehensive, but even the most pessimistic could not imagine what was to follow. The next day, right on schedule, the black van pulled up in front of the old folk's home. One eyewitness to the operation later described the van.

> Its roof was as high as the first storey. It looked like a big black coffin. Two shiny black cars brought Grabowski [chief of the Health Department] at the head of a gang of uniformed and unfamiliar Gestapo men. We had to fetch out those who were called by name, for they were mostly chronic patients and cripples. The Germans ordered us to carry them, seat the patients or stretch them on the benches within the lorry. [After the van was loaded] the metal doors were banged to, the heavy bars were dropped in place, and the large lorry set off silently but swiftly, followed by the gleaming cars.[35]

The loading procedure that day occurred without incident. The Sonderkommando showed great concern about the welfare of the patients. The next day, the gas van made two trips to the forest, each time carrying approximately 55 patients. However, all concern about patient welfare ceased. Those assisting in the loading procedure and the patients themselves were ordered to hurry and were beaten with whips for not complying fast enough. The gas van made two trips on the third and last day of the operation, October 30. The wheelchair of one old woman was returned with the explanation that "she doesn't need it any longer because she's received a new one." Following the operation, the Jewish Council was ordered to pay the cost of transporting the 290 patients at a rate of RM 4 per person. Efforts to trace the patients were unsuccessful. The Jewish Council was initially told that the patients were in transit camps and would be eventually taken to convalescent homes. Later, the council was informed that some of the patients had died of heart failure, brain fever or pneumonia. The others were in good health and in the town of Padernice. However, Padernice could not be found on any map. In July 1942, the few survivors in the Kalisz ghetto were transported to the Łódź ghetto.[36]

Henryk Mania recalled an operation in Kalisz, saying only that the gravediggers were quartered in the local jail and transported to the forest to dig the graves. He did not recall where the graves were or the number of victims. He was under the impression that the victims were mental patients.[37] Following this operation, the Sonderkommando returned to the task of exterminating the Jews of Konin County.

The victims of the second phase of the operation to exterminate the Jews of Konin County included the inhabitants of the rural ghetto in Zagórów. The killing occurred in the Wygoda section of the forest near Kazimierz Biskupi, a small town located north of Konin. In Zagórów, the Jews were assembled with their baggage at the community center and deported in trucks.[38] As opposed to the first stage of the operation, the victims were taken directly to the forest and not to an intermediate staging area (such as the synagogue in Konin).

Also as opposed to the killing conducted in Niesłusz-Rudzica, an independent observer, even participant, witnessed the operation carried out in the Kazimierz Biskupi State Forest. It was here that Lange experimented with a new form of killing. The description of the experiment comprises a portion of the testimony given by a local veterinarian, Mieczysław Sękiewicz, a Pole held in the Konin jail at the time. He had been suspected of being a member of an underground organization. Due to the size of the operation, Lange apparently felt it necessary to bring in additional laborers. In mid-November Gestapo officers ordered Sękiewicz and two fellow prisoners into a car which drove north past the town of Kazimierz Biskupi and later turned left into the woods. When he got out of the car Sękiewicz saw the following.

> [...] [T]wo large pits had been dug. The first one, closer to the dirt road in the forest, was about eight meters long, about six meters wide, and more than two meters deep. At the far edge of the clearing along its entire width was the second pit just as deep, 6 meters wide and about 15 meters long [...].
>
> Groups of Jews were standing or sitting around the entire clearing [...]. I cannot say how many of them there were, as they were standing among the trees. [...] Among the crowd were women, men and children, mothers with babies in their arms; I don't know whether they were only Polish Jews. Later I was told that they came from the village of Zagórów. Among them I recognized a tailor and a shopkeeper from Konin, but I cannot remember their names. The roads, the clearing and the surrounding forest were full of Gestapo officers. Apart from the three of us from Konin, about 30 Poles had also been brought to the site. I do not know where they came from. At the bottom of the larger trench I saw a layer of unslaked lime chunks. I do not know how thick the layer was. There was no lime in the smaller grave. The Gestapo officers warned us that they had the forest surrounded and under guard, and if we tried to escape, we would get a bullet in the head. The Gestapo officers then ordered the Jews to undress, first those standing closest to the large pit. They then ordered the naked people to walk to the area between the two pits and jump into the larger one. The screams and cries were indescribable. Some Jews jumped in themselves, in fact most of them; others resisted and they were beaten and pushed into the pit. Some of the mothers jumped holding their babies; others pushed their children aside, while others still threw their children into the pit and then jumped in themselves.
>
> Some of the women crawled at the feet of the Gestapo officers, kissing their boots, rifle butts, etc. We were ordered to walk among the Jews standing next to the graves and collect the scattered clothes and shoes. I witnessed scenes where Gestapo officers approached the places where we collected watches, rings and other pieces of jewelry in piles, grabbed handfuls of these valuables and stuffed them in their pockets. Seeing this, some of us, including me, stopped putting the valuables in piles, and instead threw the watches and rings further into the forest on purpose. At one point, the Gestapo officers ordered the Jews to stop

undressing because the pit was full. From above, the only thing visible was the heads of the people, tightly packed in the pit. Those Jews who had hurried and undressed were thrown into the pit onto the heads of those crammed inside. During this time we continued to collect and sort the scattered clothing, shoes, baggage, food, eiderdowns, etc. That lasted until midday and then a truck came from the direction of the main road and stopped near the clearing. I noticed four vat-like things on the truck. Next, the Germans set up a small engine, which was probably a pump. Using a hose, they connected it to one of the vats. Two of the Gestapo officers then dragged the hose from the motor to the large pit. They started the motor and these two Gestapo officers holding the hose began pouring something onto the Jews crowded in the pit. I think it was water, that's what it looked like but I'm not sure. As the water was pumped, the hose was moved from one vat to another. Apparently, as a result of the slaking of the lime, the people began to boil alive. The screaming was so horrible that those of us who were sitting near the clothing tore off pieces of material and put them in our ears. The horrible screams of those being boiled in the pit was joined by the screaming and wailing of those still waiting to be executed. That lasted for about two hours, possibly longer. When night fell we were taken from the clearing, along the forest road that led to the main road, towards the edge of the forest [. . .]. They gave us some coffee and 250 grams of bread. There were six or seven canvass covered trucks parked along the edge of the forest.

We were loaded into the trucks and ordered to lay face down on the floor, next to each other, and not to move. That's how we spent the night. The screams could still be heard. I heard them until I fell asleep, which happened quickly—I was horrified and exhausted. The following morning, the Gestapo officers ordered us to cover the pit with dirt. The mass of people inside had collapsed and sunk towards the bottom of the pit. The bodies were packed so tightly together that they remained in the somewhat vertical position; only their heads were tilted in all different directions. We only partly covered the grave; arms were still sticking out of the ground when we were ordered to stop, as trucks began arriving and we had to throw things onto the trucks— clothes, shoes and other items, all separately. In the afternoon a large, dark grey ambulance-like vehicle with doors in the rear drove into the clearing several times. After the doors were opened, the corpses of Jewish men, women and children fell out. I do not know whether the vehicle kept returning after I had been taken away from the clearing.

The corpses that fell out of the truck were clinging to one another, as if in convulsive grasps, in contorted positions, sometimes with mangled faces. I saw one with the teeth sunk into another's jaw, while others had their noses or fingers bitten off. Many corpses were holding hands; they were probably families. The Gestapo officers ordered us to separate the corpses, and if this did not work, then to chop them up, cutting off hands, legs and other parts. Next, we had to place the corpses in the smaller pit in the clearing, positioning them tightly together with the head of one corpse beside to the feet of the next corpse. We were ordered to stuff the body parts between the corpses. While I was there, three such layers of people were arranged and one truck had yet to be unloaded. We were then taken to sleep in the trucks just like the previous night and given potato soup and bread. The following morning I and my fellow prisoners were taken to the edge of the clearing to be searched.

[...] we were lined up along the edge of a pit which was more or less three by four meters in size. A Gestapo officer with a weapon was standing in front of each of us.

I was facing the pit. A Gestapo officer ordered me to confess to all of the charges against me, that is reading the illegal press, helping other Poles, etc. As I was explaining that the charges were false, he ordered me to turn back towards the pit and threatened me several times that he would kill me if I did not confess; if I did confess, then I could go home and would be given a good job.

When this didn't work he shot at me from a few steps away. I couldn't take it anymore and I fell into the pit. I remember thinking I was dead, yet I knew what was happening around me. Then I heard the Gestapo officer shout, "*Auf.*" I got up rapidly and crawled out of the pit. All this lasted just seconds. I was not wounded. I do not know whether the Gestapo officer missed or just shot to scare me.

When I got out of the pit, the Gestapo officers beat me about the face with riding crops and then took me and my companions back to prison in Konin. All of us were shackled just as when we were taken away. [...] The corpses were brought in a gray vehicle. It was obvious the people had been gassed. The interior of the vehicle and the clothes of the victims smelled of gas. I recall something else from the clearing when the Jews were killed; how one of the Gestapo officers took a small child from its mother's arms and, right in front of the mother, smashed the baby's head against the edge of a vehicle. When the mother started screaming, he hurled the baby's head at her so violently that its brain matter splattered in her mouth. Then he took something out of the vehicle, lime or plaster, and smeared it on her mouth. Other women who screamed loudly were given the same treatment. I witnessed one Gestapo officer grab a young attractive Jewish woman and, having torn off her dress and underwear and tied her arms behind her back, hung her naked by the arms from a tree. He then took a so-called Finnish knife and cut her right breast in slices and then cut her stomach open and rummaged around in her entrails. The Jewish woman died on the tree. I do not know any of the Gestapo officers who were there.[39]

There were undoubtedly many more cases of this sort of depravity but they remain unreported due to the fact that the witnesses to them were killed. For the perpetrators who survived the war, reporting such events would be self-incriminating and therefore they would not be inclined to relate this type of information voluntarily.

The precise number of victims murdered in the Konin County operations is not known. There are no records and the corpses of the victims were eventually dug up and burned by Sonderkommando Legath in February 1944 (Kazimierz Biskupi), and March 1944 (Niesłusz-Rudzica), as part of the operation to eliminate all evidence at the burial sites. However, based on population estimates of these ghettos, it is believed that 1,500 people were murdered in the Niesłusz-Rudzica forest and approximately 3,000 in Kazimierz Biskupi.[40]

The inhabitants of the Grodziec, Rzgów and Zagórów ghettos in Konin County were the first victims of this killing operation and were used as guinea pigs by Lange in his attempt to establish a method of mass extermination. The lime and water experiment was apparently deemed an unacceptable method of killing, no doubt due to the fact that it would require the procurement of massive quantities of lime as well as a ready supply of water. The bottled gas method also had its drawback; it relied on a continual supply of the gas-filled cylinders. This problem would be overcome with the deployment of the second generation of gas vans, developed in Berlin, which used exhaust fumes as the killing agent.

Herbert Lange was given the task of exterminating those Jews in Reichsgau Wartheland that could not contribute to the war economy. No documents have been found that specify how he was to accomplish his mission. Basically, Lange had two options. He could continue mobile operations or he could establish a static facility and bring the victims to it. According to Henryk Mania, Lange was not satisfied with his mobile operations; he found them to be inconvenient and overly labor intensive. While traveling throughout the area, Lange sought out a site to establish a permanent installation.[41] It may well be that Herbert Lange never received an order specifically stating that he establish a death camp, but did so on his own initiative. Arthur Greiser probably didn't care how Lange carried out his assignment, just that he completed it.

The establishment of the Chełmno death camp was part of an overall provincial policy aimed at the total exploitation of the Jewish population in the Warthegau. The Łódź ghetto was essentially a massive slave labor camp with its factories fueling the German war machine and private industry. The Chełmno camp was a cog in this machinery, a tool to rid the German administration of people it deemed superfluous or harmful to production schedules. Within this context the decision to employ Lange and his Sonderkommando was a logical one. The unit had considerable experience in disposing of people deemed "useless eaters."

According to Walter Burmeister, following the operation in Konin, he drove Lange to Berlin,[42] probably reporting on the results of the Konin operation and informing superiors that he had found a location to set up a static killing center. After returning from Berlin, Lange met with HSSPF Wilhelm Koppe and reported on his new assignment. Rudolf Brandt, Himmler's adjutant, also called Koppe to inform him that the "testing of Brack's gas" was planned for the Warthegau. Koppe arranged for the manpower, turning to his inspector, Ernst Damzog, for the SS personnel, and to the commander of the Order Police in the Warthegau, Oskar Knofe, for the policemen who would serve as guards.[43] According to Henryk Mania, the partially reconstituted Sonderkommando Lange did not return to Poznań, but went directly to the village of Chełmno following the operation in the Kazimierz Forest outside Konin.[44]

CHAPTER 2

Extermination: The First Period (1941–1943)

Establishing the Camp

In the autumn of 1941, Rottenführer Walter Burmeister, assigned as Lange's driver, signed an oath of secrecy to remain silent concerning his activities with the Sonderkommando.[1] While the operation in Konin was under way, Lange ordered Burmeister to drive east about 40 kilometers to the small village of Chełmno.

The war had taken its toll on the population of Chełmno and the surrounding area, which was comprised of Poles, Jews and Germans. The front lines of the military campaign in 1939, passed through the area; both Koło and Dąbie were bombed by the Luftwaffe. Dąbie's material losses exceeded the town's annual budget eight-fold. Some 15 homes, 23 farms and two industrial facilities were totally or partially destroyed. But worse was to come. As elsewhere throughout Poland, units of the Security Police (Sipo) and Security Service (SD) rounded up and arrested local citizens, both intellectuals and non-intellectuals, considered a potential threat to German rule. Those arrested in the second half of September in Dąbie included a pharmacist, a physician, and other community leaders. Locally, some 80 people were detained and held in the Koło jail until November when more than 50 of them were transported to the Rzuchów Forest and shot. This location would become the future burial site for the victims of the Chełmno camp.[2]

Towns and villages throughout occupied Poland were taken over and administered by Germans. Names of towns were changed to a German variant: Łódź was renamed Litzmannstadt and Poznań became Posen. Locally, Chełmno became Kulmhof, Koło became Warthbrücken, Dąbie became Eichstadt and Powiercie became Arnsdorf. As part of the program to Germanize the Warthegau, thousands of Poles had their land and property confiscated to make way for ethnic Germans being transplanted into the area from the Old Reich, the Baltic countries, Volhynia and other regions.

Located some 60 kilometers northwest of Łódź, Chełmno is situated in a bend of the highway between Dąbie, six kilometers to the south, and Koło,

14 kilometers to the north. The village had a population of approximately 250 residents and was comprised of some 30 to 40 houses. Several Jewish families lived in Chełmno, but when the war broke out they moved to nearby Dąbie seeking a greater sense of security. On July 15, 1940, an open ghetto with 920 inhabitants was established in Dąbie, comprising two of the town's streets.[3] As German settlers moved into the area, Poles had to relocate. Some moved out of the area, others moved in with family friends.

In 1941, Chełmno was dominated by an old estate with a dilapidated neo-Gothic mansion situated on about three hectares (7.5 acres) of land on the western edge of the village.[4] The other dominant feature was the village church, located some 100 meters down the highway, but separated by a small gully. The estate was acquired in 1837, by a Russian general, Carl Heinrich George von Bistrom, for services rendered on behalf of the Russian Tsar. The general died the following year and the estate passed to his son, Nikolaj Karl von Bistram,[5] who constructed both the mansion and the church in the 1880s. Following the First World War, the estate was confiscated by the newly reconstituted Polish state. The mansion was divided into apartments and families moved in. Ludwig Koziej, who lived in one of the apartments with his family, was the building's administrator.[6]

The *gmina* [community] administration building, or village hall, was situated approximately 50 meters down from the church and beyond that was a local grocery store. The small village school was located on the opposite side of the road. Across the road that ran in front of the mansion was the building of the volunteer fire department, which during the war was known as the German House. Behind the mansion and church the ground sloped steeply, then leveled out along the Ner River. Chełmno was a regular stop along the narrow gauge railway line that connected Dąbie with Koło. A second section of this line ran north from Koło to Sompolno.

Chełmno and 16 surrounding villages comprised the local *gmina*, the seat of which was the village of Chełmno itself. In June 1939, Franciszek Opas was elected as head of the *gmina* (called the *wójt*), Józef Ziółkowski as deputy head, and Antoni Skrobanin and Józef Woźniak as aldermen.[7] Other members of the board included Stanisław Kaszyński (secretary), Konrad Schulz and Antoni Pyszka. Czesław Potyralski and Leopold Chwiałkowski were clerks.

Franciszek Opas and Stanisław Kaszyński were long-time community public servants. Both were founding members of the local branch of the Airborne and Antigas Defense League [Liga Obrony Powietrznej i Prze-ciwgazowej, LOPP], a nationwide, civil defense organization founded in 1928. The local LOPP branch was established in Chełmno in February 1934 and located in the *gmina* administration building. Opas and Kaszyński served on the board of the organization for a number of years.[8] Konrad Schulz, as the name implies, was of German heritage. In 1922, he moved from a small village near the town of Zagórów, west of Konin, to a farm in Sobótka, a village located just south of Chełmno along the road to Dąbie. Schulz also had a history of involvement in local community politics, in the early 1930s serving as head of the local council and later sitting on the board of the Chełmno *gmina* administration.[9]

Following the invasion of Poland the Nazi regime installed Germans in the top administrative positions. Locally, Konrad Schulz was appointed administrative head of the *gmina* [Amtskommissar] by Landrat Baur from Koło and was also appointed the local head of the Nazi party. Jakob Semmler, a local farmer, was named village administrator [*sołtys*] of Chełmno.[10] A German named Kluge replaced Kaszyński as secretary. However, Kaszyński, together with Chwiałkowski and Potyralski, remained as clerks.[11]

When Burmeister drove Lange to Chełmno that autumn, the Nazi party district leader of Koło, Walter Becht, was there to meet them. Konrad Schulz, the highest-ranking local official, was not in Chełmno that day. Together Lange and Becht drove around the area for some time, inquiring about public buildings. They stopped and examined the mansion, paying particular attention to the basement area. After this inspection, they left.[12]

A few days later, Lange and Burmeister returned. The local schoolteacher, Erhard Michelsohn, one of the Germans who had recently been resettled in the area, recalled this second visit.

> One day in the winter of 1941/42 several cars drove to the town hall, opposite the school, and several SS men in field gray uniforms got out. I could observe this from the school. They went into the town hall and conferred there with Amtskommissar Schulz. Afterwards, Schulz told me that a Sonderkommando would establish a *Durchgangslager* [transit camp] in Chełmno. The SS men told him that Jews would pass through here on their way to Russia.[13]

During their meeting Lange informed Schulz precisely what his intentions were and that he was requisitioning the German House for his men. He then departed. Schulz passed on the information to the former secretary of the *gmina*, Stanisław Kaszyński. Jan Bąberski, a young boy who was frequently at the *gmina* office, heard Kaszyński say that the Germans were going to establish a camp "to kill people." Bąberski also overheard a conversation in which Schulz told Kaszyński that "things were going to heat up in Chełmno, that blood will flow and few will survive."[14]

Several days later, after the second visit and when all the necessary arrangements had been made, Lange, together with the Sonderkommando, arrived in Chełmno. At least a part of the group came directly to Chełmno from the operation in Konin.[15] The others, including new members, were picked up in Poznań by Polizeimeister Willi Lenz. Among those in this group was the policeman Karl Heinl who gave the following account.

> I was to report to Polizeimeister Lenz [at the Poznań Gestapo office] in order to be incorporated into a guard squad together with other police officials.

Revierleutnant Graf personally passed this order on to me. I do not know who from the commando of the Schutzpolizei passed on this order. I was not told, either, for what purpose or in what place this kommando was to be employed. As ordered I went to the Stapo [Gestapo] office in Poznań on the following day. The aforementioned Polizeimeister Lenz, whom I did not know, met me at the entrance. Altogether, five or six police officials met there, who like Lenz came from police districts in Poznań. As far as I remember there were:

1. Polizei-Oberwachtmeister Hannes Runge
2. Polizei-Wachtmeister Max Sommer
3. Polizei-Hauptwachtmeister [Simon] Haider
4. Polizei-Oberwachtmeister Erich Kretschmer

I cannot now recall the other persons. We asked Lenz for what purpose we were being employed but he told us that he did not know. He told us to go to the canteen and wait for him. Then he went into the Stapo office. In the afternoon, at about three o'clock, Lenz appeared and ordered us to depart. In front of the Stapo office we got into a truck, which was driven by a member of the Stapo, Oberscharführer Erwin Bürstinger. He drove us via Koło to the village of Chełmno. After we arrived there Lenz assigned us quarters in a house in the village, where we spent the night in a big room.[16]

The SS men were originally housed in the building of the local volunteer fire department, the German House, but later when the police guard arrived, they moved into private homes and the police guard was quartered in this building. Sometime later, barracks to house policemen were brought in from Konin or Koło and erected next to the German House.[17] Lange, his deputy Obersturmführer Herbert Otto and Burmeister stayed in the local administration building. In addition to the German House and the administration building, the Sonderkommando confiscated the old mansion, the church (which was closed) and the presbytery. The local priest, Father Karol Morozewicz, was arrested by the Germans and died in the Dachau concentration camp on May 3, 1942.[18] Houses were also confiscated to serve as a kitchen and a canteen.

Outside the village, about four-and-a-half kilometers along the road to Koło, was the Chełmno forest, also known as the Rzuchów and Ladorudz forest. The Sonderkommando confiscated sections 76, 77, and parts of sections 74 and 75 of this forest on the left-hand side of the road. A police guard was established around its perimeter and it was placed off limits to the public.

The Sonderkommando was composed of two groups. The first was a small group of police officials, most of whom were members of the SS and SD [SS Security Service]. They were responsible for carrying out the actual extermination process. Police ranks, not SS ranks, were generally in use among these men. Those from this group who did not belong to the SS (for example, Görlich) were given a complimentary SS rank corresponding to their police rank. The second group, which composed the bulk of the

Sonderkommando, consisted of members of the Schutzpolizei [Municipal Police]. They served primarily as guards and escorts.

The original SS contingent was assigned almost exclusively from Poznań and Łódź. Only the administration official and his replacement were transferred from Inowrocław. The SS Sonderkommando, which established the camp in November 1941, was composed of the following personnel:

Hauptsturmführer Herbert Lange, commandant
Obersturmführer Herbert Otto, deputy commandant (arrived in early January 1942)
Rottenführer Walter Burmeister, Lange's driver and adjutant
Hauptscharführer Friedrich Neumann, administrative affairs
Hauptscharführer Erwin Bürstinger, in charge of vehicles
Hauptscharführer Fritz Ismer, in charge of valuables (arrived in early January 1942)
Hauptscharführer Karl Goede, Ismer's assistant (arrived in early January 1942)
Hauptscharführer Alfred Behm, transport commander
Hauptscharführer Johannes Runge, assistant to Lenz
Unterscharführer Erich Kretschmer, transports
Oberscharführer [first name unknown] Basler, gas van driver (arrived in December or January 1942)
[Rank unknown] Franz Walter, gas van driver (arrived in December or January 1942)[19]
Polizeimeister Willi Lenz, supervisor of the forest camp

However, personnel changes soon occurred. A part of the Sonderkommando who participated in the mobile killing operations was dismissed.[20] Otto, Goede and Behm were in Chełmno only a short time and would be replaced, respectively, by Sturmscharführer Albert Plate (from the Łódź Gestapo), Unterscharführer Max Sommer and Oberscharführer Herbert Hiecke-Richter (known in Chełmno simply as Richter). Later, in April 1942 Neumann was replaced by Sturmscharführer Wilhelm Görlich. Both of these men were assigned to Chełmno from the Gestapo office in Inowrocław.

Lange served as commandant of Chełmno for a relatively brief period of time. In March 1942, he was transferred to the Reich Security Main Office (RSHA) in Berlin, whereupon he received a promotion in July. It is not known if Lange was recalled or if he requested the transfer. His replacement as commandant was Kriminalkommissar and Hauptsturmführer Hans Bothmann. Bothmann was born on November 11, 1911, in Lohe, Schleswig-Holstein. He was tall (187 centimeters or about 6 feet 2 inches), had thin blond hair, blue eyes, a freckled face and spoke in a high pitched voice.

According to his personnel file, Bothmann joined the Nazi party Security Service in 1933, but joined the party itself only two years later in 1935. Like Lange, Bothmann was married and had two children, the second child's birth coinciding with his posting to Chełmno. With Bothmann's arrival, the name of the special unit took his name and was also referred to as Sonderkommando Kulmhof.

Officially, Bothmann was transferred from the Leipzig to the Poznań Gestapo office. Again, like Lange, Bothmann moved his family to Poznań and visited them frequently on weekends. These trips were a combination of business and pleasure. On Fridays, Burmeister drove Lange, and later Bothmann, to meetings in the offices of the Gestapo and the HSSPF. Saturdays and Sundays were spent at home with the family. Richter occasionally filled in as driver for Burmeister on these trips, taking advantage of the situation to visit his own family in Poznań. There were also frequent trips to the Ghettoverwaltung and the Gestapo office in Łódź.[21]

Under Lange's command, the camp was run with an iron fist; he personally supervised all aspects of the operation. Frequent, surprise inspections were made to ensure that all duties were performed accordingly. Sadistically inclined, Lange had no qualms about using brutality toward the people in the transports in order to get the job done. When things did not go according to plan he became furious, cursing at those responsible.

Bothmann's arrival, on the other hand, must have been a welcome relief to the members of the Sonderkommando, and particularly the policemen. Compared to Lange, Bothmann was easygoing. To be sure, like Lange, he was an extremely brutal man, but he also liked to enjoy himself. He drank often and a lot. According to one account, he remained drunk his first three days in the camp. In conversations during the frequent drinking sessions, Bothmann allowed his subordinates to address him by his first name, something unthinkable with Lange.[22]

According to various accounts, establishing the camp took approximately one month (the period of time between the arrival of the Sonderkommando to Chełmno and the arrival of the first transport of victims).[23] This would appear to be plenty of time to accomplish the task as, in the simplest terms, the camp consisted of no more than the mansion and surrounding grounds and an area of forest, the perimeter of which was patrolled by members of the police guard. The primary task consisted of enclosing the grounds of the mansion with a wooden fence and adapting the building itself to the specific requirements of moving people in and out. Amtskommissar Schulz acted as intermediary between the local population and the Sonderkommando.[24] The mansion was evacuated. Under the direct supervision of the village administrator Jakob Semmler, the families who lived in the mansion were ordered to clean it thoroughly. The Sonderkommando undertook minor repairs. Basement windows were first boarded over and later bricked in. A local carpenter was ordered to make a number of benches and to modify the benches in the church for use in the mansion.[25]

The Sonderkommando employed several local women in the village as assistants to help the SK cooks in the kitchen and as maids to clean the offices. Individual members of the Sonderkommando hired other locals as maids, who cleaned their accommodations and washed their clothes—for which the women received a nominal wage.

The necessary building materials were brought in from outside. The grounds of the mansion, which included an overgrown park, were enclosed on three sides by a wooden fence about two-and-a-half meters tall. A large gate was built on the front side where the driveway met the main road. The backside of the mansion, which faced the Ner River, was sealed off with a wire fence. The ground here sloped steeply downward, so that when standing at the base of the hill, it was not possible to see the backyard of the mansion. A second wooden fence was built in front of the mansion enclosing the courtyard. This fence had two gates located in the northwest and southeast sides.[26]

Inside the mansion, near the main entrance on the left side of the building, was a door that led downstairs to the basement and a small landing. A long corridor, just over one meter wide and illuminated with gas lamps, led to the right. On the left side of the corridor were as many as seven rooms. On the right side were four rooms, about the same size as those on the other side of the corridor, as well as one other much smaller room. The corridor ended at a door that led outside on the right side of the building. A wooden ramp, enclosed on two sides, was built here.

The Polizeiwachtkommando [Police Guard Detachment] was composed of members of the Schutzpolizei from Łódź. The policemen, randomly chosen, came to Chełmno primarily from the first and second companies of Polizeibatallion Litzmannstadt. Originally the guards served for only a short time in the camp and then were transferred back to their police district. Later, the guards who found themselves in the camp would remain there until its liquidation. Initially, this detachment numbered about 30 men, but later this figure would increase in increments to as many as 120 men. There were three main periods when the guard detachment was increased. The first came after three prisoners successfully escaped from the camp in January 1942. The second came with the creation of an additional guard detachment, the so-called mill guard. The third increase occurred when the Jewish labor detail was strengthened in the summer of 1942, in order to exhume and burn the bodies that had been buried in the forest.

Polizeimeister Kurt Möbius served as transport supervisor at the mansion until his return to Łódź in September 1942. Polizeimeister Alois Häfele was placed in charge of Jewish labor at the mansion. Häfele was a major figure in the camp and was active there throughout both periods. In September 1942, he assumed Mobius's duties as supervisor of the incoming transports at the mansion, while simultaneously remaining in charge of Jewish labor. Häfele later related his arrival at the camp, possibly in January 1942, together with a group of policemen from Łódź.

> [T]he entire detachment was taken in several trucks to a place called Kulmhof. We arrived there in the evening, and were received by Hauptsturmführer Lange, who showed us our quarters. It was a large room in a building that must have been the administration building.
>
> The next morning the entire police squad had to gather in front of the quarters. Lange and his deputy Unterscharführer Plate arrived. Lange gave a speech, explaining that Kulmhof was the place where Jews from the Warthegau were gassed and that our task was to guard and blockade the forest camp, the mansion and the village, so that no unauthorized people could see what was going on. We would have nothing to do with the extermination of the Jews themselves. Finally, Plate said that anyone remiss in fulfilling his duties, or who refused to obey orders, would be immediately sent to a concentration camp. Next, we were given our assignments.[27]

Within the first month the head of the Polizeiwachtkommando was changed twice. Polizeioberleutnant Harri Maas replaced Polizeioberleutnant Harry Lang, the first head of the police guard. The day after Maas's arrival, he was accidentally sprayed in the face with disinfectant and replaced three days later. According to Maas, each member of Sonderkommando Kulmhof was, upon arrival, sprayed with disinfectant in order to prevent contagion from infectious diseases. His replacement was Polizeioberleutnant Gustav Hüfing, who served until the camp's liquidation in 1943. Polizeihauptwachtmeister Otto Böge, as sargeant of the guard, was deputy to Hüfing. Hauptwachtmeister Gustav Fiedler would later replace Böge.

The Polizeiwachtkommando was divided into three main groups, or guard detachments. Polizei-Oberwachtmeister Karl Heinl commanded the Hauskommando [Mansion Guard]. Its task was to secure the mansion area, seeing that no one from the incoming transports escaped, to insure that the process proceeded without incident, and to guard the Jewish workers in the mansion. The Waldkommando [Forest Guard] was responsible for the security of the forest camp. Polizeiwachtmeister Simon Haider from Poznań was in charge of this detachment. The Transportkommando traveled to towns and villages in outlying areas, loaded the local Jewish population into the trucks and brought them to the mansion. Oberwachtmeister Erich Kretschmer was in charge of the policemen in this detail.

The Hauskommando guarded three main positions. The first was at the front gate. The task of this group was to open and close the gates when transports arrived. Afterward, guards were to enter the mansion and watch the two rooms where the Jews were to undress. Then, as the victims were escorted downstairs to the basement, the guards went outside and around to the right side of the mansion to see that no Jews escaped while being loaded into the gas vans. They would then return to the front gate.[28]

The second position was in the basement of the mansion. The responsibilities here were to watch the doors of two workshops where Jewish tailors and shoemakers worked and to ensure that the victims, while being loaded into the gas vans, did not stop or try to go back the other way.

The third position of the Hauskommando was located behind the mansion. The Guards at this position were responsible for securing the area and watching the windows of the rooms where the Jewish tailors and shoemakers worked, as well as those where the Jewish labor squad was housed.

A total of nine to 12 policemen served at any one time in these positions. During the course of a day the guards rotated through each position. At night two policemen were assigned to watch the basement where the Jews slept. Another guard was stationed in front of the mansion.[29]

The second group of policemen, the Waldkommando, was assigned to secure the forest area. The sections of the Rzuchów Forest were bordered by forest roads within the woods and the Koło-Dąbie highway to the east. One squad of policemen was assigned to guard the outer perimeter. No one was allowed to enter this area. A second group was assigned to guard the Jewish labor squads working inside the forest. Originally, about 25 policemen served in the Polizeiwaldkommando, but this number increased as time went on.[30]

The third group of policemen composed the Transportkommando. This group escorted six to eight trucks, which were stationed in Chełmno, and brought victims to the mansion from towns and villages up to 75 kilometers away. One policeman was assigned to each truck.[31]

In return for serving in the camp, the members of the Sonderkommando were paid an extra RM 10 per day; more was paid to higher-ranking men. Bothmann received RM 15. In addition, special allotments of liquor and cigarettes were provided and, of course, service at the front could be avoided. The assignment in Chełmno also provided relief for the guards from the monotony of daily drills and exercise back at their home barracks in Łódź.

Eight of the Polish prisoners who had served as gravediggers for Sonderkommando Lange had been isolated for some time in their cell in Fort VII prior to the operation conducted by the Sonderkommando in the forests outside Konin. One day Lange appeared and remarked about the weakened physical condition of these prisoners. He procured sausages and bread for these men explaining that they had to regain their strength as they would be employed in a new operation.[32] The relationship between these eight Polish workers—Lech Jaskólski, Marian Libelt, Henryk Maliczak, Henryk Mania, Franciszek Piekarski, Stanisław Polubiński, Kajetan Skrzypczyński and Stanisław Szymański—and the members of the

Sonderkommando changed over time. As Henryk Mania later recalled, it was at this time that

> [...] A change took place in the attitude of the SS men toward us. For example, in Konin we were to be housed in the jail, but were to be provided with better conditions than the other prisoners. The head of the jail did not agree to this so the SS men took us to the apartment in town where they stayed at that time and we lived there in a room next to theirs, although we were still watched by them. During the operation in Konin the SS men took us with them to the restaurant where they eat their meals, although we sat at a separate table. There was, at that time, a certain relationship established with them resulting from the frequent direct contacts.[33]

It would have been relatively easy for the Polish prisoners to escape. As workers in Chełmno, they were dressed in civilian clothes and were housed in a room on the ground floor of the mansion. They were never shackled in leg irons, as the Jewish labor squads would be. Local residents Wanda Kropidłowska and Andrzej Miszczak, the local farmer who lived at the bottom of the hill behind the mansion, stated that these men were initially watched under armed guard as the camp was under construction but when the transports began arriving the Polish men were no longer treated as prisoners but as workers. Moreover, the Polish workers themselves were seen escorting Jewish prisoners to various assignments around the village.[34] Relations between these men and the Sonderkommando had improved to the point that they had complete freedom of movement around the local villages, as photographs taken during their outings testify. Piekarski, the senior member of the group, was on relatively friendly terms with Lange and later Bothmann. He was responsible for securing the improved relations with the Germans.[35]

According to Henryk Mania, the Polish workers remained in Chełmno due to threats that their families would suffer the consequences if they attempted to escape. This was contradicted by Henryk Maliczak, who stated that "we were on friendly terms with the Germans. They considered us employees [pracownicy]. The German administrators of the camp never spoke to us about the possibility of escape. Besides, as far as I know, none of us had any intention of escaping. Moreover, we were never threatened that our family would have a problem if one of us escaped. Objectively speaking, we had it pretty good."[36] In contradiction, at least two local villagers testified after the war that these workers feared for their lives and had considered escaping.[37]

Relations between these eight men and the local village population were quite friendly. From time to time the Polish workers would stay overnight with friends, outside the camp. Each of these workers had girlfriends in the village.[38] They were allowed to send and receive mail once a month, but also sent and received mail unofficially through Andrzej

Miszczak.[39] Officially, they were forbidden to talk about what they heard or saw in the camp. However, during parties with bottles of vodka, the locals learned much about events that took place behind the fences.[40]

The Polish workers were not paid for their services. However, they were regularly provided with a ration of vodka. According to Mania and Maliczak, they helped themselves to money and valuables that were confiscated from the victims, stating that they were never specifically told this was forbidden, but they also never made this fact known to the Germans.[41] With this disposable income, among other things, they bought food from local farmers and paid local women to have their laundry cleaned. Their clothing was provided by the people from the incoming transports.

According to one member of the Sonderkommando, Kurt Möbius, on two or three occasions the Poles kept Jewish girls in the mansion overnight with Lange's approval.[42] And later, according to Walter Burmeister, under Bothmann's command:

> It happened sometimes that a woman was selected from the Jews delivered for gassing for the work squad, which consisted of young men; probably the Poles themselves would choose her. I think that the Poles asked her if she would agree to have sexual intercourse with them. In the basement there was a room set aside for this purpose where the woman stayed one night or sometimes several days and was at the disposal of these Poles. Afterwards, she would be killed in the gas vans with the others.[43]

But was it only the Polish workers who abused these women? One of the victims was the Jewish girlfriend of Abram Rój, one of the Jewish prisoners from Izbica Kujawska assigned as a gravedigger in the forest camp. While at the mansion one day, perhaps on the way to work, he spotted her, but according to his description "she had been raped by the SS and looked wild, crazed, not of this world." The next time he saw her was in the forest, among the dead bodies of the Jews from Izbica.[44]

According to two local residents, Szymański's wife stayed in Chełmno for two weeks.[45] Photographs taken by these prisoners of themselves while on walks around the village—with a camera confiscated from the camp's victims—document their transition from prisoner to collaborator.

Upon arrival in Chełmno, the Poles were employed in establishing the camp. One of the first tasks was to build the eight-foot tall fence that enclosed the mansion and sealed it from public view. The fence was built by, among others, Maliczak and Szymański. They also constructed the wooden ramp that would lead the victims from the basement door to the interior of the gas vans. The other six Poles went to the forest each day where they were employed doing what they had done previously for Lange, digging graves.[46]

After the extermination began, six of the Poles worked around the mansion grounds. Polubiński was involved with the transports, translating the arrival speech for those groups who did not understand German. Jaskólski, and later Maliczak, serviced the vehicles of the Sonderkommando, filling them up with gas, checking the oil, and performing other related duties. Libelt, Mania, Polubiński and Szymański collected the valuables from the victims, accompanied them down to the basement and, when necessary, they also forced the victims into the gas vans. One of the Poles, Marian Libelt, attempted to coax a group of Jews from Izbica Kujawska into the van by entering it himself. He ended up caught on the wrong side of the doors, trapped inside the van, and was gassed.[47] Both local residents and camp staff stated Jaskólski drove a gas van on occasion.[48] The other two Poles, Piekarski and Skrzypczyński, went to the forest each day where they were employed in extracting gold teeth and searching the corpses of the victims for hidden valuables.

The Jewish prisoners in the camp were divided into two main labor squads. The Hauskommando operated within the grounds of the mansion. The Waldkommando performed the duties that the Poles had undertaken earlier during the mobile gassing operations: digging the mass graves, emptying and cleaning the gas vans, and burying the corpses. Later, a third labor squad would be added, consisting of a group of craftsmen that worked in the basement of the mansion.

The origin of the first Jewish labor commando is unclear. It must have been obvious to Lange that the six Poles would not be able to dig the pits for the anticipated number of victims. On December 5, 1941, members of the Sonderkommando took a car and truck and drove to the nearby town of Koło, where they forced 30 Jewish men into the truck and drove off.[49] These men may have been used to "jump-start" the digging operations. If they were the first Jewish labor kommando, they did not survive long.

It is clear from various testimonies that Jews were not employed in the forest during the initial phase of operations. Kurt Möbius, the supervisor of the incoming transports, stated that during his first visit to the forest in mid-December, he saw a large grave that had been dug by four or five Polish workers. During this visit, he witnessed the arrival of two gas vans and watched as the Poles unloaded the corpses and put them into the grave. He also stated that it was only later when more transports arrived at Chełmno that this work was taken over by Jews, while the Poles now worked in the mansion.[50] The Poles stated that it was they who initially dug the graves and later showed the Jews how to do it. However, it is not known exactly when Jews from incoming transports began to fill this role.[51] On Friday, January 2, 1942, the Kłodawa gendarmerie picked up and detained 30 strong and healthy men. The men were forced to board a truck that arrived in the evening, which then drove off in the direction of Chełmno. It is undoubtedly these men who were the first documented members of the Jewish Waldkommando.[52]

While the camp was under construction during November and the first week of December 1941, Lange sent a portion of the Sonderkommando back to the Kalisz area to conduct another operation. (In October, the Sonderkommando had gassed patients from an old folk's home in Kalisz.) On November 26, Ferdinand Göhler, the Gestapo chief in Kalisz, had conducted a selection in the Koźminek (Bornhagen) ghetto in which 700 elderly and sick adults, as well as children up to the age of 14, were loaded into the black, hermetically sealed gas van and transported to a forest outside Gołuchów and buried.[53] The operation was conducted over a period of several days. One eyewitness to the operation later recorded his recollection of events.

> In November 1941, Göhler came to Koźminek and prepared a list of the Jewish population. Everyone knew that this did not bode well. Several days later a large number of Gestapo men and military policemen arrived with Göhler and surrounded the ghetto. He then ordered all older people, unable to work according to his list, to report to the synagogue. In the meantime, a black van arrived. Göhler ordered all those assembled in the synagogue to get into the van. They were to be taken to a special camp for people unable to work. Göhler stood next to the open doors and hit each person entering the vehicle with a truncheon. Seventy people were ordered into the van. As the vehicle was full after about 40 people had entered it, Göhler began beating those standing in it until they made room for others. He even kicked the last ones in. The vehicle was extremely crowded. When the van had 70 people packed inside, Göhler then threw in children over the heads of those already inside. The doors of the van were then closed and locked. In this way, those unable to work, children and single mothers were gassed in two vehicles on the way to Gołuchów, where they were buried.[54]

This operation became the model later used in ghetto clearing operations whereby the victims were first ordered into a building, usually a church or synagogue. Once confined, the victims were then forced to wait in the overcrowded building for a number of days without food, water or basic sanitary facilities. Therefore, many of these people, physically and psychologically broken, were only too eager to leave the building and offered little resistance when ordered to board waiting vehicles.

It is not surprising that Lange chose Chełmno as the site to establish a death camp. Location was an obvious factor in making his decision. Chełmno was centrally positioned in relation to the Jewish population of the Warthegau. Moreover, it was isolated, there were no large cities in the vicinity, and yet it was easily accessible by road and by rail. Lange may have considered Chełmno the perfect location to carry out his assignment. With final preparations completed at the mansion and in the forest, Sonderkommando Lange received its initial transport of victims on December 7, 1941.

The Transports

A substantial number of the victims came to Chełmno directly from the Łódź ghetto and were among the first to be exterminated there. The history of the Łódź ghetto, including the horrible conditions in which the inhabitants worked and died, is well documented. However, the cooperation that occurred between the ghetto's German administration, the Ghettoverwaltung and Sonderkommando Kulmhof is less well known.

Łódź was an important center of Jewish life prior to the Second World War. The city itself had grown rapidly in the nineteenth century as a manufacturing center. The Jewish community, long present in the city, experienced significant growth along with the development of the industrial economy. The Germans occupied Łódź in September 1939, renamed it Litzmannstadt in April 1940, and established the second largest Jewish ghetto (the Warsaw ghetto was the largest), which was sealed in May 1940. In a top secret circular on the establishment of the ghetto, District President Friedrich Übelhör stated, "The erection of a ghetto is naturally only a temporary measure. I reserve the right to determine the time and means by which the ghetto and with it the City of Łódź will be cleansed of all Jews. It must be our final goal to eradicate this pestilent boil once and for all."[1]

The Łódź Ghetto Administration [Ghettoverwaltung Litzmannstadt], headed by Hans Biebow, a former coffee merchant from Bremen, was directly responsible for ghetto affairs. The administrative chain of command over the Łódź ghetto ran top down from Warthegau Governor [Reichsstatthalter] Arthur Greiser, District President [Regierungspräsident] Friedrich Übelhör, Lord Mayor [Oberbürgermeister] Werner Ventzki, to the Łódź Ghetto Administration chief, Hans Biebow and deputy, Friedrich Ribbe. It was the Ghettoverwaltung that interacted directly with the Jewish Council [Judenrat], headed by Chaim Rumkowski, the titular representative of the Jewish population. The head of the Gestapo office in Łódź was Hauptsturmführer Robert Schefe, who was replaced by Hauptsturmführer Dr. Otto Bradfisch in January 1943. Bradfisch was transferred to Łódź after serving in the Soviet Union as commander of mobile killing unit Einsatzkommando 8, part of Einsatzgruppe B. Bradfisch also took over Ventzki's position with the latter's departure in 1943.

As head of the ghetto administration, Biebow had a close working relationship with Sonderkommando Kulmhof from the very beginning. On October 20, 1941—prior to the establishment of the Chełmno camp, but after Lange received his extermination order—Biebow sent out a circular in which he wrote that the solution of the Jewish question was strictly a political affair that would be settled exclusively by people appointed by the Führer, and that the obligation of everyone employed by the

Ghettoverwaltung was to maintain strict secrecy for general political reasons.[2] Biebow worked closely with Sonderkommando Kulmhof coordinating the resettlement of the provincial ghetto populations, steering those considered fit for work to the Łódź ghetto and the others to Chełmno, as well as sending transports directly from the Łódź ghetto to Chełmno. Moreover, logistics for shipping the belongings of the victims sent to Chełmno had to be coordinated with Biebow. Biebow personally participated in the resettlement operations and was a frequent visitor to the Chełmno camp, as were Bradfisch and Günther Fuchs, the Łódź Gestapo's commissioner for Jewish affairs.[3]

In order for Chełmno to function with any degree of efficiency, close coordination with Biebow and the ghetto administration was vital. Members of Sonderkommando Kulmhof met with officials in Łódź on a regular basis. These meetings, hosted by Biebow, were attended by Lange, later Bothmann, Richter and others from Chełmno.[4] Coordinating the departure of transports from the ghetto and their arrival to Chełmno was a crucial link in the extermination process. The shipment of confiscated goods out of the camp to the warehouses in Dąbrowa also required logistical cooperation between the parties involved. The Łódź ghetto administration was an integral part of the Chełmno operation.

The extermination process began in early December 1941 with the liquidation of the Jewish populations of surrounding towns and villages. This method was to ensure a degree of secrecy in regard to the events that took place at the mansion in Chełmno. Nevertheless, rumors began circulating as soon as the extermination process began. While the Jewish populations in the immediate vicinity of the camp (Koło, Dąbie) were the first to be liquidated, the Jewish community in Grabów, some 12 kilometers from Dąbie, was inexplicably bypassed for four months. This is extremely significant in regard to events that later unfolded in January 1942. (Transports to Chełmno are listed chronologically in Chapter 4, page 185.)

The Jews of Koło, just 14 kilometers north of Chełmno, were the first to be exterminated. Prior to the outbreak of the war, Koło had a population of some 33,000, of which approximately 7,000 to 8,000 of the town's residents were Jewish. A few large businesses (a machine shop, brickworks and mills) were owned by Jews, but the bulk of the Jewish population made their living through small businesses, trading and crafts. The local Jewish intelligentsia was comprised of a small group of doctors, lawyers and teachers. The community was organized and represented by political groups of all persuasions, including Zionists who prepared and sent groups of settlers to Palestine.

After the German invasion and the incorporation of western Poland into the newly created Warthegau, the town's name was changed to Warthbrucken. In 1940, a large portion of the Jewish inhabitants were resettled to Izbica Lubelska in the General Government. Young men were taken away to work in the labor camps around Poznań and a Jewish ghetto was established in the town. The Germans also set up a Jewish Council, responsible for enacting all orders issued by the German administration. In October 1941, some of the Jewish residents were resettled to the nearby village of Bugaj. The next month the Judenrat was ordered to provide an alphabetical list of all the Jewish inhabitants of Koło. These residents were informed they were being resettled because they had to work. Everyone was ordered to pay a fee of RM 4 to cover travel costs "to the east." This would become standard operating procedure as the evacuations continued throughout the region. It also became a sign to many that their final days were approaching.

Michał Podchlebnik, a key Jewish figure in the history of the camp, witnessed the evacuation of Koło's Jewish community. He, his wife and children were not on the list; they were among the group resettled to Bugaj, but members of his extended family, including his mother and father, were on the list. Podchlebnik had acquired a job working for a German and a work permit that allowed him to travel between Bugaj and Koło.

> At three o'clock, everyone was entered on an A or B list [those able or those unable to work]. Then they were taken and locked in the synagogue and the Jewish school. The next day they were taken by transport to Chełmno. Everyone was told where they were going. It was said that Chełmno is an assembly point for further transports to the east. Sick people and pregnant women were treated with excessive politeness; they were taken during the last day of the ghetto's liquidation.
>
> The drivers were given special instructions, so that all could hear, to drive cautiously because they would be carrying sick people. Those leaving were ordered to take indispensable items and clothing. The trucks were loaded with between 40 and 60 people. During this time the names of the people leaving were read out loud and they were marked off from the registration list with red ink.
>
> I personally helped with the loading of the trucks. When the last transport was loaded, I asked if I could go to Chełmno to visit my family. They told me I couldn't, because it was impossible to return from there.[5]

Podchlebnik then returned to nearby Bugaj, his registered place of residence, where he heard rumors that Jews were being killed in Chełmno.

The first transport of Jews was taken to Chełmno from Koło on December 7. During the day, approximately 700 people arrived at the mansion, where they spent the night. During the course of the following day, they were loaded into a gas van, the old Kaiser's Kaffee van, taken to the forest, asphyxiated and buried. In the afternoon, the next group from Koło arrived at the mansion and spent the night. This process was repeated for four days.[6]

On December 6, approximately 1,100 Jews were transported from the rural ghetto of Czachulec, where they had been concentrated from surrounding villages, to the town of Dobra. There they were locked in the church for four days under appalling conditions. On December 10, this group was taken to Chełmno. The approximately 975 Jews in Dąbie, just six kilometers south of Chełmno, were subjected to the same fate. The ghetto inhabitants were moved to the local Catholic church and locked inside. They were forced to wait some seven days under horrible conditions, with no food or sanitary facilities, until Lange was ready to receive them. The transports to Chełmno began on December 14 and continued for five days.[7]

By the end of the year all Jews living in the immediate vicinity of the camp had been murdered and buried in the forest. The nearest concentration of Jews was located in the town of Grabów, some 20 kilometers by road, east of Chełmno.

In January, following a break for the holidays, the Roma from the Łódź Ghetto were the first victims of the new year. Arrested and concentrated in camps, the Roma were deported from Hartberg, Fürstenfeld, Mattersburg, Roten Thurm and Oberwart, Austria and arrived in the Łódź ghetto between November 5 and 9, 1941.[8] It was decided not to allow the Jews and Roma to intermingle and therefore a special so-called "Gypsy camp" was built for them within the ghetto. A small area in the southeastern corner of the ghetto was surrounded by a double row of barbed wire fences and a two meter wide moat bordered the enclosure on two sides. Some 4,996 Roma were herded into this makeshift holding pen, which comprised a mere 15 buildings and a total of 543 rooms. The most basic facilities—beds, furniture, kitchens and toilets—were lacking. It was not until December that 1,000 bowls and 2,000 spoons were delivered to the camp. The conditions created by the German authorities could only end in disaster. The first cases of typhus were recorded in mid-November. The disease spread quickly and efforts to fight it by Jewish doctors were fruitless. After some 613 Roma had died of the disease (as well as Kriminaloberassistent Eugen Jansen, the camp commandant, who contracted typhus during an inspection), the German administration decided to liquidate this camp.[9]

Between January 2 and 9, the Roma were taken, under armed escort, in trucks from the ghetto directly to Chełmno. The procedure for exterminating the Roma, varied from that of the Jews. Upon arrival at the mansion they were loaded directly into the gas vans. At least two of these transports were taken to the forest and shot.[10] Members of the Sonderkommando, no doubt, wanted to minimize their contact with the typhus-ridden Romani people. Despite the precautions, typhus did break out in the camp. All of the Polish workers contracted typhus with the exception of Maliczak and

60 units of protective clothing were subsequently procured for members of the Sonderkommando.[11]

Hauptscharführer Fritz Ismer and two other policemen had just been assigned from Łódź to the Sonderkommando. Ismer vividly recalled the extermination of the Roma in Chełmno.

> When we reported to Lange, he instructed us to go with him by car to the forest, which was about five kilometers away, in order to witness the commando in action. Lange had told us before that everything that happened there was top secret and that we had to keep absolutely silent about everything. When we arrived at the forest, one of the policemen who guarded it reported to us. The forest [camp] was a short distance off the county road and a dirt road led to it. Lange told us to come closer. We could see a clearing in the forest and a gray van that was parked there with the rear doors open. The van was full of bodies, which were taken out by a Jewish labor squad and thrown into a mass grave. The dead people looked like Gypsies. There were men, women and children there. The bodies were clothed. When I saw this I began to feel sick and had to vomit. When I rallied a little, Lange told me, "You'll get used to it." We stayed there for only about ten minutes. I think two more vans came during this time. They were also full of Gypsies.
>
> When we came back, Lange told us that he wanted to show us the mansion. In the area of the mansion we saw people go directly from the trucks into the gas vans. Those people were Gypsies too.[12]

One of the Jewish gravediggers who buried the Roma in the forest confirmed this testimony, stating that these people were fully clothed and even had their possessions with them in the vans. On January 9, 1942, Lange appeared in Łódź where he received an RM 20,000 check from the Ghetto Administration as a special allocation for the Gypsy Camp.[13]

On December 20, 1941, the German authorities in Łódź informed Chaim Rumkowski, the Eldest [leader] of the Jews, that 20,000 inhabitants were to be evacuated from the ghetto. Rumkowski eventually managed to have this number decreased by half. The inhabitants of the ghetto were led to believe that they were to be taken to small towns in the General Government where the food problem was not as acute as it was in the ghetto.[14]

Leopold Chwiałkowski and Stanisław Kaszyński were two local villagers who worked in the Chełmno local government office. In early January, the assistant commandant of Chełmno, Obersturmführer Herbert Otto, received a phone call from Łódź, which the two Poles overheard as Otto repeated what the caller was saying. Transports of 750 Jews were to arrive daily to the Koło train station from the Łódź ghetto.[15]

The Jews themselves determined who would be included in the transports through the establishment of an Outsettlement Commission. It was decided that those who had recently arrived to the ghetto from the surrounding area, the family members of people who had been sent to work in Germany in November, and "undesirable elements" of the ghetto, such as people in the ghetto prison, would be included in the transports. Each person was allowed to take 12.5 kilograms of baggage and RM 10 with them on their journey. In addition, prior to departure, the clothing department distributed 12,000 pairs of warm underwear, earmuffs, gloves, stockings, socks and clogs. Of course, this was all part of the deception; these items would be searched and sorted in the camp, stored for a time, and eventually returned to Łódź. In February, during the so-called second stage of the resettlement, the right to take money out of the ghetto was rescinded.

The death transports from the Łódź ghetto to Chełmno began on January 16, 1942. The trains, made up of approximately 20 passenger cars with 55 people per car, departed the ghetto in the early morning hours.[16] One ghetto resident noted the following in his diary on January 17.

> Early today [should be yesterday] the first transport of evacuees was sent out. Altogether, the transport numbered 780 men, 853 women and 154 children. Most of them—poor, broken, naked and starved. Their departure was extraordinarily tragic. All of them cried mournfully. Mothers embraced their children . . . and screamed aloud: If we will die, you at least [try to] stay alive in order to be able to get revenge on those who are banishing us. . . . Terror, rage, deadly turmoil combined to annihilate a community of Jews. With our own eyes we saw how Jews were going to destruction.[17]

The transports left Łódź for 14 consecutive days, beginning on January 16, during which 10,003 people (5,750 females and 5,353 males) were shipped to the death camp. On January 30, the ghetto breathed a collective sigh of relief. The deportation was halted, but only temporarily.

Transports resumed on February 22, for seven more consecutive days, carrying a further 7,043 people to their deaths. The German Reichsbahn billed the Łódź Gestapo RM 20,484.80 for transporting these victims to Koło and returning the guards to Łódź. (Each trip cost more than RM 2,900.)[18] In March, transports left the ghetto six days a week, Sundays excluded. In that month, 24,687 people were shipped to their death in Chełmno. Transport 39, on April 1, and the final transport, number 40, on April 2, left for the death camp carrying 2,349 deportees. This round of resettlement was then suspended. The number of victims from the 40 transports totaled 44,064 people.

On April 16, Reichsführer Heinrich Himmler met with Hitler at his *Wolfsschanze* headquarters near the town of Kętrzyn. Following the meeting, Himmler flew to Poznań and spent the evening in discussions with Greiser and Koppe. The next day, April 17, Himmler and Koppe, possibly accompanied by Greiser, drove to Koło and the nearby village of Osiek Moczydło (renamed Redern by the Germans) to meet with Baltic Germans recently settled in the area at the expense of Poles who had been expelled from their homes. It is not known if Himmler made the short drive to Chełmno, but it is virtually certain that on this day Himmler ordered the extermination of 10,000 German, Austrian, Czech and Luxemburg Jews confined in the Łódź ghetto.[19]

As mentioned earlier, these Western European Jews from Berlin, Vienna, Düsseldorf, Hamburg, Prague, Frankfurt and Luxemburg had been resettled into the ghetto at the end of 1941 against the wishes of Greiser. As ordered, the transports began on May 4, departing daily for 12 consecutive days. During this wave, 10,914 people (3,657 males and 7,257 females) were shipped out of the ghetto. The transports were made up of seven passenger cars in each of which the first and last compartments were assigned to the escort detachment. On May 15, only 31 percent of these Western European Jews, who had arrived only some six months earlier, remained in the ghetto.[20]

The transports from Łódź arrived in Koło primarily by train via Kutno after Koło had been "cleansed" of its Jews. At the station in Koło, the commander of the train transport would hand a large yellow envelope to a member of the Sonderkommando, possibly Richter, containing a list of the names of the people in the transport.[21] The transports arrived in Koło on a group ticket. On the basis of these tickets, the booking clerk at the Koło station estimated the number of people in each transport was approximately 1,000.[22]

When the transports arrived at the station, everyone present was ordered to leave the immediate vicinity. The baggage was put in piles. As the Jews left the train they were beaten mercilessly with sticks, so that every day a number of bodies lay on the platform. The Germans picked out several strong men from each transport and ordered them to carry these bodies or load them on a cart while the rest of the group was marched to the local synagogue. Later, the groups of people arriving at the train station would be transported to the synagogue by truck.[23]

Initially, the Jews were assembled into columns of three or four and marched from the station, through Koło, to the synagogue. Heinz May, the German forester whose responsibilities included the Rzuchów Forest, was a witness to one of these processions.

> I saw a transport of these unhappy people marching through Koło. Men, women, children and old people. A horse-drawn vehicle drove behind the column, evidently to pick up those incapable of marching. In the vicinity of the post office I saw a woman who carried in her arms a small child, obviously only several months old; she tripped and fell down. The child was probably already half frozen, because I did not hear any screams. [A policeman] grabbed the child by one leg and threw it on the vehicle like a piece of wood.
>
> Some of them whose knees shook with fright and cold and who could not keep up with the column were driven forward by rough pushes with rifle butts.

I saw two pretty, well-dressed girls who held an emaciated woman between them. It was probably their mother. The two girls dragged the woman
along with difficulty. When she could go no further and collapsed on the road,
the two girls endeavored to put her back on her feet. In so doing they fell
somewhat behind the others. One of the accompanying gendarmes immediately dashed toward the group and yelled, "You dirty bunch of Jews, you
probably would like to ride."

Silently people stood on the roads and looked at this sad line of
people.[24]

The march from the station to the synagogue covered a distance of approximately one kilometer. One of the five or six guards who accompanied
the transports from the train station to the synagogue was August Piella.
He described these people as being so stupefied that they were concerned
only with the moment and were unable to think about what the future
might hold. Their weakened condition was a result of life in the ghetto
and this made the job of the guards much easier. Piella also described their
arrival at the synagogue.

At the entrance to the synagogue, high ranking officers counted the people
entering the building and from this I knew that the transports numbered over
1,000 people. In the synagogue, Polizeimeister Draheim collected money from
the Jews for straw which was brought to the synagogue. The men who supplied
the straw and the cart which brought the weakest people were paid with the
money collected. Draheim and Polizeimeister Gerolis donated the rest of the
money for "German Policeman's Day." So they told us. The Jews were brought
in the afternoon. They spent the night in the synagogue and in the morning
trucks arrived from Chełmno and took away the people, who were packed
very tightly [together] and without their baggage. The Sonderkommando from
Chełmno took away the Jews from the synagogue because none of us were
permitted to go there.[25]

The local authorities received complaints from the public about the
brutal daily processions through Koło. An SS commission investigated
and subsequently forbid the processions to continue.[26] Trucks from the
Sonderkommando then met the transports at the train station, loaded their
cargo and drove in the direction of Chełmno. However, in March this procedure also changed. Now, after arriving at the Koło station, the Jews were
loaded directly onto a small narrow gauge train. This train took them to the
village of Powiercie, located along the narrow gauge rail line between Koło
and Chełmno. Here they were unloaded and marched, about one kilometer, to a mill house in the neighboring village of Zawadka. The mill was a
fairly substantial two-story brick building, 44 meters long and 10.5 meters
wide, situated next to the Warta River. The building was used from March
until May for the transports from Łódź and functioned as a holding pen.
Other transports that arrived during this time by truck were given priority
and taken directly to the mansion.

Wilhelm Schulte, along with 25 to 30 other policemen, was transferred from Łódź to Chełmno during this period. He arrived to begin his duty together with a transport of Jews.

We were taken by truck to the railway station in Łódź. Our commander was Polizeihauptwachtmeister Gustav Fiedler. We had to get into the first carriage of a train that stood on the platform ready to leave. There were Jews in the remaining six or seven carriages. As I recall, a railway employee had locked the doors of those carriages. I cannot remember if there was a special police or SS squad to watch the Jews. As I recall, it was not our duty to watch the transport. The train then went to Koło. The Jews had to leave the train there and get into carriages of a narrow gauge train. It proceeded under the control of SS men and young policemen, whom I had seen before in Polizeibatallion Litzmannstadt. We got into a bus and were taken to Chełmno.

The next day, Hüfing assigned us to our guard service. About 15 people, including me, were in the group that was commanded by Polizeihauptwacht-meister Fiedler. We were to guard a mill that was located outside of Chełmno. It was called "the mill guard."

In the afternoon of the same day we went by bus in the direction of Koło. Fiedler was in command. We got off the bus on a country road after about seven or eight kilometers, where the narrow gauge railroad crossed the Koło-Dąbie road. The bus went back to Kulmhof.

After a while a train with 250 to 300 Jews arrived. We took control of them and escorted them to the mill, which was about two kilometers away. Bothmann and Plate, who came by car, were present. The train was escorted by policemen who served in Kulmhof.

After we had come to the mill, the Jews were put in a large room, where they slept. The policemen from the mill guard were accommodated in a room in a house next to the mill. It also served as our guardroom.

Fiedler appointed three guard shifts, which changed every two hours. Our task was to watch the Jews, so that they did not escape. Policemen who were not on guard duty were required to be on call.

The next morning trucks from Kulmhof came to the mill and the Jews were taken away. After the mill had been cleaned, the guard detachment was taken back to Kulmhof on the bus. Then we had time off.[27]

Schulte failed to mention any specifics about the march to the mill; he may have considered this a mundane and routine affair. However, the German forester, Heinz May, in addition to witnessing a transport march through Koło, also watched a transport arrive in Powiercie. He later described what he witnessed.

Once when I was on business at the Powiercie estate administration, I went through the estate park to the unloading place of the narrow gauge rail-road and, standing behind a hedge, [I] observed the proceedings for some time.

The people were formed into a line on a dirt road behind the estate. Several sick persons were lying in the grass next to the tracks of the narrow gauge railroad. They were taken care of by others who brought them something to drink and tried to alleviate their suffering. After the line was formed, policemen appeared and made the sick ones get up by using their rifle butts. One who had helped the sick called indignantly, "One does not even treat cattle that way." From his language, I noticed he was a German. One of the officials raised his pistol against the person who made the remark. I thought that he wanted to frighten him but a shot could be heard right then. The man collapsed. He tried to get up but fell down again and remained lying with his head on the tracks. Bright red and foaming blood came from his mouth. Terrified, the sick pulled themselves together and staggered to the column. One man could not make it and fell down again. Another shot; he did not rise anymore either.

The officials got four Jews from the line. They were compelled to load the two dead persons onto a truck which stood nearby. I heard one of the officials saying, "Dirty pigs."[28]

Another account by a local villager describes how he came down the road following behind one of these processions. Two children who appeared to be about five years old were playing with sticks and collecting pebbles and had fallen behind the others in the transport. One of the guards called out to the children to catch up with the group. One of kids, instinctively trusting the adult, ran up to the guard who struck her on the head with a stick so hard it killed her instantly. The other child fled.[29] Those in the transport who were unable to walk were taken by truck directly to the forest where Lenz, Plate or Bothmann shot them.[30]

In Powiercie, the baggage was loaded onto trucks and taken directly to Chełmno. As the people in the transports entered the mill in Zawadka, the guards confiscated personal items. Many people objected but they were told, "Tomorrow you will get bowls, spoons and food."[31] Leopold Surgot, who lived in Powiercie, once heard the Germans tell the Jews that, "Tomorrow you will all be killed." The Jews laughed, thinking it was a joke.[32] The next morning the trucks from the camp arrived and transported the victims in groups to the mansion. The mill was empty by 3:00 p.m. when that day's transport of victims arrived at Powiercie for the short march to the mill building.

Between January and May 1942, transports to the camp originated not only from Łódź but also from the small towns in the Warthegau where the Jewish population had been concentrated in local ghettos. The Sonderkommando had its own transport detachment that operated in conjunction with the German ghetto administration. The Transportkommando traveled to the various towns, and in cooperation with local police officials loaded the people into the trucks and took them directly to the mansion. The guard, Wilhelm Schulte, served in this detachment on several occasions.

The group was made up of six to eight men, mostly the same ones. But from time to time Fiedler appointed other people to help them. I was appointed to this group several times.

Our task was to escort six to eight trucks, which were in Kulmhof, as the Jews were being brought from various neighboring villages. Sometimes we had to go as far as 60 kilometers from Chełmno and take the Jews from there. Polizeioberwachtmeister Kretschmer was the commanding officer of this escort. As far as I know, the transports were organized by Scharführer Richter, who drove to the villages and took over command of the Jews from the SS men and policemen who were guarding them. I do not remember from what villages we took Jews. They were always ready for the transport. Kretschmer ordered me to get into a truck with the Jews, sit on the tailgate and watch them so that no one escaped. Policemen escorting the other trucks had the same task. During the drive, Kretschmer rode in the first truck, beside the driver. Richter drove in his car in front of us. The Jews were always transported to the mansion in Kulmhof where they were taken over by Häfele or Möbius.

Our trucks left the villages at 20-minute intervals so that they did not all get to Kulmhof at the same time. Many times I also escorted Jews from the ghetto in Łódź. Gestapo men in civilian clothes handed over these Jews to Richter.

Members of the escort detachment wore coveralls during the transports. Policemen in the detachment had to have a leather whip during these trips; it was Bothmann's order. I also had such a leather whip. A Pole who worked in the mansion gave it to me; it had been made by a Jewish craftsman. It was made out of a single piece of leather, something like a dog whip. Kretschmer also had a whip like this and he ordered us to beat the Jews if they didn't walk fast enough. Many times I saw policemen beating Jews in accordance with this order. I used my whip several times in this situation, but I did not really beat them; I only touched those people who did not get onto the trucks fast enough, to make them go faster. But it surely cannot be considered a beating so that the Jews could feel pain.[33]

Working in conjunction with Sonderkommando Kulmhof, Hans Biebow of the Łódź ghetto administration assembled a special transport detachment of his own to help evacuate the Jews from the smaller towns and villages. Local policemen would surround the ghetto, securing the area. The people were then divided into two groups: those able and those unable to work. The young, the old, the sick, and those otherwise unfit for work were loaded into trucks and driven directly to the mansion in Chełmno. Those individuals deemed fit to work took a more circuitous route to Chełmno, first being directed to the Łódź ghetto to provide labor for the German war effort. They were transported to the ghetto either by train or by truck, depending on the circumstances of the operation.

From December 1941 to June 1942, the transports had been arriving from the various towns and villages along with the mass transports from the Łódź ghetto. By the time Chełmno began operations in December, the Poznań District was virtually cleared of the few Jews who had lived there. The victims of Chełmno came directly or indirectly from the other two districts of the Warthegau: Inowrocław and Łódź.

The first transports arrived to the Chełmno camp from Koło and Dąbie in December 1941. In January, the Jews from Kłodawa (January 10, 12),

Bugaj (January 13), Izbica Kujawska (January 14, 15) were sent to their death. Transports from the Łódź ghetto occupied the Sonderkommando during the second half of January (16–29) and the entire month of February. The town of Sompolno was also declared *Judenrein* at this time (February 2).

Killing operations were in full swing during March. Not only were transports sent from Łódź throughout the month, but the ghettos in Kutno County were liquidated as well. The population of the ghetto in Krośniewice numbered some 1,500 when it was established. Its liquidation was conducted in an extremely brutal manner. A kind of transit camp was established at the market hall, which had been used to house cattle. Groups of several hundred people were brought here at a time. Conditions in the barracks were appalling. These unfortunate people were brutalized before being killed. Food rations consisted of a liter of soup and bread twice a day, but eating was difficult because there were no utensils; spoons and bowls, along with all other belongings had been taken away. Those who survived the appalling conditions were eventually transported to Chełmno at the beginning of the month.[34]

The approximately 3,000 Jews in the Żychlin ghetto in Kutno County were transported to Chełmno in the first week of March. The entire Judenrat and 17 members of the Jewish police were shot on the spot.[35]

The ghetto in Kutno, established in June 1940, was located at the Konstancja sugar mill and consisted of five residential buildings located on its grounds. The mill was surrounded by a brick wall and partly by an iron rail fence. The mill's facilities had been vacant for some time as they were considered unusable. Approximately 8,000 people from Kutno and the surrounding villages were crammed into this small area comprising several hectares. The population density of this ghetto was greater than that of the Łódź ghetto.

In early March 1942, groups of several hundred people at a time were loaded into trucks and taken to the railroad station where they were transferred to trains and transported to Chełmno. The members of the local Judenrat were shot on the spot. The crew of workers brought from the Łódź ghetto to clean up the area were beaten and starved and, after their work was completed, were loaded into trucks, which drove off in an unknown direction. They were never heard from again.[36]

Łęczyca County was targeted next. The Jewish populations in the Ozorków and Poddębice ghettos were cleared in March, followed by those in Grabów and the town of Łęczyca.

The trucks arrived in Gostynin, Gostynin County, on April 17. Approximately 3,500 Jews had previously been locked in the church to await deportation. All personal items were confiscated, including food. The sick and unfit were killed on the spot; the others were loaded onto the trucks and driven to Chełmno.[37]

The ghetto of Pabianice in Łask County was liquidated in mid-May. One Jewish man who survived the deportation and the remainder of the war in the Łódź ghetto described how the "resettlement" proceeded.

[I]n March 1942 everyone had to assemble on the square where the Jewish Council was located. They were to be stamped. [Biebow], Fuchs, and a third German were there. The stamping took place in the following manner: all the people - women and men - had to completely undress, and they were stamped with the letter A, B or C. They stood there with whips. We didn't know what it meant. On May 18, during the resettlement, everyone again had to assemble on the square. There, they segregated us. They took my wife and children from me. To this day I haven't seen my children. I was directed to the ghetto in Łódź.[38]

Some 5,600 people received the designation "A" and were sent to work in the factories of the Łódź ghetto. The others, the "useless eaters," were all sent to Chełmno.

Depositions taken from survivors after the war describe the horror inflicted on the people in the Brzeziny ghetto, located in Łódź County. On May 14, 1942, all the Jewish women of Brzeziny who had children up to age ten had to assemble with them on a square near St. Anna's church. A large number of elderly Jews were also present as were Biebow, Seifert, Fuchs and other Germans. Biebow was in charge and sorted the women into different groups. They were then taken to the building at 14 St. Anna. At about three o'clock in the morning of the May 15, the Germans arrived. First, they threw empty beer and liquor bottles through the windows of the building. Then, they entered the building shouting and gesticulating with pistols and rubber truncheons. Biebow, Fuchs and Seifert were among this group and it was obvious that they were drunk. Seifert started to hit women over the head with the handle of his whip, many of them bleeding and collapsing under the blows. The Germans then proceeded to take the children outside and load them into waiting carts. One of the Jewish women inside the building, Fanny Miller described the scene.

I did not want to lose my two-and-a-half-year-old daughter, Hannah Miller, and I tried to hide her. The child was very agitated and I remember her crying, "Please mommy, do not let them do it—daddy is not here." Siefert must have heard this, for he came up to me and hit me in the face with his rubber truncheon, and I bled heavily. He then tore my baby away from me and she was taken outside with the rest. I was frantic and asked Seifert to shoot me. He only laughed and said, "You will die anyway."[39]

Another woman, Ewa Funt, fell to the floor, kissing Seifert's boots and pleading for the life of her five-year-old child. Seifert beat the woman with his truncheon and left her lying unconscious in a pool of blood. Biebow also beat women with his truncheon. Some of the women tried to hold on to their babies. Biebow grabbed the children by the legs and threw them onto the stone floor, killing some of them. They were later carried outside and thrown onto the carts. After the carts departed with all the children onboard, the Germans continued to abuse the women and make light of their predicament. By 12 o'clock on May 15, the women were allowed to return to their homes.

The Jewish ghetto police accompanied the transport of children to the Gałków train station, just south of Brzeziny. The transport arrived at about five o'clock on the morning of May 16. Biebow, Seifert, Fuchs and Albert Richter (Fuch's deputy) soon appeared on the scene. Biebow was accompanied by half a dozen SS women. He ordered the drivers to pull the carts up to about ten meters from the railroad cars. The Jewish police were then told by Biebow to throw the children into the cars. They were not allowed to carry them; the children had to be thrown the several meters into the freight wagons. The deputy head of the ghetto police, Gedalie Fuks, later related what happened next.

> I tried to ignore the order and proceeded to carry a four-week-old baby towards one of the railway cars. Biebow rushed over and hit the baby over the head with the handle of his whip. The child's head split wide open and its blood and brains splashed about. I let it drop and Biebow then gave me three savage blows across the face with his whip. My ear split open and blood poured from the wound. After this incident we tried to throw the children into the cars, but after a short while we tired and could not throw that far anymore. Some of the children therefore dropped on the hard ground between us and the cars and I saw the heads of a number of these [children] split open from the impact. Biebow and the German women with him were highly amused when this happened and they roared with laughter.[40]

The other Germans then joined in, throwing the children into the railway cars. But this soon became monotonous and some of the children were then grabbed by the legs, torn apart, and then thrown into the cars. Meanwhile, Seifert and another group of Germans unloaded the women and elderly from the carts. They were forced to enter the railway cars unassisted. Those who did not run fast enough were thrown into small pools of water where they were kicked and trampled. Those who survived were shot. The bodies of approximately 50 adults lay scattered around the area when the loading procedure was completed. The Jewish policemen had to pick up more than 40 babies who were either dead or had broken bones. They were all thrown into the cars, which were then sealed. Next, the Germans began beating the Jewish policemen and later made them perform repetitive exercises for amusement. They were finally allowed to return to the ghetto between ten and 11 o'clock that morning.

The ultimate fate of this transport is unknown but it was undoubtedly sent to Chełmno. Moreover, this is only one episode in the liquidation of the Brzeziny ghetto. Biebow, Seifert, Fuchs and the others returned to the ghetto on May 17, to continue the "resettlement." Needless to say, numerous additional atrocities were committed on this population that numbered some 7,000 individuals in 1941.

The first county in the Inowrocław District cleared of Jews was the nearest, Koło County, of which Chełmno was a part. This was followed by the counties of Kutno and Gostynin, and part of Ciechocinek County in March–April and subsequently Włocławek County in April–May. Deportations from the district of Łódź began with Kalisz County between January and March. Deportations from Łęczyca County proceeded more slowly, over the course of several months, beginning in March and extending into August. Parts of Sieradz and Łask counties were touched by the deportations before June. The Łódź ghetto had undergone three major liquidation actions during this period. But by the beginning in June, for reasons unforeseen, virtually all transports to the camp were temporarily halted.

The Mansion: Arrival, Murder, Plunder

The mansion in Chełmno was the final stop for the people in the transports. The vast majority of these people arrived totally unaware of the fate that awaited them. Rumors circulated about Chełmno, but there was nothing particularly sinister-looking about the camp. The facility was no more than a building, the mansion, surrounded by a fence. No one had any reason to suspect that they had just arrived to a "human slaughterhouse."

What follows is a description of the general procedure used in Chełmno to murder thousands of men, women and children during the first period of the camp's existence. This procedure was not fixed; there was no outlined plan to follow, but developed as a result of the experience gained from each new transport. For example, the victims arriving in the first transports from Koło spent the night in the mansion. This did not last long. Trucks arriving with victims would later stop outside the fence in front of the mansion and the victims, under armed escort, walked into the courtyard area. Later the victims were driven into the mansion grounds; the trucks then backed up to the second gate enclosing the mansion's courtyard. Finally, the trucks drove into the courtyard and exited through a second gate located on the fence opposite, making a big circle and exiting the grounds through the main gate. The line of trucks along the road in front of the mansion was a common sight in the village. During the first winter, the victims were made to wait outside in the cold while listening to the arrival speech. Consequently, the half-frozen people were eager to enter the building, seeking shelter from the cold. The undressing rooms inside the mansion were kept very warm. It was hoped this would lessen any resistance when the victims were "asked" to disrobe. Initially, the victims were not ordered to completely undress, but merely turn in their valuables.[1] Only later did the

Sonderkommando begin to confiscate the remainder of the belongings of its victims.

Polizeimeister Kurt Möbius was assigned to Chełmno from Łódź in early December. Albert Plate assigned the policeman to serve as supervisor of the transports arriving at the mansion. Möbius was responsible for ushering the victims through the mansion in the most efficient manner. This was achieved through deception in order to ease the work of the perpetrators. The victims were to be unwitting accomplices in their own murder. Deception was carried out at each stage of the process: arrival, welcome speech and disrobement. First, as the victims arrived at the mansion they were treated politely by the mansion guard: The young and elderly were helped out of the trucks that brought them. Once the transport was assembled in the courtyard the victims were put at ease with a reassuring speech given by one member of the camp staff. Several of the SS men are known to have given the arrival speech, including Lange, Bothmann, Plate, Richter, Burmeister, Häfele and Heinl. The speech was given in German. Two of the Polish workers, Piekarski and Polubiński who knew German well, translated the speech into Polish for those people in a transport who did not understand German.[2] For added effect, Walter Burmeister would, on occasion, present himself to the victims wearing a physician's white coat, the implication being that the people were in caring hands and that medical help would be available to those who needed it.[3] This behavior and the speech must have been a very welcome relief to the people in the transports after enduring the horrors of their "resettlement" and the burden of life in the Łódź ghetto.

Möbius later recounted what occurred, procedurally, under his supervision at the mansion.

> After the Jews arrived at the mansion, they waited in the yard for some time. There they heard a speech, which was given by Plate or me. They were told that they would go to a large camp in Austria where they would have to work. But first, they were told, they would have to take a bath, and their clothes would have to be deloused. Plate and I gave the speeches so that the Jews would remain unaware of their fate and do as they were told.
>
> Next, the Jewish people (men, women and children) were taken to the ground floor of the mansion. The Polish workers helped with this. They went through a straight corridor and entered two large rooms connected by a door. There the Jews undressed under my supervision. They were not separated by sex. Before this, they had to turn over their valuables. The Polish workers collected these items in baskets.
>
> Next, as many people as could fit into a gas van at one time were taken from the rooms. On one side of the corridor there was a door that led to the basement. There was a sign on it that read *Zum Bade* [To the baths]. The group that was led to the gas vans always consisted of 35 to 40 people. The stairs led down to a corridor that first went straight and then turned right. The people had to turn right and go to a platform where the gas van stood with its doors

open. There was a board wall on either side of the platform that ended at the doors of the van.

Usually the Jewish people went to the gas vans quietly, believing what they had been told. The Polish workers accompanied them. They had leather whips and beat those who were insubordinate, suspicious, or who wouldn't enter the van. [. . .]

Transports came every day except Sundays. During my stay in Kulmhof, it happened only two or three times that there were no transports at all on a weekday or that the transports were very small. When there were only a few Jews, they were kept in the basement and gassed on the following day. About five to ten transports came per day. I know this because I gave the speeches to the Jews every day and it happened five to eight, sometimes even ten times a day. On average there were about 100 people in each transport.

When there were so many of them that they could not fit in the two rooms, some of them had to wait in the yard. [. . .]

The speech was given several times by Sturmscharführer Albert Plate. In May or June 1942 Polizeimeister Alois Häfele helped me with my work in the mansion. [. . .] He also made speeches and carried out the same functions as I did. [. . .]

The number of guards in the basement depended on the size of the transport. Sometimes there was only one or two, but for larger transports there were eight to ten policemen there.[4]

As the victims were led down the corridor to the undressing room they could see signs on the walls, next to the doors, with inscriptions reassuring the people that this room was designated for "men" and that one for "women with children." Once inside the undressing room the victims turned over their valuables and were given a receipt.[5] This lasted only a brief time as receipts were deemed unnecessary in order to achieve the desired effect—putting the victims at ease. Men, women and children undressed in the same room. The guards serving at the mansion observed the daily procession of people arriving to the camp.

Two of the policemen who served at the mansion were Wilhelm Schulte and Wilhelm Heukelbach. They later gave testimony concerning this step in the extermination process and their part in it. Schulte gave this account.

I often stood at the main gate of the mansion and let in the transports of Jews. The Jews were received there by Häfele or by Polizeimeister Möbius. (As far as I know, Möbius was second in command after Häfele.) They always gave the speech to the Jews before they entered the mansion. Bothmann and Plate were also sometimes present and gave the speech. They told the Jews that they were in a transit camp where they would be washed and deloused. Afterwards, they would be transported to a labor camp. First they should go inside the mansion, take off their clothes, and deposit their valuables, because they would be taken to baths by truck.

When the Jews entered the mansion, I followed them and, in accordance with Häfele's instructions, I guarded the doors to the rooms where the Jews had to undress. Either Häfele or Möbius supervised the undressing. Several Poles who worked in the mansion collected valuables in baskets. I also saw Häfele collecting valuables from time to time, but not Möbius.

After the Jews had undressed, a Pole took them downstairs to the basement. Häfele or Möbius followed them. The Pole, Häfele, and Möbius had leather whips. I don't know if they used them to beat the Jews in the basement.

When the Jews went downstairs to the basement, I went outside to the right side of the mansion where the gas vans were parked. I could see the Jews going over the platform naked into the gas van. The back doors were closed by the gas van drivers Laabs and Hering. They then turned on the engines of their trucks, which began the process of gassing. I noticed it because the people who were inside the vans knocked against the walls and screamed, frightened to death.[6]

The recollections of the guard Heukelbach agree with and confirm those of Schulte. On his second day in the camp, two trucks with Jews arrived at the main gate where he was serving guard duty. He opened the gate and the trucks drove inside the mansion grounds. His testimony describes what happened next.

There the people had to get out of the trucks, and they were welcomed by a police officer. He gave a speech saying that they were in a transit camp where they would be washed and deloused. Next, they would be taken to a labor camp in the Reich. Before they were taken to the baths they had to go inside the mansion and remove their clothes. They had to deposit their valuables, which would be given back to them later.

The Jews went inside the mansion. There were men, women and children. I followed them and guarded the position at the doors to the two rooms. After the Jews had undressed, they were led downstairs to the basement by a police officer, who counted them.

Then, following orders, I went to the right side of the mansion, where there was a platform and a gas van. It was a truck with an enclosed compartment. The color was gray. The doors were in the back of the van. The gas van stood at the platform with its doors open. I could see the Jews, who were brought through the basement, enter the vans.

After all the people had entered the gas van, the driver closed the doors and locked them. Then he turned on the engine. Shortly after that I could hear screaming and pounding against the walls of the van. [...] After about ten minutes the screams died down and I knew the people were dead. The driver let the engine run for another few minutes and then he drove away. [...]

Many times I also stood at the position in the basement when the Jews arrived at the mansion and after undressing were led to the gas vans. The Jews mostly walked to the vans quietly, because they knew from the speech that they were going to the baths. But sometimes during my service in the basement it happened that the Jews did not want to walk into the vans. In such cases I had to use my hands to push and hit the people so that they would move on. Several times I beat Jews when they did not want to walk on. But it surely was not a real beating, so that they felt pain. Each time I only threatened them with my whip and touched some of the Jews slightly to make them walk on. I felt sorry for the poor people and it was impossible for me to beat them harshly.[7]

Hauptscharführer Gustav Laabs and Oberscharführer Oskar Hering arrived in Chełmno around the end of April or the first part of May 1942. They were assigned as the new gas van drivers. Laabs had previously worked in Berlin at the motor pool of the Reichssicherheitshauptamt (RSHA), the umbrella organization of the Gestapo, the Criminal Police and the Security Service. He was told that he was being transferred to a Sonderkommando in Poznań and that he needed to sign an oath of secrecy.

Laabs and Hering reported together to the Gestapo office in Poznań where they were examined by a doctor and then told that they were being assigned to a Sonderkommando in Chełmno. Again, they signed an oath of secrecy, but were not told the nature of their assignment. The next day they were met in Poznań by Walter Burmeister, who drove them to Chełmno. They were then assigned their quarters. The following day, Erwin Bürstinger took them to the mansion and told them to try out the empty vans, in order to get a feel for how they handled.

According to Laabs, it was only several days later that Bothmann put them to work when he ordered them to wait by the vans, which were parked at the mansion. Three trucks loaded with Jews arrived, and Bothmann gave the welcome speech. Also present were Plate, Richter, Bürstinger, Burmeister and Häfele. After the speech the Jews entered the mansion. Laabs, still claiming ignorance of the purpose of the camp, recalled what happened next.

> Shortly afterwards, Bürstinger ordered me to back up the van that had been assigned to me to the ramp, which was on the side of the mansion by the park. The ramp was made of wood and sloped down into the basement corridor. The sides were comprised of a board wall about 2.5 meters tall. The front was enclosed by the van. Bürstinger opened the doors of the van after I had backed the van up to the ramp. He had unlocked the doors with a key that hung in the driver's cab. After the doors were opened, the ramp was completely enclosed so that one could not see into it nor could one exit from it. I stayed in the cab because Bürstinger ordered me to do so. Bürstinger left the ramp through the basement corridor. [...]
>
> After about half an hour, I heard loud calls from the basement hall and saw in the rear view mirror barefooted people run into the van. I did not see the people themselves, but through the gap between the right door and the van's body I saw bare feet. From this I concluded that the people were undressed. I knew they entered the van because it shook. When the van was full, the doors were closed and locked, apparently by Bürstinger, because he then hung the keys back up in the cab. Then Bürstinger ordered a Polish civilian to get under the van and do something there. Bothmann, who came out through the basement, ordered me to start the motor and let it run for 20 minutes. I started the motor, and after about one minute I heard terrible moaning and screaming coming from inside the van.
>
> I was overcome by fear and jumped out of the cab. (It was now clear to me that the exhaust gas led into the van in order to kill people.) Bothmann yelled at me and ordered me to get back inside. I sat and waited. I couldn't

do anything, because I was afraid of Bothmann. Slowly the moans and cries faded away after several minutes.

After about ten minutes a police official sat down beside me, and Bothmann ordered me to drive. But before this the Pole again crept under the van and, as was now clear to me, disconnected the inflow of the exhaust gas into the van. [. . .] The policeman who sat beside me told me where I was to drive.

After about three kilometers we came to a clearing in a forest area that lay along the road to Koło. When we arrived there, the policeman told me to stop at a mass grave, where under the supervision of a police official, a Jewish labor squad was working. There were several other policemen standing in a circle, apparently standing guard. The police official who supervised the labor squad told me to back the van up to the mass grave. The policeman who came with me unlocked the doors. Some members of the labor squad were then ordered to open the doors. When the doors were opened, eight to ten corpses fell out of the van. The labor squad then threw the rest out of the van.

After the van had been emptied, I drove it back to the mansion. On the way, I met Hering with his van. In the van I was driving, about 50 people were gassed. The same number was probably gassed in Hering's van.

At the mansion some Jews who obviously belonged to the mansion labor squad had to clean the inside of the van with water and disinfectants. To do this, they had to take out two wooden grates from the floor of the van. [. . .] After the van had been cleaned and the grates put back in, Häfele ordered me to drive back to the ramp.[8]

Laabs took one more load of corpses to the forest that day. Over the course of his service in Chełmno, he would make that drive countless times.

As has been noted, there were two principal Jewish work details in the camp, a Hauskommando and a Waldkommando. In late January or early February 1942, after three Jews successfully escaped from the camp, all Jewish prisoners working in Chełmno were forced to wear leg irons, which severely restricted their movements and made running impossible. Alois Häfele served as supervisor of the Jewish Hauskommando. The men of the Hauskommando were kept locked in rooms in the basement of the mansion until they were needed to perform the duties assigned to them. Undoubtedly, the number of people employed varied, but approximately 20 individuals were engaged in the work at the mansion.

After the victims were led into the basement and forced to enter the gas vans, about six to ten members of the Hauskommando were ordered to remove the clothes that had been left upstairs in the undressing room. This was done quickly since the next group of victims was waiting its turn outside.

Michał Podchlebnik, the Jew from Koło who had helped load members of his own family onto the trucks destined for Chełmno, was working in a labor brigade in Bugaj for the local Jewish Council. In January 1942, the group was loaded onto a truck and taken to the mansion in Chełmno. Podchlebnik became a member of the Hauskommando. Just after their arrival he and his companions were locked in a room in the basement.

Shortly thereafter, he heard people pass through the corridor and enter a gas van.

> Then we, that is the ten Jewish workers, were called upstairs to a large room in which men's and women's clothes, coats, and shoes lay in a mess on the floor. We were ordered to quickly carry the clothes and shoes to another room. In this room there were already a lot of other clothes and shoes. We placed the shoes in a separate pile. After the work was done, we were forced back to the basement.[9]

When the transports first began to arrive in Chełmno, the victims were made to undress in rooms on the ground floor, and the clothes were removed to adjacent rooms. Later, probably when all the available rooms had been filled, the people from the transports were taken upstairs and made to undress there. The members of the Hauskommando removed the clothes from the undressing rooms took them to the rear of the mansion and simply threw them out the windows. The residents of Chełmno could see the clothes being thrown from the upstairs windows. These clothes began to pile up and remained outside in the backyard. Blankets were thrown over the pile to protect the clothing from the elements. (A Nazi welfare organization that received some of this clothing, Winterhilfswerk, would later complain about the storage methods used in Chełmno.) Later, to keep these clothes hidden from the arriving transports so as not to arouse any suspicions, the victims were probably forced to undress in rooms on the front side of the building.

As time permitted, a group of the Hauskommando worked behind the mansion searching, sorting and stacking the articles that continually piled up there. Luggage brought to the camp was searched and eventually stored in the village church. Items found in the luggage and deemed worthless were burned in pits on the mansion grounds. As the mansion filled up with the belongings of the murdered victims, the granary building located on the right side of the mansion was also used to store clothing. The Catholic church in nearby Dąbie also served to warehouse items from Chełmno. All articles were searched. Any valuables found were collected daily by the Polish workers and turned over to SS Hauptscharführer Fritz Ismer.

In March 1942, Lange assigned Häfele the task of using his labor squad to pave the road, using stones, leading from the highway to the mansion. When transports arrived Häfele took his squad behind the mansion, so as not to be seen, and the squad stacked the clothing there. This road project was completed in May.

Another task assigned to the Hauskommando was cleaning out the gas vans. As a result of the gassing, excrement and urine remained in the interiors of the vans after each trip to the graves. Originally this was done in the forest, immediately after the dead were unloaded. Later, it was not done until the vans arrived back in Chełmno. Two Jews were assigned to clean each van.

According to Häfele, both Lange and Bothmann ordered his labor squad to undergo a selection every week. Those who were considered too weak to continue working were selected, taken to the forest and shot. Replacements for those killed were taken from incoming transports.[10]

Very little is known about the small group of skilled craftsmen that were imprisoned in the basement of the mansion. They are rarely mentioned in testimony concerning the camp's first period. Bothmann may have formed this group, just after his arrival at the camp. Neither Michał Podchlebnik nor Szlama Winer, who escaped with Podchlebnik and survived long enough to give testimony, mention craftsmen working in Chełmno. The known craftsmen came from towns that were 'resettled' mainly during April 1942, although they may have arrived to the camp via the Łódź ghetto as well.

What their specific purpose was is also unclear. It is known that they made whips for camp personnel and that their professional services, such as tailoring, were rendered for members of the Sonderkommando.[11] It is not known if these men were engaged in removing the Jewish stars from the clothing of the victims and repairing this clothing prior to it being shipped out, or if they refurbished items that were personally confiscated by Bothmann and other Nazi officials.

The Jewish craftsmen working in Chełmno attempted to communicate with the outside world by writing notes on scraps of paper. The number of notes written is not known, but two survived the war. One of these notes, written in Yiddish, was found along the road near the forest. According to the reference of burning corpses, the note can be dated no earlier than July 1942.

These are the Jews who worked in the death camp Kulmhof (Chełmno) between Koło and Dąbie:

1. Josef Herszkowicz from Kutno
2. Mojżesz Plocker from Kutno
3. Fajwel Plocker from Kutno
4. Szyja Szlamowicz from Grabów near Łódź
5. Noech Wolf Judkiewicz from Łódź
6. Chaskiel Zarak from Łęczyca
7. Motel Symkie from Łęczyca
8. Chaskiel (son) Wachtel from Łęczyca
9. Beniek Jastrzębski from Łęczyca
10. Aron Nusbaum from Sanok
11. Iser Strasburg from Lutomiersk
12. Gecel Stajer from Turek.

These are the last Jews who worked for the Gestapo in Chełmno, which is located between Dąbie and Koło. These are the last days of our lives, so we are sending word about ourselves. Perhaps [this note will] find [its way to] relatives or friends of these people, so that they will know that all the Jews who were taken from Łódź were killed in a horrible manner: They were tortured and burned. Be healthy and, if you survive, avenge us.[12]

The craftsmen wrote another note just days before the liquidation of the camp in 1943. This note was found in the laundry in Pabianice. Note that virtually all the names from the first note appear on the second. This would indicate that the craftsmen were not subjected to periodic selections; at least to the degree the other Jewish workers were.

April 2, 1943

This card is written by people who have only several hours to live. Whoever reads this will find it difficult to believe whether it is the truth or not. But this is the tragic truth, for in this town are your brothers and sisters who also died the same way. It is a place called <u>Koło</u>. This "human <u>slaughterhouse</u>" [underlined in the original] is located 12 kilometers from this town. We worked as craftsmen. Among others, there were tailors, leather workers, and shoemakers. There were 17 craftsmen, and so I give you the names of these people.

1. Pinkus Grun from Włocławek
2. Jonas Lew from Brzeziny
3. Ika Szama from Brzeziny
4. Zemad Szumiraj from Włocławek
5. Geszyp Majer from Kalisz
6. Symcha Wachtel from Łęczyca
7. Smlek Wachtel from Łęczyca
8. Beniek Jastrzębski from Łęczyca
9. Aron Nusbaum from Skepe
10. Iser Strasburg from Lutomiersk
11. Moniek Plocker from Kutno
12. Felek Plocker from Kutno
13. Josef Herszkowicz from Kutno
14. Chaskiel Zarak from Łęczyca
15. Wolf Judkiewicz from Łódź
16. Szyja Szlamowicz from Kalisz
17. Gecel from Turek

So these are the names, these are the people whom I list here. They are individuals from among the hundreds of thousands who died here![13]

In 1944, during the second period of the camp's operations, Bothmann would again form a group of craftsmen from the first Łódź transport. These men lived and worked upstairs in the granary building.

Valuables taken from the victims in the undressing rooms of the mansion and those found among the belongings of the victims during the sorting and searching were turned over daily to Hauptscharführer Fritz Ismer. Together with his assistant Hauptscharführer Karl Goede, Ismer was assigned to Chełmno from Łódź. When the extermination began, Ismer set up his office in the mansion. The valuables were stored in a room on the ground floor between the two front entrances. This lasted a very short time, perhaps ten days, until he was required to move. It is not known why this move occurred; but it may have become obvious that with hundreds of people a day entering the building it was simply an inconvenient place to work. The new office was some 100 meters from the mansion, but Ismer had to move a second time when this building was taken over by the police guard. Finally, Ismer's office was located in the former presbytery, across the street from the church. He and his new assistant, Unterscharführer Max Sommer (Goede had left Chełmno), were also billeted in the building.

At the end of each day, after the last transport had been gassed, Ismer and Sommer went to the mansion and collected the day's haul of valuables, which had been put inside a large sack. Cash was received in a wicker basket. They carried the goods back to the office using a handcart. The next day the items were sorted on a large table. Watches, rings, necklaces, articles of gold and silver, even alarm clocks, were entered on itemized lists. The goods were then packed into boxes, padlocked and subsequently taken by truck to the Ghettoverwaltung in Łódź.[14]

Sturmscharführer Wilhelm Görlich, the administrative official, lived and worked in Chełmno with Ismer, after Neumann left. In addition to his administrative duties, Görlich was also responsible for the money flowing into the camp—money taken from the pockets of the victims. He periodically delivered the cash by car to Biebow in Łódź. During one of these delivery runs to the Ghetto Administration, Ismer bought two watches and a couple of rings, while Sommer bought a diamond ring.[15] Karl Heinl, the police official who commanded the mansion guard, frequently accompanied the transports of valuables to Łódź. In addition, he made many trips to Berlin, transporting boxes to the Reich Security Main Office. He claimed not to know what was inside the boxes, but the contents may have included the gold teeth torn from the mouths of the victims.[16]

At other extermination camps, the confiscated property fell into the hands of the SS, but at Chełmno most items were turned over to the Ghettoverwaltung in Łódź. The ghetto administration in Łódź engaged in a campaign to acquire control over all Jewish belongings inside and outside the Łódź ghetto. Biebow's first competitor for the plundered spoils was the Criminal Police, the Kripo, with which he reached an agreement on October 23, 1940, whereby officials of the ghetto administration took possession of the furniture, money, crystal and household appliances accumulated in the warehouses of the Kripo. It was agreed that all of the goods, valuables, etc. confiscated in Łódź by the Kripo would be turned over to the ghetto administration, according to Biebow, to cover the costs of feeding the inhabitants of the ghetto. In exchange, Kripo officials were permitted to purchase confiscated items.

The second competitor for the confiscated property was the Łódź branch of the Main Trusteeship Office East [Haupttreuhandstelle Ost, HTO]. Following long negotiations, Biebow reached an agreement with this office, on the basis of which all items of Jewish origin found outside the ghetto and not yet requisitioned were to be transferred to the Łódź branch of HTO. However, this state of affairs did not last long. On March 16, 1942, Biebow managed to conclude a new agreement whereby HTO was obligated to sell confiscated goods, following their valuation, to the ghetto administration. Therefore, Biebow's office gained the right to acquire and dispose of Jewish property, including the right to sell jewelry and items of gold on the open market to jewelry stores in Łódź. These sales are thought to have generated an income for Biebow of between RM 1 million and RM 1.3 million.

Biebow was able to acquire this authority largely by using the argument that he was feeding the Jews based on the ghetto's self-sufficiency. He also had the support of the military as the factories in the ghetto were contracted to fill orders for it. Finally, it was a convenient means to dispose of the confiscated goods as well as a legal source through which these goods could be purchased at low prices, using a very general description of the items to be sold (for example, the standard of the gold items and the number of carats for diamonds were not listed). First in the buyer's line were Kripo officials, followed by such dignitaries as the Dr. Moser and other HTO officials, the Mayor Ventzki, Gestapo Chief Bradfisch and others. There were numerous buyers. An incomplete list for the period September 11, 1941 to September 27, 1944, noted 4,654 sales of goods for private use to German officials.[17] According to a provisional account these sales involved 800 to 1,000 buyers. One of Lange's last acts before his transfer to Berlin was to inform the Ghetto Administration that he was interested in a diamond ring worth RM 500—presumably a gift for his wife.[18] Gauleiter Greiser also benefited from the confiscated goods but is not listed among the buyers because he wasn't required to purchase items. Biebow testified at Greiser's trial after the war that he delivered gold from the ghetto to the town of Chodzież so that a table service could be made for Greiser and that he shipped 40 to 50 kilograms of silver to Greiser. Biebow delivered jewelry to Greiser's office and transferred some RM 5 million to RM 6 million of the ghetto administration's "surplus" funds to a special bank account (Friends of the Warthegau) to which Greiser had access.[19] On orders of Biebow, Rudolf Kramp, who delivered supplies to Chełmno, also delivered two leather trunks and, in the presence of Bradfisch, turned them over to Bothmann who was to fill them and deliver them to Greiser.[20]

Early in 1942, while returning by car from a meeting in Poznań, Biebow told his companion Albert Meyer, a member of Biebow's staff and director of the Goods Utilization Department, that he needed to stop in at the

Chełmno camp. The camp was not receiving transports that day. The two were met by Oberscharführer Herbert Richter, who gave them a brief tour, explaining how the procedure was carried out at the mansion. While passing the gas vans parked in the mansion courtyard, Richter pointed out that these were the vans that took the Jews for "disinfection." However, the purpose of the meeting between Biebow and Richter was to work out the details of transferring the goods accumulating in Chełmno to Łódź. It was following this meeting that a facility was established in Dąbrowa, a small town just outside Łódź, to serve as a collection point for the confiscated goods.[21]

Biebow also confiscated Jewish property outside Łódź after deporting the inhabitants of the provincial ghettos either to death in Chełmno or to work in the factories of the Łódź ghetto. On the heels of the deportations, a special detachment moved into the cleared ghetto areas, collecting the belongings that remained behind and transporting them to the warehouse facility in Dąbrowa. All the items brought to the warehouses were searched, sorted and cleaned by a workforce of some 250 Jewish laborers. Franz Seifert, who headed the Dąbrowa operation, requested that members of the police detachment receive a special monetary allocation ranging from RM 6 to RM 9 per day as well as additional allocations of vodka, cigarettes and soap for their "hazardous" work. In justifying the special monthly allocation of vodka for the members of the detachment, Ribbe pointed out that the special detachment in Chełmno received the same monthly vodka allocation.[22]

The possessions of those sent to Chełmno were also transported to Dąbrowa. The trucks used to bring the Jews to Chełmno were also utilized to transport their belongings out of the camp. According to Häfele, this began after his road project at the mansion was completed in May.[23] The Chronicle of the Łódź Ghetto, a record of events kept by the Jewish administration, noted the following in an entry for May 22 and 23, 1942.

> The Jews from Pabianice who were recently settled in the ghetto say that in the village of Dąbrowa, located about three kilometers from Pabianice, in the direction of Łódź, warehouses for old clothes have recently been set up on the grounds of a factory idle since the war began. Thus far, five gigantic warehouses have been set up there. They contain clothing, linen, shoes, pots and pans, and so on. Each day, trucks deliver mountains of packages, knapsacks, and parcels of every sort to Dąbrowa. Everything is broken down into groups and put in its proper place in the warehouses. Each day, 30 or so Jews from Pabianice ghetto are sent to sort the goods. Among other things, they have noticed that, among the waste papers, there were some of our *rumkis* [ghetto money], which had fallen out of billfolds. The obvious conclusion is that some of the clothing belongs to people deported from this ghetto. Apparently, some of the residents of Brzeziny, who had been sent out to perform manual labor directly upon their arrival in the ghetto [of Łódź], had been sent to work in Dąbrowa.[24]

It is not possible to determine the quantity of goods that was shipped out of Chełmno. Records are incomplete, but one document is worth noting, a telegram from the Łódź ghetto administration, dated May 27, 1942, to the Regional Economic Office [Landeswirtschaftsamt] in Poznań. The telegram details the vehicles required to transport goods from the "de-Jewified" areas and the amount of gasoline needed to accomplish the job. It also notes that, "For transporting approximately 370 wagons of clothing stored by Lange's Sonderkommando, about 900 trucks with trailers [i.e., 900 loads] are required."[25] Albert Meyer, the official who had visited Chełmno with Biebow and inspected the goods stored there, suggested that this telegram exaggerated the situation in the camp by about 100 loads in order to receive a larger allocation of gasoline.[26] Whether or not this is true, the quantity of goods that passed through the camp was indeed enormous.

Transporting the goods to the warehouses did not occur without incident. Franz Seifert, the official in charge of the facility, complained to Friedrich Ribbe, Biebow's assistant, about the policemen from Chełmno who accompanied the trucks to the warehouses. On one occasion in May 1942, a policeman accompanying the load of goods beat up a Jew without reason and threatened him saying, "Just wait, I'll get you, too!" Siefert pointed out to Bothmann that this sort of behavior was not in anyone's best interest. Bothmann apologized and said it wouldn't happen again. Nevertheless, about a week later a truck arrived from Chełmno at quarter of five in the morning on a Sunday. Therefore the night duty officer had to summon some Jewish workers to unload the goods, forcing the policeman from Chełmno to wait. When the Jews appeared, the policeman beat each one for not saying good morning. The German official on duty was also accidentally struck. The second incident sparked correspondence regarding the problem. Seifert requested Ribbe urge Bothmann to prevent similar incidents in the future, not because of any compassion for the Jews, but because such behavior could jeopardize discipline, order and the performance of work in the camp. Seifert was later informed that while visiting Chełmno, Biebow spoke with Bothmann about the matter. Bothmann assured Biebow such events would not be repeated and that all drivers had been duly informed.[27] Such events may not have been repeated at Seifert's processing facility but more interestingly they show that those working for Hans Bothmann had no qualms whatever about beating Jews.

Another problem encountered by the Ghettoverwaltung was connected with selling the belongings of the murdered Jews. In August 1942, a relief organization in Poznań, the National Socialist People's Welfare [Nationalsozialistische Volkswohlfahrt, NSV] asked for 3,000 suits and 1,000 items of women's apparel, and some underwear and bed sheets. The items were urgently required for the settlers being brought into the area as part of the Germanization plan for the incorporated territory. The NSV was looking for a good deal and after some time an agreement was reached. (The suits sold for RM 5 each, the dresses for RM 2, and the price of the 5,000 kilograms of bed sheets was RM 4 per kilogram.) The items were duly shipped to NSV and the relief agency was billed.

On January 16, 1943, the Ghettoverwaltung received a complaint. The initial shipment of 1,500 suits had been sent to the local offices of the relief organization. After opening the crates the employees were dismayed to find that the shipment did not conform to samples they had viewed at Chełmno. Many of the suits were not suits at all but unmatched coats and pants. Worse, a large part of the clothing was soiled with dirt and bloodstains. Several hundred items of clothing still had the Jewish star attached to them. As most of the workers employed unpacking the crates were Poles, it was feared that the German settlers would find out about the origin of the items, thereby discrediting the relief agency.

The Ghettoverwaltung eventually sent a reply, acknowledging the return of 2,750 suits and 1,000 dresses. It claimed that the stains were not blood but rust and that they could not be removed. As a result a new bill would be made out only for the 250 suits and underwear. This reply generated another letter from Winter Relief stating that the welfare organization could not resign itself to the loss of the suits. If the rust spots could not be removed, then at least the Jewish stars could be removed from the clothing.[28]

It is not known if Biebow's other customers had similar problems, but this correspondence does show that clients were fully aware of the origin of the merchandise they were buying. Indeed, they were taken to Chełmno to inspect the goods prior to purchase.

Arguably the most enigmatic incident in the camp's history involves another group of visitors to Chełmno. During the summer of 1942, a "commission" of four or five Gestapo agents arrived to inspect the facility. The commission from Berlin had been expected, and although it had arrived early, the members were received with some fanfare. However, Bothmann was not present in Chełmno at the time. (One account states he was getting drunk with a Dr. König, a friend of his.) Instead, Bothmann's deputy showed them around the camp. Helena Król, a local woman employed by the Sonderkommando in the kitchen, saw the members of the commission when they came into the building. It is possible that this commission took photographs and received documents concerning the camp. Before they left, Kajetan Skrzypczyński, one of the Polish workers employed in the camp, put gas in their car. Later he stated that while doing so one of the men from this commission gave him a knowing smile.

Approximately two hours after this commission left the camp, a second group of Nazi officials, the actual commission, arrived. Naturally, this caused quite a stir among the Sonderkommando. A search was launched to find the first "commission" but this was unsuccessful. One account relates that they fled to Koło where they abandoned their car. The car was later taken away by the police. Bothmann was in despair when he learned what happened. Allegedly he got drunk again and went to Łódź. In Chełmno the guard was doubled and the following day policemen stopped everyone on the streets of Koło and checked their identity papers.

According to Andrzej Miszczak, a local farmer whose information is generally reliable, the "commission" eventually sent a card to Chełmno representing themselves as English intelligence. Miszczak later heard members of the Sonderkommando boasting that the members of the "commission" were caught "on the Turkish border." In 1944, while being given his guard assignment in the camp, Bruno Israel was told that "English agents" were once in Chełmno and that this was not to happen again.

It seems extremely unlikely that the British would have had agents infiltrating Chełmno in 1942. If in fact camp security was breached, it is much more likely to have been accomplished by agents of the Polish underground and would have required advance knowledge that a commission was expected to visit the camp. The Poles did send an agent (Jan Karski) into the Bełżec extermination camp to find out what was taking place there. The Polish government, based in London during the war, had an intelligence outpost in Istanbul, Turkey, where couriers brought reports smuggled out of Poland. General information concerning Chełmno did reach London via Istanbul but no detailed report, which such a mission would have provided, has been found. The event in Chełmno has never been acknowledged by any government and requires further investigation.[29]

The mansion was a very busy place. The transports arrived almost every day, and hundreds of people were greeted with the deceptive arrival speech. Then, the victims were forced to endure a final humiliation of disrobing in public—men, women and children together—only to be led down the stairs, through the basement, and into the gas vans. The entire process of extermination took between 60 and 90 minutes. It was a simple, yet a cunning and effective system. It was the ultimate deception and degradation.

One local man, who had illegally returned from Germany, spent most of the war hiding at his brother-in-law's house in Cichmiana, a village neighboring Chełmno. He was undoubtedly expressing the thoughts of many local residents when he recorded his reaction to the establishment of the death camp.

> [...] I still don't believe it. I can't believe something so horrible. The holocaust of a whole nation has lasted two weeks already and still I don't believe it, I can't. And often I repeat: No, it's impossible. But there is terrifying proof.

I can't believe, although I see the same trucks going back and forth everyday on the road between Dąbie and Chełmno. I can see them going, hear them. I listen to terrible stories but still I don't believe [...]. Finally I have to believe [...]. This slaughtering of thousands is being done quietly, almost unnoticeably. You can hardly hear a groan. Only in the houses that are the closest, sometimes they can hear some groans, weeping, laments. Only the movement of the big trucks can be seen. Passersby can see lots of Jews in these trucks because they are covered with canvass that isn't fastened in the back. So usually it takes place efficiently, quickly, quietly. If not for the sound of the motors, the silence would be simply terrifying. It takes place in front of all the people of Chełmno and in front of passersby because the mansion is near the road. But now the mansion is fenced in. This is why nobody knows anything for sure. Nobody knows how it is being done. But everybody knows that the murdering is taking place or starting in Chełmno, behind the fence, and the people are being buried in the Rzuchów Forest.[30]

The Forest Camp

As the first extermination camp to be established, Chełmno was also the first place to encounter the unexpected problem associated with burying thousands of bodies in mass graves. Due to expanding gasses, corpses erupted from the ground engulfing the area for miles with a putrid stench. This resulted in the camp ceasing operations in order to develop a new method for disposing of large numbers of human bodies. This new method, employed later in the Aktion Reinhard camps and across the occupied territories of the Soviet Union through Aktion 1005, was pioneered in Chełmno.

The forest camp, situated within Forestry Service sections 76, 77, and parts of sections 74 and 75 of the Rzuchów Forest, was not a camp in the traditional sense of the word. Initially there were no major structures or barracks as there was no one to house and no guard towers. Only later would a fence be built to enclose the area. The forest camp was merely a convenient location to bury and later burn the corpses of the victims. It eventually consisted of three clearings, a large one about 80 meters long and 80 meters wide (enlarged in the course of time), a middle clearing about 70 meters long and 20 meters wide, and a small clearing about 40 meters long and 15 meters wide. Strips of trees separated the clearings.[1] The earliest description of graves in the forest comes from Kurt Möbius, who was taken there the day after his arrival in mid-December 1941.

There was a large clearing in the forest surrounded by one or two cordons of guard posts. There was a large grave in the clearing that had been dug by four or five Polish workers. The grave had the following dimensions: five to six meters deep, eight meters wide and 20 meters long. About one-eighth of it was filled with bodies.[2]

Rottwachtmeister Jakob Wildermuth was among the earliest group of policemen to serve in Chełmno. His description of the graves differs only slightly from the one given by Möbius.

> In the first clearing, there were two mass graves about 30 meters long, ten meters wide, and three meters deep. In the second clearing, there was a mass grave about 30 meters long, ten meters wide, and three meters deep. In the third clearing there was a mass grave about 12 meters long, ten meters wide, and three meters deep. When I started my duty in Chełmno, the mass grave in the third clearing had already been filled with corpses. The mass grave in the second clearing was half filled with corpses. The other mass graves had only been prepared and were filled with corpses later.[3]

Another early description of the area originates from a local villager. On December 22, 1941, just two weeks after the first transport arrived, Adam Milewski snuck up to the area when fewer policemen than usual were guarding the forest camp due to the holiday break. Although unable to roam about freely, he observed one grave about ten meters wide and some 30 meters long. It was camouflaged with freshly planted trees. He also noted that trees were cut down in a second area making way for another grave. In addition, the local forest worker saw four guardhouses.[4]

Over the course of the next several months, the space taken by the graves in the forest increased and grew larger as the procession of transports continued. In the summer of 1942, when Fritz Ismer was transferred to the forest camp, he saw two large mass graves about 150 meters long, about three to four meters wide, and three meters deep. Another grave was about 50 meters long, three to four meters wide, and three meters deep. In addition there were 12 to 20 square graves, each with different dimensions.[5]

Along with about 30 other policemen from Łódź, Josef Islinger was assigned to the Polizeiwachtkommando in the spring of 1942. He gives the following description about the day after his arrival.

> [W]e were welcomed by two SS officers, Hauptsturmführer Bothmann and Untersturmführer Plate. Bothmann delivered a speech explaining to us that a secret affair of state was being carried out in Kulmhof. We were to keep silent about everything we saw and heard; otherwise we would face serious punishment. We were to become members of the Polizeiwachtkommando and serve as guards. He did not explain anything else, particularly what was going on in Kulmhof.
>
> Sergeant Otto Böge gave us our assignments. I became a member of a group under the command of Polizeimeister Haider. The task of this group was to guard a certain forest area near Chełmno. At first, we didn't know why we were guarding the forest. Haider assigned us to several positions around the forest. Our task was to ensure that no one entered the woods. [...] (Eventually, from hearsay, I found out what was happening.) A Jewish labor detachment worked in the forest. It consisted of about 15 to 20 people.

At first, I mounted guard on the outer perimeter of the forest camp. Depending on where I mounted guard, I could sometimes see the gas vans drive into the forest camp. During my service there, I could see that everything I had heard from hearsay was true. I saw two large mass graves in the forest, about 20 to 30 meters long, six to eight meters wide, and four meters deep. One of the mass graves was already filled with dead bodies and covered with earth. The other one was half filled at that time. The gas vans came many times a day and stopped at the grave. The members of the Jewish labor detachment, whose legs were shackled, opened the back doors of the gas vans and took out the bodies that were inside. Next, the bodies were stacked in layers inside the mass grave. The gas vans, full of bodies, came five to ten times a day. I estimate that there were always about 50 bodies in the smaller vans and 70 in the larger one. [. . .] The forest camp was supervised by Polizeimeister Lenz. Polizeioberwachtmeister Runge was second in command. [. . .] Lenz and Runge always urged the Jews on who were unloading the gas vans. They reviled the Jews with terms like, "swine." Sometimes, they also beat the Jews with sticks.

Almost every day, in the evening, several Jews from the labor squad were shot in the forest camp, before the group was transported back to Chełmno. Only those Jews who were unable or unwilling to work were shot. Usually there were five or six, but sometimes up to ten were shot. Polizeimeister Lenz carried out most of the executions. He ordered the Jews to lay face down on the edge of the mass grave. Then he took his gun and shot them in the back of the neck. The other Jews had to throw the bodies into the grave. [. . .] I also recall that Plate carried out those executions from time to time. He often visited the forest camp and supervised our work.[6]

In the spring of 1942, the German forester Heinz May, under whose jurisdiction the Rzuchów Forest fell, was summoned by his superior to report to Oberführer Dr. Mehlhorn in the Reichsstatthalterei, the office of the Gauleiter. There, he was informed that the events taking place in Chełmno were secret and failure to keep it so was punishable by death. May was also informed that the head of the Sonderkommando, Hauptsturmführer Bothmann, would contact him for the purpose of planting trees on the graves as part of a camouflaging operation. The entire section of the forest was also to be surrounded with a pole fence, enclosing an area approximately 250 meters wide (along the Koło-Dąbie highway) and 750 meters long (into the forest from the main road).[7] May was told that the matter was urgent and needed to be carried out immediately. Several days later, May met with Bothmann.

Together with Bothmann I drove to section 77 and for the first time I entered this horrible place. In a clearing which had been enlarged by cutting down trees, I saw first a grave of about 200 meters in length and five meters wide. The grave was covered with a mound of earth two meters high. Somewhat further, there was a similar grave of about 50 meters in length. In another clearing about 50 meters away, there was a grave about 150 meters in length. This grave was covered for about three-quarters of its length. The end furthest away from me was still open. I dared not go there and look into it. Soon afterwards another [gas van] appeared which drove to the open part of the grave and pulled up close to its rear side.

The truck was opened and I saw a pile of naked human bodies tumble down. I stood about 80 meters from the truck. Under the leadership of an official a number of workers who were employed there came running, with the upper part of their bodies naked, in order to throw the corpses into the grave. Bothmann told me that they had to be stacked neatly as otherwise not enough would go in. Perpendicular to this grave, a dredge with a motor and conveyor belt was working on the construction of another grave. The covering of the graves likewise was carried out by means of a conveyor belt operated by a motor.

About 30 persons of young and middle age worked on the place. They all worked with the upper part of their bodies naked.

Bothmann told me that he changed the workers every week. They were "mowed down" and he picked new labor from every new transport of Jews. The workers wore thin steel chains on their ankles so that they could walk, but not run fast.

Bothmann said that it happened often that people would say after only one or several days that they could not continue the work and ask to be shot. He made a cross on their backs with a red pencil. This was a sign for the guards to kill them in the evening. They had to stretch out with their faces to the ground and would be liquidated by a shot into the head from the rear. Those who did not work diligently would also receive a cross from him. I saw the workers eating rye bread during a pause. After its termination, they were driven back to work with sticks.

A man in the uniform of a captain came across the place and mentioned his name. I don't remember it. The man had the bloated face of a drunkard and debaucher. He also wore the War Service Cross, 1st Class with Swords. Bothmann told me that he was responsible for the "work" in the castle. He, Bothmann, directed the whole thing.

The police captain related that he had given strict orders to close the trucks with a padlock before they drove out of the castle. En route, the back doors had flown open and the "warm loaves of bread" had fallen on the road. The streets were immediately blocked off, but nevertheless the civilian population had seen various things and thereby much had become publicly known.

In the clearings there were guards with rifles and machine pistols every-where. Bothmann told me that they were excellent sharpshooters. He told me further that it had happened several times that some attempted to run away. However, they had not got very far since the bullets of these sharpshooters reached them. One evening during the departure one person was missing at the roll call. The guards declared that nobody had run away. After a long search it was discovered that he was lying under a bundle of faggots. Naturally he was immediately liquidated.

I ordered a large amount of furze seed at a seed store in order to sow it around the place. Pines and birches were supposed to be planted in between.[8]

Shortly after the camp began operations the head of the Gestapo, Grup-penführer Heinrich Müller, ordered his subordinate Adolf Eichmann, in charge of the Gestapo's Jewish Affairs Office, to go to Chełmno and report back to him on the camp's operations. During an interrogation prior to his trial in Israel many years later, Eichmann recounted this event.

> *Eichmann:* I received orders from Müller to go to Litzmannstadt and report back to him on what was going on there. He didn't put it the same way as ... as Heydrich ... not as crassly. "An action against the Jews is under way there, Eichmann. Go take a look. And then report to me." I went to Gestapo headquarters in Litzmannstadt – now it's Łódź again – and there I was told. It was a special team, put in by the Reichsführer [Himmler]. And they told me exactly where this Kulm[hof] is situated. I saw the following: a room, perhaps, if I remember right, about five times as big as this one here. There were Jews in it. They had to undress, and then a sealed truck drove up. The doors were opened; it drove up to a kind of ramp. The naked Jews had to get in. Then the doors were closed and the truck drove off.
> *[Israeli interrogator Avner] Less:* How many people did this truck hold?
> *Eichmann:* I don't know exactly. The whole time it was there, I didn't look inside. I couldn't. Couldn't! What I saw and heard was enough. The screaming and ... I was much too shaken and so on. I told Müller that in my report. He didn't get much out of it. I drove after the truck ... and there I saw the most horrible sight I had seen in all my life. It drove up to a fairly long trench. The doors were opened and the corpses were thrown out. The limbs were as supple as if they'd been alive. Just thrown in. I can still see a civilian with pliers pulling out teeth. And then I beat it. I got into my car and drove off. I didn't say another word. I sat there for hours without saying a word to my driver. I'd had enough. I was through. The only other thing I remember is that a doctor in a white smock wanted me to look through the peephole and watch the people inside the truck. I refused. I couldn't, I couldn't say another word, I had to get out of there. In Berlin, I reported to Gruppenführer Müller. I told him the same as I've told you now. Terrible, an inferno. I can't. It's ... I can't do it ... I told him.[9]

According to Heydrich's orders, Eichmann did not file a written report, but only reported orally to Müller. He may or may not have been affected by his brief visit to Chełmno, but it was just another 'ordinary' day for members of the Sonderkommando.

Up to this point, the forest camp has been viewed through the eyes of Germans: members of the camp staff and outsiders, individuals not directly threatened by what they saw there. But what was it like for the members of the Jewish Waldkommando, the gravediggers? A very different picture emerges when viewed from this perspective.

Three of these prisoners managed to escape during the camp's second month in operation. Two of these men, Abram Rój and Szlama Winer, came from the town of Izbica Kujawska, located north of Koło. Abram Rój was born on January 8, 1916, in Przedecz,[10] the son of Icek and Sura Rój, but grew up in Izbica Kujawska. The Rój family lived a modest life but with the death of the head of the household the family's situation worsened. After completing seventh grade, Abram became a tailor's apprentice to help support his mother, four sisters and brother (all of whom died in

Chełmno). As the likelihood of war approached, Rój was called up for military service in August 1938, and in March 1939, he was assigned to the 69th Infantry Regiment, stationed in Gniezno.[11] During the September campaign, Rój's unit was captured by the Germans and he was interned in Stalag XIA, located at Altengrabow. Rój was singled out by his fellow soldiers as being a Jew and so, according to German practice at the time, he was released in March 1940, and went home to Izbica where he continued to work as a tailor. It is not certain if Rój arrived in Chełmno together with Winer (January 6, 1942) or if he arrived with the second group of men from Izbica (January 9), but he was assigned to the Waldkommando as a gravedigger.[12] The only record of Rój's experiences in Chełmno is his oral testimony told to friends and family.

On the other hand, Szlama Winer, Rój's companion from Izbica, did record his experiences in Chełmno. Following his escape and arrival in the Warsaw ghetto, Winer's story was written down, later buried for safe keeping and eventually recovered after the war. His description of events in the death camp has no equal.[13]

Monday, January 5, 1942

On Monday, January 5, 1942, the guards in Izbica [Kujawska] summoned members of the Jewish Council and demanded people for work. They declared that this order, unlike other orders issued by the *Arbeitsamt* [labor office] and, as they put it, disregarded by the Jews, must be carried out immediately.

The same day, about 40 men, including elderly and the infirm, drawn by the guards from the list of names, arrived at the police station. Their documents were taken and they were ordered to return the next day with shovels or spades and enough bread for one or two days. They were told that they would return home after a couple of days. I was among them. I know the names of some of the guards: (1) Lieutenant Johann (last name uncertain), (2) Meister (name uncertain), (3) Schmalz, a guard and *Volksdeutscher* [ethnic German]. There were seven of them. I am convinced that they knew what we were going to be used for. I repeat: They knew very well, without a doubt, what was going on, but despite this, none of the Jews were warned. Just the opposite, we were bitterly deceived.

Frankly speaking, I didn't want to show up for work. My parents persuaded me, believing that in this way I would avoid being sent to a labor camp. I admit that I had already succeeded in avoiding this three times.

Tuesday, January 6

On Tuesday morning 15 people showed up. They waited until eight o'clock, but no one else showed up, so the guards conducted a roundup. Another 19 people were caught in the street and in their houses. Five of them were let go, they were either infirm or too young. So 14 remained, but together with those who showed up on their own, there were 29 people. The names of these 29 people were written down. Meanwhile, a truck with guards arrived. We were counted once again and loaded into the truck. Everyone had a knapsack with him. The truck drew everyone's attention. Our families were convinced that we were going to a labor camp. Poles, passing by, behaved in different ways. The young ones sometimes laughed at and mocked us, but the older ones weep.

We went in the direction of Koło. Later we turned onto the Dąbie road towards Chełmno. This place was already at that time known in the whole area, because four weeks before the resettlements from Koło and Dąbie had taken place. Various disturbing rumors were circulated that anyone sent to Chełmno never returned. However, we didn't know what happened there. We heard vague rumors from messengers but not any details.

We waited on the highway in Chełmno about half an hour, then we drove up to the mansion. It's an unusual, dilapidated building dating back to the previous war. It is located on the right side of the highway while to the left is the church and the village. The Gestapo requisitioned all the buildings around the church.

We arrived in Chełmno at half past twelve in the afternoon. Gestapo men stood at both gates of the mansion, which was guarded by the field police.

Behind the second gate we were driven out of the truck, ordered to put our knapsacks aside and line up in double file. From then on we were at the mercy of black uniformed SS men, all of them high ranking Reich Germans. We were ordered to hand over all the money and valuables we had. Next, 15 people were selected, I among them, and taken under guard to one of the cells in the basement. I found out later that there were several such basement cells. The 15 of us were locked into one cell, the remaining 14 people in another.

Although it was sunny outside, it was dark in the basement. We got some straw from the Volksdeutsche on the staff.[14] For the night we were given a lantern for the cell. In the evening at about eight o'clock, we were given unsweetened black coffee and nothing else. We were depressed, preparing for the worst. Everyone weep, kissed one another, and said their good-byes. It was very cold so we huddled up next to one another and in this way spent this freezing night without shutting our eyes. We talked continuously about the Jews who were deported from Koło and Dąbie. Judging from what we knew, we became convinced that we wouldn't get out of here.

Wednesday, January 7

On Wednesday, January 7, at seven in the morning, the guard on duty banged on the door screaming: "Get up." But none of us had slept anyway because of the cold. After an hour they brought unsweetened black coffee and bread from our packs. It comforted us a little; we whispered that there is still a God in heaven and that we will be going to work.

At half past eight (the reason it was so late was that the nights were long), they led us into the courtyard. Several people were left behind. They were taken to the neighboring cell in the basement. They carried out two Jews who had hung themselves. (I don't know their names.) They were prisoner/gravediggers from Kłodawa. The corpses were thrown onto a truck. We met again with the other prisoners from Izbica. As soon as we came out of the basement, we were surrounded by 12 guards and Gestapo men with machine guns. There were 29 prisoners in the truck as well as the two corpses and six guards. A vehicle with ten guards and two civilians followed behind us.

We drove down the highway in the direction of Koło. After going about seven kilometers the truck suddenly turned left into the forest. There was a half kilometer long well-worn path. At the end of the path the SS men stopped the truck and ordered us to get out, undress and line up double file. (We remained in our shoes, underwear, pants and shirts.) Although there was a severe frost, we had to leave our overcoats, hats, sweaters and gloves on the ground. The two civilians brought shovels and pickaxes and gave each of us one of them. Only eight of us didn't get a tool. They were ordered to take the two corpses from the truck.

As we arrived in the forest we immediately saw the prisoners from Kłodawa who had arrived before us. They were already at work in their shirt-sleeves. The scene looked as follows: 21 people with pickaxes and shovels, behind them eight people and two corpses, and all around us Germans with machine guns. Those from Kłodawa were also guarded by about 12 guards. Therefore we were surrounded by 30 guards.

As we approached the ditch, those from Kłodawa greeted us in a whisper: "Where are you from?" "From Izbica," we answered. They asked, "You know how bad it is here? How many of you are there?" "Twenty-nine," we said. We talked while working. We threw both bodies down into the ditch. Shovels were brought from the truck for those who still didn't have one. However, we didn't have to wait long before the next van arrived with fresh victims. The van was specially constructed and appeared normal: the size of a normal truck, gray, hermetically sealed with two rear doors. The inside was covered with sheet metal. There were no seats inside. The floor was covered with a wooden grating, as in public baths, and with a straw mat. Between the driver's cab and the rear compartment were two peepholes. Using a flashlight one could observe whether the victims were dead or not. Under the wooden grating were two tubes about 15 centimeters long that came out of the cab. The tubes had openings on the end from which gas came out. The gas apparatus was located in the cab, in which only the driver sat. It was always the same driver who wore a uniform with the SS skull and crossbones. He was about 40 years old. There were two of these vans.

The van stopped about eight meters from the grave. The leader of the guard detail, a high ranking SS man, was an absolute sadist. He ordered eight men to open the doors of the vehicle and the strong, sharp odor of gas hit us immediately. Dead Gypsies from Łódź were in the van. Their things lay inside: accordions, violins, eiderdown, and even watches and gold jewelry. After waiting about five minutes by the doors, the SS man screamed, *"Ihr Juden, herein und schmeisst alles raus."* [You Jews, get in and throw everything out.] The Jews ran to the van and threw out the corpses. As the work initially didn't go quickly enough for them, the supervising SS man pulled out his whip and screamed, *"Hellblaue, ich komme sofort zu euch"* [I'm coming for you now], beating us about our heads, ears, eyes, in all directions, until everyone collapsed on the ground. Whoever couldn't get up was immediately shot with a machine gun. Seeing this, the others, with the last of their strength, managed to get up and continue to work.

The corpses were thrown out of the vans like garbage onto a heap. They were dragged by the feet and the hair. Two people stood at the edge and threw the bodies into the grave. Two others were in the ditch and placed them in layers, face down, in such a way that the head of one was placed next to the feet of another. A special SS man directed this. If there was an empty place, the corpse of a child was stuffed in there. The SS man stood up above with a pine branch in his hand and directed where to place the heads, legs, children, and things. All this was accompanied by malicious screams: "*Du Sakrament!*" [You bastard!]. A layer numbered from 180 to 200 corpses. After every three van loads about 20 of the gravediggers were used to cover up the corpses. At first this was done twice. Later when the number of van loads rose to nine (nine times sixty corpses) it was done three times.

At twelve o'clock the SS leader "Bykowiec" ["The Whip," probably Polizeimeister Willi Lenz] ordered, "*Spadel stehen lassen*" [Put your shovels down]. He lined us up in two rows and counted us. Then he ordered us to get out of the ditch. The guards still stood around us and didn't leave us for even a moment. We even had to relieve ourselves where we worked.

We were taken to our belongings and ordered to sit on the bags. We were continually guarded. We were given a cup of cold coffee and a piece of frozen bread. That was lunch. We sat like this for half an hour. Afterwards we lined up, were counted and taken back to work.

How did the dead look? They weren't singed or blackened. The color of the faces was unchanged. Almost all the dead were soiled with excrement.

We stopped working at about five o'clock. The eight who worked with the corpses were ordered to lie on top of them, face down. An SS man then shot each of them in the head with a machine gun.

"The Whip" screamed, "*Hellblaue, flick sich anziehen!*" [Get dressed quickly!] We dressed quickly and took our shovels with us. We were counted and led to the trucks by the guards and SS men. Here we were ordered to put the shovels away. Once again we were counted and driven into the truck. The trip back to the mansion took about 15 minutes. On the way back, we were together with those from Kłodawa. We talked discreetly in the truck. I said to my colleagues, "My mother dreamed about leading me to a white wedding canopy; now she won't even accompany me to a black one." Everyone broke out weeping, but so the guards sitting with us didn't hear. We spoke very quietly.

On the first day the following event took place. At ten in the morning a fat man named Bitter from Bydgoszcz, who had lived in Izbica during the war, one of the eight, failed to keep up with the pace of work. The SS man with the whip ordered him to undress completely and then beat him unconscious. His body looked black as spleen. Later, he was ordered to lie down in the open pit where he was shot.

It turned out that there were other rooms in the mansion. There were 20 people in our cell, 15 in the other. At that time, there were no other gravediggers. Back in the cold and dark basement, we threw ourselves onto the scanty straw and burst into tears. Fathers cried over the fate of their children, who they would never see again. One of the prisoners, Moniek Halter, a 15-year-old boy from Izbica, embraced me and sobbed, "Ah, Szlojme, I can die, but at least let my mother and sister survive." Meir Piotrkowski, a 40-year-old from Izbica, my neighbor on the straw, embraced, hugged, kissed me and said, "I have left my dear wife and eight children at home; who knows if I'll ever see them again, and what is going to happen to them?" Gerszon Praszker, age 55, from Izbica said, "We have a great God in heaven and we must pray to Him. He will not abandon us. But nevertheless, we all must recite the prayer of penitence. Everyone formed a circle, with Gerszon Praszker in the middle, and recited the prayer. We repeated after him, sobbing and weeping profusely. The mood was very depressed. Then the Wachtmeister pounded on the door, shouting; "*Hej, Juden, still bleiben, sonst schiesse ich*" [Hey, Jews, quiet or I shoot]. So with breaking voices, we quietly ended our prayers.

At half past seven in the evening, they brought us a pot of watery cold turnip soup. We couldn't swallow the food, but cried quietly, shedding bitter tears. After half an hour, black, unsweetened, barely warm coffee and a little bit of bread was brought. Again, no one could eat because of our pain and suffering. It was cold and we didn't have any covers. Someone said, "Who knows which of us will be missing tomorrow?" Finally, terribly exhausted, we pressed closer to each other. Our nightmares were full of hallucinations. We slept about four hours. Then, because of the cold, we stood up and walked around the cell, talking about the horrible fate that awaited us.

Thursday, January 8

On Thursday, January 8, at seven in the morning, the guard on duty knocked and asked angrily, "*O, ihr Juden, hat ihr euch ausgeschlafen?*" [Hey, you Jews, did you get enough sleep?] We answered, "*Wir konnten nicht schlafen wegen der kalte*" [We couldn't sleep because of the cold]. At half past seven, the cook brought warm but unsweetened coffee and bread. Some of us drank but the majority didn't have breakfast, saying that we were going to die anyway. At eight o'clock, we heard SS men approaching in the corridor. The guard reported that nothing had happened during the night. The SS man ordered the cell door opened. (It had three locks and a bolt.) Standing in the corridor the officer ordered, "*Alle Juden raus!*" [All Jews out!] (We assumed that the SS were afraid of some desperate move on our part. He counted us in the courtyard, ordered us to line up in twos and get into the truck. Generally, two vehicles took us to work and brought us back: a tarpaulin-covered truck and a passenger vehicle with windows along the sides (a bus). We stood in the truck and behind us were six guards with machine guns. During my entire stay in Chełmno, the area of the courtyard, into which we came from out of the basement, was closely watched by guards with machine guns ready to shoot. During the trip to work, a car with SS men followed us.

At work everything was just as it had been the day before. After getting out of the truck we were counted, lined up in a row and counted again. Then eight of us were selected (those who weren't able to dig energetically enough). These people, silently and with lowered heads, stepped out of the line. Before returning to the previous day's work stations, everyone had to undress. We remained in our shoes, pants and shirts. (One man who wore two shirts was beaten severely.) We put our things in one spot. After half an hour, the second group of gravediggers arrived, those from the neighboring cell. They also went through the same procedure. The whole area was surrounded by guards with machine guns. The forest was full of guard patrols. The guards were ordered to be increasingly vigilant. The chosen eight worked in the grave, about twenty steps from us. One of them, 19-year-old Mechl Wilczyński from Izbica, said to me, "Farewell, you all will remain alive. We will die, but you should try to get out of this hell." The others were silent and only sighed.

After two hours, the first van arrived with Gypsies. I state unequivocally that the executions were carried out in the forest. The gas van usually stopped about 100 meters from the mass grave, but twice it stopped about 20 meters away. As those in the ditch told us, there was a special device with buttons in the driver's cab. Two tubes led from this device into the van. The driver (there were two gas vans and two drivers, always the same ones) pressed a button and then got out of the cab. Just after that screams, frightful shouting and banging on the walls could be heard. It continued for about 15 minutes. Then the driver returned to the cab where he shone a flashlight through a peep-hole inside to check if everyone was dead. Then he drove the van to within about six meters of the grave. After an additional five minutes "The Whip" (the SS leader) ordered four of those working in the grave to open the doors. A strong smell of gas belched out. After another wait of about five minutes "The Whip" shouted, "*Ihr Juden, geht tefilin legen*" [literally, Jews go put on your phylacteries], by which he meant to throw the corpses out.

They [the dead] lay intertwined, in the filth of their own excrement. They looked as if they'd just gone to sleep, with rosy cheeks and natural skin color. The bodies were still warm and, as those working in the grave told us, they [the gravediggers] warmed themselves on the corpses. This was the method of work: four men, from the eight working in the grave, threw out the corpses from the van, driven on with shouts and beatings, of course. The corpses were thrown out onto a heap. Two others pulled the corpses to the grave and threw them in. Then, in the grave, two others arranged them according to the instructions of an SS man. After the van was emptied, those workers from the ditch cleaned out the excrement. The straw mat and wooden grating were removed, and they cleaned the van using their own shirts. Then the mat and grating were put back in. The doors were locked with an outside bolt. Locking the doors required some experience, but because it was done daily by new people, they were savagely beaten by "The Whip."

After the van left and the bodies were arranged, those [working] in the grave, in order to warm themselves, put on the colorful clothes of the Gypsies and sat on the corpses in the graves. It was a tragic, but also comical sight. Generally these prisoners weren't allowed to have contact with the other workers. During lunch, they stayed in the grave where they got only bitter, black coffee but not a crumb of bread. It was done like this: A guard filled a small pot with coffee, using a long ladle. After it was drunk by the first man, the guard refilled it and the second one drank. These eight men were treated like lepers.

After half an hour passed, the second van with Gypsies arrived. It stopped about 100 meters from us so that we didn't hear anything. (The muffled screams of despair unnerved us.) Before lunch, we "processed" three van loads; after lunch four. (We usually counted them.)

Again our lunch consisted of cold, black, unsweetened coffee and frozen bread. At five in the afternoon, we ended our workday. The eight in the hole weren't allowed out of the grave. They were ordered to lie face down on top of the corpses of the Gypsies. A guard shot them with a machine gun.

After ending our day of "work" and returning to the mansion, the gate was quickly closed behind us, so that the local villagers didn't see anything. We were led again to the basement. The same cold and darkness. Someone said, "It's a real paradise compared to that horrible cemetery." At first we sat down in the dark on the straw. After a moment, the immensity of our tragic fate shook us.

Fifteen-year-old Moniek Halter from Izbica, who held on to me the whole time, hugged and kissed me, and said, "It is hopeless." He repeated that his death would be a sacrifice for the lives of his mother and sisters.

In the darkness, voices were saying, "Again, eight innocent people among us have left this world." There was no end to the sobbing and tears.

About seven o'clock the cook brought a bucket of turnip soup and poured it into our bowls. Some of us, the most hungry, ate a little, but the majority didn't touch the food. Bitter tears flowed into the bowls of cold soup. An oil lamp was brought along with the soup. Nearly everyone was prepared to reconcile themselves to their fate, even to spend the rest of their lives in this horrifying prison if it would save their loved ones and if they might live to see these criminals punished. At a certain point, the guard ordered us to sing. We didn't hear him. Only when he threatened to shoot us, and even opened the cell door to do it, did my two companions on the straw—Meir Piotrkowski from Izbica and Jehuda Jakubowicz from Włocławek (recently he had been living in Izbica)—beg me to stand up and sing. Despite incredible fatigue I stood up—I don't know where I got the strength—turned to my companions, and with a feeble voice said, "Friends and companions, get up and sing with me. First we will cover our heads." Everyone stood up. The slop pail was covered with a shirt. The impatient guard who stood in the open door threatened us with an angry voice. So I intoned [the Shema], "Hear, O Israel! The Eternal One is our God, the Eternal One is unique." My companions repeated these words with emotion. Then I continued, "Praised be His name and the splendor of His realm forever and ever." The others repeated this three times. We felt as if our lives would soon be over. An unusual grief and trembling seized us. We were as solemn as if we were standing before the Last Judgment. We deluded ourselves into thinking that we had now sung enough. The guard demanded more. So I said, "Friends and companions, we will now sing "Hatikva" [the Hope]! With covered heads, we sang this poem and anthem, which sounded like a prayer. Then the guard left and locked the door with the three locks. There was no way to keep [ourselves] from sobbing. We said that the world had never known such cruelty, to murder innocent people and then force us to sing. We hoped that it would end for him as it did for Haman [a reference to an arch enemy of the Jews]. If only the Lord God would avert His punishing hand from us! Mojżesz Asz from Izbica said, "It has fallen to us to be victims, because the time of the Messiah is approaching."

The guard again opened the door and the civilian German cook brought a bucket of unsweetened, black coffee, which was ladled into a bowl. The uneaten soup was poured into the slop bucket. We each took a piece of bread and some coffee.

After 15 minutes, the guard again demanded that we sing. We tried to decline, pleading exhaustion. He ordered us to repeat, "*Wir Juden danken Adolf Hitler für diese Sachen.*" [We Jews thank Adolf Hitler for these things.] We repeated it. Then he added, "*Wir Juden danken Adolf Hitler für das essen.*" [We Jews thank Adolf Hitler for this food.] And we repeated this too. Finally, he demanded a song. We sang "Hatikva" and then "Beszuw Adonaj" [the 26th Psalm]. It was in response to our torment. Then again he locked the door.

We slept like logs. Whether from the nightmares or from the cold, I woke up in the darkness and began to think over the situation: O, despair, if there is a God in heaven, how is it possible to permit the murder of innocent people! Couldn't He perform a miracle? Suddenly I thought I must get out of this prison. With the flickering lamplight, I went to the bricked-up window and, with the help of a knife, tried to loosen a brick, but it was in vain. The frost, which also penetrated into the room, had frozen the bricks in place. After two hours of fruitless effort, I went back and lay down on the straw.

About five in the morning everyone was awake because of the cold. We began talking. Gecel Chrząstkowski, a member of the Bund, and Ajzensztab (Ajzensztab owned a fur shop in Włocławek)—both from Kłodawa—had lost their faith in God. The others, however, myself included, were strengthened in our belief, repeating after Mojżesz Asz that the time of the Messiah was approaching.

Friday, January 9

On Friday, January 9, 1942, at seven in the morning, bitter coffee was again brought. Asked if we had enough bread we answered yes, because we hadn't eaten what we had been given before. At eight o'clock the SS men came. We were ordered to come out and we were counted. About 20 guards with machine guns already surrounded the courtyard. Again we were counted. (It was the first day when the barrels of the guns were pointed at us. We were gripped with a terrible fear thinking that they were about to shoot us.) In the courtyard, we saw two large open trucks full of Gypsies: men, women, and children together with their belongings. We were quickly loaded into our covered truck so that we couldn't talk with them. It was the only time we ever saw victims alive. We stood in the front of the truck with seven armed guards in the back. A car with SS men followed behind us.

At the work site, the guards surrounded us again. We undressed as usual for work, then we were counted and eight of us were selected for the hole. We took the pickaxes and shovels and began to work. The bottom of the grave was about one-and-a-half meters wide. The sides slanted so that the width at ground level was five meters. The hole was five meters deep and extended out in a straight line. If a tree was in the way, it was cut down. The third day of work passed in a particularly cruel and harsh way. After an hour, the first van load of Gypsies came and 20 minutes later the next one arrived. "The Whip" was in a rage. During work, we were able to get somewhat closer to the eight in the hole. Among them were Abram Zieliński from Izbica, age 32; Brafman from Izbica, age 17; Zalman Jakubowski from Izbica, age 55; and Gerszon Praszker from Izbica. At about three o'clock, when there wasn't much to do (at this moment, they didn't hurry us), Gerszon Praszker, standing in the bottom of the hole, took out a prayer book, covered his head with his hand and began to pray. At about eleven in the morning, they had told us, "Ours is a horrible death. Let this be redemption for our loved ones, for the whole world. We shall be in this world no more."

That day we ate lunch at half past one. The temperature was 20 degrees below zero [centigrade]. The guards lit a fire to thaw out our bread. It tasted smoky and burnt. Lunch was cut short because a van with Gypsy victims came. After lunch, "The Whip" went into the forest and drank a bottle of vodka. When he returned he began screaming, "*O, ihr Hellblaue, ihr wollt nicht arbeiten!*" [Oh, you bastards, you don't want to work!] and began to crack his whip. He treated the prisoners cruelly. Heads, noses, foreheads, and faces dripped with blood, eyes were swollen. That day eight or nine transports of Gypsies were buried. We stopped work at half past five. As usual, the eight were killed. We were ordered to quickly dress and were rushed back to the truck. The whole time, the repeated head counting was scrupulously observed.

In the Chełmno mansion we saw, to our painful surprise, a new group, probably gravediggers: 16 people from Izbica and 16 from Bugaj. Among those from Izbica were Mojżesz Łepek, about 40 years old; Awigdor Polański, about 20 years old; Sztajer, about 55 years old; Król, about 45; Icchak Prajs, about 45; Jehuda Lubiński, 31 years old; Kałman Radziejewski, 32; Menachem Arcichowski, about 40; and from Bugaj, my friend and colleague, Chaim Ruwen Izbicki, 33 years old.

Twenty of the gravediggers and five of the new ones (25 in all) were taken to a cell in the basement that was smaller than the other one. In it, we found sheets, underwear, pants, jackets and food (bread, sugar, lard). These things belonged to the new gravediggers. Exhausted and broken, we sat down on the belongings. The first thing we wanted to know from the new arrivals was if any of our relatives were among them. We wept and heard voices from the next room. I went to the wall at the ventilation duct, where a brick was missing. I knocked, shouting into the hole asking if Chaim Ruwen Izbicki from Bugaj was in the room. He came to the wall. I asked him if, at least, his parents and sisters managed to escape. The guard interrupted the conversation.

During supper, Sztajer shared his lard with us, and said, "I wish God would let me die tomorrow, so I wouldn't have to look at this suffering." Indeed, the next day he was shot. Mojżesz Łepek shared his sugar. After supper we covered the slop bucket and recited evening prayers. The prayers mingled with tears. Later the new arrivals told us some news. They said that the Russians had already retaken Smolensk and Kiev and that they are advancing toward us. We wished they would come and bomb this terrible place. Some pointed out the places where they would hide during the bombing. Others, however, judged that it would take at least a month and by then we would all be dead. No one believed that we would get out of this hell in some normal way. Some, even older people among them, completely lost their faith in God. They said that those are fairy tales. There was no God. How could He see our suffering and do nothing. But people who remained firm in their faith, myself included, said that we are not able to understand God's actions. Finally we covered ourselves with our clothes and went to sleep.

One more important remark: On Thursday and Friday, January 8 and 9, in each van's last load of the day, the victims were Jews . There were men, young and old, with a star of David sewn on the front and back of their clothes. They had suitcases and knapsacks with them. We assumed that they were sick prisoners from camps. They were buried together with all their belongings. This shocked us because, until then, we had hoped that the Jews in the camps were surviving these tragic times.

Saturday, January 10

On Saturday, January 10, breakfast of bitter coffee and bread was brought at seven in the morning. After breakfast, Mojżesz Łepek recited the prayer of penitence, and we repeated it after him. Then there was the hell of being counted several times and seeing the rifle barrels pointed at us until we were in the truck. We told five of the newcomers to stick close to us. Together, with the new group, there were 53 of us. We stood crushed together in the truck. Behind us, as usual, the car with SS men followed. At the work site, the usual group of prisoners were selected and prepared to start work. Meanwhile the new group had to undergo all the tortures we knew so well. This time the eight weren't selected immediately. About eleven o'clock the first van appeared with Jewish victims.

The victims, men, women, and children, were in their underwear. After they were thrown out of the van, two German civilians approached and carried out a thorough search of the corpses, looking for valuables. They tore off necklaces, pulled rings off fingers, pulled out gold teeth. They even looked into anuses and, with women, genitalia. The rest of the procedure was done according to the established plan. Only after the arrival of the Jewish transport were the eight chosen for the hole. In the transport were Jews from Kłodawa, according to Gecel Chrząstkowski, who was himself from Kłodawa. After getting through with this first van, those in the hole returned to their previous work of burying the bodies. At half past one, the second van came. At a certain moment, Ajzensztab, also from Kłodawa, began to cry silently, saying that he no longer had anything to live for because he saw the corpses of his wife and only child, his 15-year-old daughter. He was going to ask the Germans to shoot him because he wanted to lie in the same grave as his loved ones. We persuaded him, however, that there was no hurry and meanwhile he could escape and take revenge.

At quarter of two, during our lunch (unsweetened black coffee and frozen bread) and as the eight in the hole finished arranging the corpses, two cars arrived with high ranking SS officers. They got out and, with satisfied expressions, observed the graves, listened to a report by "The Whip," shook his hand in appreciation, and left. After lunch we buried, with great speed, the next five transports. At about six o'clock everyone worked to fill in the grave until it was level with the ground. In the evening, we returned to the mansion as usual. Accidentally, Chaim Ruwen Izbicki was included in our group.

Back in our cell, everyone burst into tears. At first, I didn't even recognize my best friend, Izbicki. The widower, Ajzensztab, wept the most. After supper (a quarter liter of potato soup per person and unsweetened coffee with bread) we carried the slop bucket outside and said the evening prayers under a smoking lamp. Then Ajzensztab recited Kaddish [the mourner's prayer]. We spoke only about the great misfortune that had befallen our people. With our own eyes we saw the whole Jewish community being swept away. Nobody slept a wink. Suddenly Ajzensztab jumped up from the mat and very nervously began to sob. He screamed that there was nothing left to live for, that all hope had been taken away. He beat his head against the wall and despaired that he couldn't take his own life. Finally, exhausted, he lay down and went to sleep. I was awake all night. I embraced my two companions on the straw, Meir Piotrkowski and Jehuda Jakubowicz. I hugged them and wept silently.

Sunday, January 11

On Sunday, January 11, we were informed at seven in the morning that today we would not have to work. After the morning prayers and the prayer for the dead we remained in our basement "paradise." Again, we talked about politics, God and our situation. Everyone wanted to live to see the liberation, but our greatest desire was the rescue of our people. Everyone would gladly give their life if only our people would survive. At eleven in the morning, we were taken out to push a gas van which was stuck due to the frost. There was a gray gas van in the courtyard. Suddenly, I had an urge to escape, but at the last moment I lost the courage. After this work, we were taken back into the basement. Following lunch, we stretched out on our packs. Some took off their shoes. Finally we slept for several hours. At six in the evening, after the guard was changed, we were again ordered to sing. It wasn't a song, but a cry of voices broken with emotion, reciting the Shema and "Hatikva." Afterwards a high ranking SS officer appeared who scolded the guard because the Jews weren't allowed to sing. At seven o'clock, we ate our supper. Then we took out the slop bucket. We recited the evening prayers together with the Kaddish. Then we lay down on the mat, covered ourselves with our coats and fell asleep.

Monday, January 12

On Monday, January 12, at five in the morning, six people gathered and recited the Psalms, weeping bitterly. The others lay still, completely indifferent. Some even mocked us for our piety saying that there is certainly no God and that all attempts to console ourselves seemed childish. But we responded that our lives are in the hands of God and that, if this was His will, we would accept it with humility. All the more so, since the time of the Messiah was coming. After the morning prayers and reciting Kaddish, in which even Ajzensztab took part, we recited the prayer of penitence. At seven, they brought us coffee and bread. Several of the men from Izbica (lately they had been living in Kutno) took all the coffee for themselves. All the others condemned this and said that in the face of death we should behave with dignity. It was decided to share the coffee in the future. We were all at work by half past eight. At half past nine, the first gas van arrived. Among the eight in the hole were Aron Rozental, Szlojme Babiacki, and Samuel Bibergal—all of them aged between 50 and 60.

That day we were driven with particular cruelty. After opening the gas van doors, we weren't even allowed to wait for the gas to dissipate before entering. Our cries of torture were indescribable. Immediately after the first gas van, the second one arrived, and before noon the third van load had already come. When we went to lunch, the eight remained in the hole, finishing a transport. A black limousine with four SS officers arrived. They listened to a report by "The Whip" and clasped his hand with great appreciation. Showing his satisfaction "The Whip" once again tortured the eight. After the SS officers left, the eight also received their wretched lunch: bitter coffee and frozen bread. About one o'clock, the next gas van with victims arrived. That day, work lasted until six o'clock in the evening; nine van loads, each with 60 Jews, were buried. In all, there were five hundred victims from Kłodawa.

At a certain moment, my friend Gecel Chrząstkowski saw his 14-year-old son, who had been thrown into the grave.[15] He wanted to ask the Germans to shoot him, but we succeeded in stopping him. We argued that it was necessary to survive this suffering, to think about revenge, and that later the Germans would pay.

After work, three of the old workers in the hole were killed, and we were ordered to quickly fill in the graves. Because of the late hour—it was almost completely dark and the Germans probably feared some act of resistance—they hurriedly divided us into groups and hustled us to the truck. Seven guards traveled with us. We reached our "asylum" late in the evening. In despair, the sons of two of those killed, Rozental and Bibergal, wept loudly. We comforted them by saying that we will all die and in the end it's all the same who dies first. This time those two joined in saying Kaddish.

After supper, which as usual consisted of turnip soup, unsweetened black coffee and bread (which, as agreed, was fairly shared), Mojżesz Łepek recited the prayer of penitence. He decided to take his own life, not wanting to see the suffering of his beloved ones any longer. He gave away everything he had: bread, honey and clothes. Meanwhile some noise was heard in the corridor. The other group in the next cell told us through the wall that the Germans had caught a Jew from Kłodawa. The next day, they told us the details: Goldman from Kłodawa was caught by the Germans. He described exactly how the Jews were driven into the gas vans.

While being led into the mansion they were treated very politely. An elderly German, about 60 years old and with a long pipe in his mouth helped mothers take their children out of the truck. He took the babies in his arms so it would be easier for the mothers to get down. He helped the old people get to the mansion and he moved them with his tenderness and politeness. They were taken to a warm room which was heated by two stoves. The floor was covered with a wooden grating like in public baths. Here the elderly German and an SS officer spoke to the Jews, assuring them that they would be going to the ghetto in Litzmannstadt where they would work and become productive people. The women would care for the household while the children went to school.

Beforehand, however, they had to undergo delousing. For this purpose everyone had to undress down to their underwear. The clothes would be steamed. Valuables and documents had to be taken out, wrapped into a handkerchief and turned over for safekeeping. If somebody had bank notes hidden or sown into their clothes, they absolutely had to be removed; otherwise they would be ruined by the steam. Everyone had to shower. The elderly German very politely asked everyone to proceed to the showers. He opened a door that led down 15 to 20 steps. It was very cold down there. The German gently assured them that further on it would be warmer. Further on was a long corridor leading to a ramp. The gas van had backed up to it.

At this moment all politeness vanished. With furious brutality, the people were driven into the van. The Jews now understood that death was at hand and desperately called out, "Hear, O Israel!" On the right side at the exit of the warm room was a small closet. It was here that Goldman hid. After spending 24 hours in the shivering frost, already almost completely stiff, he decided to look for something to cover himself. He was caught and thrown in with the gravediggers. There they tried to revive him. They gave him some food, pants and a coat. We talked about this very excitedly. Everyone said that they'd have done much better in his place. About three in the morning Mojżesz Łepek woke everyone up, kissed them, said his farewells, and prepared a rope to hang himself. He already had the noose around his neck when he lost his courage. He just couldn't take his own life.

Tuesday, January 13

On Tuesday, January 13, at seven in the morning we had hardly recited the prayer of penitence after breakfast when everyone, including Goldman, was loaded into the truck. At the work site, as we prepared for work, Goldman was ordered to lie down in the grave where he was shot. By eight o'clock a van had already arrived. That day all of the van loads were especially large, 90 corpses in each. After the doors were opened, the corpses would just fall out. Despite the murderous pace, the unloading of the vans took longer than usual. That day, the Jewish community of Bugaj was liquidated. The vans arrived one after the other. During the fourth load, an infant wrapped in a pillow was thrown out and suddenly began to cry. The SS men laughed. They shot the child with a machine gun and threw it into the grave.[16] About 800 Jews from Bugaj were buried on Tuesday. We worked in the icy cold until six in the evening and buried nine van loads of victims. After work, five of those in the hole were shot.

After arriving back in the basement Michał Podchlebnik from Bugaj burst into tears. He had lost his wife, two children and his parents. After supper, the slop bucket was emptied. Some of us prayed and then we talked. And again the subject of escaping was discussed. The yearning for freedom in order to warn all the Jewish people was so overpowering that no price was too high for it. Some wanted to dig a tunnel about 50 meters long. The problem was what to do with all the dirt that was dug out. Others wanted to open the bricked-up window (one brick thick). Because of the severe frost, the strong young men weren't able to move even one brick. Resigned, we went to sleep.

Wednesday, January 14

On Wednesday, January 14, unsweetened coffee and bread was brought. Just after breakfast, Krzewacki from Kłodawa, who had long contemplated suicide, quickly made a noose and put it around his neck. He asked Chrząstkowski to take the small bundle from under his feet and shove it into his mouth to stop him from breathing. Chrząstkowski did as he was asked and Krzewacki died an easy death. He committed suicide because, as he told us, he could no longer bear to watch the murderous deeds. We cut him down and placed the body against the wall.

Gerszon Swiętopławski from Izbica then announced he also wanted to commit suicide. He had been Krzewacki's digging partner. He said he had worked together with Krzewacki and wanted to be buried with him. Nobody wanted to help him because there was no time. The guard was expected at any moment. He quickly took a rope and tied a noose around his neck. Standing with his feet on the ground he bent forward to throttle himself more quickly. While torturing himself in this way, there was a knock on the door.

Young Moniek Halter quickly cut the rope. Swiętopławski fell to the ground and began to gasp horribly as he got his breath back. After the guard had gone—while we didn't want to save him (what for?), we also couldn't bear to watch his torment—we asked Gecel Chrząstkowski to put an end to it. Chrząstkowski tied the noose tightly around Swiętopławski's neck, pinned the body down with his feet, and pulled on the rope until Swiętopławski was dead. We left both corpses lying uncovered in the basement where they remained for several days.

At eight o'clock, we were already at the ditches. At ten o'clock, the first van arrived with victims from Izbica. By noon, we had buried the bodies from three overcrowded vans. From one of the vans, the corpse of a German civilian was pulled out. He was one of the cooks. He probably thought that one of the Jews had some valuables, and so ran into the van wanting to get them. At this moment, however, the doors were locked. His shouting and screaming was ignored and he was killed together with the others. As he was pulled out of the van, a special car with an orderly arrived from the mansion. The corpse was taken back there.[17] Some said that he was killed on purpose and that the Germans would kill all the witnesses to their crimes.

In the afternoon, SS men arrived in two cars and amused themselves by looking at the death factory. After lunch, another five van loads of victims were buried. From one of the vans a young woman with an infant at her breast was thrown out. The child had died while drinking its mother's milk. That day, we worked until seven in the evening with the aid of headlights.

Also that day one of the vans, by mistake, drove up so close to the ditch that we could hear the muffled screams, desperate cries and pounding on the doors. Before work ended, six of those in the hole were shot. As we entered our cell, we burst into tears. After supper, we said the evening prayers and recited Kaddish. We slept like rocks until morning.

Thursday, January 15

On Thursday, January 15, we were again taken to work very early, this time in the bus. Moniek Halter told me that a window could be opened easily with the help of a crank. I constantly thought about escaping. More than anything I wanted to reach other Jews and warn them with the news about the horrors of Chełmno. We were already at work by eight o'clock. At ten o'clock the first van load of victims came, again from Izbica. By lunch, we had dispatched the bodies from four overcrowded vans. They waited one after the other. I must once again describe the horror of searching the corpses. Imagine for yourself such a scene. From the pile of victims, a German pulls a corpse to one side, another to the other side. Women's necks are examined for gold chains. If found, they are immediately torn off. Rings are pulled off of fingers. Gold teeth are pulled out with pliers. The corpse is arranged, the legs spread apart, and the anus is searched by hand. With women's corpses, the same is done in the front. Although this happened every day and all day long, every time it happened our blood boiled and filled us with rage.

During lunch, I received the sad news that my dear parents and my brother were lying in the grave. We were back at work by one o'clock. I tried to get closer to the corpses to see my loved ones for the last time. I was hit by a frozen clod of dirt from the "kind-hearted" German with the pipe, and "The Whip" shot at me. I don't know if he wanted to miss or if he just didn't hit me, but I survived. Ignoring my pain I worked very quickly so that for the moment I could forget about my horrible loss. I was completely alone in the world. From my family, which had numbered 60 people, I am the only one alive. Towards evening, as we helped the gravediggers to cover the dead, I put down my shovel and together with Podchlebnik silently said Kaddish. Before leaving the ditch, three of those from the hole were shot. In the evening we were taken back to our cells. The people from Izbica were in despair. We realized that we would never see our loved ones again. I, too, broke down; nothing mattered anymore. After the evening prayers, everyone from Izbica said Kaddish.

Meanwhile, we found out that 18 gravediggers from Łódź were in the next cell. Through the wall, they told us that 750 families were deported from the Łódź ghetto, according to Rumkowski's list. That night was full of nightmares and wild dreams. During the night, the strongest among us tried again to break through the bricked-up window.

Friday, January 16

On Friday, January 16, we woke up at five in the morning. We again talked about this hopeless situation. What was the point of living without friends or relatives, without hope of being freed or even of having somebody to talk to? At work the new gravediggers from Łódź were beaten without mercy by "The Whip." This was meant to be instructions in how to work. At about ten, the first van arrived. By one o'clock, we had buried four van loads. All the victims came from Łódź. We saw the degree of starvation in Łódź by how thin they were and by how their bodies were covered with wounds and abscesses. We felt pity for them that they had suffered and starved so long in the ghetto, surviving such difficult times, only to die such a horrible death. The dead hardly weighed anything at all. Normally, three van loads were placed in one layer: now four loads could be placed in the same space. After lunch, "The Whip" drank a bottle of vodka and, like a beast, tortured the workers. We buried four more van loads. At the end of the workday, seven gravediggers were shot.

Beginning on Friday, we started to pour chloride on the graves because of the strong odor from the decomposing bodies.

In our cell were three people from Łódź from whom we found out more details of the fate of the 750 families from the Łódź ghetto. They came by train on Thursday to Koło, where they were placed in the synagogue. Eighteen of the strongest men were selected and sent away as gravediggers. The three men from Łódź were so hungry that they ate everyone's supper.

Saturday, January 17

On Saturday, January 17, before leaving for work, we said the prayer of penitence. That day we buried seven tightly packed van loads of victims from Łódź. After lunch, five SS officers arrived and watched the proceedings. At 5:00, before ending work, a car arrived with an order to shoot 16 people. We supposed that this was a punishment for the escape of Abram Rój. (He had escaped on Friday at ten in the evening.) Sixteen people were selected. They were ordered to lie down in groups of eight, face down on the corpses, and were shot in the head with machine guns. Back in the basement, we thought that, like last week, we wouldn't work on Sunday. The men from Łódź told us that a newspaper cost ten marks in the Łódź ghetto. After supper, we fell into a deep sleep.

Sunday, January 18

On Sunday, January 18, we found out that it would be a working day. At eight, we were already at the site. Twenty new shovels and four new pickaxes were taken down from the truck. We realized that not only was "production" not slowing down but it was in fact increasing. Surely all the Jews from the Warthegau would be gassed. The turn of the Łódź Jews had already come. By lunch, we had buried five transports. On Sunday, there was not a full complement of guards, but there was so much work that we ate lunch in the ditch. Apparently, they were concerned that we might act against our torturers. But the machine gun barrels leveled at us paralyzed us with fear. During the nighttime conversations we often accused each other of cowardice. Even today I don't know why healthy people, who had nothing to lose, didn't do something. Maybe it was because we didn't think about heroic gestures, but about escape, so that we could warn the Jews.

Several words about the guards who watched us: Usually they were either hostile or indifferent to us. There was only one of them who, the entire time, was very sad and never screamed at us or harassed us at work. We said to each other, "Look, a humane German. He can't even look at the crimes being committed here."

In the afternoon, we buried four more van loads. None of us were killed that day. After the evening prayers and Kaddish, we decided to escape, whatever the cost.[18]

Szlama Winer's remarkable and moving testimony illustrates the atrocious conditions and impossible situation under which the gravediggers in Chełmno labored. The account also puts a human face on at least some of these unfortunate individuals. The mass grave which these men dug and in which they buried the corpses, including friends and family, would eventually reach a length of 62 meters. This was short, by comparison with the next grave which would grow to a length of 254 meters.[19]

Michał Podchlebnik's testimony, though not as detailed as Winer's, covers this same period of time, January 1942, the camp's second month of operation. It will be recalled that Podchlebnik, upon arrival to the mansion, was incorporated into the Hauskommando, which removed the clothing from the undressing rooms. Not wanting to sit in the basement during the day and thinking that he would have a better chance of escaping, he volunteered to work in the forest.

The next day I volunteered to work in the forest. Going out, on the side of the yard, I saw the big van backed up to the mansion. The doors of the van were open and there was a ramp that facilitated entry into the van. I noticed that there was a wooden grating on the floor like one sees in public baths. We, that is the 30 workers, were loaded into two vehicles, a truck and a bus, and were taken to the forest outside of Chełmno. About 30 SS men escorted us. In the forest, a ditch had been dug, which served as a mass grave for the executed Jews. We were given shovels and pickaxes and ordered to continue digging this ditch. At about eight in the morning, the first van from Chełmno arrived. The doors of the van were opened. A dark smoke with a whitish hue burst out. At this time, we were not allowed to approach the van, and it was not allowed even to look in the direction of the open doors. I noticed how the Germans ran from the van after opening the doors. I'm not able to say whether exhaust gas or some other gas was coming out of the van. Usually we stood so far away that I couldn't smell the gas. Gas masks were not used. After three or four minutes, three Jews entered the van: Neumuller from Koło, Chaim Kiwer from Babiak and a third one whose name I don't remember. They threw the corpses out of the van onto the ground. The corpses in the van were lying one on top of the other and reached about half way up the van. Some died holding the persons dear to them in their arms. The corpses looked normal. I didn't notice tongues sticking out or any unnatural blueness. The corpses were still warm. I didn't notice any smell characteristic of gas. Some of them were still alive. Those were finished off by the SS men.

They were shot in the head, usually at the back of the head. After the corpses were thrown out of the van, it drove back to Chełmno. Two Jews passed the corpses to two "Ukrainians."[20] (I don't know their names. They spoke fluent Polish and dressed in civilian clothes.) There had been a third "Ukrainian" but that day he accidentally got into the van and was poisoned by the gas, along with the Jews. They tried to save him by artificial respiration, but it was no use. I was there and I saw the attempt to resuscitate him. The "Ukrainians" pulled gold teeth out of the mouths of the corpses, tore bags of money off their necks, removed wedding rings, watches, etc. The corpses were searched very thoroughly, looking for gold and valuables, even in the women's reproductive organs [sic], anuses, etc. They didn't use rubber gloves during the search. The recovered valuables were put into a special suitcase. The SS men did not search the corpses. However, they carefully watched the "Ukrainians" doing this work. After being searched the corpses were arranged in the ditch, along the side, in layers. The corpses were arranged alternately, in such a way that the head of one corpse touched the legs of the one next to it. The corpses were arranged very tightly, face down. Underwear was not removed from the bodies. The ditch was six meters deep and about six or seven meters wide (at the top). Four or five corpses were placed in the first, bottom layer, up to 30 in the last, top layer. The corpses were covered with a layer of sand about one meter deep. Several times I saw that the next day the sand was stirred up and one could see the corpses that had been covered the previous day.

It was said that, at that time, the area was not guarded at night. When I worked there, the length of the ditch/grave was between 10 and 20 meters. During the course of a day about 1,000 people were buried. This amount of corpses took up three or four meters of the length of the ditch. The van in which the people were gassed could carry 80 to 90 people at a time. During my stay in Chełmno, two vans were used simultaneously. Besides these, there was a third larger van, which was broken and parked in the courtyard [of the mansion] in Chełmno. (I saw that a wheel had been removed.) Every day, 12 to 13 van loads arrived to the forest. In this way, I figured that about 1,000 people a day were gassed. The Jews who took the corpses out of the van also had the task of removing the wooden floor grating and cleaning the van thoroughly. Valuables [found inside the van] were also placed in a suitcase. The towels and soap were separated and taken back every day.

That day (Tuesday), the bodies of my wife and my two children—a seven-year-old boy and a four-year-old girl—were thrown out of the third van load that arrived in the Chełmno forest. I lay down next to the body of my wife. I wanted them to shoot me. An SS man approached me and said, "This big guy can still work hard." He whipped me three times forcing me to return to work. At noon, we were given something to eat. We had to get out of the ditch without the shovels and form a circle. The SS men also formed a circle around us. We were given black coffee and food that had been brought by the Jews in their bundles. Generally we were well fed. That evening after work, Krzewacki from Kłodawa (I don't remember his first name) and one other Jew, whose name I also don't remember, hung themselves in the basement. I also intended to hang myself but I was persuaded not to.

I worked in Chełmno for ten days. The process of executing the Jews was the same every day. The area of the forest was not fenced at that time, nor was there an oven for burning corpses. While I was there, the Jews from Bugaj were executed and later the Jews from Izbica. On Friday, Gypsies from Łódź were brought. On Saturday, the first transport [of Jews] from the Łódź ghetto arrived. Our group underwent a "selection" when the transport from Łódź arrived. Twenty of the weakest of us were killed and replaced with Jews from Łódź. At night we talked with our new work companions. They were locked in the neighboring cell. They asked if this was a good camp and if there was a lot of bread. When I told them how it was, they said: "We volunteered for work in Koło." From the beginning I tried to persuade my companions to escape but they were so despondent that they couldn't decide.

During my stay in Chełmno, I saw Zimmermann of the NSKK [National Socialist Motor Corps] in Koło come to the forest with two Germans unknown to me. He looked at the corpses, spoke with the SS officers, and laughed. Shortly afterwards, he left. I didn't see anybody from the local population contacting the SS men. The area of the Chełmno forest was guarded by about 80 SS men. Judging from my observations, I think that about 120 to 130 SS men served in Chełmno. These men were sober while on duty. The same people always guarded us so their faces were well known to me. The SS men were dressed in police uniforms with the SS insignia on the collar. It seems to me that they were billeted in the village, but I'm not exactly sure. Our work continued until dusk. During work we were beaten; if somebody did not work hard enough he was ordered to lie on the pile of corpses and was shot with a revolver in the back of the head. The guards near us didn't talk among themselves and they spoke with us only curtly. Sometimes they threw packs of cigarettes to us in the ditch. [I think] the drivers were Germans—but I'm not sure about this. They wore civilian clothes. In any case, they were not from Koło. I don't know where the SS men serving in Chełmno came from. I don't remember any names. The killing process was the same every day. The SS men treated the Jewish workers cruelly and punished them for the slightest offense. They were killed for any reason.[21]

The incredible testimonies of Winer and Podchlebnik chronicle for the historical record the suffering of the Jewish prisoners at the hands of sadists like Lange and Lenz. They offer a very unique perspective, one not gained from the testimonies of the guards or other non-victim eyewitnesses. Fortunately for the chroniclers who managed to escape, but unfortunately for the historical record, they cover a very brief period during January, just after the camp began functioning.

Numerous graves were dug in the forest. Witnesses relate what they saw at the time. Guards who served in the forest do not provide a comprehensive overview of the number of these graves or insight into the process of deciding their locations. As Winer and Podchlebnik relate, the graves were dug by hand, using pickaxes and shovels—a feat made even more difficult by the sub-zero weather conditions. Later, in the spring, Bothmann brought in machinery to dig the pits and cover them over, a fact mentioned by the forester Heinz May when he visited the forest together with Bothmann.[22]

Following the escapes of Winer and Podchlebnik while on the way to work in the forest, at least two changes were made in regard to the Jewish labor squads. All Jews working in Chełmno were soon shackled in leg irons, which made walking difficult and escape all but impossible. The Jewish labor detail working in the forest was henceforth transported to and from the graves in a gas van. Both changes greatly diminished any chances for others to escape. The situation for the Jewish workers in Chełmno was a living hell. Incredibly, for those men left working in the forest, their situation was about to get even worse.

According to the German forester, Heinz May, an order was issued sometime in the spring to camouflage the graves in the forest. Trees were to be planted on top of the graves, and a fence was to be built around the forest camp to provide greater security. Such an order, or at least part of it, soon became impossible to carry out. The corpses, buried in the ground for several months, began decomposing. The mounds of earth that covered the graves began to swell and the whole area was engulfed in a wretched stench.

The problem of the decomposing corpses was so acute that all transports to Chełmno were stopped. The last known transport, with 630 Jews, arrived from Radziejów Kujawski on June 11.[23] May was a witness to a Dantesque scene when he visited the forest camp during this time.

> When during the summer of 1942, during the erection of the post fence, I again, together with Bothman, saw the graves, there was a nauseating sweet-strong odor above the whole place. I had to hold my nose and left the place as quickly as possible. Bothmann showed me great round bulges which had developed on the long graves, if one looked closely one could see a light mist rise in the sunshine. Bothmann told me that 250,000 [corpses] were buried there. However, there was still room for at least 100,000 [more].[24]

To solve the problem, the notorious Standartenführer Paul Blobel soon arrived in Chełmno. Blobel's connection to Chełmno dated back a year earlier, to June 22, 1941, when the German army launched Operation Barbarossa, the invasion of the Soviet Union. Blobel commanded Einsatzkommando 4A, one of the mobile killing units that followed the German army into the Soviet Union. These groups of executioners fanned out across occupied territory with orders to kill, among others, the Nazi arch enemies: communist activists and Jews. Perhaps the most notorious of these operations was the murder of more than 33,000 Jews in Kiev (Babi Yar) during a two-day period in late September 1941. The victims were shot and buried in pits. Early counter-offenses by the Russians led to the discovery of mass graves and accounts of the atrocities began appearing in the press. As a result, Himmler ordered the eradication of the graves throughout the region. The top secret operation tasked to Blobel was code named Aktion 1005.[25] Blobel required a location to experiment and develop a method to employ throughout the East and Chełmno proved ideal; it was far from the front and therefore secure and the site offered an abundance of material with which to work. Bothmann also needed Blobel to solve his immediate problem of the decomposing corpses, as well as the longer term issue of erasing evidence of the mass murder in the forest.

One of Blobel's experiments involved blowing up the bodies with thermite bombs. This proved unsuccessful as body parts were left hanging from tree limbs. During these trials, a part of the forest caught fire. The Koło fire department arrived on the scene, but was not allowed to enter the restricted area. The Jewish Waldkommando eventually extinguished the fire. Blobel ultimately decided that the best course of action for Bothmann's problem was to simply dig up the corpses and to burn them in specially built crematoria. In order to burn the thousands of bodies already in the forest, huge quantities of wood were needed. Bothmann went to see the forester May, who gave the following account.

> One day Bothmann appeared in the forestry office and told me that he had orders from higher authority to burn all the corpses. He had already had the graves opened and attempted to burn the bodies with thermite bombs. Now he wished to try to carry out the order with firewood and he requested great amounts of it. During the burning with thermite bombs, a forest fire had been caused whereby a portion of the woods surrounding the field of graves burned down. The charred woods could not be cut down since otherwise a view of the field of graves would have become possible [to see] from the road.
>
> I approached the Landesforstamt in regard to the ordered firewood and I was advised to deliver the wood.
>
> At first I ordered all young woods in question to be searched and delivered great quantities of branches and faggots. However, this was not sufficient and I had to deliver cordwood. Finally, the consumption became so great that I changed over to making clearings in older woods. [...]
>
> For many months, a terrible stench laid over the entire vicinity. When the wind was blowing from the west, the sickening odor could be noticed up to the forestry house in Bilice. This is about 15 kilometers from the graves by air. [...]
>
> After several experiments, the cremation of the bodies took place in a circular hole in the earth, about three meters deep and with a diameter of four meters; it was lined all around with stones. A strong fire was built in the hole and the bodies were simply thrown in.[26]

This "hole in the earth" is apparently a description of one of the field furnaces constructed by Blobel. At least four such crematoria were built, measuring roughly eight meters by eight meters.[27] Testimonies indicate experiments using these furnaces were in operation by the middle of July.[28]

Friedrich Maderholz, a guard transferred to the forest camp in August, described the crematorium he saw in operation at that time as being approximately eight meters long and eight meters wide, made of stones and buried deep in the ground.[29] According to the guard Wildermuth, who served in the forest camp, these ovens did not work very well.

It is assumed that the solution to eliminate the danger posed by the thousands of decomposing, stinking corpses with the field furnaces was inadequate and therefore two more efficient crematoria were built. These ovens were more elaborately constructed and featured tall chimneys that towered over the forest. Local residents could see these chimneys and the smoke belching from them. One brief description of the new more efficient crematoria, albeit secondhand, comes from Rozalia Peham, the wife of one of the guards.

> Two crematoria were built. I don't know how they were installed because, of course, I was never there. I know only that the ovens had tall chimneys and were so constructed that they had a very strong draught. The bodies were arranged in layers in these ovens. Between each layer of bodies was a layer of wood. Gasoline was poured over the pile of bodies and wood when the corpses were to be burned in the fire.[30]

The guard Maderholz stated that later in the autumn another furnace was built and put into service. Hauptscharführer Fritz Ismer—who was in charge of the valuables for the Sonderkommando, and who was transferred to the forest camp by Bothmann in the fall because transports were no longer arriving—confirms that another furnace was built. "When I began to serve in the forest camp, one crematorium was being used. There were two more of them but they were not used anymore."[31] Although the testimonies are limited, it generally appears that a number of temporary furnaces were constructed by Blobel and tested over a period of time. Hauptscharführer Johannes Runge, Lenz's assistant, subsequently carried out the construction of the new ovens. He acquired 60,000 bricks from the firm of Freudenreich in Koło. His superiors were apparently pleased with his work as, according to one of the guards, he received the War Service Cross for building the ovens.[32] These two furnaces were built following the visit of Rudolf Höss, the commandant of Auschwitz, to the camp.

Heinrich Himmler had inspected the Auschwitz concentration camp in the summer of 1942, observing the entire extermination process. Standartenführer Blobel arrived in Auschwitz shortly afterwards informing Höss that the mass graves were to be opened and the bodies cremated. The ashes were also to be disposed of so that in the future it would be impossible to calculate the number of victims. Blobel was to show Höss how this was being carried out in Chełmno. The visit took place on September 16, 1942. Höss was not impressed with the technology Bothmann had inherited from Lange, later recalling, "During my visit in Kulmhof, I saw the extermination installations with the gas vans which were prepared for killing by exhaust fumes. The chief of the command there described this method as very unreliable, because the gas was produced very irregularly, and often was not enough for killing."[33]

Once the crematoria were ready, the unimaginable and nauseating task of exhuming the mass graves began. The corpses were dug out of the graves by the Jewish Waldkommando, the size of which was increased for this purpose. The corpses were then transported to the crematoria by the Jewish workers using specially constructed wooden stretchers as well as by a small tram that ran from the graves to the crematoria.[34]

Blobel was not satisfied with simply burning the corpses. All traces were to be destroyed. After the corpses were burned, small bone fragments remained. These too had to be disposed of. It was decided to crush the bone fragments into powder. A bone grinder was required for this purpose. Blobel turned to Hans Biebow of the Ghettoverwaltung in Łódź for help.

On July 16, 1942, Biebow's assistant, the deputy chief of the Ghettoverwaltung, Friedrich Ribbe, wrote a letter to the head of the Council of Elders, Chaim Rumkowski, in the Łódź ghetto.

July 16, 1942

To the Eldest of the Jews, Litzmannstadt Ghetto

Regarding: Machines in the Ghetto

I request an immediate assessment of whether inside the ghetto there is a Bone Mill either manually operated or motor driven.

By Order of: Fr. W. Ribbe

Sonderkommando Kulmhof is interested in such a mill.[35]

Apparently there was no bone mill in the ghetto at the time, as one was eventually bought from the Hannover firm of Schriever and Company.[36] On Blobel's order, Walter Burmeister assisted in bringing the bone mill and a compressor to the forest camp. The mill weighed about five-and-a-half tons and was transported on a five-ton truck and trailer. The grinder was powered by a gas-driven generator.[37] According to one of the guards, Hauptwachtmeister Gustav Fiedler and Revieroberwachtmeister Kurt Hoffman supervised the operation of the bone grinder.[38]

The guard Wilhelm Heukelbach served not only at the mansion but as well in the forest camp. He remembered the bone grinder as follows.

I had heard there was a bone grinder in the forest camp where the bone fragments from the crematoria were ground. One night, when I was standing sentry in the forest camp, I had a closer look. It was situated not far from the crematoria and was covered with a roof. There was a large funnel on the top where the bone fragments must have been poured in. There were several bags full of ground up bones near the mill. The bags were open so I could see what was inside.[39]

Heinz May, the forester, also saw the bone grinder while on one of his visits to the forest camp.

The hollow, cylindrical bones which were not burnt were taken out and pulverized in a bone mill driven by a motor, which was located in an especially built wooden barrack. I don't know where they took this bone flour. There must have been great quantities [...] Bothmann showed me the bone meal. There were a number of filled sacks in the barracks. Bothmann said to one of the chained men employed there, "Izig, get me a handful of flour from the sack." The elderly man hurried to a sack and brought two handfuls of snow-white, finely ground bone flour. Bothmann said to him: "These are members of your race." The man said quietly and submissively, "Well, what can we do?" I could tell from his voice that he, too, was a German.[40]

The sounds of machinery emanating from the forest camp could be heard by the people who lived nearby.[41] Initially the ashes and ground bones were simply buried in pits four meters deep and eight to ten meters wide. Later, they were sprinkled around the area on the forest floor. A postwar investigation noted that where the cremains had been sprinkled, the vegetation was very abundant and of a more intense green color than the surrounding area.[42] The guard Jakob Wildermuth adds that the bone meal was put into sacks and transported away from time to time. He did not know where it was taken, but heard that it was used as fertilizer.[43]

More workers were now needed to carry out the additional tasks. A crew was formed to cut wood and transport it to the vicinity of the crematoria. Other crews dug up the corpses, transported them and stacked them onto the ovens. Still another group operated the bone grinder. In order to accomplish this added work, the size of the Jewish Waldkommando was increased. It is not known how many Jews were employed at this work. However, an estimate can be made based on information from two of the local Polish women who prepared meals for the Jewish workers. One of them was told to prepare coffee for 200 to 300 Jews, while another kitchen worker mentioned the figure 380.[44]

All transports to the camp were stopped for a period of over one month following the destruction of the Jews from Radziejów Kujawski, giving the Sonderkommando, both literally and figuratively, some breathing space to solve the problem of the stench emanating from the decomposing corpses. When transports resumed in July, the victims continued to be buried as Blobel experimented until the final transport arrived from Zelów. The first "industrial" crematorium was ready for service, probably in the second half of September 1942, following the Höss visit. A second crematorium was constructed and readied shortly afterwards. During the months ahead, the Sonderkommando, or more precisely the Jewish Waldkommando, exhumed the previously buried bodies, transported them to the crematoria, stacked and burned them, and ground the bone fragments into powder. Having established a method of eliminating the evidence of the mass killings, Blobel headed east to begin his own massive and grisly task.

Resumption of Transports

After a break of more than a month, transports from the small towns in the region began arriving to Chełmno again. These transports began to arrive even before the method of burning the corpses had been fully worked out, but before the bone mill arrived.

The murder began again with the liquidation of at least two ghettos in July. The final liquidation of the remaining 2,700 Jews from the rural ghetto in Czachulec began about July 20. It might be recalled that a portion of the people concentrated in Czachulec were among Chełmno's first victims. The 750 Jews of Lutomiersk, in Łask County, were also exterminated at this time.

In August, the remaining Jews in Łask County were either resettled to the Łódź ghetto or transported to Chełmno. The Jewish population of two other counties was also decimated at this time. The 10,000 Jews from the villages of Praszka, Czernice, Działoszyn and Bolesławiec in Wieluń County were all deported that month. The liquidation of the Jewish communities from Sieradz County—including those in the ghettos of Sieradz, Szadek, Warta (where during the ghetto clearing operation Hans Biebow found a woman who had just given birth lying in bed, shot her in the genitals and threw the baby on the floor),[1] and Zduńska Wola—began on August 11 and continued through the month.

During these deportations, and working in conjunction with Chełmno's own transport commando, Biebow's special ghetto clearing unit evacuated the Jews from the smaller towns in the area. Generally, those who were strong and able to work were diverted to the Łódź ghetto to become slave laborers in the factories there. The weak, ill, old and very young were sent to Chełmno in the transport commando's trucks.

As has been pointed out, Biebow, Seifert, Fuchs and others personally participated in many of these operations. The ghetto in Zduńska Wola was the second largest ghetto, after Łódź, in the Wartheland. Established in January 1940, some 8,700 people initially registered as inhabitants within the barbed wired enclosure. Population transfers occurred over the following two years, with some people being deported to other ghettos and approximately 3,000 people from Sieradz, Pabianice, Kalisz, Poddębice, Szadek, Widawa, Burzenin, Klonowy and other towns and villages being relocated to Zduńska Wola. In 1942, some 10,000 to 13,000 people inhabited the ghetto. Rafał Lewkowicz, an eyewitness, later recounted the events that transpired in connection with the liquidation of the ghetto in Zduńska Wola.

In June 1942, the Germans issued an order that everyone was to assemble at the Hilfskomitet building. There, people entered the building one at a time where four or five uniformed officials conducted a selection. Men and women from the age of 14 were forced to march past this commission, naked, each of whom were stamped with the letter "H" or "B." This was done in a denigrating way, stamping each person on the buttocks, stomach or breasts, with members of the commission laughing as it proceeded. As a result of this selection, 397 people were sent to the Łódź ghetto on June 26.

The liquidation of the ghetto began in the early morning hours of August 24. This did not cause a panic among the inhabitants because most already knew what was in store for them. Many had known since the winter of 1941 when, according to the son of Dr. Lemberg,[2] "two Polish railroad men came one night to see my father. They said they had confidential information for him. Later they said that the Nazi's had evacuated several villages around Chełmno and that the trucks arrived there with Jews but left stuffed with clothing. They were convinced that the mass extermination of Jews was occurring there. My father decided to inform the local Jewish communities about this horrible discovery. He wrote anonymous letters with the information that the Jews were not going to work, as the Germans said, but to their death. We also sent word about this to Łódź."

Aware of the fate that awaited them, many hid in basements and attics, while others went to the assembly point at Stęszydzka Street, completely resigned or in despair. This behavior had an influence on the particularly aggressive course of the ghetto's liquidation.

A significantly strong contingent of SS, police, including a special unit known as the Rollkommando, and the entire unit of the Schutzpolizei in Zduńska Wola, with its chief Hermann Funke, were mobilized for the operation. Also participating in the operation were Gestapo officials from Łódź, Günter Fuchs and Albert Richter, as well as the head of the Ghettoverwaltung, Hans Biebow, and section heads Erich Czarnulla, Wilhelm Ribbe and Franz Seifert. Biebow and his associates were there to conduct the selection of the Jews, who were to strengthen the workshops of the Łódź ghetto and to secure the property of Zduńska Wola's Jews.

Following the initial segregation of the Jews at the assembly point on Stęszydzka Street and murdering the sick, infirm and many elderly, the others were hustled through the streets to the Jewish cemetery, where a cordon of SS-men was waiting. Another selection was conducted here, among screams and beatings, by among others Biebow and the Gestapo officers. Everyone was divided into two groups. One group comprised young people, able to work, while the other included the elderly, children and the sick. Horrible scenes played out here when children were taken away from their mothers. Many chose death rather than separation from their loved ones.

While this selection was occurring at the cemetery, other SS and police detachments, with the help of the Jewish police, searched the ghetto murdering anyone who crossed their path. Those murdered in this way included elderly people and children as well as all the patients of the Jewish hospital on Ogrodowa Street. Dozens were killed on the first day of the operation. Dozens more were killed in the following two days. The corpses of those killed were taken to the cemetery and buried in prepared graves.

Those assembled at the cemetery languished there for two days without food or water. The cemetery was illuminated at night to prevent the two groups from intermingling. Those who tried [to mingle] were killed. The guards also shot into the crowd without reason, killing several dozen people.

On August 25 and 26, the larger of the two groups, comprising 8,594 people, were loaded into trucks and transported to Chełmno. The smaller group, 1,169 people, was taken by train to the ghetto in Łódź.[3]

This was one of those times, which Bothmann referred to as a boom period, when the camp "eliminated" as many as 3,000 people a day.[4] The personal participation of Hans Biebow in the liquidation of the ghetto in Zduńska Wola is provided by the same eyewitness, Rafał Lewkowicz, who managed to survive the war and testify at Biebow's trial.

At four o'clock in the morning the Gestapo and Biebow entered the ghetto. All Jews were ordered to assemble in the square. There were 11,000 of us and everyone had to run to the designated assembly point. Those who didn't make it were shot. We were taken from the square to the Jewish cemetery where we were divided into two groups, on the right side and at the back of the cemetery. I stood next to Dr. Lemberg. Biebow lined up the Gestapo and SS men. Those earmarked for death were beaten, kicked and tripped. People couldn't run fast enough and one Jew fell down. Biebow walked up and shot him on the spot. Then he went to Dr. Lemberg and said: "Am I not a humanitarian? I do not allow these Jews to suffer." We were held for two days and two nights without any water. And then on Wednesday, at half past ten, we were taken to the station and Biebow gave a speech. There were 700 of us. We were loaded into wagons, and Biebow said: "You had everything here, contraband, bread. Now you are going to your homeland, your promised land. They will deal with you there." Later, he ordered all money, gold and diamonds to be turned over and said: "You know me; you saw what I can do. Those who don't give voluntarily will be hanged." We were loaded into freight wagons, 700 people in six cars. There were 27 dead when we got to Łódź. In the end, ten Jews were hanged in Zduńska Wola. He [Biebow] said it was for sabotage so they will no longer be a threat. He also said: "If you have a God, pray to Him." [. . .] [Biebow] conducted the selection himself. He stood there in a short-sleeved shirt, with a riding-crop in his hand. He and a guard walked up to Dr. Lemberg, called him out, and said this is his final journey. [. . .] I understood that we were going to our death. Biebow personally conducted the selection. Each Jew had to pass by him while he indicated this one to the left, that one to the right. In this way, he selected 1,200 of the 11,000 people for the ghetto in Łódź.[5]

Sasza Lewiatin was one of the truck drivers employed in Biebow's transport group. He was present during many of these resettlement operations and, after the war, he recounted his experiences.

I was called into service during the resettlements from the small towns. The first resettlement was from Ozorków. Biebow, Fuchs, Stromberg, Schmidt and other Gestapo men arrived. There was one more from the police in Ozorków, a certain Fritz. They began the resettlement of the Jews at twelve midnight.

Everyone was allowed to take a small suitcase. Children were separated from their mothers. It was said that the children were going to a summer camp in Skalmierzyce and that healthy workers were going to work in Częstochowa. One mother, who didn't want to give up her child, was shot.

I was also in Zduńska Wola during the resettlement and in Pabianice where at midnight everyone was forced into Church Square, where they began the evacuation. Children were shot. Everyone was ordered to completely undress within five minutes. Some women didn't want to. I sat in the cab of the truck. When one woman didn't want to undress, she was beaten with a riding crop and told, "*Wir haben schon Solches gesehen.*" [We've seen such things before.] Some were sent to Chełmno. The healthy ones were sent from Pabianice to the Łódź ghetto.

I was also at the liquidation in Dąbrowa, where the Eldest [leader] of the Jews was a man named Francuz. He had a daughter, wife and son. Biebow turned to him, demanding that he hand over the valuables of all the Jews. Francuz replied that he could only give that which was his. Biebow was indignant at such a reply. He drew his revolver and shot the man.

I was in Zduńska Wola, in Wieluń and Osiek. After each transport Biebow and the whole gang got drunk on vodka. There was Miller, Schwindt [probably Heinrich Schwind], and others. They were all employed in Einsatz zur Räumung Warthegau [Operation for Clearing the Warthegau].

[W]hen we arrived at Chełmno, we were ordered to get out of the trucks and lock them. Other personnel got in the trucks and after some time, they brought them back. Only Biebow and Kramp had access to Chełmno.[6]

Another driver employed by Biebow was Stanisław Kapica, who was present at many of the provincial ghetto operations. He stated that some 24 trucks were used in the operations. Initially, he and the other drivers were not told specifically what the purpose of the ghetto clearing operations was, but after some time it wasn't difficult to figure it out. The drivers were told not to speak to anyone about what happened during these operations. His own truck carried some 80 people each trip and was guarded by two policemen who sat in the back and a Gestapo official who rode in the cab. Kapica admitted to beating people on occasion. Once he beat a Jew with a wooden bat, because he had asked for a cigarette. On another occasion, he beat Jewish children with his fist, because they didn't want to get into his truck. According to the driver, the elderly, women and children he transported had a sense of foreboding the closer his truck came to the town of Koło, and they began to scream and weep. On arriving in Chełmno, he saw Jewish workers, on a number of occasions, walking with their legs in chains. As he arrived at the gate in front of the mansion, a policeman from the Sonderkommando took his place and drove the vehicle through the gate and into the camp. Later, the truck was returned, loaded with shoes and clothing. Kapica then drove the truck to the warehouse facility in Dąbrowa.[7]

Between May and August 1942, a total of 14,441 Jews from the provincial ghettos (Pabianice, Ozorków, Brzeziny, Kalisz, Łask, Bełchatów, Turek and others) were sent to the Łódź ghetto.[8] The others, if not shot on the spot, were sent to Chełmno as part of the Operation for Clearing the Warthegau.

A new round of deportations from Łódź began on September 1, 1942. This operation was considered by many to be the ghetto's most horrific. The transports consisted almost exclusively of the sick, the elderly and children under the age of ten. The police surrounded the hospitals in the ghetto, including the children's hospital. The transport unit literally attacked the facilities. The manner in which the Germans took away the patients left no doubt at all regarding the fate of the unfortunates. They threw them down stairs, took them off operating tables, beat them and laid the patients one on top of the other in the trucks. No one knew where they were being taken, but it was clear to everyone that they were going to their deaths.[9] The trucks drove out of the ghetto on September 1 and 2. On this second day 200 randomly selected people, the number purported to have escaped from the hospitals, were deported. Panic and shock reigned in the ghetto.[10]

On September 4, 1942, Rumkowski spoke before a huge crowd assembled in Fire Brigade Square and delivered what has come to be known as his "Give Me Your Children" speech:

> A severe blow has befallen the ghetto. They [the Nazis] are asking from it the best that we possess—[our] children and old people. I have not had the privilege of having a child of my own and therefore I devoted the best of my years to children. I lived and breathed together with the children. I never imagined that my own hands would have to deliver the sacrifice to the altar. In my old age, I must stretch out my hands and beg: "Brothers and sisters, give them to me! Fathers and mothers, give me your children... "[11]

Rumkowski went on to tell the ghetto dwellers that he managed to reduce the number of people to be deported from 25,000 to 20,000 people: children under ten and the elderly over 65 years of age. Rumkowski proposed including the sick in an effort to try and save the healthy.[12] Transports left the ghetto on September 1–2 and September 7–12. A total of 15,685 people, 6,016 males and 9,669 females, were deported to the death camp during those eight days.[13]

After these September transports Biebow announced that the resettlement was over. While there were no further mass deportations to Chełmno, several more transports did arrive. The origins of these transports are not known.

The guard Friedrich Maderholz had been transferred from the mansion to the forest, because there were no more transports arriving and thus there was no one to guard. Then, in October, he was transferred back to the mansion, because Jews began arriving again, though not as often as before.[14]

Theodore Malzmüller, a guard who only began his service in Chełmno in September, recalled that three different transports arrived during his stay: a train transport with about 200 Jews, a transport of five or six trucks with 150 to 180 Jews and a transport of four trucks with about 100 Jews. This last group was taken directly to the forest and shot by Bothmann, Plate and Lenz. Malzmüller heard that these people were mentally ill.[15]

Rudolf Otto was another guard who arrived in the camp in September, possibly together with Malzmüller. He also remembered only three transports, probably the same ones. He described them as a transport with about 120 Jews, a transport of three trucks with about 80 to 90 Jews and a transport of three trucks with about 120 Jews.[16]

The gas van driver Laabs stated that in February 1943, a total of about 1,000 people were brought from the Łódź ghetto by truck and were gassed and burned.[17] The Chronicle of the Łódź Ghetto, under the March 30, 1943, entry, makes reference to a 20-car train that was assembled and loaded that afternoon, mostly with hopelessly sick people.[18] While there is no proof that this transport was directed to Chełmno, it may be connected to Laab's recollections.

Stanisław Rubach, a journalist who lived just outside of Koło in the neighboring town of Kościelec, kept notes about the events taking place in Chełmno as he heard them from members of the local community. In his notes of mid-October, he mentioned that a very elegantly dressed and well-fed group of French Jews were brought to Chełmno.[19] Józef Czupryński, a local resident, said that at the end of 1942, a transport of rich foreign Jews arrived at the camp. They were well treated with cigarettes and friendly conversation.[20] It may have been this same group that was seen outside of Chełmno on its way to the camp. Three large luxurious buses were seen stopped on the Turek-Dąbie road. Fashionable suitcases were packed on top of the bus and elegantly dressed men and women were inside. Police guards stood outside around the buses and were very polite to the passengers. They spoke French among themselves. One account claimed they came from France, another from Belgium.[21]

Not only Jews and Roma were killed in Chełmno. Throughout the entire existence of the camp, an unknown number of small groups of non-Jews were brought to the village. While no official documents have been found to support this, many people from the area around Chełmno reported seeing "unusual" transports. It is often claimed that Russian POWs were killed in Chełmno. Indeed, Russians were killed in the camp, but the evidence can only account for about 60. For example, in February 1942, Józef Przybylski saw two trucks arrive

[...] from the direction of Dąbie with soldiers in them. The soldiers were emaciated. One of them had only one leg. Several of them had rolled-up blankets thrown across their shoulders. Mess kits were fastened to the blankets. They were dressed in light green uniforms with a light blue tint. I didn't notice shoulder straps or insignias. I didn't know at that time what type of uniform it was. Later, when I was working in Germany, I saw this same uniform on Russian prisoners many times. [...] The trucks stopped on the highway in front of the mansion. The drivers got out and the Sonderkommando drivers drove the trucks directly to the forest. After about 25 minutes, the trucks returned empty. The drivers were exchanged and the trucks headed toward Dąbie. [...] The trucks had extended cabs and in each of them were at most about 20 prisoners. I was about 15 to 20 meters from the trucks.[22]

The Poles, Henryk Mania and Henryk Maliczak, confirm that two truckloads of Russian soldiers were brought to the camp. Maliczak said that they were gassed and then buried in the forest. In addition, he remembered a separate occasion when six Russian officers were brought to the mansion. Lenz took them aside and shot them all with his pistol. Maliczak had to load the corpses onto a truck which then drove to the forest.[23] Apparently the same incident, one of the policemen saw Lenz shoot five or six Russian soldiers who had escaped from a POW camp.[24] Buttons from Soviet military uniforms were recovered from the area of the forest camp after the war.

Not only Russian but also Polish soldiers appear to have been killed in Chełmno. Marianna Woźniak saw five men in Polish army uniforms with packs arrive at the village. They were taken directly to the forest.[25] Wiktoria Adamczyk saw a group of about ten men in civilian clothes (without Jewish stars) standing on the highway in front of the mansion. They were handcuffed. The next day, Adamczyk was told by three members of the Jewish Hauskommando, all of whom worked in the camp kitchen, that these individuals were Polish officers.[26]

On April 28, 1942, trucks arrived at two nursing homes in Włocławek. The Germans forced the elderly patients, as well as the nuns who cared for them, into the trucks and drove away. This procedure was repeated on August 5, when two more nursing homes were evacuated.[27] Many people in Chełmno witnessed the arrival of the elderly people and nuns at the camp. Zygmunt Szkobel saw Toni Wornshofer, a Sonderkommando truck driver, behind the wheel of the kommando's bus carrying a transport of Poles to Chełmno. First, four trucks and then the bus drove by. He noticed they weren't wearing Jewish stars; they looked like Poles. They shouted from the truck, "Is it far to Koło?" Women with white kerchiefs on their heads were in the bus. There were a lot of them. The bus was full.[28]

Zygmunt Antecki saw a transport of four trucks and a bus escorted by the Sonderkommando. It contained young and old people. The next day, he was told by a man named Majewski, who sold gasoline to the Sonderkommando and knew them by sight, that he saw members of Sonderkommando Kulmhof in Włocławek that day. The old people had been taken from a nursing home and the young people had been caught in a roundup.[29] Wornshofer, the driver of the bus, told a local, Stanisław

Śliwiński, that he had been in Włocławek that day. Rubach duly recorded this in his notes between August 13 and 16, 1942.[30]

Just before the liquidation of the camp Stanisław Polubiński, one of the Polish workers, told a local villager, Jan Krysiński, that Poles had been brought to Chełmno. Special vehicles, which held 15 people, were used for this purpose. They were sent directly to the forest, indicating that the Poles were shot, not gassed.[31] Polubiński also told Józef Grabowski that Poles were brought to the camp. Once he told him, "Today was a sad affair; they brought priests. What could we do?"[32]

As mentioned above, these non-Jewish transports were taken directly to the forest where they were shot. People who lived near the forest camp heard those shots, mostly at night. Screams and cries, in Polish, were also heard emanating from the forest: "Jesus, Mary, Joseph, save us!"[33] Józef Czupryński recalled that at night, when sounds carried a great distance, he could distinctly hear voices and shots coming from the forest. One night he heard what he estimated to be the sounds of about 100 people, screams of "O Jesus, Jesus, Mother of God who lives, save us." This was followed by machine gun fire and then silence. It was repeated on the following night.[34]

The number of Poles murdered in Chełmno will never be established. Several groups of Poles were certainly murdered in the camp, but this was minimal, in terms of numbers, in comparison to the average daily death toll of 1,000 Jews.

On June 10, 1942, the Nazis destroyed the Czech village of Lidice in reprisal for the assassination of Reinhard Heydrich, the top Nazi official of Bohemia and Moravia, and the chief administrator of the Final Solution. The men from the village were shot on the spot, and the women were sent to concentration camps. The 88 children from the village were transported by train to Łódź. Dr. Walter Robert Dongus examined the children at the Rasse und Siedlungsamt [Race and Settlement Office]. Those who did not qualify for "Germanization," apparently all but seven, were loaded onto trucks during the night and driven away. There are no documents showing that these children were shipped to the camp; yet the evidence supports the contention that they were murdered in Chełmno as the young people were marked for "special treatment."[35]

Local residents in Chełmno do recall a children's transport, although it cannot be established if it was in fact the children from Lidice. Some believed that these were Polish children deported from the area around Zamość in the General Government.

> Once—it was summer—I saw children brought in trucks from the direction of Dąbie. There were four trucks, one with a trailer. There were dozens of children. They were ten to 12 years old, mainly girls. I didn't see Jewish stars [on their clothes]. The children were dressed as though for a trip. It was eight

in the morning. They looked like Polish children. It was during the time when children from the Lublin area [in the General Government] were expected. People had applied to take them and raise them.[36]

Wiktoria Adamczyk also saw the transport. She asked one of the Jews who worked in the kitchen, Toporski, about it. He told her that they were from the Protectorate.[37] Another local villager remembered a transport of children from the Protectorate. She was with her sister who worked in the barracks next to the German House. A policeman entered the building and said a transport of children had arrived. He ordered the girls to collect apples and give them to the children in the truck, which they did.[38] After the war, Mania told a reporter that he placed the steps at the back of the truck and helped the Czech children disembark.[39] These accounts may well be the most direct evidence that the Czech children were brought to the death camp.

Wilhelm Orlowski, one of the policemen serving in the camp, witnessed the arrival of a group of children to Chełmno. About 20 small children, approximately five years of age, arrived by truck and were driven onto the grounds of the mansion.[40] Hauptscharführer Fritz Ismer also remembered a transport of children. He said it stood out in his memory.

> It must have been in 1942. From my quarters, I could see three trucks with children standing on the road that lead to the mansion. The children were well dressed, at any rate, better than Jews usually were. I estimate that there were about 200 of them in those trucks. I do not know if more trucks with children came to Kulmhof. Most likely, the children were also gassed, but I do not know for sure.[41]

A group of 200 children would seem to be a memorable event. This is the only account of such a large transport of children. Other members of the Sonderkommando may not have wanted to remember these children. It is difficult to establish whether or not the above testimonies refer to separate transports.

The large-scale mass murder campaign in Chełmno ended with the September 7–12, 1942 transports from Łódź, although several smaller transports did arrive at the camp before it was closed in April 1943. By the end of September 1942, virtually all of the Jews from the provincial ghettos in the Warthegau had been exterminated or sent to the Łódź ghetto. Only small isolated groups working in labor camps scattered across the region, individuals in hiding and those surviving Jews in the Łódź ghetto remained alive.[42] Chełmno had essentially completed its mission.

Escapes

It is not known how many escape attempts were made during the first period of the camp's operations, but specific information exists concerning five prisoners who successfully fled from Chełmno. Information also exists regarding three other men who managed to escape, but there are no specific details concerning these latter individuals; it would appear that they did not survive the war, or they chose not to step forward publicly to relate their experiences following the war.

The first three escapes occurred days apart in January 1942, just weeks after the camp began functioning. The first to successfully escape was Abram Rój, a tailor from Izbica Kujawska, who was forced to work in the camp as a gravedigger. Rój was the first person to escape from a Nazi death camp, a fact he himself may not have realized. On the evening of Friday, January 16, Rój and a couple of other prisoners were taken to a room in the basement of the mansion, probably the kitchen, where large meat hooks hung from the ceiling. The guards, perhaps out of boredom and for their own amusement, told the men that they were to impale themselves on the meat hooks by the time they returned and if they had not done so they would do it for them or shoot them. The guards then left the room and locked the door. The men inside became hysterical. Given a choice, Rój preferred to be shot while trying to escape rather than to die such a horrible death. The room had a small window, but large enough for him to crawl through (Rój was a physically small man), which is just what he did.

Once outside the mansion Rój managed to slip outside the camp and flee to nearby woods. He spent the night in a barn and then made his way to a nearby town, presumably Koło, but this is not certain. Rój's precise movements at this point are not clear, although it is known he traveled to Krośniewice, some 40 kilometers east of Koło, where he spoke with members of the local Jewish community. The news he brought about the events transpiring in Chełmno was not well received and threats were made against him. However, at least one person took him seriously. On January 21, Róża Kapłan sent a postcard to her husband in the Warsaw ghetto informing him that she had just spoken with an escapee from Chełmno.[1] It was on this same day that news started spreading from the town of Grabów, approximately 20 kilometers southwest of Krośniewice, about what escapees from Chełmno were saying there about the fate of the Jews. After hearing that others had escaped from Chełmno, it is believed Rój set out to find them.

After Michał Podchlebnik buried his wife and children in the forest on January 13, and after Rój's successful escape, he became determined to get out of the camp. He began to discuss the possibilities with his fellow prisoners, including Szlama Winer.[2]

> I noticed while going to work in the bus that one of the windows could be opened. I told my companion Winer (I don't remember his first name) from Izbica about this and suggested that we escape. The next day on the way to work we were going to jump out of the window and escape into the forest;

however, we were separated while boarding. I was placed in the truck and Winer in the bus. I decided to escape alone. When the truck was in the forest, I approached the guard and asked for cigarettes. I got them and went back to my place. Then my companions surrounded the guard also asking for cigarettes. With a sudden movement, I cut the canvas on the right side by the cab with a knife that I had hidden on me and jumped out of the truck. They shot at me, but missed. Luckily the bus was not following us, so that the shooting came only from the truck. The absence of the bus led me to believe that Winer had escaped and in connection with this, the bus had stopped. As I escaped through the forest, a civilian on a bicycle tried to stop me, shooting at me with a pistol. I escaped from him as well. I hid in a barn and buried myself in the hay. In the morning, I heard some peasants talking near the barn, saying that the Germans were looking for some Jews who had escaped. After two days during which I didn't eat anything, I left the barn and went in the direction of Grabów. On the way, I stopped at the home of a peasant whose name I don't know. He fed me and gave me a hat. I shaved and he showed me the way [to Grabów].[3]

Podchlebnik gave two primary postwar testimonies, one in 1945 and another in 1963. At this point in his testimonies, the versions vary slightly. In the later testimony, he stated that he stayed in the barn for 48 hours. At night, he came out of the barn and went to the owner's house. The man fed him and gave him a cap. Podchlebnik then left. After the war, Michał Radoszewski stated, "Klein from Grzegorzewa jumped out of a vehicle going to Chełmno. He hid at my place for a number of days. Later, he made his way to Grabów."[4] Podchlebnik was obviously using a false name and from the account above it would appear that Podchlebnik stayed those couple of days at Radoszewski's farm. Podchlebnik seems to have been in contact with several local Poles during his escape to Grabów. Stanisława Testkowska stated that around nine o'clock in the evening [Podchlebnik] came to her house and asked for a cap, but she didn't have one.[5] Władysława Bielińska stated that Podchlebnik came to her house during the evening with a cap on his head. He told her someone had given it to him.[6] Eventually, Podchlebnik reached Grabów without incident.

In testimony given in 1963, Podchlebnik continued the story of his escape. After reaching Grabów, he had two reunions.

The first was with Winer. It is difficult to describe that meeting in which we alternately wept and rejoiced that we had survived. The second meeting was no less moving, because I met my brother-in-law and later my sister and nephew.

In Grabów, I told the Jews about the atrocities in Chełmno. But they not only didn't want to believe it, they threatened that they would turn me over to the German authorities for spreading such stories.

Under these conditions, I hid in Grabów for several days. Together with my family, we made it to Piotrków Trybunalski [approximately 100 kilometers south of Grabów]. From there, with Aryan papers and travel permits, the two of us, my nephew and I, went in the company of a Christian by train to

Rzeszów. The trip, however, was not successful. In Tarnów, we were taken off the train and handed over to the Gestapo. After an interrogation, we were led outside where the Gestapo official shot dead my nephew and then came for me. However, what he got was a punch in the stomach, which made possible my escape. A bullet just missed my ear and I got away.

Alone, I walked to Rzeszów and succeeded in entering the ghetto. My sister also arrived, having paid some Christian a lot of money. [...] Again I began to trade in cattle, and I must admit that I earned a lot of money. I knew, however, that life in the ghetto was hopeless, so I went to the countryside and gave everything I had to a peasant. I hid at this farm for 11 months. I was lucky that he didn't turn me in. It's hard to describe in words how it was to hide for such a long time in that rat hole. In 1944, the Russians came and I was liberated.[7]

Such is the story of Podchlebnik's escape as told by Podchlebnik himself from testimonies spanning almost 20 years. However, an independent, seemingly reliable source suggests there is much more to the story of Podchlebnik's escape prior to reaching Rzeszów. Yehoshua Moshe Aronson, the rabbi of Sanniki, a small town some 100 kilometers east of Koło, was deported to the Konin labor camp in the summer of 1942, where he secretly kept a journal, meticulously documenting his experiences for posterity. Miraculously, both the rabbi and his writings survived the war.[8] Rabbi Aronson recorded meeting with another Sanniki resident, a Mr. Kohn, in January 1942 (prior to his deportation to Konin), who told him details of the Chełmno death camp. Mr. Kohn's source was an escapee named Michał Podchlebnik. The details about the death camp written down by the rabbi could only have come from an eyewitness and indeed are consistent with Podchlebnik's experiences while in the camp, including the death of his wife and children. Of significance here is the information about Podchlebnik's movements after his escape. According to this account, Podchlebnik first went to the town of Grabów, and from there to Krośniewice and Gostynin, before traveling to Warsaw.[9]

Podchlebnik never mentioned escaping in this direction, to the east of Chełmno and Grabów. According to his own testimony, he went to Piotrków Trybunalski (with relatives) after leaving Grabów, and then taking a train to Tarnów and eventually walking to Rzeszów, where he spent the rest of the war. In other words, he travelled south of Chełmno and Grabów to Piotrków and then east to Rzeszów. It is not clear where, or precisely when, Kohn spoke with Podchlebnik. Kohn was able to travel, so the meeting could have occurred in virtually any town in the area. Before moving to Sanniki, Kohn lived in Gostynin and probably met Podchlebnik there, which is how he could have known the sequence of towns Podchlebnik traveled to "before leaving for Warsaw." However, Podchlebnik never mentioned being in Warsaw and there are no accounts of his being there. Without additional facts, the discrepancy in the two accounts of Podchlebnik's movements following his escape cannot be rectified.[10]

Podchlebnik and Winer had planned to escape together but were separated while being loaded into the vehicles to go to work in the forest. Winer's testimony is continued here with his last night in the basement of the mansion.

Not having a penny to my name, I asked Kalman Radziejewski from Izbica for several marks. He pulled out RM 50 he had sewn into his clothing and gave them to me. Rój's escape had made such an impression on me—he escaped through a basement window—that before dawn I tried to pull out a brick from the window. Again, however, without success.

On Monday, January 19, we were loaded into the bus. I let everyone get on in front of me and I got on last. The guards sat in the front. That day there were no guards following behind. On my right side was a window which opened very easily. I opened it and a stream of air rushed in. I got scared and closed the window. But my companions, particularly Moniek Halter, encouraged me. I was determined. I asked my companions, in a whisper, to stand up so that the stream of air wouldn't reach the guards. I quickly rolled down the window, put my legs out and lowered myself down. I grasped the body with my hand and supported my feet on the door hinge. I had told my companions to close the window immediately after I jumped out. I slipped down and tumbled several times, scraping my hand. I hoped I wouldn't break my leg. I would have rather broken my arm, because the most important thing was to run and reach the first Jewish settlement. I saw that the bus continued on. Without wasting time, I set out as fast as possible across fields and forests. After an hour, I came upon a Polish house. I went inside greeting them with "Blessed be Jesus Christ!" I asked how far it was to Chełmno. It was only three kilometers. I got a large piece of bread that I put in my pocket. As I was leaving the house, the peasant asked me if I wasn't, by chance, a Jew. I boldly denied it and asked him why he suspected me. In response I heard, "In Chełmno, they are gassing Jews and Gypsies." I said good-bye to him using a Polish expression and left. I continued on for an hour and again came to a Polish house. Here I was treated to white sweetened coffee and a big hunk of bread. The hosts showed me the way. I went on until I reached a German village. (German farms were easy to distinguish from Polish ones, because they were well equipped and had aerials on the roofs.) I made myself walk boldly through the village. Only at the end of it did I see a Polish house. Here, it turned out that I was ten kilometers from Grabów, where Jews lived. I introduced myself as a Polish butcher on the way to Grabów in search of work. The host sent me to a neighboring village, to a certain Grabowski, who had a horse and cart and might give me a lift. I always kept off the roads, but at one point I had to walk along one. Suddenly I saw a military vehicle and my heart nearly stopped. I already saw myself caught by the Germans. At the last moment I grabbed a peasant woman passing by me by the arm and took her down a side road. I asked her if by chance she didn't have some butter to sell. The vehicle passed by. I breathed a sigh of relief.

The whole time, I asked God and my parents to help me save the Jewish people. At the Grabowskis' house, I introduced myself as Wojciechowski, going to Grabów to work. It happened that he was going to the market in Dąbie. His neighbor, to whom I was sent, had already left for the market. So, I went further along the road, thinking of the bad luck that was haunting me. I asked directions along the way, avoiding sentry posts, because

I didn't have any documents. Finally, I reached a village seven kilometers from Grabów. I convinced a Polish peasant to take me to Grabów for RM 15. I put on a sheepskin coat and fur hat. We reached Grabów on Monday, January 19, at two in the afternoon.

The Jews thought I was a Volksdeutsch because I wasn't wearing the Jewish badge, the star of David. I searched for the rabbi. I looked pretty rough. (In Chełmno we couldn't wash or shave.) I asked, "Does the Rabbi live here?" "Who are you?" "Rabbi, I come from another world." His look told me that he thought I was a madman. I said, "Rabbi, don't think that I am mad or have lost my reason. I am a Jew. I was in another world. The extermination of the Jewish people is taking place. I myself have buried an entire Jewish community, including my parents, brothers, and entire family. I am completely alone." I sobbed as I said this. The Rabbi asked, "Where are they being murdered?" I answered, "In Chełmno. Everyone is poisoned with gas in the forest and buried in a mass grave."

The maid (the rabbi was a widower), whose eyes were swollen from crying, brought me a bowl of water. As I began to wash my hands, the wound on my right hand started to hurt. When my news made the rounds in the town, many Jews came to the Rabbi's and I told them the details about these horrible events. Everyone wept. I ate bread and butter, drank some tea, and said a prayer of thanks.[11]

The rabbi was shocked at what he heard. That same day, after hearing Winer's story, he wrote a postcard to his brother-in-law. The postcard made its way to the Łódź ghetto and eventually survived the war.

My Dearest Ones!

I have not replied to your letters, since I did not know exactly what was being rumored. Now, to our great misfortune, we know everything. An eyewitness who by chance was able to escape from hell has been to see me. ... I learned everything from him. The place where everyone is being put to death is called Chełmno, not far from Dąbie; people are buried in the nearby forest of Łochów. People are killed in one of two ways: either by shooting or by gassing. This is what happened to the towns of Dąbie, Izbica Kujawska, Kłodawa and others. Recently, thousands of Gypsies have been brought there from the so-called Gypsy camp in Łódź and for several days thousands of Jews from Łódź are being brought and the same is done to them. Do not think that a madman is writing; unfortunately, it is the cruel and tragic truth (Good God!). O man, throw off your rags, sprinkle your head with ashes, or run through the streets and dance in madness ... I am so wearied by the sufferings of Israel, my pen can write no more. I feel my heart is breaking. But perhaps the Almighty will take pity and save the "last remnants of our people."

Help us, O Creator of the world!

Grabów, January 19, 1942
Jakub Szulman[12]

Two days later Rabbi Szulman spoke with a second escapee, Pod-chlebnik, confirming what Winer had told him. Afterwards, he sat down and wrote another letter, dated January 21, similar in content to the first.

Dear relatives and loved ones,

We can now tell you of the dreadful occurrences near our town, which were a heavily guarded secret until today. For your information, four weeks ago all the Jews, without exception, were deported from the town of Koło—men, women, and children—and were taken by trucks in an unknown direction. The same happened in Dąbie, Kłodawa, Izbica and other towns in that district. Despite all efforts that were made, we heard nothing about them, and we received no word of what had happened to them. This week, however, some Jewish refugees who had fled from that place came and said that they are all being killed, down to the last one. They are asphyxiated with gas, after which about 50 to 60 people bury them en masse in a single grave. New victims are being brought in incessantly every day, and the danger of a similar fate hovers over everyone's head. Obviously, this horrific news caused us terrible panic and indescribable fear. We declared a fast day today, the third of Shevat, and we gave charity for the release of deportees.

You should know, however, that what was kept secret until today must from now on be publicized everywhere. You must raise an outcry. Do not rest and do not be silent. Take counsel and come up with stratagems regarding how to save those who are still alive from the dreadful decrees! You must not sit with folded arms! Do not be silent! You have to take action to save the lives of thousands of Jews. Every moment counts. You constitute a certain force of what used to be the largest community.

Ask the leading Jewish sages, too, whether we—the relatives of those who were murdered—have to sit shiva [observe a period of mourning], and what we should do about this.

And may God, blessed be He, have mercy on all the Jews, save us from all evil... and send us the proper help. May we hear and send you good news... Please reply immediately and tell us what is happening with you.[13]

The rabbi wrote and sent a number of such letters and postcards as he appreciated the gravity of the situation in which the Jewish community as a whole found itself as related by Winer and reinforced by Podchleb-nik. Indeed, the Rabbi of Grabów received at least one more visitor and additional letters would be written. Some six weeks after Winer and Pod-chlebnik spoke to the rabbi, Fiszel Brejtsztajn arrived in Grabów. At the encouragement of his own family, Brejtsztajn escaped from a transport as the Jewish community of Żychlin was being deported to Chełmno. Brejtsztajn informed Rabbi Szulman of the tragic events he had witnessed in his own hometown and on the way to Chełmno. According to Brejtsztajn, the rabbi summoned local Jewish community leaders who wrote letters to other towns in the area (with local Poles acting as couriers) as well as a letter to Mordechai Chaim Rumkowski in the Łódź ghetto, who reportedly did not believe the contents.[14] However, Rabbi Szulman and his colleagues were not the only ones to inform friends, family and others about what was happening in nearby Chełmno. As the shocking news spread through Grabów, other residents began sending news to friends and relatives, including a Mr. Zontag, who wrote to his parents in the Warsaw ghetto informing them that the men, women and children of Koło County had been killed.[15] The postcard was sent two days after Winer's arrival. Another letter sent from Grabów, also to Warsaw, informed the reader, "Our brothers and sisters no longer live in their homes and now live in the same house as our mother. It was Judgment Day here today."[16]

From Winer's testimony and from the date of the rabbi's first piece of correspondence, it is known that Winer arrived in Grabów on the day of his escape, January 19. Podchlebnik, after escaping, spent two nights in a barn and then arrived in Grabów no earlier than January 21. Podchlebnik never mentioned meeting Rój in Grabów, but he did meet Winer and suggested that the two of them continue on together. According to Podchlebnik, Winer declined.[17]

Based on correspondence that Winer eventually received in Warsaw, he and Rój met up at some point, perhaps in Grabów[18] following Podchlebnik's departure, but it is not known precisely where. The movements of Winer and Rój between January 21 and February 5 are not known. However, it is known that on January 21, Winer was in Grabów and Rój in Krośniewice. Having heard that other prisoners had escaped from Chełmno, Rój probably set out for Grabów, the source of the information.[19] If Winer had already left, Rój eventually caught up with him at another location, but where? It is not until February 5 that Winer appeared in Piotrków Trybunalski, where he registered with the local Jewish Council as Jakub Grojnowski.[20] It is not known when Winer arrived in Piotrków, but while there he met an acquaintance from Dąbie, Bajla Alszuld. After the war, she recalled, "In the winter of 1942, I met my friend Winer from Izbica in Piotrków. He told me that he escaped from the "death camp" in Chełmno. [He] escaped from a vehicle while going to work and another Jew escaped the same day."[21] The other Jew, of course, was Podchlebnik. The fact that she did not mention a third escapee suggests that Rój had not yet caught up with Winer. If the two had recently met, wouldn't Winer have mentioned this "latest news" to his friend Alszuld? There is no evidence that Winer or Podchlebnik spoke with Jewish community leaders while in Piotrków. The chief rabbi of the city, Moshe Hayim Lau, would not learn about Chełmno until months later when other escapees from the camp spoke with him directly.[22]

Winer left Piotrków for Warsaw in the second week of February. Based on the data available, it appears Winer met Rój, either in Piotrków, after speaking with Alszuld, or in Koluszki, on his way to Warsaw. Rój left

Koluszki on approximately February 10, and went to Wierzbnik, now part of Starachowice, in the district of Radom. From there, he sent a desperate letter to Winer in Warsaw on February 20.

Wierzbnik, February 20, 1942

Dear Szlamek,

I can tell you that I'm at Helcia's now. I'm fine, which I wish from all my heart for you too, dear Szlamek. I can tell you that I received a letter from your sister in Zamość. She wrote you telling you that you must come. She will take good care of you. She wrote me that she's worried about you and would very much like to be with you, dear Szlamek. I also received a postcard from Mr. Herber and from Grabów. They are still there and send their regards. Dear Szlamek, I regret very much that we parted. I am at Helcia's; it's very bad. It's very bad for Helcia. She can't help me at all. It's worse for me here than in Koluszki. You can imagine what's going on with me. I don't have any more money. I don't know what will happen, what to think [?], better not to have survived.

Kind regards, I remain your sincere friend, Abram[23]

Like Podchlebnik and Winer, Rój also used a false name, or possibly a series of names, after escaping from Chełmno. Details concerning Rój's experiences during the war are very limited. It appears Rój stayed in Starachowice, probably working in one or several of the slave labor camps established in the town. In July 1944, he was deported from there to Auschwitz,[24] but subsequently escaped, either from the camp itself or during the death marches when the camp was being evacuated. Abram Rój, sick and emaciated, was hiding in a barn when he was liberated by Russian soldiers in 1945.

Meanwhile, Winer, now using the name Jakub Grojnowski, left Piotrków Trybunalski and arrived in Warsaw during the second week of February. Shortly after arriving he met with Hersz Wasser, a lawyer, economist and secretary of Oneg Shabbat, an organization headed by the Warsaw historian, Dr. Emanuel Ringelblum. Oneg Shabbat had been clandestinely collecting information concerning, among other things, the tumultuous events engulfing the Jewish people. Wasser directed the archive's activities concerned with reports coming from ghettos outside Warsaw.

Winer related his experiences in Chełmno to Wasser. The testimony was written down and added to the archive. It was also sent to London as evidence of the genocide taking place against the Jews in Poland. Wasser considered Winer a valuable eyewitness to the tragic events unfolding around them and took care of Winer while he was in Warsaw. Winer began sending and receiving mail during his stay in Warsaw, which lasted approximately five weeks.

Winer, however, was restless and wanted to go to Zamość to be with his sister-in-law, Felicja Bajler. She advised him to wait for the appropriate time before coming. Wasser probably also advised against such a trip because of the obvious risk involved. Winer remained in Warsaw until at least March 18, based on a dated photograph that he gave to the Wassers before leaving, possibly that same day.[25]

Winer was in Zamość by March 20. The move there indeed proved to be a mistake. Wasser received letters from Winer in Zamość, the last one written in a very desperate tone, informing him that a death camp, like Chełmno, also existed in Bełżec. He also wrote that he very much wanted to return to Warsaw. Wasser responded with a letter to Winer, telling him to come back. He received a reply, not from Winer, but from his 14-year-old nephew Abram, Felicja's son. He informed Wasser that his uncle and mother had been taken away two weeks earlier. He did not know where they were.

On April 11, 1942, some 3,000 Jews were deported from Zamość to the Bełżec death camp. Knowing what awaited him, one can only wonder what Szlama Winer's thoughts were upon his arrival to a second death camp. Did he attempt to volunteer to serve in a labor detail hoping once more to try and escape, or did he resign himself to the seemingly inevitable? Regardless, due to the eyewitness testimony of Szlama Winer given in Warsaw just after his escape, the world found out that genocide was taking place in Chełmno.[26]

There was another escape from the Chełmno camp about which there is some specific information. Unfortunately, the escapee did not meet with the same kindness that Winer and Podchlebnik encountered upon their eastward flight from the camp. After the war, Natalia M., a Pole who lived in the village of Majdany, just west of the forest camp, provided testimony about the escape.

> On March 11, 1942, a Jew escaped from the forest [camp] and came to our house. I gave the Jew something to eat and some tea. The Jew was very tired. He said that he was a cap maker from Łódź. He had a Jewish star on his coat. While the Jew was at my house, the village administrator came and took him away.[27]

How did the village administrator know that a Jew was in Natalia M.'s house? Her own sister provided the answer.

> My sister or her husband went and got the village administrator, Mundt, who took the Jew to the Gestapo in Chełmno. I know this from my sister. [...] [She] said that she regretted turning in the Jew, but that she had to; otherwise she could have been killed.[28]

Yet another escape from the camp during the first period took place during the night of May 15–16, 1942. At half past two in the morning, guards discovered that six Jews had escaped from the basement of the mansion. Police units were notified throughout the area and a search was launched.[29] It would appear that this is the same escape later recalled by Henryk Mania.

> [D]uring the time I was in the camp in Chełmno, there was one instance of escape from the mansion. The Jewish prisoners, who worked in the forest, were locked in the basement. One of the walls was weak and by bolting through a hole, several, or a dozen, prisoners escaped one night. Some of them were caught. We [Polish prisoners] also took part in the pursuit, acting as translators. The group I was with didn't catch any prisoners. I heard that the Gestapo took those that they caught to the forest and shot them. The policemen told me about this.[30]

Rozalia Peham, the wife of one of the German guards, also recalled that in the summer of 1942, six Jews escaped from the camp. She stated that her husband took part in the search for them. He told her that four of them were caught and killed, but that the other two were not found.[31] The names as well as the fates of those two prisoners who succeeded in fleeing from the camp are unknown.

The third escapee for which there is no specific information concerning his fate is provided by Kurt Möbius, the transport supervisor at the mansion. In postwar testimony, Möbius stated the following.

> Under my supervision, straw was brought from a silo to five Jewish craftsmen who had been brought in late in the evening and were about to enter the [basement] of the [mansion]. In the course of this one of the Jews fled and it was impossible to give chase, as we had no illumination apart from one lantern.[32]

The man successfully fled the camp, but no further information about this individual is known. The date of the event is also not clear. The first known craftsmen in the camp came from towns "resettled" in April 1942.

Two other men successfully escaped from the camp during the first period, but are absent from the Chełmno literature. They decided not to come forward and publicly relive the painful events from their past. These men were Yerachmiel Widawski and Yitzhak Justmann. Yerachmiel Widawski, the son of Joshua and Chaya Widawski, was born into a large family in Sieradz, Poland, in May 1913. Joshua Widawski was employed in the spirits business.[33] No information concerning Yitzhak Justmann's pre-war history is known.

Details are also lacking on how the two men arrived at Chełmno, their stay there, and how they managed to escape from the camp. It is assumed they were transported to Chełmno during the deportation of the Sieradz Jewish community at the end of August 1942, and spent approximately one week in the camp. The two men were assigned to the Waldkommando, working as gravediggers in the forest camp.[34] After escaping from the immediate area of the camp, they made their way to Piotrków Trybunalski, since they were determined to flee the Reich and Piotrków was the nearest large city across the border. The only published account of these events is by Naphtali Lau-Lavie, the son of Moshe Hayim Lau, the rabbi of Piotrków at the time, in whose home the escapees found temporary refuge.[35]

> [...] Two young men in their twenties—Chaim Jerachmiel Widawski [sic] and Yitzhak Justmann—arrived in the ghetto seeking shelter. On the way to our home, they noticed that the Volksdeutsch Gestapo agent Emmering was following them. In order to lose him, they went in separate directions: Justmann went in the direction of the Great Synagogue and lost Emmering [and found sanctuary in the Wajsberg home, where he was well hidden], while Widawski arrived at our home with the Jewish policeman Checinski on his tail who tried to stop him. Hearing the commotion on the stairs, my father went out to see what was happening and with a firm voice ordered the policeman to leave the man alone, who, crying, thanked my father for saving him. [Distraught and weeping, Widawski asked for water and the opportunity to tell his story.]
>
> A calmer Widawski said that, together with Justmann, he escaped from a "commando" that buried victims of the death camp in Chełmno. No one in the ghetto had yet heard the name of that place.
>
> My father took Widawski into his office and closed the door. After about an hour, he came out and told me to summon several of his friends, among whom were members of the pre-war community council: Mosze Nordman, Baruch Zylberszac, [Hirsch-Leib Krakowski,] Meir Abramson, Fiszel Lubliner, [Mordechai Michelson,] Bunim Kaminski, Rabbi Mosze Temkin and Dr. Sztajn. Soon everyone was gathered in my father's study (with his permission I stayed also), to hear Widawski recount his experience in Chełmno. My father wrote down his every word and asked many questions to check the veracity of his story.
>
> Widawski told about murdering people with exhaust fumes in special trucks, the exhaust pipes of which were directed into the hermetically sealed rear compartment full of people. In the course of half an hour trip from the mansion in Chełmno, where they were imprisoned, to the clearing in the forest, where large rectangular pits were dug, everyone was murdered with the exhaust fumes from the vehicle's engine. Widawski and his friend were among the group whose task was throwing the corpses from the truck and carrying them to the pit. There, four other people threw the corpses into the hole where another group arranged the bodies so as many as possible could be packed together. Infants and babies were placed into any empty spaces. Lime was poured over each layer of bodies, on which the next layer of bodies was placed. After the final layer was placed in the grave, the Germans ordered the eight men in the hole to lay face down after which they were shot.
>
> Among the tasks assigned to the group throwing the corpses out of the vans was cleaning them before they left for a new transport.
>
> "We worked like machines, unaware of what we were doing. The entire time I recited the Kaddish for the victims whom the van brought regularly every hour. Among the bodies that we pulled from the van I recognized relatives from Sieradz, and worst of all my fiancée, to whom I had proposed two months previously," Widawski said, his voice breaking.
>
> That tragic day while returning to the mansion in Chełmno, where they were isolated from those designated for death, Widawski and Justmann

decided to escape from that hell at any price and whatever the consequences. That very night, they managed to escape and after four days reached us in Piotrków.

[Naively, I believed that nothing could horrify me after my own experiences at Auschwitz. But Widawski's story, halted by sobs, dispelled that illusion. He talked compulsively, with Father writing everything in his notebook, pressing him for further details. The others listened, petrified. No one moved or spoke.] At one point my father told me to take Widawski to the dining room where my mother had prepared some food for him. When he was eating his first hot meal since who knows when, my father prepared a plan of escape for Widawski and his friend Justmann who was hiding in the Wajsberg's apartment, not far from the synagogue. Both were near the psychological breaking point, but as the Gestapo was aware of their presence, they had to escape from Piotrków as soon as possible. It was already curfew when I took Widawski to the nearby Goldring's home. There, the two fugitives were dressed in uniforms of Polish railroad employees and given the necessary documents and money. Widawski held my hand convulsively not wanting to let go.[36]

Contrary to the impression given in the account, Widawski and Justmann spent four or five days in Piotrków. Widawski stayed two nights in the library of the Lau's home (21 Piłsudski Street) before moving to another location, while Justmann, initially at the Wajsberg's, stayed with the Goldring family (17 Piłsudski Street).[37] Widawski and Justmann did not share the details of their escape plan with their facilitators in Piotrków. It is not known at what point the two men separated after leaving the city, but Widawski was eventually caught by the Germans and deported to Auschwitz. Along the way, he jumped off the train, seriously injuring himself. He laid on the tracks for three days and survived only because no other trains came down this line. Partisans found the injured man and nursed him back to health. Widawski subsequently made his way to Žilina, Slovakia, more than 300 kilometers south of Łódź, where his fortunes turned around when he met Meir Jacob Grünfeld.[38]

Meir Grünfeld, a Slovakian Jew from Medzilaborce, was living in Žilina under the alias Stefan Slivka, a Grünfeld family friend (and gentile) who had emigrated to the United States before the war. Grünfeld adopted the man's identity and acquired a permit to work as a traveling salesman of shirts and hats. But Grünfeld was engaged in more than just selling men's clothing. Together with a couple of friends, each man acquired a vacated apartment building in town and adapted it by constructing a false wall in one of the rooms. Each of these men took the risk of hiding a fellow Jew within their clandestine shelters. Grünfeld also acquired a permit to procure food and wine for a local church. The wine was then sold in order to buy food for the people in his "bunker," which eventually sheltered 13 Jews. The food was brought almost daily after returning from his travels as a salesman. It is not known precisely when Widawski reached Žilina (probably not earlier than late September 1942) or how he met Meir Grünfeld.

Widawski was physically and mentally exhausted, as well as extremely depressed because of the murder of his family and fiancée in Chełmno. Those already hiding in the bunker did not want Widawski to join them because they feared he could not be trusted. After all he had already endured, "he appeared unstable," and they believed he would put them at risk of being discovered. Nevertheless, Grünfeld overruled the men and Widawski spent the rest of the war hiding in the bunker.[39]

Yitzhak Justmann's trail after separating from Widawski is speculative at best. According to one account, an escapee from Chełmno arrived in the Częstochowa ghetto and spoke with Rabbi Henoch Gad Justman about the camp and the extermination of the Jews. The rabbi was shocked and encouraged young people to save their lives by fleeing the ghetto.[40] Neither the date of the event nor the identity of the escapee are known. Based on the timeline, the escapee could have been Widawski or Justmann. The two left Piotrków on about September 13 or 14, and the next mass deportation from Częstochowa began on September 22. The victims, including the rabbi, were sent to the Treblinka death camp. According to one source, Rabbi Justman had a grandson named Itzhak.[41] The fact that one of the escapees and the rabbi's grandson had the same first and last names raises an interesting question: Was the grandson seeking out his grandfather, the rabbi, to tell him the horrible truth about the extermination of the Jewish people?

One other account of a multiple escape from Chełmno has been published, yet the veracity of the account is questionable. The tale originates from Kłodawa. In January 1942, the Jews of the town were assembled at the church and firehouse for deportation to Chełmno. One woman fled to Grabów, but later returned and stated that while there she met two brothers, the Krzewackis, also from Kłodawa, who told her they escaped from the camp where they worked, together with their father, digging graves in the forest. The brothers also told her they helped hang their father because he didn't want to be gassed.

The problem with the account is that neither Podchlebnik nor Winer mentions the two brothers in their own accounts, although both mention Krzewacki's suicide. Winer even states that it was Chrząstkowski who assisted in the January 14 hanging. Considering the detailed nature of Winer's account of his experiences in the camp, it is highly suspicious that he would omit, or forget, that the man's own two sons participated in the hanging of their father. The details provided by the woman could have been part of the information circulating in Grabów following the arrival there of Winer and Podchlebnik. Without additional documentation, the authenticity of this story is doubtful. The fate of these two brothers is unknown, as is the fate of the woman who allegedly met the two brothers in Grabów.[42]

1. General view of Chełmno from the south. The mansion is visible to the left of the church (pre-1943). *IPN 47407*

2. Chełmno local government. Seated from left: Andrzej Miszczak (2nd), Stanisław Biskupski (3rd - senior official), Stanisław Kaszyński (5th). Standing from left: Czesław Potyralski (3rd), Konrad Schulz (7th), Franciszek Opas (8th), Leopold Chwiałkowski (11th) (Jan 1939). *ZL*

3. Back of the mansion; Ludwig and Hanna Koziej at top of stairs. The granary building is visible in the background (1939). *ŁPN*

4. Chełmno church and Ludwicki home; the mansion is located to the left of photo (ca. 1940). *FORUM*

5. Local government office. Lange, and later Bothmann, lived in this building (1945). *IPN 11294*

6. The church rectory was used by the Sonderkommando as its administrative office. Valuables taken from the victims were stored here (1945). *IPN 11289*

7. Building of the volunteer fire department referred to as the German House during the war. Policemen were quartered in this building (1945). *IPN 11292*

8. The Banaszewski's house was requisitioned by the Sonderkommando and used as a canteen. The building was located across the street from the German House and the entrance to the mansion grounds (1945). *IPN 11230*

Sonderkommando Kulmhof and other key perpetrators

9. Herbert Lange *BDC*

10. Hans Bothmann *BDC*

11. Herbert Otto *BA*

12. Albert Plate *BDC*

13. Walter Piller *BDC*

14. Herbert Hiecke-Richter *BDC*

15. Walter Burmeister *BDC*

16. Erwin Bürstinger *IPN* 47421

17. Gustav Laabs *IPN* 47422

18. Johannes Runge *IPN* 47423

19. Erich Kretschmer *IPN* 47424

20. Wilhelm Görlich *BDC*

21. Fritz Ismer *BDC*

22. Alois Häfele *BDC*

23. Ernst Burmeister *YV 4577_605*

24. Arthur Greiser *IPN* 05019

25. Wilhelm Koppe *IPN* 58846

26. Hans Biebow *YV* 36EO9

27. Policemen and Polish workers drinking beer in front of the mansion. Seated from left: Henryk Mania (1st), Policeman Friedrich Maderholz (3rd), Sergeant of the Guard Otto Böge (7th) (1942–43). *IPN 50378*

28. Poles employed in Chełmno. From left: Henryk Mania, Stanisław Polubiński, Lech Jaskól-ski, Kajetan Skrzypczyński, Henryk Maliczak (1942–43). *IPN 47430*

Transports

29. Passenger train from Łódź ghetto arrives at Koło station (1942). *IPN 50377*

30. Victims transferring to narrow-gauge train (1942). *IPN 00498*

31. Victims loaded and waiting for departure to Powiercie (1942). *ŻIH*

32. Close-up of victims in narrow-gauge freight wagon (1942). *ŻIH*

33. Victims arriving at Powiercie (1942). *IPN 00499*

34. Transfer of belongings to trucks for transport from Powiercie to Chełmno (1942). *ZL*

Mansion grounds

35. View of the mansion grounds from the Koło-Dąbie highway (Oct 1945). *YV 4063_7*

36. The granary building housed the Jewish laborers and craftsmen during the second period of the camp's operation (Feb 1945). *IPN 50380*

37. Interior of the granary building (Feb 1945). *IPN 50381*

38. Remains of the last Jewish workers and two Sonderkommando members killed during the final liquidation of the camp (Feb 1945). *IPN 50385*

Forest camp

39. Remnants of the crematoria (May 1945). *IPN 50390*

40. Rails used in the construction of the crematoria (May 1945). *IPN 50391*

41. Remnants of the main guard house (May 1945). *IPN 11253*

42. Remnants of unidentified structures on the edge of the main clearing (May 1945). *IPN 11296*

Members of Jewish labor squads who escaped from the camp.

43. Abram Rój (1946). *SR*

44. Szlama Winer (1942). *ŻIH*

45. Michał Podchlebnik (1945). *AGO*

46. Yerachmiel Widawski (1946). *HW*

47. Szymon Srebrnik (1961). *GPO D409-018*

48. Mieczysław Żurawski (1961). *GPO*

49. Death camp survivors at the Chełmno trial in Bonn, West Germany. Seated from left: Mieczysław Żurawski, Michał Podchlebnik, Max Podchlebnik (relative from US), Szymon Srebrnik (Jan 1963). *YV 7452_12*

Monument in memory of the victims of the Chełmno death camp in the Rzuchów Forest.

50. Monument under construction (Jul 1964). *ZL*

51. Monument completed: *Pamiętamy* - We Remember (1987). *PM*

The penalty for successfully escaping or attempting to escape from the camp was severe. After the escape of Abram Rój, Szlama Winer stated 16 men from the labor squad were called out and shot in reprisal for his flight. Winer and Podchlebnik knew then the price their companions would pay as a direct result of their escape. They also realized that all the men were doomed anyway. The question was not if, but when they would all be killed. It is not known how many men had to step forward and pay the ultimate price as a result of their escape.

As preventative measures against future escape attempts, two changes were made in the way the camp operated. All the men in the Jewish labor squads were forced to wear leg irons. Jan Oliskiewicz, the Pole who was held prisoner in the basement of the mansion in connection with the Kaszyński affair, reported hearing the clanging of chains just two weeks after the first three men escaped. The prisoners in the Waldkommando were henceforth transported to and from the forest camp inside the gas vans. Nevertheless, these measures did not deter the prisoners from trying, and even succeeding, to escape from the death camp.

First Liquidation of the Camp

At the beginning of March 1943, Arthur Greiser had already informed Hans Bothmann that the camp would be closed. There are no documents specifically stating why this decision was made, yet the fact that Chełmno was closed at this time even as the extermination program continued to devour thousands of Jewish victims daily in the Aktion Reinhard camps is evidence of the administrative divide between Chełmno and the death camps of Treblinka, Sobibór and Bełżec, and the control exercised by Greiser within his Gau.

As stated in the Höppner memorandum, Chełmno was established to solve a local problem of feeding an estimated 100,000 unproductive, "useless eaters" in the Warthegau. This mission was deemed accomplished following the deportations from Łódź in September 1942. All Jews remaining in the territory were sealed in the Łódź ghetto or labor camps. However, Chełmno was not closed for another seven months. Greiser continued to push his plan to exterminate 35,000 (non-Jewish) Poles suffering from tuberculosis, with Chełmno being the obvious destination for these intended victims.[1] Moreover, the task of digging up and destroying the bodies in the Rzuchów Forest was only getting started in the fall of 1942. The fact that neither Hitler nor Himmler ordered Greiser to accept further transports originating from areas outside his Gau testifies that the Gauleiter was given broad authority regarding his Jewish problem.

On September 11, 1942, the order to halt the extermination campaign in the Wartheland came down from Poznań.[2] The following day Biebow informed the residents of the Łódź ghetto that the transports would cease. This meant that the *raison d'etre* of Chełmno—the murder of the so-called unproductive population—had also come to an end. While a few additional transports did arrive at the camp, it appears that these arrived due to the "convenience" that the Sonderkommando was still in place, rather than as part of a continuing systematic campaign.

Bothmann's tasks now became expediting the plundered belongings of the victims and eventually eliminating all traces of the camp. In the forest the exhumation and burning of the corpses probably continued until February 1943, when the last crematorium was blown up and the bricks collected and hauled away. All the equipment, including the excavator and the bone grinder, was removed and shipped out by train from Koło. All structures were destroyed, except the wooden fence that surrounded the forest camp.

Trees were planted over areas in the clearings where the graves had been in order to eliminate all traces that a death factory had once functioned there. By November 1942, 50,000 bundles of seedlings had been acquired. Another 22,000 birch seedlings were taken from the nearby village of Gaj toward the end of March.[3] The planting of the seedlings in the area completed the clean-up and cover-up in the forest. The gates to the former forest camp were locked and the keys given to the forester.[4] Meanwhile, at the mansion, the belongings of the victims had to be searched, sorted, packed and shipped to the warehouses in Dąbrowa.

These tasks took some seven months, from September 1942 until March 1943, and were not actually completed even by that time. Many corpses remained buried in the forest. The length of time involved, some seven months, was not due so much to the amount of work that needed to be done, as to the fact that, according to Walter Burmeister, Bothmann was in no hurry to complete his assignment and be sent to the front.[5]

Members of the Sonderkommando had no complaints about their assignment in Chełmno. They earned extra money for the duty and received extra rations. On weekends, they went to the movie house in Koło, and they enjoyed numerous drunken parties with female companions in the local restaurants. At one of these celebrations, a member of the Sonderkommando went into the kitchen and demanded some bullion. When the cook refused, the SS man drew his revolver and said "You have to give it to me; I am from Chełmno."[6] Bothmann hosted his own share of parties as the local schoolteacher recalled.

> I taught in the old school in Chełmno located just opposite the quarters of the SS Kommando. Bothmann and his men arranged orgies there almost every day with German girls and women who were, as far as I know, mainly nurses from the hospital in Koło. In the morning Bothmann would throw these women, frequently drunk and unclothed, out into the street so that the schoolchildren

could see them. I complained about this to the inspector of schools. The result was that at first the school was moved into the rectory and finally closed in October 1942.[7]

Perhaps Walter Burmeister best conveyed how SS Sonderkommando Kulmhof felt about its assignment. Killing 1,000 men, women and children a day was not considered a particularly depressing task.

> The SS men did not have to stay in their houses at night; they could go wherever they wanted. The atmosphere in the camp was not depressing. We were all doing well. Sometimes we went to see a movie in Koło. Many of us played skat when we were off-duty. We drank relatively large amounts of alcohol because everyone's ration was half a liter of vodka per week. There was also beer, which we could buy without any problem. Practically all of us had girlfriends and they were allowed to stay with us for the night. The mood among us was mostly good.[8]

On March 5, 1943, Gauleiter Greiser arrived in Chełmno with an entourage of SS officials. The SS Sonderkommando and the Polizeiwachtkommando were ordered to assemble in the courtyard of the mansion. Greiser announced that the camp would shortly be liquidated. In the name of the Führer, he thanked everyone for the work they had done and each man was rewarded with a special four-week vacation. Greiser proposed that they spend it, free of charge, on one of his estates. Everyone was then invited to a final farewell party that evening in Koło.

The party took place in a large room in the Riga restaurant. It began with a dinner and was followed with speeches by Greiser and Bothmann. Dr. Otto Bradfisch, the head of the Łódź Gestapo, was also in attendance. According to one of the guards, Alois Häfele was personally promoted by Greiser to Revierleutnant. The party ended about one or two in the morning with everyone drunk and asleep at the tables.[9]

After the party, Greiser returned to Poznań and, on March 19, wrote a letter to Reichsführer Heinrich Himmler praising the Sonderkommando for a job well done.

Reichsführer!

A couple of days ago I visited the former Sonderkommando Lange, which is presently under the command of Hauptsturmführer and Kriminalkommissar Bothmann, as the Sonderkommando in Kulmhof, Warthbrücken County, will have ended their activity by the end of the month. Moreover, I found the attitude of the members of the Sonderkommando such that I would like to inform you, Reichsführer, about this. They not only faithfully and bravely fulfilled their duties, but also represented the best of *Soldatentum*.

For example, at the fellowship evening to which I invited them, they handed me a donation of RM 15,150, which they had spontaneously collected that same day. This means that each of the 85 men of the Sonderkommando gave RM 180. I gave this money to the Fund for the Children of Murdered Volksdeutsche, if you, Reichsführer, do not wish to use this money for any other purpose.

The men have also shown their desire to remain under the direct command of Hauptsturmführer Bothmann. I have promised them, Reichsführer, to pass this wish on to you.

I also ask you to allow me to invite these men, during the vacation due them, partly as guests on my estate and also to give them financial help in order to embellish their vacation.

Heil Hitler, Greiser[10]

Several days after the party, most of the Polizeiwachtkommando and some members of the Sonderkommando left Chełmno for their four-week vacation. Those who remained began the final physical liquidation of the camp.

The Jewish labor squads, including the craftsmen living and working in the basement, were killed as their work was completed. May, the forester, reported that they were "eliminated" and burned.[11] According to one member of the Sonderkommando they were shot by Albert Plate.[12] During the last few months, people who lived in the area frequently heard shooting coming from the forest camp. Henryk Maliczak stated that the final group of Jewish workers was shot. He and his fellow workers then buried them.[13]

On September 19, 1942, Stanisław Szymański, one of the Polish workers, was taken to Bothmann's office and questioned in regard to stealing jewelry that the Sonderkommando had "confiscated" from the victims. It is not known how Szymański responded to the charge but following the meeting he returned to the apartment in the mansion and told his colleagues that he was being taken back to Poznań and probably wouldn't return. Szymański was driven off, but the vehicle returned after 60 to 90 minutes, too short a period for a round trip to Poznań.[14] Szymański is believed to have been shot in the forest. Bothmann apparently found out that Szymański was providing jewelry to a local woman who he frequently visited. (Szymański's wife stayed with this person when she came to Chełmno earlier for a two week visit.) This friend had two sisters who lived in Łódź and who sold the goods to a German jeweler in town. The jeweler is believed to have brought the matter to the attention of the authorities. Szymański's friend was arrested and sent to Auschwitz. She survived the war.[15]

The six remaining Polish workers stayed to the end, eventually replacing the Jewish labor squads. These men had considered stealing a car and escaping to Warsaw, but feared what would happen to their families if they did.[16] It was during the liquidation of the camp that one of the drunken German soldiers accidentally shot Mania in the leg. He was taken to the hospital in Koło (admitted as 'Heinrich' Mania), where he was treated.[17] The other Poles were taken back to the Fort VII prison in Poznań,[18] where Mania joined them after his release from the hospital.

At the mansion, everything was removed that would indicate a camp had once existed there. The board fence surrounding the mansion grounds was dismantled and taken away. Laabs and Hering drove the gas vans to the train station in Koło. Burmeister and Bürstinger loaded them on a train and then returned to Chełmno.[19]

On April 7, 1943, the villagers in Chełmno were told to open all the windows of their houses, take their livestock to the other side of the river and wait. At about noon, a loud explosion was heard. Standartenführer Paul Blobel had returned. Despite extensive preparations, he only partly succeeded in blowing up the mansion.[20]

That same evening Fritz Herkner, the administrator of the Powiercie estate and a friend of Bothmann[21], arrived on the scene with a group of his workers. Their task was to dismantle what remained of the structure and to salvage what they could from the smoldering ruins. First, they removed ten wagon loads of wood. Then bricks were hauled off, followed by tools, bowls and chains. Everything was carted off to the estate in Powiercie. Inside the granary, which was not destroyed, the upper floor was full of clothes and shoes. These too were taken to Powiercie and probably distributed among the local German population or sold to the local Poles.[22]

Later, rummaging through the ruins of the mansion, items found by local villagers included Christian religious relics, including pictures, crucifixes, rosaries and medals. This confirmed that non-Jews were also victims of the camp.[23] A local farmer was allowed to plow over the area and cultivate it. He also uncovered various items, including spoons, knives and destroyed papers.[24]

A small guard detachment, composed of 13 policemen, was organized from several local police posts. They occupied the presbytery in Chełmno. The head of the detachment is said to have come from Sompolno. Their assignment was to guard the forest area as it remained "off limits" to the public.[25] On April 11, 1943, the remaining members of SS Sonderkommando Kulmhof drove out of the village and returned to their respective police districts.[26]

Two weeks earlier, on March 29, after receiving Greiser's letter in praise of SS Sonderkommando Kulmhof, Himmler's office sent a letter to Ernst Kaltenbrunner, the head of RSHA.

Dear Gruppenführer,

Enclosed I am sending to you a copy of a letter written on March 19, 1943 by Gauleiter and Reichsstatthalter Greiser to the Reichsführer SS.

The Reichsführer SS wishes that the 85 men under the command of Hauptsturmführer Bothmann, after their leave, will be employed as a unit of the SS Volunteer Division Prinz Eugen.

The Reichsführer SS asks you to assemble these men once again before they start their service and categorically oblige them to strike out the period of their membership in the Sonderkommando and not to mention it even in conversations.

The head of the Führerungshauptamt Gruppenführer Jüttner received only the information that in the course of April the 85-man unit, together with their commander, may be assigned to the SS Volunteer Division "Prinz Eugen."

SS Obersturmbannführer[27]

Shortly afterwards, each member of the Sonderkommando received an order to report to the RSHA in Berlin. They were met there by Bothmann and Hüfing, who had brought the Polizeiwachtkommando from Łódź. In a speech given by Obergruppenführer Ernst Kaltenbrunner (Heydrich's replacement), the assembled Sonderkommando was thanked once more for its service in the name of the Führer and the German nation. They were again reminded that in the future they were to remain silent about everything they knew concerning Chełmno. Finally, he informed them that they would all be going on a new assignment under Bothmann's command.[28]

The Sonderkommando was later assembled in Vienna and together they went to the Banat, where they were outfitted and then marched on foot to Belgrade. In Belgrade, the men were loaded onto a train and taken to Sarajevo, where the group was divided into two military field police detachments. Later, the Sonderkommando served in Mostar in Bosnia and Hercegovina, as well as in Croatia. The commanding officers were Bothmann and Hüfing.[29]

The break in the camp's activity lasted almost one year, from April 11, 1943, to March 19, 1944. The Sonderkommando, incorporated into the Waffen-SS as part of the 7th SS Volunteer Mountain Division Prinz Eugen, was transferred to the Balkans to engage in anti-partisan warfare. It is not known why the Sonderkommando received this particular assignment, only that, according to the above-cited letter, it was Himmler's wish. If Bothmann's superiors in Berlin hoped this would eliminate many of the eyewitnesses to their policy of genocide, they would not be disappointed. Deputy commandant Albert Plate, gas van driver Oskar Hering and several of the policemen were killed and many others wounded. Following the closure of the other death camps, personnel from Treblinka, Sobibór and Bełżec were also sent to the Balkans where many of them were killed, most notably SS Hauptsturmführer Christian Wirth, the inspector of those camps. Despite these assignments, others previously involved in the extermination of the Jews, such as Einsatzkommando personnel, were not assigned to hazardous duty; Otto Bradfisch being just one example. Regardless of the motives of RSHA, Bothmann was undoubtedly not pleased with his new orders. As noted earlier, the commandant of Chełmno was not eager to see frontline duty.

Polizeimeister Willi Lenz, the supervisor of the forest camp, was not sent to Yugoslavia with the rest of the Sonderkommando. In November 1943, he was assigned, on the basis of his expertise in burning human bodies, to a new formation: Sonderkommando Legath.[30]

This group was assembled in the Gestapo office in Inowrocław (Hohensalza) and commanded by Kriminalkommissar and Hauptsturmführer Dr. Johannes Legath. Other members included Kriminalobersekretare and Sturmscharführere Wilhelm Schmerse, Erich Michaelis and Walter Piller, as well as a 30-man police detachment, commanded by Polizeileutnant Ernst "Max" Burmeister (no relation to Walter Burmeister), which was transferred from Łódź and assigned to guard duty for the "Wetterkommando," as the unit was also known. Drivers for the Sonderkommando were Hauptscharführere Ernst Thiele, who had previously served in the Fort VII prison, and Hermann Gielow.

The task of the Wetterkommando was to exhume and burn the bodies of those victims of the mass executions carried out by Sonderkommando Lange and others since the beginning of the war. The SS personnel, of course, did not dig up the corpses. A Jewish labor squad of 30 men was assembled from the Łódź ghetto to do the actual dirty work. They had to accomplish this task while shackled in leg irons to prevent escape. Twice during the course of the operation, 50 Jews were brought by truck for this purpose.

Four Poles were employed to supervise the Jewish workers. Polizeimeister Willi Lenz drove to Poznań and picked up Leszek Jaskólski, Henryk Maliczak, Henryk Mania and Kajetan Skrzypczyński, all well trained for such work.[31] Maps of the gravesites were obtained from the Inspector of the Security Police in Poznań, Brigadeführer Ernst Damzog, and the hideous work began. Even with the maps, Piller later stated that finding some of these sites would have been impossible without the help of these Poles who had been to the locations earlier when the victims were buried. The work of this squad was periodically subject to inspection by the head of the Poznań Gestapo, Obersturmbannführer Heinz Stossberg and the aforementioned Inspector of the Security Police and Security Service, Brigadeführer Ernst Damzog.[32]

The Wetterkommando was disbanded in the spring of 1944, although the more appropriate word would be "transferred," for almost the entire unit was sent to Chełmno to reopen the camp. Legath's Jewish labor squad was shot, stacked up and burned when they were no longer needed.[33] Schmerse, Piller, Lenz, Thiele, Gielow, along with Burmeister and his police detachment all served in Chełmno during the second period of the camp's operation. The four Poles were returned to Fort VII and later transferred to the Żabikowo (Poggenburg) transit camp of the Poznań Gestapo.[34] (For the subsequent fate of the Polish workers see Appendix III: Fates of Key Figures.)

In August 1943, Erwin Bürstinger, Max Sommer and Alois Häfele were dismissed from the Prinz Eugen Division in Yugoslavia, according to Häfele, because they were over the age of 45. They were then assigned to a reserve detachment in Weimar. In April 1944, they received a teletype from Bothmann ordering them to report back to Chełmno.[35]

CHAPTER 3

Extermination: The Second Period (1944–1945)

Re-Establishing the Camp

B etween the closure of Chełmno in April 1943 and its re-establishment a year later, Germany faced a number of defeats on the battlefield. German forces had already surrendered at Stalingrad, the Red Army's long march to Berlin had begun and Allied bombing over the Reich intensified. In May 1943, German and Italian forces surrendered in North Africa. By the end of 1943, the Allies were pressing up the Italian boot and the Russians had retaken Kiev.

Gauleiter Arthur Greiser was also under pressure. Himmler opposed the idea of employing Jews in ghettos for the manufacturing industry, particularly with respect to war materiel. Following the Warsaw Ghetto Uprising in April-May 1943, the Reichsführer was intent on closing all ghettos and labor camps or at least placing them under control of the SS. By the end of 1943, numerous labor camps had closed and the Jewish laborers were deported to Auschwitz. As a result, Greiser lost substantial income from the terminated projects.

Himmler also had his eye on the Łódź ghetto. In June 1943, he declared the ghetto was to be reclassified as a concentration camp and placed under the authority of Gruppenführer Odilo Globocnik, the SS and Police Leader in Lublin, and recommended transferring the ghetto's skilled labor and machinery to concentration camps under his control. Greiser found allies to maintain control of the ghetto with the Wehrmacht's Weapons Inspectorate and the Ministry of Armament and War Production (Albert Speer). The issue remained unresolved until the end of the year when Himmler again stated the ghetto would become a concentration camp administered by Obergruppenführer Oswald Pohl's Economic and Administrative Main Office [Wirtschafts Verwaltungshauptamt, WVHA], responsible for the concentration camps. Both sides of the conflict pushed their positions on the ghetto's profitability or lack thereof. At a meeting on February 9, 1944, Greiser's representatives demanded some RM 20 million for the ghetto's machinery and a portion of future profits should the ghetto transfer to

SS control. Three days later, Himmler was in Poznań discussing the issue personally with Greiser. As a result of this meeting, Greiser maintained control over the ghetto but, in exchange, he agreed to begin closing the Jewish enclave. The meeting also led to reactivating SS Sonderkommando Kulmhof. Details have been preserved in the following document, a letter by Greiser to his adversary in the matter, Oswald Pohl.

Posen, February 14, 1944

Top Secret!

Dear Party Comrade Pohl,

On the occasion of the Reichsführer's visit to Posen yesterday and today, I had the opportunity to discuss and clear up two issues concerning your sphere of activity. The first issue is this:

The ghetto in Litzmannstadt is not to be transformed into a concentration camp, as was pointed out by Oberführer Beier and Hauptsturmführer Dr. Volk, who were sent to my Gau by your office. Their discussions took place in my office, in the Reichsstatthalter in Posen, on the 5th of February. The decree issued by the Reichsführer on June 11, 1943, will therefore not be carried out. I have arranged the following with the Reichsführer:

(a) The ghetto's manpower will be reduced to a minimum and retain only as many Jews as are essential to the war economy.
(b) The ghetto therefore remains a Gau ghetto of the Wartheland.
(c) The reduction will be carried out by Hauptsturmführer Bothmann's special Sonderkommando, which has already had prior experience in the Gau. The Reichsführer will give orders to withdraw Hauptsturmführer Bothmann and his Sonderkommando from his mission in Croatia and again place him at the disposal of the Wartheland.
(d) The utilization and administration of the contents of the ghetto remains in the hands of the Wartheland.
(e) After all Jews are removed from the ghetto and it is liquidated, the entire grounds of the ghetto are to go to the town of Litzmannstadt. The Reichsführer will then give appropriate instructions to the Main Trustee Office East [Haupttreuhandstelle Ost].

May I ask you to send me your suggestions in this matter as soon as possible.

With comradely greetings and

Heil Hitler
Yours

Greiser[1]

According to point (c) of the above letter, it was Himmler who ordered Bothmann to return to Chełmno. In Croatia, Bothmann assembled most of the members of the Sonderkommando and informed them that they would be returning to Chełmno to reestablish the camp and resume their former activities. Initially the Sonderkommando traveled to Berlin where Bothmann announced that they would be notified where and when to assemble. He then dismissed them. Shortly thereafter, they individually received orders to report to the Gestapo office in Poznań. Once assembled in Poznań, Bothmann informed them that they would go to Koło by train and from there by truck to Chełmno.[2] Bothmann was officially assigned to head Section C in Department IV of the Poznań Gestapo Office, which dealt with enemies of the regime.[3]

In his notes for mid-March, Stanisław Rubach, the journalist from the nearby town of Kościelec, recorded that the Sonderkommando was back in Chełmno.

> March 19, 1944, after a yearlong break, the news is circulating about the resumption of the camp in Chełmno. Basically preparations at the old granary on the estate are in full swing; it's being fenced, etc. The people living in the houses nearby were removed. There are already more than 100 of the butchers [in the village].[4]

The reassembled SS Sonderkommando Kulmhof, once back in Chełmno, resumed their old duties with the following personnel:

Hauptsturmführer Hans Bothmann - commandant
Unterscharführer [promoted] Walter Burmeister - Bothmann's driver and adjutant
Hauptscharführer Herbert Hiecke-Richter - valuables[5]
Hauptscharführer Wilhelm Görlich - administration
Hauptscharführer Erwin Bürstinger - motor pool
Hauptscharführer Gustav Laabs - gas van driver
Hauptscharführer Erwin (Erich) Schmidt - canteen and provisions
Hauptscharführer Johannes Runge - supervisor of crematorium
Unterscharführer Erich Kretschmer - supervisor of crematorium
Unterscharführer Max Sommer - assistant to Görlich
Sturmscharführer Alois Häfele - supervisor of Jewish labor
Polizeimeister Willi Lenz - supervisor of the forest camp

In addition, the following individuals were transferred to SS Sonderkommando Kulmhof, having previously served together in Legath's "Wetterkommando":

Oberscharführer Walter Piller - deputy commandant
Hauptscharführer Hermann Gielow - driver
Hauptscharführer Ernst Thiele - driver
Scharführer Stefan Seidenglanz - driver

Bothmann was again commander of the Sonderkommando. Walter Piller served as deputy commander. Albert Plate, Bothmann's deputy during the first period of the camp's operations, remained in the Balkans and died there on October 4, 1944.[6] According to Piller, Sturmscharführer Wilhelm Schmerse who was transferred to Chełmno with him from the Wetterkommando was to be Bothmann's deputy. Schmerse stayed only two days in Chełmno and then left due to a stomach ailment.[7]

Members of the Sonderkommando were well provided for, receiving the largest ration allotment permitted, as well as washing powder and soap. In addition, every ten days, each member received a bottle of liquor and 100 cigarettes. Every 15 days, Görlich distributed an extra pay allotment to the men serving in the camp. The police guard received RM 12 per day, members of the SS and Revierleutnant Ernst Burmeister, the head of the Polizeiwachtkommando, received RM 15 per day, and Bothmann received RM 18 per day. Bothmann also received an additional allotment of liquor and cigarettes for entertaining guests such as Gauleiter Greiser and officials from Łódź. The costs for these benefits were covered by the GSV and Governor's Office in Poznań.[8]

As the camp was completely liquidated in 1943, the first task of the Sonderkommando was to re-establish it. Rudolf Kramp from the Łódź Ghetto Administration, a frequent visitor who had total access to the camp, was one of those who delivered supplies, as well as victims, to Chełmno. He later gave the following account.

> In March 1944, I delivered furniture to Chełmno, which I unloaded in front of the staff building. Several days later, I delivered cement, which I unloaded next to the granary on the grounds of the former mansion. Burmeister, Richter and Runge took the cement from me. At this time, there were no Jewish workers in Chełmno. They carried the cement themselves. The area of the mansion was not fenced. There were no sentries. Several days later, I delivered more furniture. Altogether, at this time, I made about six trips. Besides me, Oswald Gossele also drove to Chełmno. I saw that barracks were being built and that the terrain was being fenced in. I delivered boards several times. The fence was being built by the SS men. At the end of April, Jewish workers were brought to Chełmno. Tusst and Schwind from the Gestapo brought them. About this same time, I brought a load of iron rails and thick sheet iron. I believe that this was at the end of April 1944. Policemen and SS men were brought in to supplement the Sonderkommando. At this time, other than Bothmann, I met Piller (Bothmann's deputy), Richter, Runge, Schmidt, Görlich, Lenz, Sommer, Laabs, Bürstinger and two others from Łódź.[9]

The Sonderkommando enclosed the grounds of the former mansion not with a wooden fence as in the first period, but with a barbed wire fence supported by concrete posts. Every few meters a sign was attached to the fence with a skull and crossbones and the inscription "electrified," although in fact the fence was not electrified.[10] Inside the enclosure, a second fence surrounded the granary building.

As in the first period, Bothmann maintained a group of skilled Jewish craftsmen in the camp. As the mansion no longer existed, the Jewish work details and the craftsmen were quartered in the granary building. Again little is known about these craftsmen during this second period. None survived the final liquidation of the camp and they are seldom mentioned in testimonies. However, a document did survive the war and found its way into the State Central Archives in Moscow. Part of the Anti-Fascist Jewish Committee Collection, the document comprises a notebook written by the craftsmen themselves. Its contents, as can be expected, are a final farewell to family members and pleas for revenge rather than a chronicle of events that occurred in the camp. The notebook was given to a Polish farmer for safekeeping and turned over to the Red Army when it entered Chełmno. The craftsmen worked on the upper floor in the granary. The door leading upstairs may have been kept locked so as to limit direct contact with the other Jewish workers. (They could, however, communicate by talking through the floor.) It is not known what freedom of movement was available to them or if these people were ever let out of that upstairs room.

This group was composed of approximately 15 tailors and five shoe-makers (the numbers, of course, varied with every execution). They worked not only for the Sonderkommando, making civilian clothes and uniforms, but also for other German dignitaries, such as Greiser and Biebow. (During this period Greiser visited Chełmno at least once, and Biebow visited several times.) The raw materials used by the craftsmen were provided by the incoming transports. It was said that Bothmann had 17 pairs of boots.[11] These craftsmen, as a group, would survive until the final liquidation of the camp.

Next to the granary a large wooden barrack was built. Inside it were two rooms. The walls of the first room were lined with shelves and served as a temporary storeroom for various items taken from the victims. The other room served as an office for Walter Burmeister.[12]

A shredding machine was brought to the camp from the Łódź ghetto. Nicknamed "the wolf," it was positioned on the side of the barrack facing the river, on a 3-by-5 meter platform, and used to shred the low-quality clothing into rags, which were packed and shipped to the Łódź ghetto.

A huge tent was erected on the opposite side of the barrack. According to Piller it was approximately 80 meters long, 15 meters wide and six meters high[13] and served as the sorting room and a storage area for the items brought into the camp.

Next to the tent, a deep hole was dug in the ground. A fire was kept burning in it to serve as an incinerator for "worthless" personal items (such as photographs, personal papers, passports, letters, etc.) discovered among the belongings of the victims during the searching and sorting process.[14] Several such pits would be dug.

Meanwhile, two wooden barracks were built in the forest, some 150 to 200 meters from the main road.[15] In this second period, these barracks served the function that the mansion had filled in the first period - that of a reception area for undressing and an antechamber to the gas vans. The barracks were approximately ten meters wide by 20 meters long and stood side by side. They were located in the forest near the large field in which the new crematoria would be built. There were no windows on the sides facing the field. The barracks were entered through doors on the opposite side, away from the field. A wooden fence was built to enclose these two barracks.[16]

Two weeks after the Sonderkommando arrived back in Chełmno, the gas vans arrived by train in Koło.[17] Gustav Laabs, the gas van driver, would later recall those first days back in the village:

> In Chełmno, we returned to our old quarters in the village houses. On the days that followed, I had no work at all nor was I given any. As far as I remember, nothing had been built or started in the village including the area of the former mansion. [...] After a short time Hering[18] and I were ordered by Bothmann to go to the railroad station in Koło and pick up the two gas vans. [...] Walter Burmeister drove us by car to the Koło train station where two gas vans stood on a freight train. In my opinion, they were the same gas vans which we had driven during 1942–3. We brought the vans to Chełmno and parked them on the grounds of the former mansion.[19]

After the two barracks were built in the forest and the grounds of the former mansion were secured with a barbed wire fence, the first transport of Jewish workers from the Łódź ghetto was brought to the camp by truck. (In contrast to the first period, there were no Polish prisoners in the camp during the second period.) Included in this first transport was 13-year-old Szymon Srebrnik:

> In March 1944, I was caught in a surprise roundup organized in the ghetto while riding a tram and taken to Bałucki market. Trucks from Chełmno were there. Together with 50 other Jews caught in the roundup, we were loaded into the trucks and driven away. [...]
>
> They took us to Chełmno and put us in the granary on the grounds of the [former] mansion. There were no other Jews there. We found out that we were in a camp of a Sonderkommando. After an hour, we were divided into two groups. The stronger and better workers were sent to the forest, creating the so-called "Waldkommando." The weaker and younger workers, including me, stayed and worked as the so-called "Hauskommando." [...] About 40 Jews were assigned to the Waldkommando, the others to the Hauskommando. Everyone was shackled in leg-irons. The chains restricted the legs in such a way that it was not possible to take normal steps, only small ones. [...]
>
> The workers were given 20 dekagrams [about seven ounces] of bread a day, coffee in the morning and half a liter of soup for lunch. Only after the arrival of the first transport [of victims] did we receive blankets.[20]

Unique among all the Jewish workers in Chełmno, Srebrnik managed to survive the camp's entire second period, approximately eight-and-a-half months. His survival was due mainly to Walter Burmeister, who took a special liking to the boy. Burmeister personally intervened many times during the "selections" which the workers underwent approximately every week. Once during a selection, when Srebrnik had been in the camp for three months, he was asked how long he had been there. When he said two days the German began swearing at him, calling him a liar. Srebrnik began crying. Burmeister stepped up and said something to the man and Srebrnik was left alone. Another time when Bothmann was going to shoot 15 workers, as retribution for an escape attempt, Burmeister told Srebrnik to go to the office and scrub the floor, in order to get him out of Bothmann's sight.[21] Burmeister told Srebrnik that "when the war is over, you can come home with me and be my son."[22]

Srebrnik had a beautiful singing voice and sang often for the amusement of the camp staff. Among the various tasks assigned to him in the camp, he gathered food for rabbits that Bothmann kept. During these guarded food-gathering excursions, sometimes in a boat along the river, Srebrnik would sing. His voice carried a great distance and the people in the village could hear the singing. They nicknamed him "Śpiewak" [the singer].[23]

Srebrnik primarily worked for Burmeister. In the mornings, after the Waldkommando had left for the forest, Srebrnik cleaned the granary. Together with Burmeister, he would take drinking water to those working in the forest and occasionally collect that day's haul of gold teeth which had been extracted from the mouths of the victims. Then back at "Burmeister's office" he sat on a little chair and separated the gold from the teeth with a small hammer. As the camp had no running water, Srebrnik also hauled drinking water from the river up to the camp.

The initial task of the Hauskommando was a grisly one. The immediate area of the former mansion reeked with a foul stench. The commando was ordered to remove the rubble from the basement of the ruins. After digging down into the basement area, they discovered a number of rotting corpses, and pieces of corpses, including those of children. The workers were ordered to load these corpses onto a truck that subsequently took them to the forest camp.[24] The ground was then filled in again. It is not known who these victims were. In his notes, Rubach stated that people were inside the mansion when it was blown up. He was under the impression that they were the last group of Jewish workers.[25] According to Srebrnik, as the bodies were being removed, it was said that they were mental patients.

Meanwhile, the group of Jewish workers who were taken each morning to the forest, the Waldkommando, began building two large crematoria. Initially, the workers did not know what they were building but simply followed the instructions given to them. Runge supervised the construction, choosing to build the ovens just a couple of meters north of the location of the last ovens constructed in 1942. Runge received an extra bottle of liquor when the crematoria were completed.[26]

The foundations of the crematoria were approximately three-and-a-half meters below ground. The walls widened as they approached ground level, reaching dimensions of approximately 17 meters long by 17 meters wide. They were made of fireproofed bricks brought from a factory in Koło. The grating was made of rails for train track, the ones brought from Łódź by Rudolf Kramp. To ventilate the fire, each oven had air vents on either side. The vents provided a flow of air down into the ash pit. To clean out the oven, the workers had to pass through a chute, about eight meters long, which led down to the ash pit. The chute was tall enough so that a man could, while stooping, walk through it.[27] The entire apparatus was underground. There were no chimneys. When the ovens were not in use, a removable roof made of pine branches was placed over them as camouflage from aerial observation.[28]

The Jews employed in building the crematoria were often killed for the amusement of the Sonderkommando. Bothmann and Lenz particularly distinguished themselves in these atrocities. Srebrnik recalled one such "game."

> Bothmann would select a group of Jews and say, "You see this finger? If I move it this way, you will stand and if it moves that way, you will lie down." It was up and down, and up and down, until we were completely out of breath. When he wasn't looking I wouldn't get up [...] so that I was not so tired. Finally, he would whip out his pistol and shoot all those who remained lying down.[29]

Mieczysław (or Mordechai, but known in the camp as Max) Żurawski, the only other Jewish survivor from the second period, arrived in Chełmno with Transport VII from the Łódź ghetto. He survived another game played by the SS. Sundays were generally a day of rest in the camp. Bored members of the Sonderkommando would order a few of the prisoners to line up so that, "[...] we were placed in a row; each man had a bottle on his head and they amused themselves by shooting at the bottles. When the bottle was hit the man survived, but if the bullet was low of the mark he was killed."[30]

Of the approximately 30 workers sent to the forest each day, it was not uncommon that only half of them would return to the granary at the end of the day. The group of workers was continually supplemented with new workers brought from Łódź. Eight times during the initial period of re-establishing the camp, fresh workers, in groups of 30, were brought to the camp from Łódź.[31] When the first transport of victims arrived on June 23, only 18 Jewish workers remained alive in the camp. The others had all been killed. The bodies were buried in a sand pile together with the corpses that had been removed from the basement area of the former mansion. Later, when the crematoria were ready, these bodies were burned along with approximately 15 German officers, who were brought to the forest camp in leg irons and shot.[32]

Revierleutnant Ernst Burmeister initially headed the Polizeiwachtkommando during this second period. He and his 40-man police squad had just completed their service in Legath's Sonderkommando, which exhumed and burnt the bodies of victims of earlier atrocities. Burmeister later recounted his arrival to Chełmno.

[Bothmann] assigned us some empty houses in the village as accommodation. Then I asked Bothmann what was going on in Kulmhof and what the task of my squad would be. He explained to me that an extermination camp for Jews had been set up near Kulmhof in the forest. He and a squad of SS men had just been building several barracks and a crematorium there. When this was completed, transports of Jews would come to Kulmhof. These Jews would first be accommodated in the church in the village and then transported to the forest camp and killed there. The corpses would be burnt in the crematorium. My task was merely to secure the entire forest camp from outside. He then ordered me to place sentries around the forest camp. [...] On the first day [in Kulmhof], Bothmann drove me to the so-called forest camp. [...] Two barracks and a crematorium were constructed in a clearing. The clearing was about 120 meters long and 80 meters wide. Bothmann told me to place a line of sentries around the camp [...] and I did so. Later, when the actual extermination of the Jews was being carried out, he told me that more sentries would have to be placed inside the forest camp. [...] After about 14 days or three weeks, the forest camp was ready and the first transports of Jews arrived.[33]

Approximately 40 additional policemen were transferred from Łódź to the camp. When the area around the former mansion was prepared and secured, and all preparations in the forest were completed, transports again began to arrive at the camp.

A New Killing Procedure

With the preparations for the camp complete, Proclamation 416 appeared in the Łódź ghetto on June 16, 1944, calling for voluntary registration for labor outside the ghetto. Incentives for volunteering included gifts of clothing, shoes, linen, socks and the immediate opportunity to collect food rations. The Gestapo issued instructions concerning these transports to the Jewish Administration in the ghetto. The instructions were duly noted in the ghetto Chronicle.

Memorandum:

On Monday, Wednesday and Friday of each week, a shipment of 1,000 people is to depart for labor outside the ghetto. The first transport is to leave on Wednesday, June 21, 1944 (about 600). The transports are to be numbered (with roman numerals: Transport I, and so forth). Each departing worker is assigned a transport number. The individual is to wear his number, and it is also to be attached to his luggage. Fifteen to 20 kilograms of luggage per person are allowed. [...][1]

After a delay of two days from the original start date (due allegedly to the unavailability of freight cars), the first transport departed for "work outside the ghetto." From the Chronicle:

Friday, June 23, 1944

[...] The first transport of 562 people left Radogoszcz station this morning at eight o'clock in the morning. Before their departure, Gestapo Commissioner [Gunter] Fuchs made a few reassuring remarks. He stated that they would be working in the Reich and that decent food would be provided. For lack of passenger cars, they would initially be loaded onto freight cars but be transferred to passenger cars en route. No one had anything to fear.[2]

Of course, the speech Fuchs gave was a complete deception. There would be no food, no passenger cars; the Jews had everything to fear. After the departure of this transport, Biebow is said to have remarked, "We've got the first 600 in the can."[3] Ernst Burmeister recalled the arrival of this first transport of victims to the Koło train station as follows.

Train transports with Jews arrived at the railway station in Warthbrücken [Koło]. There the Jews had to change to the narrow gauge track which went to Kulmhof. When the first transport arrived in Warthbrücken, Bothmann told me to accompany and guard this transport of Jews from Warthbrücken to Kulmhof with about 20 policemen from my squad. Bothmann himself drove me and the squad to Warthbrücken. As we arrived, a transport with about 500 to 600 Jews arrived. It was accompanied by a police squad under the command of a police officer. [...] Bothmann took over this transport from the police officer, and afterwards, under the command of Bothmann, we took the Jewish people [by the narrow gauge train] to Kulmhof, where they were accommodated in the village church. Then I had to assign sentries to guard the church.[4]

During this period, the narrow gauge train continued past Powiercie, where it had stopped during the first period, and skirted past the edge of the forest camp before arriving at the train station in Chełmno, located just beyond where the railroad tracks crossed the road near the policemen's canteen. The march to the church in Chełmno was a short one, some 400 meters. After the transport arrived, Häfele assured everyone that there was nothing to worry about. The people were then locked in the church. The size of the transports during this period was based on the number of people the church could hold, approximately 700. Srebrnik and other members of the Hauskommando were then ordered to assemble. Srebrnik later recalled the routine that followed.

They ordered us to carry the baggage, which was found by the narrow gauge railway where it intersects with the road. The people were already locked in the church. We took the things to the two barracks located in the park. One of them was very big [the tent], the other was smaller. The things were sorted in the larger one. The bundles were put on one side and then sorted on the other side. The Hauskommando sorted the belongings. The most valuable items were put in the small barrack [Burmeister's office]—new clothes and the like. Valuables were given to Burmeister.[5]

It was very crowded in the church. Srebrnik would bring bread and water to the people locked inside. On one occasion someone inside the church started screaming, trying to warn the others that they would all be gassed the following morning. In order to keep the people in the transport calm, this individual was taken out, led away and shot. According to Srebrnik, the individual claimed to have previously been in Chełmno.[6]

The next morning, trucks arrived in front of the church. Again, Häfele was on hand to reassure the victims that everything was fine. Beginning at about six or seven o'clock in the morning, the trucks were loaded one at a time so as not to cause a backup at the barracks in the forest. Everyone was told that they would be taking a bath. The number of people loaded onto each truck was determined by the capacity of the gas vans. The trucks were driven from the church to the barracks in the forest, primarily by the drivers, Seidenglanz and Gielow. Two guards accompanied each truck transport. When the last victims of the day had been removed from the church, generally around two o'clock in the afternoon, a group of Jewish workers, under Häfele's supervision, cleaned up the building in preparation for the next transport.

After the trucks arrived at the barracks in the forest, Kretschmer ordered the people to get out and line up in front of the buildings within the fenced enclosure. In order to create the impression that this was an actual transit camp and that there was more to the camp than just these two barracks, a sign with the number of the barracks was painted on each building—not numbers one and two, but, for example, eight and nine. (The actual numbers have not been established.)

It was here, in front of the barracks, that the transports were given the "arrival speech." Various members of the Sonderkommando, including Piller and Bothmann gave the speeches. First, they were told that they would be going to Germany to work rebuilding bombed cities. Specific cities were mentioned. Everything had been coordinated with Biebow's ghetto administration so that the same city mentioned in the ghetto, upon departure, was also mentioned in front of the barracks in the forest. The city name was included with the name list of passengers that accompanied the transports. Transport VII, which brought Mordechai Żurawski to Chełmno, was told that it would be going to Leipzig.[7] Other cities mentioned were Munich, Hannover and Cologne.

The speech painted a rosy picture of how life would be in Germany: There would be work, families would live together in newly built barracks, etc. But first everyone was to be examined by a doctor to make sure that each person was capable of working. Then everyone was to be taken to a bath to be deloused, so as to arrive in Germany clean and fit. During the bath, their clothes were to be disinfected. The speech was so effective— people were told just what they wanted to hear—that they often applauded and cheered when the speech concluded.[8] There must have been a great sense of relief after the dread and chaos of events in the ghetto.

The victims then entered the first barrack. A sign reading "To the doctor" was written on the door. They were told that they had to hurry because the transport to Germany was leaving that same day. Items of value were to be placed on the shelves above the hooks upon which they would hang their clothes. Bread and tobacco, as well as matches and lighters, were to be placed separately in a handkerchief or bag because the clothing was going to be chemically disinfected and, if anything was left in the clothing, it would be ruined by the chemicals.

Everyone undressed together, men, women and children. According to Srebrnik, women were allowed to remain in their underpants. According to Żurawski, everyone had to completely undress. (This step in the process may have varied depending on the "mood" of the transport.) After the un- dressing, the "medical examination" was conducted by Oberwachtmeister Bruno Simon.[9] Simon wore a white doctor's coat to lend authenticity to the charade, just as Walter Burmeister had during the first period of the camp's operation. The examination consisted of a quick visual observation. Everyone was deemed fit to work in Germany. After the examination, with their soap and towels in hand (which they brought with them), everyone was politely asked to proceed, still naked, to the next barrack for the ride to the bath.

On the door of the second barrack was the reassuring sign "To the bath." According to Herman Gielow, there was an opening in the wall of the second barrack and the people were ordered to go through it; from inside the barrack it looked like a bath, but it was in fact a gas van. After the vehicle was loaded, it pulled away from the wall, the doors were closed and the van headed slowly toward the crematoria. The drive took about six minutes.[10] According to Walter Piller, once inside the room, everyone was asked to proceed through the passageway on the other side of the room. This passageway, which led outside, was a corridor about two meters wide and approximately 25 meters long. It was enclosed on the sides by a wooden fence. There was a right-hand turn near the end of the corridor, which hid the small wooden steps that facilitated entry into the gas van.[11]

The description of this stage of the killing process given by Żurawski contains elements concurring with the descriptions given by both Gielow and Piller. However, Żurawski stated he witnessed the procedure from the area of the crematoria, some 200 meters away. It is not known if Żurawski was ever actually at the barracks. Ernst Burmeister also mentions this corridor in his testimony (see below). The procedure as described by Gielow had an obvious shortcoming. The act of pulling away from the wall in order to close the van's doors provided an opportunity for people with second thoughts to jump out of the vehicle. After experiencing this or similar problems, the procedure was probably adapted to that described by Piller: A chute was built to channel the people into the vans, allowing the doors to be closed without the necessity of pulling the van forward.

Four policemen were stationed at the end of the corridor. In the event that someone refused to enter the van, the policemen would beat the person with clubs.[12] The German forester Heinz May personally witnessed this stage of the extermination procedure and how the camp staff dealt with individuals who refused to enter the van.

> A young woman who was supposed to enter the [gas van] broke into wild screams and kept calling, "I do not want to suffocate. I prefer to be shot." "You can have that [wish], girl," said Bothmann who raised his pistol and shot her down.
>
> An elderly woman with her daughter, their faces ash-gray with terror and fright, asked to be allowed to kill themselves. She asked for a rope. Bothmann tossed her a brassiere from a pile of clothes nearby. The daughter lay down on the ground while her mother placed the straps around her throat. When the mother pulled, the daughter screamed with fright and the mother let go again. Bothmann and his hangmen looked on with diabolical grin[s]. "We are still more humane, aren't we; therefore, into the truck," he said.[13]

Ernst Burmeister, commander of the Polizeiwachtkommando, was also present and witnessed this stage of the killing procedure with Transport I.

> The next morning members of the Sonderkommando took these Jews, men and women, in trucks to the forest camp. I went to the forest camp to see what happened to these people. The Jews had to get off the vehicles in front of the big barracks in the forest camp. They were gathered together in the yard in front of the barracks, which was surrounded by a fence the height of a man. Bothmann told them that they would go to work in Germany, but first they would have to be examined by a doctor and, in order to prevent an epidemic, to take a bath. For this purpose they would have to undress in the barrack, take soap and a towel, and enter a van, which would drive them to the bath. And so it happened. The Jews entered the barrack and afterward they came out naked. Then they had to enter a van, after having been led through a gangway enclosed by a wooden fence. The van was a so-called gas van, which had an enclosed body and was similar to a furniture van. After they had gotten inside this van the doors in the back were closed by an SS man. After the doors were closed, the van drove immediately in the direction of the crematorium.[14]

When the van was full, the doors were closed and locked. The driver would then start the motor. During this period, as in the first, Laabs was the official gas van driver. Generally, one van was used, but when the size of a transport required it, the other van was also used, which according to one guard was driven by Erwin Bürstinger.[15] But they were not the only ones to drive these vans. According to Srebrnik, "everyone" drove the vans at some time; Piller, Gielow and Walter Burmeister all helped with the driving.[16]

There were two vans in Chełmno during this period. Most testimonies state there was one larger in size and one smaller.[17] Thus it would appear that one Sauer van and one Opel-Blitz van were in service during the second period. There was a third van in the camp, which has led to a discrepancy in the number of gas vans reportedly used during this period. The confusion appears to arise from the fact that only two of them were used for gassing. The third van served a different purpose, disinfecting clothing.

The number of people gassed at one time varies from testimony to testimony. The numbers may differ, partly, based on which van was being used. Walter Piller gave lower figures, 70 to 90 victims at a time. Srebrnik and Żurawski each gave higher figures. Srebrnik stated that the smaller van, which was used most often, held 100 to 120 people. The larger van, with a capacity of 170 people, was used only occasionally. Żurawski's figures were 90 for the smaller van and 110 for the larger one. Nevertheless, the results were the same as in the first period. Srebrnik witnessed the gassings on numerous occasions during this period.

> The doors were closed, locked and bolted. The motor was started. The exhaust gas was directed into the van by a special exhaust pipe and it poisoned the people inside. [. . .] Screams and knocking on the walls of the van continued for about four minutes. During this time the van didn't move. When the screams ceased, the van moved and took the bodies to the crematorium.[18]

Several people who were able to write in German were selected from each transport. This occurred during the undressing in the first barrack. These people remained in the barrack, while the others proceeded to the second barrack. Once isolated from the group, they were forced to write postcards to friends and family back in the ghetto. The postcards contained information about their arrival in Germany, the good living conditions, the good food—everything the people in the ghetto wanted to hear.

After writing the cards these people were forced to undress and were then led outside and down a narrow path that led to the crematoria. They were then shot, in most cases by Bothmann, Lenz or Ernst Burmeister. The bodies were burnt in the crematoria, together with the rest of the transport.[19]

The postcards were later proofread and taken to Biebow in Łódź. He personally showed these cards to people in the ghetto, encouraging others to report for "labor in the Reich."[20] The "Chronicle" recorded the reaction the postcards had in the ghetto, even at this late date.

Tuesday, July 25, 1944

The ghetto has received its first messages from people who left to perform manual labor outside the ghetto in the recent resettlement. Thirty-one post-cards have arrived, all of them postmarked July 19, 1944. Fortunately, it is apparent from these cards that the people are faring well and, what is more, that the families have stayed together. Here and there, a card mentions good rations. One card addressed to a kitchen manager says in plain Yiddish, "Mir lakhn fun ayere zupn!" [We laugh at your soups!]

The ghetto is elated and hopes that similar reports will soon be arriving from all the other resettled workers. It appears to be confirmed that labor brigades are truly required in the Old Reich.

It should be recalled that before the departure of Transport I, there was mention of Munich as its destination. One group may well have gone there, too.

It is also worth noting that the postcards indicate that our people are housed in comfortable barracks.[21]

The medical staff that accompanied each transport, comprised of a physician and one or two nurses, was separated from the transport when it arrived at the barracks. They were informed that next to the baths was a "doctor's office," where they would examine everyone and determine what type of work each individual was capable of performing. Kretschmer then escorted them toward the crematoria where they were shot.[22]

The gas vans stopped near the ovens. The driver would get out, put his ear to the wall, and when it was quiet inside open the doors. Corpses leaning against the doors fell to the ground. The van would sit for approx-imately five minutes to air out. Then, two members of the Jewish Wald-kommando would climb into the van and begin to throw the dead bodies out. If anyone was still alive, which happened frequently, they would be shot. Żurawski saw the driver Gielow shoot these people with his pistol as they tried to regain their senses. Two Jews, Frydland and Moniek Reich, searched the bodies removing rings and pulling out gold teeth.[23]

Lenz supervised the activity occurring in the area of the ovens and was assisted by Runge. The behavior of these two men was particularly brutal. It was reported that Runge killed prisoners by plunging an ax into their backs.[24] After the corpses were searched, about 100 bodies would then be stacked on the grating, alternating each layer of bodies with a layer of wood. All of the bodies from one van load could be placed at one time on the grating. The fire would then be lit. Żurawski, who was assigned to perform this work for a period of time, provided additional details in his postwar testimony:

There were two identical crematoria in the forest. They were on ground level (forming a kind of hole). These ovens were four meters deep, six meters wide and ten meters long. The walls of the oven narrowed gradually and at the bottom, where the grating was, they were maybe one-and-a-half meters wide and two meters long. The grating was made from narrow gauge train track rails. [. . .] The walls of the ovens were made with fireproof bricks and were lined with concrete. The ash pit was under the grating. A long ditch led to it facilitating air to the oven. The oven was lit with wood, then a layer of corpses was arranged on the burning wood. The corpses had to be placed in such a way that they did not touch each other. In one layer (the lowest), 12 bodies were arranged. Small pieces of dry wood were placed on the corpses and then the next layer of corpses was arranged. In this way, up to 100 bodies could be placed in an oven at one time. In the course of burning, space was made at the top and filled with the next layers of corpses and wood. The corpses burned quickly, in about 15 minutes. The ashes from the ash pit were removed with a special type of pokers. They were long iron poles that ended with a perpendicular iron plate about 40 centimeters wide.[25]

The work at the ovens was extremely difficult in every sense. The mental and emotional stress of performing such a task can never be fully appreciated. The work was also physically demanding, carrying and stacking hundreds of corpses a day, and working in close proximity to the huge fires. These men were dirty; black from the smoke and soot, their arms scorched from the heat; they smelled badly. There were no baths or showers for the workers. Upon arrival at the camp, they were shackled in leg irons. These were never removed and so they could neither change nor clean their clothes.

The firewood for the ovens came from a nearby forest. Upon his arrival at the camp, Żurawski was assigned to the group of prisoners, a part of the Waldkommando, who chopped the wood, brought it to the ovens and stacked it. Hauptscharführer Ernst Thiele and four to five policemen supervised this group of workers.[26]

The exact procedure for burning the bodies is not clear. Piller stated that when transports of 700 people arrived (which would have been typical), both ovens were used. He also testified that in order to have Sundays free, on Saturday the workers would burn the entire transport which had arrived on Friday and had spent the night in the church.[27] This implies that, for example, in a transport that was gassed on Tuesday, perhaps only half the bodies were cremated that day, and the rest were cremated the following day. The guard Bruno Israel stated that on occasion only half of the transport would be killed that day. The second half would be killed the next day, before the arrival of the new transport.[28] Thus, it is not clear if the cremation began while the people were still being shuttled from the church to the barracks, or if it began only after the last victims of the day had been gassed.

The ashes and bits of bones that were not completely burned were periodically removed from the ash pits, and scattered around the area of the crematoria. After these ashes had cooled, they were loaded into a two-handled chest and carried to a nearby concrete slab. A group of five or six prisoners worked there, grinding the bone fragments into a fine powder. The work was accomplished by hand, using grinding tools.

Bothmann had "borrowed" a grinding mill from the mill in the village of Zawadka. Apparently, this grinder proved to be ineffective. After three months, it was cleaned, oiled, disinfected and returned. Herkner, the administrator of the estate at Powiercie, then sold it to a nearby estate at Głębokie.[29]

The ashes and bone powder were then poured into sacks. Periodically they were loaded onto a truck and driven at night to the mill in Zawadka by Runge, Kretschmer or Laabs. On multiple occasions, Franciszek Kazmierski, who lived in Zawadka, witnessed

> ...a truck from Chełmno arrive about eleven o'clock at night. The policemen, using flashlights, removed bags from the truck and threw their contents from the bridge into the river. After dumping the whole load, the bridge was carefully cleaned with brooms. However, I found bones that had been smashed into small pieces.[30]

According to Walter Piller, a portion of the ashes and bone powder were bagged and taken to Poznań where they were used as fertilizer on vegetable gardens at concentration camps.[31]

After the victims had been loaded into the gas van, their belongings, which remained in the barracks, were quickly gathered together by a group of six to eight prisoners under Piller's supervision and loaded onto a truck before the next group arrived from the church. These workers were kept behind the second barrack, out of sight, until the victims were in the van. The truck drove to Chełmno, where the belongings were transferred to the sorting tent on the grounds of the former mansion.

The clothing was thoroughly searched for hidden valuables, and the stars of David were removed. Shoes were ripped apart in the hope of finding something of value hidden in a hollowed-out heel. Herbert Richter and Walter Burmeister supervised the Jews performing this work. From time to time, they would double check clothing to insure the search had been properly performed. The clothing was then disinfected. The gas vans were used for this purpose because they were hermetically sealed. At first, one van was used (probably the one found in Koło after the war). Later the others were used as well, presumably after the transports stopped. The clothes were hung inside the vans; underwear was placed on specially constructed shelves. Before closing the doors, a pot with dimethan, a powdered chemical, was placed inside and lit. The items were left inside the vans for eight to ten hours.[32]

The disinfected clothing was taken to Koło and distributed among German settlers. Lower quality items found their way to the Polish population. The poorest quality clothing and clothing on which the outline of the six-pointed Star of David was visible was shredded into rags. Two workers from the Hauskommando operated the shredding machine. The rags were then bundled and shipped back to Łódź by truck.

Valuables collected from among the belongings of the victims were turned over to Görlich. As in the first period he delivered them periodically to the Gettoverwaltung in Łódź.

During the second period, "only" ten main transports were sent to the camp. The reason the camp was reactivated was to exterminate the remaining inhabitants in the Łódź ghetto, the origin of the ten transports. The above-described extermination procedure was repeated for the nine subsequent transports that were sent to Chełmno from the ghetto. Information concerning each departing transport was duly noted in the ghetto Chronicle.[33]

Monday, June 26, 1944

Today, Transport II, with 912 persons left the ghetto (accompanying physician, Dr. Adolf Wittenberg, Berlin). The same train as last time was used under the same circumstances. Once again, Gestapo Commissioner [Gunter] Fuchs said a few words. This transport included a large contingent of young people, several of them volunteers, leaving the ghetto in high spirits. On the other hand, there were a great many feeble and sickly people.

Wednesday, June 28, 1944

Early this morning Transport III departed with 803 people. The accompanying physician is Dr. Walter Schwerin of Berlin.

Friday, June 30, 1944

In the morning, there was some uncertainty whether today's transport would be leaving, since the train was not delivered punctually to Radogoszcz station. But the Reich railroad did provide the train toward nine in the morning, whereupon the 700 people could board. This transport included Dr. Elisabeth Singer (Prague) as its physician. [. . .] All told, 2,976 people have left the ghetto, a figure that breaks down as follows:

	Total	Men	Women
June 23	561	268	293
June 26	912	361	551
June 28	803	261	542
June 30	700	204	496
	2,976	1,094	1,882

Monday, July 3, 1944

Early this morning, Transport V left Radogoszcz station with 700 people. The accompanying physician was Dr. Fritz Heine (Berlin).

Wednesday, July 5, 1944

A total of 700 people were shipped out of the ghetto on Transport VI, with 214 males and 486 females.

Friday, July 7, 1944

Early this morning, Transport VII left the ghetto with 700 people. The accompanying physician was Dr. Hugo Natannsen, originally from Hamburg, but resettled to this ghetto from Prague. His wife and daughter left with him.

Monday, July 10, 1944

Today, Transport VIII, under the leadership of the physician Dr. Felix Proskauer (Berlin), left the ghetto with 700 people. The dispatch took place as usual, without incident. Today's transport was composed of 202 men and 498 women. [...]

Wednesday, July 12, 1944

This morning, Transport IX left the ghetto. No physician accompanied it. The designated physician, Dr. Grödel of Cologne, was called back at the last minute and will presumably go with the next transport. Again, 700 people have departed, bringing the current total to 6,496.

Friday, July 14, 1944

This morning, Transport X left the ghetto with another 700 people. The accompanying physician was Dr. Grödel (of Cologne). [...] With today's transport, the ghetto has so far yielded a total of 7,196 persons.

Saturday, July 15, 1944

Never has the ghetto been so happy. Today toward noon, the Eldest [Chaim Rumkowski, chairman of the Council of Elders] was instructed to halt the resettlement.

No other documentation exists that any major transports, other than the ten transports from Łódź, which arrived at Chełmno between June 23 and July 14, were sent to the camp during this period. However, both Srebrnik and Żurawski reported that, following these ten Łódź transports, small groups of people were brought by truck to the camp and executed.

Srebrnik remembered several smaller transports of 40 to 50 people that arrived in trucks from the Łódź ghetto. He even recognized some of the people as Jewish ghetto officials. He also recalled a group of nuns being brought to the camp.[34] The arrival of the nuns appears to have been witnessed by Józef Przybylski, a local resident.

> In the summer of 1944, I saw one truck carrying Polish women coming from the direction of Dąbie. They were young, 23 or 24 years old, dressed in light colored outfits. They had white kerchiefs on their heads and wore shoes with low heels that laced high up. They were dressed alike, as if from a school. They didn't wear Jewish stars. They spoke Polish among themselves. There were about 30 of them. The truck went to where the mansion used to be. I don't know what happened [to them] after that.[35]

Żurawski, who worked in the forest camp, remembered other small transports. "After the last transport [Transport X], from time to time, several people were brought to the area of the crematorium and shot. We burnt the bodies. They were not Jews because they were not circumcised."[36]

The only known escape attempt during the second period took place sometime during the summer. Finkelsztajn was a member of the Wald-kommando. He carried the corpses from the gas vans to the crematoria. One day he saw that his sister's corpse had been thrown out of the van. He then had to throw her into the fire.

Early that evening, after returning to the granary, he was one of six prisoners assigned to take some garbage to the dump. The group was lightly guarded. At an opportune moment, he removed the chains from around one of his legs and fled toward the river. Several local villagers saw Finkelsztajn escaping. Roman T., Adam L. and Henryk B. chased after him. Roman T. caught the fleeing man on the other side of the river, brought him back and turned him over to the Sonderkommando. According to Srebrnik and the policeman Bruno Israel, Finkelsztajn was then shot by the guard Arthur Sliwke.[37] There was a RM 100 reward for catching Finkelsztajn. Roman T. later said that he acted in fear of the Gestapo.[38]

At eight o'clock that evening, Piller came to the granary and ordered everyone out. A headcount was taken: One person was missing. Piller asked where the missing person was. He then ordered four of the prisoners to go and retrieve the body. When the body was returned, Piller said, "You see, he escaped; this is his fate."[39]

Bothmann came to the granary an hour later and ordered fifteen people to come out. He then took his pistol and shot them. Bothmann then said to the others, "You know why I did it? Because a man had run away and if any of you try to run away, I will kill you all."[40]

Final Liquidation of the Camp

Following the ten transports sent to Chełmno in June and July 1944, the "resettlement" from the Łódź ghetto was temporarily stopped. The decision to end the transports to Chełmno was, no doubt, based on the time factor. From the Gestapo's perspective, Chełmno's capacity to "process" less than 1,000 people daily was inadequate to accomplish the task at hand. In addition, some time would be required in order to dismantle the camp and erase all traces of what happened there before control over this territory was lost to the approaching front.

Time was running out for the Nazis in Łódź. By the end of July 1944, the Red Army had reached—and in some places crossed—the Vistula River, some 130 kilometers east of Łódź. If Stalin had not stopped the Soviet advance at Warsaw, allowing the Germans to crush the Polish underground army's Warsaw uprising, begun on August 1, the Red Army could have been in Łódź within a matter of days. This might have saved the lives of more than 50,000 people still living in the Łódź ghetto. As for Chełmno, a swift Soviet advance into the area would have resulted in the Sonderkommando killing all the remaining Jewish prisoners and fleeing the camp, just as it did when the front approached the area several months later. However, a rapid move into this area, with no time for the Sonderkommando to dismantle the facility, could have resulted in the death camp remaining intact. Had this occurred, it would have been the only such facility not to have been dismantled by the Nazi perpetrators.

The Łódź ghetto was finally liquidated during the month of August. The 54,500 people remaining in the ghetto were sent to Auschwitz, while some 500 were evacuated to the Sachsenhausen-Oranienburg and Ravensbrück concentration camps in Germany. A group of some 700 people remained to clean up the former ghetto area. Additionally, there were some 200 people in hiding within the ghetto.[1]

The liquidation of the camp in Chełmno began in August, following the decision to evacuate the remainder of the Łódź ghetto inhabitants primarily to Auschwitz. The Chełmno death camp, for a second time, no longer had a *raison d'etre*. There remained only the tasks of disposing of the victim's belongings, dismantling the camp and erasing all traces of its existence.

First, the size of the Polizeiwachtkommando was reduced. With no more transports arriving, their presence was no longer required. Bothmann ordered Ernst Burmeister to select 40 members of his police guard to be transferred. They were assigned, under Burmeister's command, by the police commander in Łódź to perform guard duty along the border between the Warthegau and the General Government. Burmeister and his squad, however, would soon participate in crushing the Warsaw uprising. A police squad of approximately 40 men remained in Chełmno to guard the Jewish Haus- and Waldkommandos, which at this time numbered about 100 prisoners.

During August, the Waldkommando dismantled the barracks. The building materials were transported to Koło and shipped from there, by train, in an unknown direction. As opposed to the end of the first period of the camp when the crematoria were blown up, in the second period the crematoria were dismantled. But this occurred in stages. Only one of the crematoria was initially dismantled. The second one was dismantled later, in December or early January, just before the departure of the Sonderkommando. The dismantlement of the crematoria was supervised by Runge, who had previously supervised their construction. A special commission arrived to see that the work was carried out correctly. They found that the concrete foundation from the first crematorium was still in the ground. They ordered it dug out and destroyed. According to Żurawski, this inspection tour was headed by Arthur Greiser.[2]

Some of the bricks from the crematoria were scattered around the forest; others were taken away to the estate in Powiercie. There they were used to make a drainage channel in a greenhouse.[3]

When the work in the forest camp was finished and the installations, except for the one remaining crematorium, were dismantled, a large group of the Waldkommando, approximately 40 men, was informed that they were being transferred to another camp. Häfele told them that they would be well off, better than in Chełmno. After having seen and experiencing so much, they were skeptical. Before they left, they told Srebrnik that they would try to leave a note in the truck with information as to where they were taken. When the truck returned, Srebrnik checked and found a note with the message "to death" written on it.[4] Later, Żurawski found their clothing in the forest. They had all been shot by Bothmann, Lenz and Piller.[5]

Żurawski survived the liquidation of the Waldkommando because of his profession. He was a butcher and was transferred to work in the kitchen that prepared the meals for the Jewish workers. The Jewish kitchen staff included a cook and two or three assistants. Toward the end, Srebrnik also worked in the kitchen as one of the assistants.[6]

On Bothmann's order, Laabs and Runge loaded the two gas vans on a freight train in Koło and accompanied them to Berlin. From Berlin, they drove the vans to a large motor pool in Oranienburg. The trip lasted about one week after which they returned to Chełmno.[7]

It was during this period that Bothmann increased the number of skilled craftsmen working in the camp. On September 15, Łódź Ghetto Administration head Hans Biebow ordered six tailors to board a truck. They were to be taken on an eight day assignment. After a three hour journey, the truck stopped in the village of Chełmno. The tailors Mordkiewicz, Oberferst (both highly regarded for their professional skills, these two tailors worked exclusively for German and Jewish dignitaries in the ghetto, including Biebow and Bradfisch) and four others were ordered to take their sewing machines and get out of the vehicle. The tailors were escorted through the gate and into the camp. They were shocked by what they saw and pondered, "Are these people savages or really human beings?" They were informed that they were in a labor camp and anyone who does not work, or avoids work, will be shot; that they had to help the Germans win the war that the Jews had wanted. The men had to turn over all personal belongings; those wearing clothing deemed usable, were ordered to strip and put on older, worn out clothing. The new arrivals were then shackled in leg irons and escorted to the old granary building. Once inside, and with the door locked behind them, they were able to talk with the other prisoners. According to the account, eight tailors, five cobblers, one boot maker, two carpenters and four others who worked in the kitchen were inside the building. The two groups exchanged information, the new prisoners were told what was happening in the camp and they shared the latest news about events in the ghetto.[8]

Also on board of this transport of tailors were Dr. Sima Mandels, her husband and two children. Dr. Mandels was the director of the pediatric department at the Łódź ghetto hospital on Lagiewnicka Street. The family was sent to their death by Hans Biebow. During a visit to the hospital one evening Biebow, who was drunk at the time, encountered the Mandels' 16-year-old daughter in a hallway. He grabbed her and forced her into an office. The girl rejected Biebow's sexual advances and, screaming, attempted to fight him off. It is not clear whether the girl was actually raped before Biebow drew his pistol and shot her in the face. She survived the assault and attempted murder, but not for long. In order to cover up the affair, Biebow ordered the entire family deported to Chełmno. When the truck arrived and the tailors climbed out of the vehicle the Mandels family was ordered to remain in the truck, which subsequently drove in the direction of the forest camp.[9]

The Hauskommando spent the following months searching, sorting and shipping the belongings of the victims of the camp. The belongings were periodically loaded onto trucks and driven to Łódź by the driver Gielow. As winter approached, the Jewish prisoners chopped wood in the forest to heat the homes in which members of the Sonderkommando lived.

Bothmann prolonged this clean-up phase as long as possible. As in the first period, he was content to sit in Chełmno and thereby avoid service at the front. Walter Piller summed up this period in the camp by describing it as a "lazy" period.[10] It may have been a time of relaxation for Piller, but the work and constant terror continued for the Jewish prisoners. They had to be on constant guard against their tormentors, such as Herbert Richter who "had a habit of killing anyone who ate a piece of bread while working."[11]

Rudolf Kramp from the Łódź Ghetto Administration returned to the camp sometime in November or December. His truck and trailer was loaded with office equipment and, allegedly, at least some of the camp records. After returning to Łódź, Kramp parked the vehicle at the office of the Ghetto Administration building. That evening several inquisitive Poles, employed by the Ghetto Administration, snuck up to the truck and, using flashlights, began looking around inside the vehicle. After noting that the file cabinets were under seal, they were afraid to open them and withdrew. The next day when the truck was being unloaded, one of these Poles, Adam Rapaport, was told by a driver that archives were in the truck. Overcome by curiosity, Rapaport opened a cabinet and saw a number of ledgers and records bound together with string. Kramp told him to keep working and therefore he couldn't examine them more closely. The next day, the records were taken to the city (away from the ghetto).[12]

It was not the Nazis, but the advance of the Red Army, that determined when the final liquidation of the camp took place. Eventually, sounds of artillery began to be heard, which grew louder as the front approached the area of Chełmno. The remaining Jews knew that for them this meant not so much the end of the war, as the end of their lives. On December 1, 1944, they wrote a letter as their final testimony to the world and then buried it for safekeeping.

Announcement to our future nation:

I describe to you the life of the Jewish nation from September 1, 1939 to December 1, 1944 and in what way they oppressed us. We were taken, young and old, to between the towns of Koło and Dąbie. We were taken to the forest, there we were gassed, shot, and burned. And so we ask so that our future brothers [word illegible] for our German murderers. Witnesses to our oppression are the Poles who live in this area. Once again we ask that this murder be made known throughout the whole world and to all the press. The last Jews who [word illegible] here wrote this. We survived until December 1, 1944.

[illegible signature][13]

On January 17, 1945, 47 Jews remained imprisoned in the granary, 25 from the Hauskommando and 22 craftsmen. That night, Bruno Israel was on guard duty at the granary. Having received the final evacuation order, Bothmann arrived at the guardhouse around one o'clock in the morning and ordered drivers. The entire Sonderkommando was summoned to roll call. Bothmann informed them that the Red Army was in Łódź and that the Sonderkommando was to be disbanded. The remaining Jewish workers were to be shot immediately and burned in the forest the following morning. The final liquidation was underway. Bothmann's Mercedes and a truck drove to the granary and stopped, their headlights illuminating the building. The entire area was surrounded by the police guard.

Inside the granary, the Jews were awakened by the sound of the approaching vehicles. Polizeimeister Lenz opened the door and demanded, "Five outside!" Those inside knew immediately that this was the end.

Szymon Srebrnik saw no reason to delay the inevitable any longer and went outside with the first group. Also among this first group of five was a Czech named Yvo (possibly Ime Rozenblum) who began to sing. Bothmann indicated to Lenz where he wanted the executions carried out. Lenz ordered the five to lie face down in the snow about 15 meters in front of the granary building. The Czech refused and continued to sing. Lenz walked up to him, pointed a pistol at his head and pulled the trigger. Srebrnik, wearing only his underwear, lay on the snow shaking in fear.[14] After hearing three shots, he lost consciousness. As fate would have it, Srebrnik was only wounded; Lenz shot him not in the head but in the neck, the bullet exiting through his mouth. Moments later he regained consciousness. As he lay there, Lenz forced two more groups of five outside and shot them. Srebrnik later recalled the following.

> I was laying on the ground and he would pass by, and when he heard some signs of life—there were all sorts of movements—he would finish them off with a second shot. After a few minutes, I regained consciousness, and when he passed by, I stopped breathing, so that he should think that I am dead. I was just lying there. And then there was another group of five. They shot them, and then the third group of five, in turn, and they were also shot. There was one soldier who was just guarding the groups of dead people and finishing off those who still showed signs of life.[15]

Żurawski was due to go out with the next group, but he had no intention of laying down and being shot. He took his knife, which he had "acquired" from the kitchen, stood behind the blanket covering the door and waited. When Lenz came in for the next group, Żurawski twisted the flashlight from his hand and, like a madman, ran out of the building striking out wildly with his knife. One of the guards struck him on the leg with the butt of his rifle but he kept running. He forced his way over the fence, injuring his right hand, and continued running into the darkness.

Bothmann, Kretschmer and others pursued Żurawski. Hiding in a ditch, Żurawski heard the guard Rufenach and another guard riding by on bicycles informing locals about the escape. He eventually made his way to the nearby village of Ostrów, northeast of Chełmno. There he hid in the barn of Marja Przybylska until the Red Army arrived.

Accounts vary slightly as to how exactly Żurawski got out of the granary and what happened next. The following is the version given by Walter Piller. Before leaving briefly to look for Żurawski, Bothmann ordered Piller to kill the remaining workers.

> [...] Lenz removed the remaining five Jews from the lower cell, and they were shot by Lenz and myself. Only the 20 craftsmen remained in the upper cell. Without my orders, Lenz proceeded to the upper cell, together with a Wachtmeister from the Schutzpolizei, in order to remove five of the Jews so that they might be shot like the others. As he opened the door to the cell, four Jews immediately threw themselves on Lenz and pulled him into the cell. There they took his pistol and started shooting at the two guards who were posted at the lower door. Bothmann, who in the meantime had returned after the unsuccessful hunt of the escapee, ordered the lower door locked. After Bothmann, Häfele and I repeatedly ordered the Jews to release Lenz and come out from the upper cell in groups of five, the answer was renewed fire from the pistol stolen from Lenz. Furthermore, one Jew yelled that Lenz had hanged himself. It was impossible to determine if this was true, because the craftsmen had set the prison on fire and the flames were already coming through the roof. The fire found additional fuel because the attic above the cell contained wood that was stored there to be dried. Then Häfele unlocked the exterior door because it was assumed that the craftsmen would now come out on their own. Only two tailors managed to reach the staircase, where they collapsed

unconscious, apparently because of the smoke. It was impossible to extinguish the fire.[16]

It is doubtful whether the Jews themselves started the fire. Other accounts say that Bothmann ordered guards to bring gasoline from Dąbie to set the building on fire. Those who tried to escape were shot at the doorway. Furthermore, it is difficult to believe that Lenz hanged himself. A more likely scenario is that he was dealt with swiftly by the Jews who had suffered so much at the hands of the sadist. Though the details vary, all agree that Lenz and the guard Haase died that night in the granary.

When those inside had been consumed in the flames, the other groups of five that had already been shot were thrown back into the burning building. The corpses of Lenz and Haase were also consumed in the fire.

During the shootout and the ensuing confusion at the granary, Srebrnik began to crawl away. "Like a dog" on all fours, he made his way through the fence and down the hill toward the river. Eventually, he crawled through a pigpen and into the barn of a local farmer, Józef Wieczorek. There he buried himself in the hay.[17]

Hearing his pigs squealing, Wieczorek went out to check on them and found Srebrnik in the barn. The farmer was afraid that he would be killed if the Germans discovered Srebrnik there, so he went to his neighbor Andrzej Miszczak, and asked him what to do. Miszczak advised him to leave for a few days, until the Red Army arrived, and that he would take care of his livestock.

Miszczak brought Srebrnik milk and bread, but he was too weak to eat or drink. Srebrnik's life was probably saved with a mouthful of snow that clotted the blood from his wound. Afraid to come out, he remained in the barn until the Red Army entered Chełmno.

Later that same morning, Bothmann ordered Görlich and Piller to remove all the documents from the safe and burn them. The ashes from the papers were scattered over an open field.[18] Then, at ten in the morning on January 18, 1945, after packing up their personal belongings, Sonderkommando Kulmhof left the village of Chełmno driving in the direction of Poznań.

CHAPTER 4

Epilogue

Chelmno: 1945 to the Present

The Sonderkommando fled Chełmno just before the arrival of the Red Army. The remaining members of the Polizeiwachtkommando were placed under the command of the local police in Koło. The SS contingent drove to Konin and spent the night there. Bothmann attempted to contact Dr. Bradfisch of the Łódź Gestapo, but was unsuccessful. Contact was established with the Inspector of the Security Police and Security Service Brigadeführer Damzog in Poznań. The events of the previous day, including the evacuation of the camp, were reported. Bothmann was then ordered to report as quickly as possible with his Sonderkommando to the Poznań Gestapo office where SS Sonderkommando Kulmhof was then disbanded.[1] (For the subsequent fate of the members of the Sonderkommando see Appendix III: Fates of Key Figures.)

What remained of the camp consisted of a couple of structures, the smoldering granary building and the barbed wire fence that surrounded it. (The walls remained standing but the roof had collapsed and was partially consumed in the flames.) Inside the granary were the remains of the 45 Jews and the two policemen, Lenz and Haase. The corpses were eventually removed by locals and buried in a common grave just to the east of where the mansion had once stood. The earliest known description of the former camp originates from a local villager.

> Immediately after the Germans fled I went to Chełmno. For the first time, I passed through the gate of the enclosed area. [. . .]
> Ahead of me groups of people are going there. Behind me are new groups, some of them are coming, others leaving. All of them in rapt attention. And nearby, along the road, are endless columns of Russian tanks, tanks, tanks going west toward Berlin.
> I go to all the barracks that remain. They are empty. There are four of them. One is larger. In one of them, the butchers parked their cars. In the second one was a repair shop. In the third one, the small one, the valuables of the murdered people were stored. I don't know the purpose of the fourth building. The fifth one [sic], the granary, was changed into a camp for the chained Jews, who worked mainly, or partly, in the forest burning their brothers. The floor in the old granary was removed and they made a new one of tiles. Above, they arranged two floors. On the second floor, tailors and shoemakers slept and

worked, obviously for their butchers. On the third floor was a storeroom for shoes, stolen linen, and the better clothing, etc. Those who worked in the forest at the crematoria and here at this place slept on the ground floor. [...]

So I approached this camp. Already from a distance I can smell a burnt odor. The walls are charred. The roof is destroyed. The little windows with bars are burnt. The door is burnt.

I go inside. A terrible sight. A hellish view. On the left side in the corner is a column of smoke, something is still burning. Everything inside is burnt— people, sewing machines, beams, everything. Forty-seven people burnt. The corpses are completely charred, deformed. Separate torsos, arms, heads. It is all revolting, black, horrible! One of the torsos is still a little white. A bit of white flesh in the burned blackness. The poor remains of humanity. Everywhere blackness, horror, hell. The rolled tin roof is mixed with the burnt remains.

Most of the burnt remains of the human bodies are near the door. This is understandable. Deathly suffering and fear led everyone to the door. It forced them against the door. It wanted to breakdown the door, to breakdown the walls. Unfortunately the door and the walls were stronger than the scorching muscles of the 47 people burning alive. They withstood the pressure. They didn't break. They didn't let the victims out.

I go further. Here, a pot of unfinished soup. There, farther, another one. Here, the remains of a sewing machine. Here, rolled tin. But fewer and fewer human remains. Everybody died closer to the door, closer to the last illusive hope.

The view is so horrible that no one goes farther. The spectators stop at the door only for a moment. They glance horrified inside, horrified, and run away. No one can bear this view.[2]

In the forest outside the village, the wooden fence that surrounded sections of the woods remained standing. Inside, on the large field where the crematoria had stood, some brushwood was piled up, and bricks and grating (train track rails) from the last oven destroyed lay scattered around the area. It is not known what eventually became of these bricks and rails but it is assumed they were pilfered by local residents.

A brief investigation was immediately undertaken by the political administration of the first Belorussian front and submitted on February 1, 1945.[3] This report merely sketched out that a death camp, which had utilized gas vans, had existed in Chełmno. It included a minimum of basic facts and some errors as well.

The first concerted effort to document what occurred at Chełmno was begun by a Jewish survivor who had lost his family in the camp. Jakub Waldman began collecting testimonies from local villagers and from the three survivors in the area. He later participated in the initial visit to the former camp by a delegation comprising members of the Main Commission for the Investigation of German Crimes in Poland and the Central Jewish Historical Commission in May 1945. These documents are now located in the archives of the Jewish Historical Institute in Warsaw. Waldman died in Turek on September 1, 1945.[4]

On May 24, 1945, the above-mentioned commission traveled from Łódź, making brief stops in Poddębice, Uniejów and Dąbie, to Chełmno where they examined the grounds of the former mansion and the forest camp. The synagogue and Ostrowski Works, where a vehicle thought to be a gas van was parked, were also visited in Koło. On June 6, 1945, the Polish Ministry of Justice appointed Judge Władysław Bednarz to conduct an official investigation of the former camp. He set to work immediately collecting evidence and taking testimonies from people in the area who witnessed the activities of the Sonderkommando as well as from the survivors Podchlebnik (who had returned to Koło), Srebrnik and Żurawski (who was located in his hometown of Włocławek).

On the grounds of the former mansion, a "garbage pit" was excavated in which items considered worthless by the Sonderkommando were burned. Recovered from the pit were partially burned papers, including a 31-page journal, apparently kept by a member of the Jewish Waldkommando. Only 11 of the pages contain entries, written in pencil. One still legible portion reads, "The next morning we were taken to the forest where ovens for burning people were being built.... "[5] Also found in the hole were about 24,200 spoons, 4,500 knives, 2,500 forks, large quantities of pots and pans, hair clippers, eye glasses and many other items. Additionally, various types of jewelry (rings, necklaces, ear rings, watches) and paper money, including US dollars, Soviet rubles and German marks were uncovered.[6]

The fact that items of obvious value were found in the garbage pit indicates that whenever possible the members of the Hauskommando who searched the belongings of the victims took the opportunity to discard these items rather than to turn them over to the Sonderkommando. This act of resistance must have given the prisoners some measure of satisfaction, however small.

The money, jewelry and other objects of value that were dug up were placed in boxes, eventually catalogued and deposited in a bank in Łódź. In January 1960, the contents of the boxes were checked. The inventory list agreed with the contents and the boxes were again deposited in the bank, but only for a short time. Two months later, the items were turned over to the Polish national treasury.[7]

In the forest, Bednarz attempted to secure the area. Locals were dismantling the fence that surrounded the area and had carted off some of the more than one dozen rails used as grating for the crematoria; eventually, all would be lost. The site, like the other death camps, began to attract treasure hunters. Bednarz excavated an area used in 1942 as one of the mass graves. This portion of the investigation is missing from the record; however, Bednarz does state in his book that in the lowest layers bodies were discovered, confirming the testimony of Podchlebnik in regard to the method of placing the corpses.[8]

In Koło, Judge Bednarz secured the old synagogue and the Jewish Committee building located next door. The walls inside were covered with handwritten notes left by the people who had passed through it before and during the first period of the camp's existence. Among the hundreds of inscriptions only one was found which indicated that the writer knew the fate that awaited them. It read, "... Jews, don't wait—you will be here one day, then you will be taken to the ovens—transport 13."[9]

The floor of the synagogue was littered with more than 5,000 pairs of shoes. They had arrived, like other shipments before them, via Poznań for repairs. The items were sent by the Nationalsozialistische Volkswohlfahrt, a Nazi welfare organization, which bought goods originating from the camp. The origin of the shoes was common knowledge among the workers. The eventual fate of the shoes is not known. (It is believed that they were eventually thrown away.) The synagogue itself was later demolished. Today, the site of the synagogue is an empty lot. A monument stands across the street, in a park, dedicated to the memory of the former Koło Jewish community.

Also in Koło, at the former Ostrowski Works, Judge Bednarz examined a van that had been brought there and left by the Sonderkommando in the fall of 1944. This vehicle is commonly referred to as a gas van, but this was never established as fact. Srebrnik said this van was used for gassing, but according to the guard Bruno Israel and Mordechai Żurawski, the van was not used to gas people, but rather to disinfect clothing.[10] Walter Piller testified that originally one van was used to disinfect the clothing and that only later were the other vans also used for this purpose.[11] Based on this and other information, the vehicle does not appear to have been used as a van to gas people during the second period.

On July 30, 1945, during the Bednarz investigation, three mass graves containing the remains of 55 Poles were exhumed in the area of the forest camp. These Poles had been taken from jail in Koło and shot in the forest before the camp was established. On Sunday, August 5, the corpses were placed in caskets and given an on-site Christian burial during a county-wide solemn ceremony, attended by representatives of the administration, various political parties and social organizations. A large wooden cross was erected over the grave in memory of these Poles, victims of the Nazi occupation.

In 1946, Judge Bednarz published his findings about the camp in a 74-page book, "Obóz Straceń w Chełmnie nad Nerem" [The Death Camp in Chełmno-on-Ner]. On March 29, 1947, despite having sufficient material to go to trial, the District Court in Łódź decided to suspend criminal proceedings against "Häfele and others" until such time as they were apprehended and turned over to Polish authorities.[12]

The grounds of the former mansion were used as a soccer field by local youth until 1956, when an agricultural cooperative was established on the site. The old granary building was re-roofed and widened, and became a warehouse for storing fodder. Bullet holes, which resulted from the firefight during the final night of the camp, could still be seen around the door over sixty years later.

In 1957, a small monument was erected over the common grave of the last members of the Jewish labor squad who died in the early morning hours of January 18, 1945. The remnants of the Jewish communities from Łódź and Włocławek erected the memorial. On it is inscribed in Polish and Hebrew, "A place sanctified by the blood of thousands of victims of the genocidal Nazi murderers. Honor their memory." The bodies of the Hauskommando members were never exhumed and given a proper burial. Many people do not realize that the remains of the policeman Haase and of the sadist Willi Lenz, the most brutal of all the members of the Sonderkommando, are buried together with these Jewish victims. For several decades, the small monument was the only indication of the genocide that occurred on the grounds of the former mansion.

In the early 1960s, the Polish government decided to build a monument on the grounds of the former forest camp. The monument was dedicated on September 27, 1964. Consisting of a concrete structure six to seven meters thick, the construction, approximately 35 meters by 36 meters, is supported on five pyramid-shaped legs. The front (the side facing the highway) features a bas-relief representing the victims. To the right is inscribed the Polish word, *Pamiętamy* [we remember]. Portions of the note written on December 1, 1944, allegedly by Izaak Sigelman, a member of the Jewish labor squad, are inscribed on the back of the monument. (For a translation of the entire note see Chapter 3, page 172.)

Beginning in 1959—with the establishment of the Central Office of the State Justice Administration for the Investigation of National Socialist Crimes [Zentrale Stelle der Landesjustizverwaltungen zur Aufklärung Nationalsozialistischer Verbrechen] a year earlier— authorities in the Federal Republic of Germany began collecting information concerning the Chełmno death camp.[13] Formal charges of complicity in mass murder were brought against 12 former members of Sonderkommando Kulmhof on July 5, 1962. Once located, several of the defendants were held in custody throughout the course of the trial; Laabs since November 26, 1960; Häfele since December 8, 1960; Walter Burmeister since January 24, 1961; Heinl since September 7, 1961; Möbius since November 9, 1961; Ernst Burmeister since April 13, 1962. The other defendants, Bock, Heukelbach, Maderholz,

Mehring, Schulte and Steinke, all former guards of the Polizeiwachtkom-mando, remained free until the final two weeks of the trial, March 14–30, 1963.[14]

The trial began on November 26, 1962, and the verdicts were handed down on March 30, 1963. The guards Bock, Mehring and Steinke were acquitted. Heukelbach, Maderholz and Schulte each received a sentence of 13 months and two weeks in prison. On appeal, these sentences were dropped. Basing its judgment on the Military Penal Code, the court felt that the legal minimum sentence of three years imprisonment was unjust.[15]

For complicity in mass murder, the following sentences were handed down to the other defendants who were found guilty: Laabs,15 years in prison and loss of civil rights for ten years; Walter Burmeister, 13 years in prison and loss of civil rights for ten years; Häfele, 15 years in prison and loss of civil rights for ten years; Möbius, eight years in prison and loss of civil rights for six years; Heinl, seven years in prison and loss of civil rights for five years; Ernst Burmeister, three-and-a-half years in prison.[16]

On appeal, the sentences of Laabs and Häfele were each reduced to 13 years. Reasons given by the court to justify the reductions included the fact that Laabs did not want to be in Chełmno and Häfele had given cigarettes to the Jewish workers in the camp. Ernst Burmeister's appeal was later dropped due to his ill health.[17]

In 1964, Professor Edward Serwański published an 87-page book on Chełmno entitled, *Obóz zagłady w Chełmnie nad Nerem 1941–1945* [The Extermination Camp in Chełmno-on-Ner 1941–1945]. The book, largely based on the Bednarz investigation, but also including the testimony of the German forester Heinz May, was published in conjunction with the dedication of the monument in the former forest camp. The book was also to affect the debate then underway in the German Bundestag concerning, in effect, extending the statute of limitations for Nazi war crimes.[18]

In 1975, the area of the former forest camp underwent a general land-scaping. An asphalt road, paths and squares were laid out—further ham-pering future archeological work. Decorative shrubs were planted around the area. Additional work was carried out in the early 1980s.

During the summers of 1986 and 1987, the District Museum in Konin began archeological work in the area of the former forest camp as part of an initiative to establish a museum on the site of the former death camp.

On June 17, 1990, a small museum was opened on the grounds of the former forest camp. In the forest, where the crematoria stood dur-ing the first period, fragments from one of the crematorium's founda-tions discovered during the excavations were put on display. A "Wall of Remembrance," 37.5 meters long and 2.20 meters high, was erected nearby, inscribed with the words, "To the memory of the Jews murdered in Chełmno

1941–1945." The concrete wall features a gate over which is inscribed in Hebrew "The gate through which the just will pass." The structure serves as a memorial wall where the names of the victims can be displayed, helping to end the anonymity of the camp and, more importantly, its victims. In addition to the wall of remembrance, memorials have been erected in subsequent years by various associations representing the Jewish communities murdered on these grounds, including Łódź, Bełchatów, Brzeziny and Gąbin.

On August 7, 1991, an updated tablet was unveiled at the gravesite of the Poles who were shot in the forest in 1939. The same day, a new monument was unveiled, an obelisk in memory of Stanisław Kaszyński. Kaszyński was betrayed and killed in 1942 for filing reports with the Polish underground about the events occurring in his village. (See Appendix II: The Kaszyński Affair.)

On August 22, 1994, a memorial cemetery was unveiled on the grounds of the former forest camp in conjunction with the 50th anniversary of the liquidation of the Łódź ghetto. The initiative was headed by the Turek Compatriots' Association from Israel and features Jewish headstones salvaged from the nearby town of Turek. Three plaques in Polish, English and Hebrew bear the following text: "To mark the 50th anniversary of extermination. In memory of our ancestors, who lived on this land and our brothers and sisters brutally murdered in Chełmno by the German Nazis. The lapidarium of tombstones from the destroyed Jewish cemetery in Turek was constructed by Compatriots' Association of Turek Residents in Israel."

The District Museum in Konin was able to locate two important objects in the former forest camp through analyzing aerial photographs taken of the area in 1958 and 1979; a field furnace from the first period of the camp's operation and a crematorium from the second period. In 1998, the museum purchased the land comprising the grounds of the former mansion.

Between 1997 and 2001, the museum located waste pits on the grounds of the former mansion, used to burn discarded items. The area of the former mansion itself was excavated down to the foundation, where numerous items of daily use were discovered, including tools of the tailors and shoemakers who worked in the basement. The excavation also revealed the floor plan of the basement area. The visitor to the site can now see the stairs leading down to the basement and the corridor through which thousands of victims were driven into the gas vans.

In 2003 and 2004, further archeological work was conducted in the former forest camp. The precise locations of the mass graves and individual objects were identified, as were the locations of the two main crematoria from the first period and two crematoria from the second period. This work continues as funds allow.

The district museum plans to develop the grounds of the former mansion as a memorial site to the victims of the Chełmno death camp as financial resources become available. In addition to those who escaped from the camp, among those victims are the individuals who worked as members of the Haus- and Waldkommandos.

The following list includes the names of those men and one woman, as well as their hometown or country, when known, as recalled by Michał Podchlebnik, Szlama Winer, Mordechai Żurawski, Szymon Srebrnik and others.[19] (The possibility of duplication exists.)

1941–1943

Ajzensztab (Kłodawa)

Menachem Arcichowski (Izbica)

Mojżesz Asz (Izbica)

Szlojme Babiacki

Samuel Bibergal

Bitter (Bydgoszcz)

Moszek Brafman (Izbica)

Gecel Chrząstkowski (Kłodawa)

Eisensztab (Kłodawa)

Gawerman (Izbica)

Pinkus Grun (Włocławek)

Moniek Halter (Izbica)

Josef Herszkowicz (Kutno)

Chaim Ruwen Izbicki (Bugaj)

Jehuda Jakubowski (Włocławek)

Zalman Jakubowski (Izbica)

Beniek Jastrzębski (Łęczyca)

Noech Wolf Judkiewicz (Łódź)

Kaliski (Dąbie)

Chaim Kiwer (Babiak)

Król (Izbica)

Krzewacki (Kłodawa)

Jonas Lew (Brzeziny)

Jehuda Lubiński (Izbica)

Mojżesz Łepek (Izbica)

Geszyp Majer (Kalisz)

Neumuller (Koło)

Aron Nusbaum (Sanok or Skepe)

Meir Piotrkowski (Izbica)

Mojżesz Plocker (Kutno)

Felek Plocker (Kutno)

Awigdor Polański (Izbica)

Icchak Prajs (Izbica)

Gerszon Praszker (Izbica)

Kałman Radziejewski (Izbica)

Aron Rozental

Gecel Stajer (Turek)

Iser Strasburg (Lutomiersk)

Gerszon Swiętopławski (Izbica)

Motel Symkie (Łęczyca)

Szmul Sztajer (Izbica)

Ika Szama (Brzeziny)

Szyja Szlamowicz (Grabów or Kalisz)

Zemad Szumiraj (Włocławek)

Toporski

Chaskiel Wachtel (Łęczyca)

Smlek Wachtel (Łęczyca)

Symcha Wachtel (Łęczyca)

Mechl Wilczyński (Izbica)

Michal Worbleznik

Chaskiel Zarak (Łęczyca)

Abram Zieliński (Izbica)

1944–1945

Paweł Akin (Łódź)

Alex (England)

Israel Bełchatowski (Bełchatów?)

Dawid Bendkowski (Łódź)

Fulek Berger (Zduńska Wola)

Bromberg

Icek Brzeziński

Henoch Erlich

Wolek Erlich

Finkelsztajn (Pabianice)

Moniek Fogiel

Frydland

Bendet Gliksman (Szczerców)

Laj Goldberg

Gringlum

Mojsie Gutman

Berek Himelfarb (Łódź)

Bern Jakobowicz

Israel Jakobowicz

Srul Jakubowicz (Bełchatów)

Huskiel Kalmuszewicz

Icie and Mojsie Kołton
   (brothers, Łódź)

Imom Koszkowicz

Hela Kowalska (Włocławek)

Bocian Lejb (Łódź)

Walter Lichtstein (Germany)

Franek Markiewicz

Beldyt (Abram?) Micenmacher
   (Bełchatów)

Miodownik

Abram Mordkiewicz (Łódź)

Mordka (Leizer?) Mordkiewicz
   (Łódź)

Shmul Nasadzki (Osieków)

Berek Oberferst (Łódź)

Noah Oberferst (Łódź)

Mordka Orzelek

Szmul Pasalski

Mojsie Ptaszkowski

Icek and Nathan Rapoport
   (brothers, Łódź)

Moniek Reich

Ime Rozenblum (Yvo?)
   (Czechoslovakia)

Izaak Sigelman

Berek Sitenfeld (Łódź)

Zawek Srebrnik (Łódź)

Jakub Szlamkowicz (Sieradz)

Geniek Szlamkowicz (Sieradz)

Weber

Szaja Weinblum (Łódź)

Werner

Jankiel Ziemniak

Berek Zytenfeld

Israel Zygelman (Łódź)

The Number of Victims

The exact number of people murdered in Chełmno will never be known. A debate on this subject, like many others regarding the camp, continues to this day. The lists of names that were turned over to the Sonderkommando when transports arrived to the camp have never been found and were probably destroyed at the end of the war. Some other records did survive the war, notably the daily chronicle of events in the Łódź ghetto as recorded in the Archives of the Jewish Administration. Also saved were file cards of the Łódź ghetto's statistical department containing information about the 1944 transports. These cards, however, provide figures only for those ten major transports that arrived during the second period.

Since the end of the war, the estimates of the number of victims murdered in the camp have steadily declined. This is not due to any attempt to minimize the horror that took place in that small village or to deny that people were exterminated there. Rather, it is due to the availability of documents and more accurate studies of the events that took place.

In the period immediately following the arrival of the Red Army to Chełmno, local villagers began speaking of one million victims. After a brief investigation the Red Army filed a preliminary report on Chełmno, dated February 1, 1945, in which a figure of "hundreds of thousands" of victims was given, based on what local residents had told investigators.[1] Four months later, on June 6, 1945, the Polish government began its own investigation of Chełmno, headed by Judge Władysław Bednarz from the district court in Łódź. He concluded that between 350,000 and 360,000 could have died there. This figure became the most widely accepted estimate, the official estimate of the Polish government and the most often repeated figure of the number of Chełmno victims.[2]

But is this number accurate? How did Bednarz arrive at it? Based on the testimonies of various witnesses, including the ticket agent at the Koło train station, the judge concluded that during the first period, on average, 1,000 people a day were killed. There was even a saying in the camp: *Ein tag, ein tausend* [one day, one thousand]. After subtracting Sundays, holidays, short breaks, etc., he then calculated the number of days the camp was active at 330. Bednarz then calculated the number of victims for the first period may well have been between 330,000 and 350,000. For the second period, he used the Łódź ghetto statistical department records of the ten transports (7,196). In addition, Bednarz estimated that the number of victims who came to Chełmno by truck brought the total for the second period to 10,000. Therefore, the number of victims for both periods totaled between 350,000 and 360,000.

This figure is obviously inflated. Although the camp was active between September 1942 and April 1943, few transports were sent there during those months. Moreover, by the time Chełmno became operational, at the end of 1941, the Jewish population of the Warthegau had been reduced to approximately 260,000, possibly even less.[3] If Bednarz's estimate were to take into account the relative inactivity of the period from mid-September 1942 through March 1943, it would reduce his total by approximately 195,000, that is to approximately 165,000.

The number of victims adopted at the trial of 12 former members of the Sonderkommando, held in Bonn, West Germany, in 1962, was 152,000. This figure was considered a minimum number of victims (the number for which there existed some sort of documentation). There are three sources for this documentation. The first is from the so-called Korherr Report, an SS statistical report on the Final Solution of the Jewish Question, prepared by the head of the SS Statistics Department, Dr. Richard Korherr.[4] In it, the figure 145,301 is given as the number of Jews who passed through "camps in the Warthegau" (in other words, Chełmno), up to December 31, 1942. The second source is the Łódź ghetto statistical records of the 7,196 victims from the ten 1944 transports. Adding these two sources together the total number of Chełmno victims comes to approximately 152,000.

The third source of official figures is an SS report concerning modifications to be made to the gas vans. The report states that 97,000 people had been exterminated in Chełmno as of June 5, 1942.[5] Thus, based on German documents concerning the first period of the camp, it appears that from December 1941 to June 1942 there were 97,000 victims, while 48,000 people died in Chełmno during the June through December 1942 time period. As has already been pointed out, there were few victims during the January through April 1943 period. Therefore, based on German documents, the number of victims during the first period is approximately 145,000.

Another method to determine the number of people who died in Chełmno is to construct a calendar that includes the dates, origins and sizes of the transports, as well as can be established. Such a calendar has, by and large, already been constructed, geographically rather than chronologically, by Danuta Dąbrowska.[6] The following chronological table is based largely upon her work.

	Date of Deportation	Origin of Transport	Number of People Deported
1941	Dec. 7	Koło	700
	Dec. 8	Koło	700
	Dec. 9	Koło	700
	Dec. 10	Koło	700
	Dec. 11	Koło	700
	Dec. 14[7]	Dąbie	975
	Dec. (second half)	Dobra	1,100

	Date of Deportation	Origin of Transport	Number of People Deported
1942	Jan. 2–9	Łódź (Roma)	4,300
	Jan. 10, 12	Kłodawa	1,000
	Jan. 13	Bugaj	600
	Jan. 14–15	Izbica Kujawska	1,000
	Jan. 16–29	Łódź	10,003
	Feb. 2	Sompolno	1,000
	Feb. 22–28	Łódź	7,025
	Mar. 1–31	Łódź	24,699
	Mar. 2	Krośniewice	900
	Mar. 3	Żychlin	3,200
	Mar. (first half)	Ozorków	500
	Mar. (second half)	Poddębice	2,008
	Mar. 26[8]	Kutno	6,000
	Apr. 1–2	Łódź	2,349[9]
	Apr. 10	Grabów	1,240
	Apr. 10–11	Łęczyca	1,750
	Apr. 16–17[10]	Gostynin	2,000
	Apr. 16–17[11]	Gąbin	2,150
	Apr. 17	Sanniki	250
	Apr. 22	Osięciny	300
	Apr. (mid-month)[12]	Brześć Kujawski	< 200[13]
	Apr. (mid-month)	Piotrków Kujawski	< 550
	Apr. 30–May 2	Włocławek	3,500
	May 4–15	Łódź	10,914
	May 17–18	Pabianice	4,000
	May 19–20[14]	Brzeziny	3,000

	Date of Deportation	Origin of Transport	Number of People Deported
	May 22[15]	Ozorków	300
	June 10–11	Radziejów Kujawski	630
	July 20	Czachulec	10,000[16]
	July (end)	Lutomiersk	750
	Aug. 11–13[17]	Bełchatów	4,953
	Aug. 14	Szadek	450
	Aug. 22	Sieradz	1,400
	Aug. 22–24	Warta	1,353
	Aug. 24–28	Łask	2,600[18]
	Aug.[19] (last week)	Wieluń	10,000
	Aug. 25–26[20]	Zduńska Wola	10,900
	Sept. 1–2, 7–12	Łódź	15,685[21]
	Sept. 14[22]	Zelów	6,000[23]
1944	June 23	Łódź	562
	June 26	Łódź	912
	June 28	Łódź	803
	June 30	Łódź	700
	July 3	Łódź	700
	July 5	Łódź	709
	July 7	Łódź	700
	July 10	Łódź	700
	July 12	Łódź	700
	July 14	Łódź	700
		Total for 1941–43:	165,034
		Total for 1944:	7,196
		Grand Total:	172,230

Using independent sources, the above table does provide figures similar to the German statistics. For the period from December 1941 to June 5, 1942, the table indicates 100,580 people were killed in Chełmno in comparison to the 97,000 figure given in the SS gas van document. Likewise, the figure in the table corresponding to the period noted in the Korherr report (145,301 victims) is 165,034. The localities listed in the table cannot be considered complete, although all major locations are included, and some figures in the table are merely an approximation of the number of people comprising the known transports. The result should be treated as a very rough estimate. Moreover, in addition to these transports listed in the table, forced laborers, unable to work any longer, were also sent to Chełmno from the labor camps scattered around the Warthegau. For example, 149 sick and unfit Jews were sent to Chełmno from the Konin labor camp between April and September 1942.[24] However, the table, as well as German documents, does indicate that the official Polish government estimate of 350,000 victims is simply too high. The figures mentioned in the German documents appear to reflect more accurately the actual number of victims.

The debate on the number of people murdered in Chełmno continues. One of the more recent studies supports the theory of approximately 151,000 victims while another has given a figure of 225,000.[25] The exact number of people who perished in Chełmno is not known and probably never will be. Based on German documents, a minimum of 152,000 people were killed in the camp; the actual number was no doubt somewhat higher.

Conclusion and Reflection

The history of the Chełmno death camp chronicles how much of the Jewish population of today's western Poland, as well as Roma and others, were murdered as a matter of government policy in the first death camp established by the Third Reich during the Second World War. The origin of the camp can be directly traced to the use of poison gas by the Nazi regime to kill mentally disabled patients in Germany. This so-called Euthanasia Program, whose planning began in the late 1930s and whose implementation coincided with the outbreak of the war, established institutes to kill those individuals whom the program deemed "unproductive." The toxic agent employed was carbon monoxide gas pumped into specially constructed chambers. With the outbreak of the war and subsequent occupation of Poland, the newly annexed territory of the Warthegau (roughly today's western Poland) where Chełmno was later established was incorporated into the program.

To conduct the killing program in the Warthegau a special squad, or commando, was created known as Sonderkommando Lange, named after Hauptsturmführer Herbert Lange who headed the unit. (Following Lange's transfer to Berlin in April 1942, the unit was referred to as Sonderkommando Kulmhof, after the Germanized name of the village where the camp was located.) The major difference between how the Euthanasia Program was conducted in the "Old Reich" and in the Warthegau was the use of Sonderkommando Lange as a mobile euthanasia institute. From December 1939 to June 1940, this unit traveled throughout the region to hospitals and other facilities murdering the disabled using what was, in effect, a gas chamber on wheels.

By July 1941—five months before Chełmno became operational on December 7, 1941—Greiser had developed a new program for his region's Jewish population. The plan, approved at the highest level of the Nazi government, envisioned the establishment of a single massive slave labor camp—the Łódź Ghetto—where productive Jews would be exploited to support the war effort, and a "quick-working device"—the Chełmno death camp—to exterminate the young, old and feeble, or as termed during the Euthanasia Program, the unproductive "useless eaters."

When Greiser received Hitler's permission to implement his plan and kill 100,000 Jews in the Warthegau, Lange was selected to head the project because of his experience gained during his mobile killing operations conducted within this same area. The direct prelude to the establishment of the Chełmno camp was the extermination of the Konin County Jews, a two-phased operation conducted during September and October 1941. This operation was experimental in nature, an effort to ascertain the best method of carrying out the murder of entire populations and to test the reaction of the victims to the reality of what was about to happen to them. With the experience gained from this experiment, Lange was ready to establish a static killing facility to which the victims would be transported, killed and disposed—a literal death factory, the first of its kind. The village of Chełmno was selected based on its relatively isolated location, proximity to the victims and access to roads and rail lines.

The Chełmno death camp as established was a primitive facility probably due to the fact that it served a limited purpose. Lange was tasked with murdering 100,000 people. With a killing capacity of approximately 1,000 people per day, the camp was probably expected to function for a relatively short period of time—some 100 working days. Once operational, and minor adjustments made to the killing procedure, the camp functioned without major incident until the summer of 1942 when the ground over the corpses buried in the forest began to swell and gasses from the decomposing bodies began escaping and polluting the surrounding area. The odor was so foul and pervasive, the camp had to cease operations until, after some experimentation, crematoria were constructed in the forest to dispose of the decomposing bodies. Henceforth, after gassing, all victims were burned, their bones ground into power and buried in pits, scattered around the forest floor and poured into the Warta River.

When virtually the entire Jewish population in the provincial ghettos of the Warthegau—including a portion of the residents in the Łódź ghetto— had been exterminated in Chełmno, the camp was closed. Following a mission-accomplished party in Koło and an official thank-you ceremony in Berlin, Sonderkommando Kulmhof was transferred to the Balkan theatre to fight partisans. Almost a year later, in March 1944, it was decided to reactivate the camp to exterminate those Jews remaining in the Łódź ghetto as agreed to by Oswald Pohl and Arthur Greiser. A reconstituted Sonderkommando Kulmhof returned to the village and re-established the facility, but due to the unfolding military situation and the limited capacity of the gas vans, "only" ten transports with a total of 7,196 people were directed to Chełmno. The remaining inhabitants of the Łódź ghetto (excluding a clean-up crew of several hundred Jews and those in hiding) were deported to Auschwitz, providing them, ironically, with a greater chance of survival than if they had been sent to Chełmno. As horrific as Auschwitz was, people in the transports were subjected to a selection process offering the possibility of survival. No such selection process existed in Chełmno.

By mid-January 1945, 47 Jews remained locked in the granary building, virtually the only structure left of the camp. As the final liquidation of these men began, they managed to overpower two of their German tormentors, a guard and the supervisor of the forest camp, Willi Lenz, taking their weapons and killing them. A firefight then broke out which ended when the granary was set on fire and those inside were consumed in the flames. This marked the end of Chełmno's operations.

The plan to murder Jews living in the Warthegau was conceived in the Governor's office, on the local level, in July 1941. It was a plan of genocide to be enacted in three stages. Stage one called for concentrating the Jewish population in a single labor camp to work for the German economy. Stage two involved providing a "humane solution" for that portion of the population whom the government could not feed. The authorities determined that approximately 25 percent of the Jewish inhabitants of the Gau (100,000 people) fell into this category. Stage three called for sterilizing all Jewish women of child-bearing age living in the labor camp. Implementation of the plan would result in the Jewish problem in the Warthegau being solved within one generation.

It may have sounded "fantastic" at the time, but with approval from Hitler, stages one and two were eventually implemented and completed by September 1942. The Łódź ghetto became the labor camp for all Jews living in the province and Chełmno was established as the "humane solution" for a quarter of the population. The plan was unique; nowhere else had genocide been proposed as a "feasible" solution of the Jewish problem. It was a prelude of things to come.

The plan was born out of frustration. With the outbreak of the war in 1939, and the acquisition of occupied territories, the thrust of racial policy focused on the expulsion of "sub-humans" from the Reich to these newly-controlled German areas. Arthur Greiser worked feverishly to expel his Poles and Jews from the Warthegau. However, the deportation programs failed for a number of reasons. In the first half of 1941, it was acknowledged that the Poles were indispensable; their labor was required to keep the economy from collapsing. Under Hans Biebow's administration, the Łódź ghetto had also become a critical component of the economy and a profitable venture for Greiser. He now supported the "productionists" over the "attritionists." Unproductive Jews had no advocate.

The decision to commit mass murder at Chełmno was not precedent setting. Within the Warthegau itself, Sonderkommando Lange broke the psychological barrier of murdering the mentally disabled in health care facilities. Later, Einsatzgruppen were dispatched behind the front lines of Operation Barbarossa, the invasion of the Soviet Union, to murder Jews and communists.

While what has become known as the Holocaust began much earlier, neither the Euthanasia Program, Operation Barbarossa nor Chełmno mark the beginning of the Final Solution. Each of these initiatives, and others, were limited in scope, but signal the cumulative radicalization of thought and policy at the highest level. These and other initiatives as well as Hitler's frustration on the military front—he would no longer wait for military victory in Russia to deport Jews to the East—eventually led to a comprehensive Final Solution for all of Europe's Jews. Experience gained at Chełmno provided a template for the establishment of the Aktion Reinhard camps of Bełżec, Sobibór and Treblinka. Chełmno was a primitive facility, but adequate to accomplish its limited purpose. The other extermination camps were built on the experience of the first death camp to accomplish their goal of murdering millions of people. This is Chełmno's legacy in the history of the Holocaust.

During the two decades following the Second World War, the Communist government of Poland dutifully followed the Soviet line of downplaying the uniqueness of the Holocaust as a Jewish genocide. The very first memorial and museum to be established in Poland, at the former Majdanek concentration camp, became the model for the manner of commemoration at subsequent sites. While the vast majority of people who died at Majdanek were Jews, with respect to commemorating the dead, they shared an equal place among the camp's other victims, which included Poles, communists and Soviet POWs. No monuments were erected by the Polish government at the sites of the former extermination centers immediately after the war.

By the early 1960s, an agricultural cooperative had been established on the grounds of the former Chełmno death camp. The granary building, the only structure of the camp not destroyed, was renovated and used as a warehouse. The small monument to the camp's victims, erected in 1957, was overshadowed and symbolically cast aside in a corner of the former mansion grounds. At the site of the former forest camp, local Poles erected a wooden cross in 1945 to commemorate the 55 Poles who were executed and buried in the forest in 1939. Also in 1957, a delegation of Czechs planted rose bushes on the grounds of the former forest camp as a memorial to the children from the village of Lidice.

The Soviet Union, along with its socialist bloc countries including Poland, launched a campaign in the early 1960s to ensure that Germany would not allow the statute of limitations for crimes of murder to lapse, with the intention that war criminals would continue to be brought to justice. The Adolf Eichmann trial occurred at this time and also attracted world attention. The government of Poland was focused on the criminals; memorialization of the sites of the death camps was to be a tangible reminder of the guilt and crimes committed by Nazi Germany. However, the Chełmno site memorialized 55 Poles and 82 Czech children, but did not mention the 350,000 Jews (according to its own estimate) who died here. How could Poland ask Germany "to remember" and amend the law while its own government had not bothered to memorialize the real catastrophe that occurred at the sites of the death camps? This should have been an embarrassment to the Polish government.

Thus, the Polish government (through the Department of Culture in the Voivodship Office in Poznań and the Council for the Protection of Monuments to Struggle and Martyrdom) decided to build a monument in 1961, which was completed and unveiled in 1964. Today, the monument stands in the Rzuchów Forest, on the grounds of the former forest camp. Inscribed on the front, in bold letters, is a single word written in Polish: *Pamiętamy* [we remember]. But why is the message only in the Polish language? The camp's victims came from many different countries. Was the monument only intended for Polish speaking people? Next to the inscription is a bas-relief frieze representing a line of persecuted people with no suggestion indicating who they are. The side of the monument facing the forest features a portion of the letter, again only in Polish, written by the final group of Jewish prisoners—but it has been edited; both references to Jews are redacted. The monument completely erases the uniqueness of the Holocaust as the genocide of the Jewish people.

The above cited letter called for remembrance and justice for the camp's victims. The Polish government failed to properly memorialize the people who died in the camp, but has justice been served for these victims? This is a much more complex issue, beginning with the question "what constitutes justice?"

Numerous trials were held after the war involving defendants who, to one degree or another, were responsible for the mass murder committed in Chełmno. Those brought to court included the highest ranking Reich officials, such as Hermann Göring, the Gauleiter Arthur Greiser, Łódź ghetto administrator Hans Biebow and numerous other bureaucrats and police officials. In regard to Chełmno camp personnel, almost all of the perpetrators fled, or tried to flee, Poland at the end of the war. Some died in combat, others were taken captive by Soviet or other Allied forces, and others simply disappeared. A total of 16 former camp personnel faced justice in six postwar trials, two of which were held in Germany (Laabs et al and Fiedler) and four in Poland (Israel, Gielow, Piller, Mania). A 15 year prison sentence (reduced on appeal) for Gustav Laabs, the gas van driver, was the most severe penalty handed down in a German court. Polish courts initially showed little sympathy for Chełmno defendants. Israel was arrested in Łódź by Polish authorities, while Piller and Gielow surrendered to Soviet forces in Poznań, were deported to the Soviet Union and eventually returned to Poland to stand trial. Justice was swift for these men; Israel received the death penalty, later reduced to life, while the death sentences handed down to Piller and Gielow were carried out, in 1949 and 1951 respectively. The final case in Poland came to trial 56 years after the end of the Second World War.

Henryk Mania, one of the eight Polish men who worked in Chełmno, was liberated from a subcamp of the Mauthausen concentration camp in May, 1945. Mania returned home to the town of Wolsztyn and eventually settled in the city of Szczecin in the northwest corner of Poland, where he lived an unremarkable life for the next five decades.

In May 1949, a man living in Kalisz, who had worked as a driver for the hospital in Koło during the war and remembered Mania from his stay there, attended a business meeting with an associate from Poznań. The associate's name was Mania and he looked like the "Gestapo official" he remembered in the hospital. During the course of the meeting, the man asked his associate if he had worked in Koło during the war. The reply was no; he had spent the war in Kraków. The man remained suspicious and went to the police. This begins the strange history of Henryk Mania's legal problems.

The police launched an investigation of this man, interviewing Koło hospital employees and residents of Chełmno. The investigation showed this to be a case of mistaken identity, but it did set the wheels in motion for a closer look at Henryk Mania. In 1953, the police in Poznań began an investigation into the wartime and present activities of Henryk Mania, suspected of being a member of the SS. In 1956, the police concluded that it could not find any witnesses to confirm that Mania had cooperated with the Nazis, but the case continued. In 1957, the police determined that Henryk Mania had been an employee [*pracownik*] of the SS Sonderkommando in the "concentration camp" located in Chełmno. Witnesses stated that Mania participated in the murder and persecution of the Polish population. Based on this information the case materials were transferred to the archive of Department X.

In 1962, a correspondent for Czechoslovakia's *Rudeho Prava* requested and received permission from the police to interview Mania and his former co-worker at Chełmno, Henryk Maliczak, in connection with the murder of the Czech children from Lidice. The interviews were conducted in August 1962, in the presence of a police official. Perhaps as a result of these interviews, a new investigation was launched on November 14, 1963, into the activities of Mania, Maliczak and other Poles who worked in Chełmno. This investigation was halted on April 30, 1964, two weeks after new interviews were conducted with Mania and Maliczak, due to "the considerable amount of time that had passed since the crimes were committed and the death of many witnesses to the criminal activity of the suspects."

Mania and Maliczak were again interviewed in 1967 in connection with an investigation conducted by Marian Kaczmarek into the extermination of the mentally ill in the Warthegau. No charges were filed. Mania was interviewed again on February 8, 1977, concerning his arrest and imprisonment in Wolsztyn at the beginning of the war. In August 1991, the Institute of National Remembrance (IPN) launched an investigation into the activities of the Poles who worked in Chełmno. In 1995, Mania accompanied investigators to the site of the former death camp for orientation purposes.

Henryk Mania was arrested on November 3, 2000, and charged with complicity in genocide for his activities at Chełmno. During his trial, Mania claimed to be a prisoner and only followed orders under threat of reprisals against himself and his family. The prosecution maintained that Mania had shown an eagerness to beat victims and rob them of their belongings. In June 2001, the court found Mania guilty and sentenced him to eight years in prison. (The prosecution had demanded 15 years.) The sentence was upheld by the Court of Appeals (2002) and Supreme Court (2003).

Why did it take so long to arrest and charge Mania? (Maliczak, the only other of the four Poles to return to Poland after the war, died in 1982.) Why were earlier investigations discontinued? It has been suggested that these two Poles were protected from prosecution as the son of one of the Polish gravediggers for Sonderkommando Lange became a top-ranking official of the Justice Department in the Communist government of the People's Republic of Poland; it would not have been in his or the family's interest to bring the issue to light. However, no documentation has been found indicating that the official interfered in any investigation.[1]

Has justice been served in the case of those individuals who worked in the Chełmno death camp? Are the scales of justice, truth and fairness, balanced? These are questions each person must answer for him or herself.

Since the collapse of Communism in Poland, efforts to correct the distortion of history manifested in the design of the Rzuchów Forest monument have been undertaken by the District Museum in Konin and its branch affiliate, the Museum of the Former Death Camp in Chełmno-on-Ner. The monument still stands but a lapadarium has been established, as has a Wall of Remembrance. In the field near the site of the crematoria, survivor communities have erected small monuments to their friends and family who died here. The museum has also conducted important archeological research to ensure that the truth about Chełmno and the Holocaust is not lost to future generations.

It is important to remember Chełmno and the road that led to it, beginning with the perpetrators Adolf Hitler and those who chose to follow him including those "ordinary men" stationed in Chełmno who routinely committed murder as a matter of course, the majority of whom were never held accountable for doing so. This book also remembers: the pain and suffering endured by millions of people at the hands of these perpetrators; the weakest and most vulnerable, the mentally ill, who in their time of greatest need fell victim to those who were suppose to protect them; the civil servant and social activist Stanisław Kaszyński, who gave his life in the service of his country and humanity, and others who worked with him in the Polish underground movement; Szlama Winer, whose testimony remains a singular contribution to our knowledge of the camp and a reminder of the crucial importance of bearing witness; the triumph of the human spirit manifested through the escape and survival of Abram Rój, Michał Podchlebnik, Yerachmiel Widawski, Yitzhak Justmann, Szymon Srebrnik and Mieczysław Żurawski, who under impossible conditions never surrendered and later bore witness, publicly and privately, to the best and worst in mankind; the tens of thousands of anonymous men, women and children who suffocated to death in the crowded gas vans of Chełmno. They should be remembered not only for how they died, but for how they lived; as fathers and mothers, sons and daughters, husbands and wives.

Chełmno must be understood not only as a horrible event of human history. It also stands as an unambiguous warning of what can happen when we fail to maintain eternal vigilance against the dehumanization of others and as a plea to embrace and defend the sanctity of life.

Appendices

The Gas Vans

The role played by the gas vans in the extermination process conducted in Chełmno is central and therefore requires a brief review of their development and examination of the men who drove them.

The gas van is a product of the Third Reich, although the term was coined following the Second World War. The Germans referred to these vans as Sonderwagen, Spezialwagen or S-wagen—special vehicles. The origin of the gas van is traced back to 1939 when Herbert Lange traveled from Poznań to Berlin for consultations concerning the development of a mobile euthanasia institute or gas chamber on wheels. However, the precise contribution, if any, made by the Reich Security Main Office (Reichssicherheitshauptamt – RSHA) in its construction is not known. Henryk Maliczak testified he assisted in converting a van at the Gestapo office in Poznań by paneling the interior,[1] but it is not known if the entire conversion process, which was not highly technical in nature, occurred there. Nevertheless, RSHA was certainly aware of this vehicle and was aware of its shortcomings in regard to the task assigned to Lange. The supply of bottled carbon monoxide proved to be a problem and occasionally the killing process had to be delayed until new cylinders were brought from Berlin.[2]

Some 20 months after Lange began mobile killing operations with a single van, a program to develop gas vans was conducted in the technical department of RSHA in Berlin for use in the mobile killing operations of the Einsatzgruppen, which followed the German Army into the Soviet Union. In August 1941, Reichsführer Heinrich Himmler witnessed a mass shooting conducted by Einsatzgruppen B in Minsk, Byelorussia.[3] Shaken by the experience, he ordered Arthur Nebe, the head of Einsatzgruppen B and simultaneously head of the Criminal Police (Kripo, Department V at RSHA), to find a more "humane" method of killing. Himmler felt the psychological "hardship" suffered by the executioners, the German soldiers in the Einsatzgruppen, was too great. Due to the scale of the operation and logistics involved with transporting cylinders of carbon monoxide to the Soviet Union, the version of the gas van used by Lange was considered impractical. A new solution was required.

Nebe turned to Dr. Walter Heess, the head of the Kripo's Technical Institute for the Detection of Crime (KTI). KTI had previously been instrumental in developing the gas chambers used by the euthanasia institutes. The idea of using exhaust gases had already been discussed by Nebe and Heess. Nebe had come up with the idea after almost killing himself when returning home drunk from a party and falling asleep in his garage with the engine running.[4] The concept circulated around the halls of KTI, but no specific steps were taken at the time.

Dr. Albert Widmann, a toxicology expert and head of KTI's chemical section, was summoned to Minsk to conduct experiments in order to find the most practical killing method. One of these trials involved blowing up victims with explosives, but this was deemed a failure. Another test involved attaching hoses to exhaust pipes of vehicles and to pipes leading into a sealed room. The exhaust fumes killed the victims inside and this experiment was considered a success.

Back in Berlin, Reinhard Heydrich signed off on the report filed by Heess, who informed Widmann that gas vans employing exhaust fumes instead of cylinders of carbon monoxide would be constructed.[5] The task of constructing the gas vans fell to Obersturmbannführer Walter Rauff, the head of RSHA's office for technical affairs (Department II D). Rauff was responsible for all motor vehicles of the Security Police. He discussed the idea of converting trucks into mobile gas chambers with his subordinate Friedrich Pradel, the head of the transportation service. Pradel, in turn, consulted with Harry Wentritt, his chief mechanic who ran the motor pool. The idea was deemed feasible and Rauff ordered appropriate vehicles be found and converted in Wentritt's garage.

Pradel acquired five or six trucks from the Wehrmacht and ordered hermetically sealed cargo compartments from Gaubschat, a firm in Berlin. Wentritt later described the conversion process.

> A removable exhaust hose, which led from the outside to the floor of the van, was fixed to the exhaust. We bored a hole in the van about 58 to 60 millimeters in diameter, the size of the exhaust pipe. Over this hole, to the inside of the van, was welded a metal pipe, which was attached to, or could be attached to, the exhaust hose that came from the outside. When the engine was switched on and the connections made, the engine's exhaust fumes went through the exhaust pipe into the exhaust hose and from there into the pipe that led to the inside of the van. Thus the van filled with gas. [... Pradel] instructed me to fix the vans in such a way that the engine exhaust fumes could be introduced into the van. This was possible with the help of the hose that was attached to the exhaust. Pradel then told me that another pipe had to be fitted inside the van to prevent the occupants from interfering with the admission of the gas. Thus, the work carried out in our motor pool was essentially determined by Pradel or his superiors.[6]

With the conversion of the first van completed, Wentritt drove it to the courtyard of KTI. The vehicle was examined by technical experts and a test was conducted to measure the amount of carbon monoxide gas in the rear compartment. Days later, the vehicle was taken to the Sachsen-hausen concentration camp, outside Berlin, where 40 Russian prisoners were ordered into the truck. The engine was started and the gas van drove to the crematorium. The experts followed on foot. After reaching the vehicle, they could still hear the victims moaning and banging on the walls inside. After a subsequent 20 minute wait, observation through the peephole in the driver's cab confirmed all inside were dead. Heess and the other SS officials deemed the experiment a success.

Production of the gas vans now moved forward at the SS garage in Berlin. The process took eight to fourteen days, with only one van under conversion at a time. The garage converted two models of vans. The smaller version, converted from three-ton Diamond and Opel-Blitz vans, had a two-by-four meter hermetically sealed compartment and was designed to carry 25 to 30 people. The larger van, a Sauer truck, was an eight-ton vehicle with a 5.8-meter long "cargo" compartment. The specified load capacity of this model was 50 people.[7] Approximately two months had passed from conception to production, which began in November 1941.

Rauff's department in RSHA converted vans for the Einsatzgruppen operating on the eastern front. However, three vans were directed to Chełmno; two of the smaller three-ton models (only six were produced) and later a larger Sauer van. The fact that Chełmno received two of the first vans off the production line testifies to the importance placed on this camp.

Literature on the gas vans used in Chełmno has cited an invoice issued by the Leipzig-based company Motoren Heyne to Sonderkommando X in Kulmhof as evidence that the gas vans originated from this source.[8] However, this document is an invoice for a used, 18 horsepower diesel engine and not a vehicle of any kind. An engine of this sort would have more likely been used, for example, to power a bone grinder, or provide power for other equipment used in either the forest camp or at the mansion.

Gustav Laabs and Oskar Hering were assigned to Chełmno from the RSHA in Berlin and arrived there together at about the end of April or the beginning of May 1942, after Lange's departure. They reported to Both-mann and were assigned to drive the gas vans, which they did until the camp was closed in 1943. Hering remains a bit of an enigma as he did not survive the war and is rarely mentioned in testimonies by local villagers or former members of the Sonderkommando. The arrival of the two new gas van drivers raises the issue of the identity of the previous gas van drivers. This is one of many areas concerning the gas vans that remain unclear and quite remarkable considering the key role these individuals played in the extermination process. The identity of the original drivers has never been definitively established, although several members of the Sonderkommando mention two other SS men as having been gas van drivers.

Laabs stated that two SS men were transferred out of the camp to Berlin three or four weeks after his arrival. According to him one of them was named Franz Walter. The only fact he recalled about the other driver was that he suffered from rheumatism.[9] Alois Häfele, who had been in Chełmno since at least January, stated that one of these men was named Walter, the other Basler or Batzler.[10] Walter Burmeister, stationed in Chełmno from the very beginning, recalled only one name - Baseler.[11] Fritz Ismer also remembered only one name: Basler.[12] Josef Islinger, a guard who arrived in Chełmno around April, identified Oberscharführer Basler as a gas van driver.[13] On the other hand, people like Möbius and Heinl, who had been in Chełmno since December, did not remember these names at all. The two Poles who worked in the camp and gave postwar testimony did not mention the names of the gas van drivers. These drivers lived together in the Radoszewski's house, not far from the mansion. In February 1942, they employed a local young woman to bring them meals from the camp kitchen, clean the house and wash their clothes. She remembered their last names as Walter and Pasler and stated that both of them were SS men.[14] Other local residents of Chełmno who gave postwar testimony do not shed light on the question of the identity of the original gas van drivers.

Szlama Winer and Michał Podchlebnik, two members of the Jewish Waldkommando who escaped from the camp, said little to help identify the drivers. Winer stated only that the same two men in SS uniforms drove the vans and that one of them was about 40 years old.[15] Podchlebnik mentioned German drivers in civilian clothes, but it is not clear if the reference is to the gas van drivers.[16] If he was referring to gas vans, these drivers may have been the Polish workers who, in fact, wore civilian clothes and spoke German (and Polish) in the camp.

While the identity of these individuals has not been fully resolved, some details concerning the vehicles themselves can be clarified, though major questions still remain unanswered. One of the few people to give eyewitness testimony that transcends both Lange's mobile killing operations of the mentally ill and the static Chełmno killings was Henryk Maliczak. He stated that a van used by Sonderkommando Lange during the euthanasia killings was a furniture van that had been converted into a gas van at the headquarters of the Poznań Gestapo. Several of the Poles who worked in Chełmno, including Szymański and Maliczak, participated in its conversion by, among other things, paneling the interior.[17]

During the Euthanasia Program conducted in 1940, the converted van carried a cylinder of pure carbon monoxide gas, which served as the lethal agent. Henryk Mania, present during the gassings of the mentally ill by Sonderkommando Lange, testified how this first gas van was used in

1940 to kill mental patients in a forest outside of Kościan, approximately 40 kilometers southwest of Poznań. The Polish labor detail was taken to the forest to dig the burial pits. Mania described how the gas van subsequently arrived on site.

> It was a kind of furniture van, hermetically sealed with a separate cab. It seems to me that the inside was covered with sheeting. I don't remember if there was any inscription on it. The exterior was painted a dark color. Inside were benches. The contents of two [normal] trucks could be placed in it, that is 50 to 60 people, maybe more. The [Polish] prisoners carried a cylinder that was placed near the vehicle and then connected to a hose (or two hoses), the outlet of which was located inside the vehicle, under the bench. One of the SS men operated the cylinder, opening the valve. After approximately half an hour, the same SS man opened the rear doors of the vehicle. We were ordered to throw out the corpses of those gassed.[18]

The murder of the Jews in the forests outside of Konin was the penultimate operation carried out by Sonderkommando Lange as a mobile unit. The operation was conducted in stages during the months of September, October and November, after which the Sonderkommando preceded directly to Chełmno and began to establish the camp.[19] Both Maliczak and Mania stated that initially, for a short time, the victims were murdered in Chełmno by using the bottled gas method. Mania stated that after the victims were loaded into the van and the doors closed, they were killed with gas from the cylinders while still at the ramp.[20] This testimony is supported by the policeman Karl Heinl, who recalled that initially only one gas van, which looked like a furniture van, was used in Chełmno and that two new vans from Berlin arrived in the camp later.[21]

Other testimony confirming that Lange continued using cylinders of carbon monoxide originates from an interesting source, Heinz May, the local German forester. May stated that he had access to the forest camp. He never mentioned that he was present on the grounds of the mansion. However, he described this early method of gassing.

> After [the victims] had undressed they were driven into an adjacent small room in which a small electric bulb was burning. In this room, they were densely packed together. Thereupon the two doors of the room were locked and the electric light was turned off. This room was nothing else but a truck built especially for this purpose. Bottles with carbon monoxide were attached to the truck and the gas poured into the interior of the truck through narrow pipes after a valve had been opened.[22]

Based on the evidence above, the Chełmno camp began operations with a van using cylinders of carbon monoxide to carry out the killings, no doubt the same vehicle referred to as the Kaiser's Kaffee van. (The logos on the vehicle are believed to have been painted over.) This vehicle was used in Chełmno for only a short period of time.

The original gas van was not the only van used in the camp. RSHA sent two of its smaller vans to Chełmno in early January at the latest, presumably the Opel-Blitz vans. Numerous accounts refer to these gas vans, which are generally described as identical to each other, but smaller than the third van. The driver of the original van, the Kaiser's Kaffee van, has never been identified; Walter and Basler were probably the initial drivers of these two other smaller vans. The existence of three vans in the camp in the initial stage is confirmed by the testimonies of Winer and Podchlebnik. Podchlebnik stated that two vans were used simultaneously and that, in addition, there was a third larger van that was broken down and parked in the yard at the mansion.[23] This is most likely a reference to the original van that had temporarily broken down, as a larger Sauer arrived only later. Kurt Möbius and other newcomers were taken to the forest for the first time the day after their arrival in the camp. While there, Möbius watched two vans drive up to a pit and the Polish workers empty them.[24] This event occurred in December, during the first or second week of operations, and therefore these vans must have arrived shortly after the camp began functioning.

It would seem to have been apparent not only to Lange, but also to everyone else in the chain of command up through RSHA, that additional vans would be needed in order to carry out his assignment. The original van was not particularly efficient; victims often survived the gassing and were finished off with a bullet in the head. The van also required cylinders of gas, which had to be transported to the camp. In essence, this van had become obsolete with the development of the new gas vans coming out of Wentritt's garage in Berlin.[25]

Unfortunately, even the make of the two vans, driven by Walter and Basler and subsequently Laabs and Hering, have never been definitively identified. Were the Chełmno vans the smaller Opel-Blitz version? Not according to Walter Burmeister. He identified them as Wehrmacht-gray Renault vans that Walter and Basler had brought with them from RSHA in Berlin. He also stated that they appeared to be new. His brief description of the construction of the exhaust pipe on these vans matches those given by other witnesses describing the Sauer van.[26] If Burmeister is correct, the RSHA gas van program in Berlin converted not only Opels, Diamonds and Sauers, but at least one other type of van as well. Laabs stated that the vans he drove were American-made Dodge vans.[27] Whether the new vans were Opels, Renaults, or Dodges, two vehicles together with a larger Sauer operated in Chełmno until the camp was temporarily closed in 1943. According to Walter Burmeister, the clothing shipped out of the camp was first disinfected in an old furniture van, hinting at the subsequent use of the original Kaiser's Kaffee van but not its ultimate fate.[28]

The fact that four vans were in Chełmno is supported by a number of civilian bystanders. Several local residents observed two larger and two smaller vans. This would account for the presence of the Kaiser's Kaffee van, the Sauer and the two smaller Opel-Blitz models. Wiktoria Adamczyk worked in the kitchen as a cook for the Sonderkommando during the first period. She said that there were two identical vans, a larger van, and a fourth van was used when larger transports arrived. Zygmunt Szkobel, a laborer who worked on the road between Koło and Chełmno, noted that the fourth van was lighter in color and transported Jewish workers to the forest. A resident of Chełmno, Stanisław Śliwiński, stated simply that there were four vans; two larger and two smaller. Józef Dziegielewski, a civilian who worked for the forest service, noted that three vans took victims to the forest—one larger, two smaller—but occasionally a fourth van, more or less the size of the larger van, also transported victims. Alexander Woźniak remembered three vans, but stated that a fourth van, somewhat different than the others, was used in the spring of 1942.[29]

The gassing procedure practiced in Chełmno was more horrific, if such is possible, than one might imagine. Death did not come quickly. The victims were loaded into the van, the doors locked, and the engine started. After some minutes, as the screaming and knocking on the sides of the van diminished, the victims were driven off to the pits in the forest for burial. One early account states the van remained at the mansion gassing its load of victims for 15 minutes before driving to the forest.[30] However, from the observations of Winer and Podchlebnik, it is also known that once the van entered the forest camp it stopped some distance away from the grave. The driver then made some manipulations in the cab that, presumably, opened the valve on the gas cylinder. Only at this time did the members of the Jewish Waldkommando hear screams and knocking coming from inside the van. Finally, after some minutes, all was quiet and the van pulled up to the burial pit. The simplest explanation for the discrepancies in the testimonies concerning where the victims were gassed is that the procedure was not fixed. The driver of the van may have had the discretion as to where he wanted to turn on the gas, either while still at the mansion or after arriving in the forest.

Observers indicate that during the early months of activity the gas vans carried living people to the forest. The gas vans were driven between the mansion and the forest almost daily along a public road, the Koło-Dąbie highway. The local population had repeated opportunities to observe them. Józef Klonowski, a Pole who lived in the area, once saw a gas van overturned on the highway near the forest, and Jews standing around it.[31] In the winter of 1942, another local Pole was riding his bicycle down the highway when he saw that a gas van had broken down and the engine was being repaired. As he passed by, he heard screams coming from inside.

The van was started up and drove past him only to stop once more. As he pedaled by the van a second time, he again heard screams.[32] On March 23, 1942, Bolesław Antkiewicz, while on his way to Chełmno, saw a gas van broken down on the highway near the forest. Antkiewicz recalled that, "Despite the fact that the van had stopped, the body moved as if something inside of it were rocking back and forth."[33] Marianna Woźniak observed a gas van which had broken down in front of her house. "Cries were heard from inside the van. They were hitting the walls with their fists. This unnerved the Germans, so one of them struck the walls of the van with a stick screaming at them to be quiet."[34]

In order to relieve the drivers of the gas vans, as well as the general public, from the burden of listening to the victims' screams while driving to the forest and to prevent the possibility of escape in transit or after an accident, greater efforts were made to ensure the victims were killed immediately after their entry into the van, while still at the mansion. These efforts would have included a longer waiting time and revving the engine to force more exhaust into the rear compartment. Indeed, this was the procedure as described by Laabs. Evidence of this adjustment is supported by an incident that occurred after those described above. During the summer of 1942, Józef Budynek was working on the highway between Chełmno and the forest. He noticed a gas van stopped on the road with its rear doors open. Two Jews had fallen out of it. The bodies were thrown into the truck and the doors were closed.[35] Despite the efforts taken by the Sonderkommando, various accounts of the unloading procedure mention individuals who survived the gassing and who were killed with bullets.

The change in the gassing procedure and the dismissal of the original gas van drivers occurred at approximately the same time, March and April 1942. These changes may have been instituted following the arrival of the new leader of the Sonderkommando, Kriminalkommissar and Hauptsturmführer Hans Bothmann. Walter Burmeister testified that just after Bothmann's arrival, the original gas van drivers were relieved, perhaps because of some "incident."[36]

The incident may have been the explosion of the Sauer van as it was backed up to the ramp at the basement door. The victims had just been loaded inside. When the motor was started an explosion blew open the rear doors.[37] The victims inside were badly burned and at least one guard, Alexander Steinke, was injured. Little is known about the event, but it is referred to in an SS report concerning modifications to the vans. The incident was attributed to operator error and perhaps this was the reason, or one of them, that the drivers were replaced.[38]

As mentioned above, the gas vans broke down from time to time. In such cases, Hauptscharführer Bürstinger, who was in charge of the vehicles, would send them to garages in Koło for repairs. The Sonderkommando used the garage at the firm Reichsstrassenbauamt, which employed Poles as mechanics, to repair its vehicles. From the testimonies of these mechanics, it can be seen how these specific vans used in the Chełmno camp had been converted into gas vans.

During the winter of 1941–42, two vans arrived to Reichsstrassenbauamt, "one larger, the other smaller." The Sauer needed repairs; it had a damaged radiator. Józef Piaskowski, one of the mechanics at the shop, repaired it.

> I was entrusted with its repair. The smaller van left. During the repairs, two guards watched me, not allowing me to examine the construction of the van. I have been a mechanic since 1928. I have driven various types of vehicles and have a lot of experience in gauging the size of vehicles. The van that I repaired was about two meters 30 centimeters high, about 5.5 meters long and two meters wide, maybe a little more. I figure it could carry about 80 to 100 people at a time. The doors of the van, in the back, were locked and bolted. In the cab were two military-type gas masks. The exterior walls were not made of sheet metal but were wooden, made of tongue and groove boards (like furniture vans). I didn't notice any markings or inscriptions. The engine was huge. Repairing the radiator, I looked under the van and saw that the exhaust pipe was specially constructed. In particular, more or less half way down the van, about a one-meter section of the exhaust pipe was flexible, like a hydraulic hose [wąż hydrauliczny]. This flexible part of the exhaust pipe could be screwed into the end section of the exhaust pipe so that the exhaust gas would be led out, as in all normal vehicles. It was also possible to screw the flexible part of the pipe into a hole in the floor of the van. Then, the exhaust gas went into the van.[39]

The following statement was given by Bronisław Falborski who, before taking a job as a mechanic, was the driver for the forester Heinz May. Falborski had often seen the vans in and near the forest camp. Note that the exhaust pipe was connected to channel the gas into the van when it arrived for repairs.

> [T]he van was black and box-shaped. The roof was almost flat and met the sidewalls at nearly right angles. It seems to me that it was covered with sheet metal, but I'm not sure about this. I didn't look at the motor and I didn't notice the make of the van. The doors were locked and bolted. The vehicle was guarded and we weren't allowed to look at its construction. [...] The repair consisted of changing a gasket between the flexible part of the exhaust pipe and the part leading inside the van. The exhaust pipe was not normal. Instead of a single pipe, it was composed of three sections. The middle one was flexible like a hydraulic hose. This middle section of the exhaust pipe could be connected with the pipe going to the floor so that the gas would flow into the van. When it was connected to the end pipe, it would function as a normal exhaust pipe. When it was brought in for repairs the pipe was connected to go inside the van. However, the gasket between the two couplers was worn out and I was instructed to change it. I changed the gasket, installing an asbestos one, and fastened the couplers with four screws.[40]

Another mechanic, Zenon Rossa, also changed the gasket on the Sauer. His description of the van agrees with the one given by Falborski.[41] Michał Lewandowski repaired the brakes on the Sauer. His description of the exhaust pipe configuration agrees with the above descriptions. He also states that the exhaust pipe on the smaller, different type of van, which was brought in for repair, was identical to the Sauer.[42] Bronisław Mańkowski, a blacksmith and fitter employed at one of the repair shops, opened the rear doors of one of the vans while it was being repaired. He noticed "that in the middle of the wooden floor was an opening which was secured with a perforated metal plate. (It looked like a colander.) There was no wooden grating on the floor."[43] Still another mechanic noticed that in the cabs of the vans was an annotation "Berlin, Baujahr 1940" [Berlin, built in 1940] and that the six-cylinder motors were large, similar to Citroens.[44]

The testimonies of the Polish mechanics show clearly how the vans had been converted by installing a special exhaust pipe under the vehicle. The question of how the vans worked is clear. Numerous postwar testimonies collected by Judge Bednarz confirm that the two smaller vans were in general use, the larger Sauer was used less frequently and that a fourth van, about the size of the Sauer, also operated in the camp during the first period.

Another issue connected with the gas vans is the question of the type of gasoline these vehicles used. The firm "Lauf" in Koło initially supplied gasoline and oil to the Sonderkommando. According to one of the employees, the unit received 2,000 to 2,600 liters per month and much more in the summer of 1942.[45] Later, a firm in Włocławek supplied the gasoline. The fuel was brought directly to the camp in 600-liter cisterns about once a week, but large shipments, comprising a cistern and trailer were also received about every other week. The capacity of the trailers varied from 1,500 to 4,000 liters.[46] There is no evidence that the gasoline originating from these sources had been altered in any way.

Unidentified chemicals were shipped to the Sonderkommando through regular commercial channels. The freight company Maks Sado in Koło frequently received such shipments for the Sonderkommando, which included 50-liter glass bottles containing unknown "acids" and other glass containers marked with the words "caution glass."[47] An employee of another company reported the Sonderkommando receiving small, heavy boxes about 50 centimeters long, 25 centimeters tall and about 30 centimeters wide, containing some kind of brick-red colored powder. The boxes, heavy in relation to their size, were addressed to the firm Lado with the notation "For Sonderkommando Kulmhof." On at least one occasion, the boxes were not hermetically sealed and the powder poured out when the box was shaken. These boxes arrived less than ten times, each time in consignments of four to seven boxes. The company also once received iron containers with an unknown fluid. One of the containers was full; the other was half empty. The containers were sealed and allegedly contained oil.[48]

Józef Grabowski, the driver for Dr. Konig who was a frequent visitor in Chełmno and the physician who gave the SK members injections against typhus, noted the following.

> Once I got gas for the car from the Sonderkommando. I started the motor when the car was in the garage. Momentarily, I began to lose consciousness; I became lightheaded and had a sweet taste in my mouth. With my last bit of strength I managed to open the garage door and escape. Later, I had a terrible headache. [...] When I told Dr Konig about this, he categorically forbid me to start the motor in the garage when the car had gas in it from the Sonderkommando. Normally, I often started the car in the garage and it did not produce the mentioned effects. It seems to me that some substance was added to the gas.[49]

While these reports do not prove chemicals were added to the gasoline used by the gas vans, they do open the possibility that chemicals may have been used, if only on an experimental basis, and that a great deal remains unknown about the specific workings inside Sonderkommando Kulmhof.

One of the most prevalent misconceptions concerning Chełmno and the gas vans involves a vehicle found after the war in Koło. This vehicle was photographed and is often described as a van used to gas people in Chełmno. The historical evidence does not support this conclusion. The following is the record of the examination of this vehicle that the Sonderkommando left behind at the Ostrowski Works in Koło. The examination was part of the investigation carried out by Judge Władysław Bednarz in 1945. The Ostrowski Works routinely undertook repairs on the vehicles of SS Sonderkommando Kulmhof.

> Record of the Examination
> Koło. November 13, 1945. The acting district examining magistrate of the district court in Łódź, J. Bronowski, under article 123 of the Criminal Law Code, carried out an examination of the vehicle found in Koło at the former Ostrowski Works, currently the District Vehicle Office in Koło. During the examination the following was established:
> On the protective radiator screen, the vehicle has the inscription "Magirus." The length of the van is 8.3 meters, frontal width is 2.1 meters, rear width is 2.32 meters, motor length is 1.65 meters, radiator width is 67 centimeters, radiator height is 80 centimeters, the rear compartment length is 5.25 meters, height is 2.43 meters and width is 2.32 meters. The rear compartment is box-shaped, covered with tongue and groove boards, and painted lead gray. The roof is convex and partially covered with impregnated canvass. On each side wall are two rectangular openings, 46 centimeters by 15 centimeters, two meters above the bottom edge of the van. They are boarded up and sealed

with the impregnated canvass. On the back of the rear compartment are double doors, which cover the entire width of the van and hang from three pairs of hinges. On the doors, under the gray paint, the inscription, "Otto Köhn Spedition Ruf 516 Zeulen....da i.TH" can be seen. On the front fenders is the inscription "Atü 5.8" and on the doors of the cab, within a white circle, "40 km" is written in black paint.

The two-door cab is 1.55 meters high, 1.4 meters long and 2.3 meters wide. There are no seats or steering wheel and the tachometer is missing from the dashboard. After opening the hood covering the motor, the following was established: The motor is a "Deutz" six cylinder, diesel. There are no spark plugs, generator, starter, radiator fan, air filter or fuel pump. On the plate of the motor is written: "Humboldt-Deutz A.G. 'Magirus-Werke' Ulm /Donau/Baujahr - 1939 Lieferdat 739 Abn-Stempel. Fahrgstell Nr. 9282/38 Nutzlast kg 2700 Fahrgestell-Baumuster 023. Eingewicht 4980 kg. Motor-Baumuster FoM 513 zul. Gesamt gew. 7900 Leistung P.S.105 cm^3 7412. Zulassige Achsendrücke vorn kg 2400 hinten 5500."

The front wheels, differential and headlights are missing. The doors are seven centimeters thick. The rear compartment walls are eight centimeters thick. The internal walls, floor, ceiling and inside portion of the doors are covered with two millimeters thick iron sheeting. The external edges [inside the van where the ceiling and floor meet the sides, front and back, as well as the corners] are sealed by a wooden triangular molding. At a height of 52 centimeters from the floor, there is wooden molding along the walls, six centimeters wide by four centimeters thick. In the front part of the rear compartment, a grating 2.04 meters wide is leaning against the side molding. The interior sheeting is badly corroded. Fragments of the sheeting were taken. The doors were locked with a round iron rod. The rod is the length of the two doors with two hooks on the ends, and a staple in the middle for securing the lock. The doors were sealed with impregnated canvass. On the frame in the back is a hitch for a trailer.

At this point the record of the examination is concluded.

[signed] J. Bronowski

The investigation also includes testimonies from the Polish mechanics who worked at the garage. Several of them undertook repairs on this particular van. Below are portions of their testimonies relevant to the vehicle.

Josef Piaskowski: "I saw the van presently at the old Ostrowski Works for the first time in the spring of 1942. At that time it was a normal furniture van. The inside was lined with canvas. I felt hay under the canvas. The van had a crack in the frame of the chassis. Mańkowski and I repaired it. It was taken away after several days. During the repairs the police didn't guard us. The doors were open."[50]

Bronisław Mańkowski: "The van currently located at Ostrowski's was brought from Chełmno at the end of 1944. This van was to be dismantled. The Germans themselves removed the wheels. A mechanic rigged up a kind of couch inside the van and slept there. An electric light was even installed."[51]

Jan Grudziński: "The van now located at Ostrowski's was towed from Chełmno in the fall of 1944. This van was once brought to the repair shop, but it didn't undergo any repairs. It was painted in the garage. The doors were not locked and the inside was in the same condition that it is now."[52]

Jerzy Fojcik: "This van was not airtight [in 1942–43]. The van was painted and taken to Chełmno."[53]

According to the guard Bruno Israel, who served in Chełmno during the second period only, this van was not used for gassing, but for disinfecting clothing.[54]

From the examination of the vehicle and from the testimonies of the mechanics and guard, there is no proof that this particular vehicle served as a van to gas people. Judge Bednarz was aware of the gas vans equipped with the specially constructed exhaust systems, which were used in Chełmno during the first and second periods of the camp's operations. The examination fails to mention the construction of the exhaust system on this vehicle. No mention is made of a hole, sealed or otherwise, in the floor of the rear compartment that could have channeled gas into this compartment. There is also no mention of a peep hole in the cab of the vehicle, which allowed the drivers to verify whether or not the victims inside the rear compartment were dead. Other testimony by Laabs and Israel indicates that the vans of this type used in Chełmno were sent to Berlin after the transports were halted.[55]

Could this vehicle be the notorious Kaiser's Kaffee van? The dimensions of the rear compartment would classify it as a van of the larger type, similar in size to the Sauer. It is not known if Bednarz was aware that a van using bottled gas was initially employed in the camp. Mention is made in the examination of sealed openings on the sides of the vehicle. Testimony given by Henryk Mania on the method of gassing in use before and just after the Chełmno camp was activated indicates that the pipes which channeled the gas into the rear compartment could have entered through these holes, but in fact these openings are too high, too difficult to reach, and impractical to serve this function. While the ultimate fate of the Kaiser's Kaffee van is unknown there simply is no evidence that this vehicle was used to gas human beings.[56]

APPENDIX II:

The Kaszyński Affair

The arrest and death of Stanisław Kaszyński is a key event in the Chełmno death camp's early history. The story is one of heroism, courage, personal responsibility, friendship and betrayal.

Stanisław Kaszyński was born on November 16, 1903, in Brudzew. After graduating from high school he eventually began working as secretary in Chełmno's local government in 1928. The next year he married Karolina Posłowska and the couple had four children, two boys and two girls. Kaszyński was active in the local community, serving as the head of the volunteer fire brigade and founding an amateur theater group. By all accounts, he was well-liked and respected by those who knew him.

Just after the Chełmno death camp became operational on December 7, 1941, the former secretary of the Chełmno *gmina*, Stanisław Kaszyński, wrote a letter to the Swiss consulate in Łódź, containing information about the establishment of an extermination center in his village. It is not known how, but the camp commandant, Herbert Lange, found out about this letter and arrested Kaszyński at the *gmina* office on January 31, 1942. He was held in the mansion for several days. On February 3, as he was being led to Lange's office, he turned and started to run down the gully between the church and the mansion. One of the guards accompanying Kaszyński raised his rifle, shot three times and killed him.[1] A couple of local villagers were ordered to carry the corpse back to the mansion. The body was probably taken to the forest and buried. Kaszyński's wife, Karolina, was later arrested and taken to Łódź. She wrote letters to her four children from two different prisons in Łódź and then was never heard from again.[2] With the death of their parents, the four young children were taken in and raised by relatives and family friends.

Jan Oliskiewicz worked in the Landratsamt (county administration office) in Koło and knew Kaszyński through official contacts. He became embroiled in the affair because Kaszyński had passed the letter to him. Oliskiewicz later recalled the affair.

> On December 13, 1941—but I'm not sure of the date—Kaszyński came to me with a request to translate a letter into German. This letter was to be sent to the Swiss consulate in Łódź. It contained information about the liquidation,

by gas, of the Jews in the camp at Chełmno, as well as the murder, in the same way, of the Gypsies. The letter also touched upon a whole series of questions not connected with the camp at Chełmno.

On February 5, 1942, members of the Sonderkommando took me to Chełmno where I was interrogated in the matter of Kaszyński's letter. The day before I was arrested, I found out that Kaszyński had been shot. I stubbornly maintained that I burned the translation of the letter; that it had not been sent. I was badly beaten and put into a cell in the basement of the mansion.

In the neighboring cells were Jews, women and men, whose voices I heard because the guards forced them to sing constantly. This singing continued for a couple of days. One morning, before dawn, I heard the sound of clanging chains; a clanging as if something was being taken from the basement. A couple of times a Jew was brought to my cell, wearing only a shirt despite the frost. This Jew took the [excrement] bucket from the cell.

I heard voices outside in a mumbled language, not exactly Polish and not exactly German. In fragments of conversations among the guards, I heard about some bodies laying *durcheinander* [strewn in a mess] in the trucks. During the day, I heard shots, in series of four or five. I had been arrested on February 5, 1942; I heard the shots on February 8 and 9, 1942. In the morning I heard a vehicle driving up to the mansion. Afterward I heard the sound of a lot of bare feet running above me. After shouts of *"genug, genug"* [enough, enough] the footsteps stopped. I heard the sound of slamming doors; then for some five minutes, the sound of a motor. Then it drove off. I had the impression that as one vehicle left, another one arrived.[3]

After spending some 16 days in the basement of the mansion, Oliskiewicz was freed on condition that he "forget" everything he had seen in the camp.

Oliskiewicz's story of Kaszyński's arrest and death is the version that has been related for more than 60 years, and is still repeated today. The story is only partly true[4] and raises more questions than it answers. Kaszyński felt morally obligated to inform the outside world of the horrible events transpiring in his village, writing and sending letters to foreign diplomatic missions and the International Red Cross in Switzerland. Details surrounding these letters are lacking. The number of letters written is not known, nor for the most part is it known to whom specifically they were addressed. No institution has acknowledged receiving a letter from Kaszyński. No one, other than Oliskiewicz and Kaszyński's eldest son, claims to have seen one of these letters. Did Kaszyński, in fact, write such letters? The answer is probably yes. Were they all intercepted and, if so, why was he allowed to continue to write letters before his eventual arrest? The best direct evidence of such letters originates from Kaczyński's eldest child, 13 years old at the time, who stated, according to one source, that he assisted his father in writing one of the letters to the International Red Cross in Switzerland.[5]

Alongside this private initiative and at great risk to both himself and his family, Kaszyński was working with the intelligence network of one of the main military resistance organizations in Poland, Związek Walki Zbrojnej (ZWZ) [Union of Armed Struggle] to inform the Polish government about events unfolding in Chełmno. Other underground organizations, including Komenda Obrońców Polski [Defenders of Poland Command] and Narodowa Organizacja Wojskowa [National Military Organization], operated in the area around Chełmno as well. The man who Colonel Leopold Okulicki charged with setting up the ZWZ intelligence network in the Łódź district reported he obtained information about the camp in Chełmno quickly and that this information was passed on to headquarters in Warsaw.[6] It is not known how many reports containing information about Chełmno made their way to Łódź, but one report subsequently passed on to Warsaw gives information on events in Chełmno that occurred in December 1941 and January 1942. The report reached Łódź from Koło, Oliskiewicz's place of residence, and included information about the transports of Jews from Koło and Dobra to Chełmno. It described how the victims had to undress in the basement of the mansion and were killed in a special gassing van, which transported the dead to the forest where they were buried. The report also mentions that some 2,000 Roma were brought to the mansion from the Łódź ghetto and that "an employee of the *gmina*, a member of the underground, overheard a telephone conversation to Łódź that 800 Gypsies had been taken care of without incident."[7] Leopold Chwiałkowski and Stanisław Kaszyński, *gmina* employees, had overheard an earlier telephone conversation by Obersturmführer Herbert Otto that Roma were going to be sent to Chełmno.

The report that led to Kaszyński's arrest was not intercepted by the Germans. Kaszyński was betrayed. According to a very close relative of an individual directly involved,[8] Kaczyński was arrested for his work with the underground and not because of letters he had written to foreign institutions and representatives of foreign institutions. Jan Szałek worked for Józef G., one of the local farmers in Chełmno who was a friend of Kaszyński and the godfather of one of his children. On weekends, Szałek took the farmer's horse-drawn wagon to Łódź in the early morning hours to sell the farmer's fruits and vegetables at the market. Józef G. took the bus on Saturday mornings to Łódź and would meet Szałek at the market. One day, the farmer saw Szałek at the market speaking with strangers and something passing between them. He was convinced that Szałek was selling some of his fruits and vegetables on his own behalf and keeping the money for himself. The farmer searched Szałek, looking for his money, and found Kaszyński's report. Knowing that Kaszyński and the farmer were friends, Szałek thought he could trust him and explained the situation.

Another version of this story is told by Stanisław Kaczyński's daughter, Maria. After the war, her brother spoke with Józef G. who said he received the letter from Kaszyński and passed it on to an employee who was to mail it. This employee supposedly had a German girlfriend and it was this woman who turned the letter over to the Gestapo.[9] The farmer's story generally supports the employee's account, but also puts the farmer in the best possible light; he was cooperating with Kaszyński and it was not his fault that the letter fell into the hands of the Gestapo. Whether the details of this story are true or not, Józef G. does implicate himself in the affair. The farmer was on friendly terms with the local Germans and members of the Sonderkommando, but it is not known why he turned in his compatriot. Józef G. was arrested after the war for collaborating with the enemy, but was not convicted. According to locals, bribes of gold from the camp's Jewish victims made that problem go away.[10] Józef G. denied it was he who betrayed Kaszyński until the day he died.

Konrad Schulz (the *gmina* administrator) and Jakob Semmler (the village administrator) learned of the betrayal either from Szałek or through the *gmina* office and informed Kaszyński that the farmer, his friend, had compromised him to the Germans, but Kaszyński didn't believe it. The next day when he went to work, Kaszyński was arrested and imprisoned in the mansion. Karolina Kaszyńska went to the *gmina* office several times to plead on her husband's behalf, without success. There are no accounts of what Kaszyński was forced to endure during the three days he spent in custody. It is also not known why Kaszyński remained in Chełmno. Whether he was arrested for writing letters to a foreign institution or for espionage, it is not known why he remained in the village, rather than being transferred to the Gestapo in Łódź.

The circumstances surrounding the death of Stanisław Kaszyński are also disputed by eyewitnesses. In addition to the most frequently cited sequence of events noted above (that Kaszyński was shot while being taken to Lange's office in the *gmina* administration building), a second version begins somewhat differently. Zofia Szałek was at her grandfather's house, located in the small ravine between the mansion and the church, at the time of Kaszyński's escape attempt. Szałek, her grandfather, her grandmother and her uncle were standing in the yard when they saw Kaszyński jump over the fence surrounding the mansion and begin running across the road toward the house. He was dressed only in long johns and an undershirt. Szałek's grandfather told the fugitive to go around toward the back of the house, which would obstruct the view of pursuers and provide more time to get further away by running around the back of the church. However, three uniformed Germans followed in close pursuit. A shot rang out and Kaszyński fell to the ground.[11]

The death of Stanisław Kaszyński was investigated in 1948 by the municipal court in Koło at the request of his eldest surviving son and again in 1994 by the District Commission for the Investigation of Crimes against the Polish People in Łódź. During the initial inquiry, one of the key witnesses questioned during the proceedings stated the following.

> If I remember correctly it was in February, probably 1942, that I found out the secretary of the *gmina*, Stanisław Kaszyński, [...] had been arrested by the Germans. Several days later [...], it was a Thursday, I went to Dąbie and when returning home I stopped in at the *gmina* office in Chełmno and found out that Stanisław Kaszyński had been shot by the Germans "while trying to escape." I went to the spot where the body was lying on the ground and recognized it as being Kaszyński. While looking at the body, an SS commissar approached and ordered me to take the body to the basement of the mansion in Chełmno. Weremski and Ludwicki assisted me in doing this.[12]

Chwiałkowski and Potyralski fled to the General Government following Kaszyński's arrest. They had been informed that their own arrest was imminent. As mentioned above, Oliskiewicz was arrested, but eventually released. His story is the most problematic. The first problem with the story is the fact that, if Kaszyński was writing to foreign diplomatic missions, he didn't need to have the letters translated. Even if he wanted to have them translated, he could have done it himself, since he was fluent in German. It was Oliskiewicz who came up with the translator story when he was arrested, no doubt in order to lessen his own role in the affair. He offered virtually no details of the affair or his own participation in it, saying only that he burned the translated version of the letter, but he does not mention the original letter. If this were true, why did he burn the translation and what became of the original letter? How did the Germans learn of his involvement in the affair? Oliskiewicz offers no insight into his interrogation by Lange. Why? Did Kaszyński betray him during his interrogation? According to his own version of events, he admitted to participating in a conspiracy to inform the outside world of what was happening in Chełmno (though he also claimed to have destroyed the letter). Lange considered his options and decided to release the prisoner. Many people lost their lives at the hands of Herbert Lange for much less serious offenses.

Together with Kaszyński, Oliskiewicz was probably also working with the anti-communist ZWZ, which in February 1942 was transformed into Armia Krajowa (Home Army), the largest armed resistance movement in Europe and the military arm of the Polish underground state. Oliskiewicz's version of events was first told when he provided testimony to the Polish government's investigation of the death camp in Chełmno. When Judge Bednarz was conducting this investigation in the immediate postwar period, it was clearly not in the best interest of a witness to admit membership in or even cooperation with an anti-communist organization. Armed units of the anti-communist Polish underground remained active in the area. As a member, or even as an active sympathizer, Oliskiewicz could have been arrested by the Soviet security apparatus. None of the men involved in

this affair who provided testimony to Judge Bednarz—Chwiałkowski, Potyralski and Oliskiewicz (co-conspirators with Kaszyński)—admitted their
roles in the underground. Interestingly, on January 24, 1945, four days after
Soviet forces entered Koło, the county's military commander appointed
Oliskiewicz county commissioner [*Starosta*] of Koło County, thus beginning his long political career in postwar communist Poland.

APPENDIX III:

Fates of Key Figures

The Survivors

Yitzhak Justmann left Piotrków Trybunalski in September 1942 dressed as a Polish railroad employee. His further movements are not documented. According to the Widawski family, Justmann and his fellow escapee Yerachmiel Widawski met in Tel Aviv, Israel in 1955. According to Naphtali Lau-Lavie, Justmann immigrated to the United States, settled in Chicago, and died a few years before Widawski.[1]

Michał Podchlebnik returned to Koło after the war and cooperated with the Bednarz investigation of the camp, providing key testimony. After resuming his pre-war profession of cattle trader in Koło, he decided to leave Poland. After several years of living in Zeilsheim, Germany, he finally emigrated to Israel in 1949, working initially in a confectionary plant and later as a partner in a laundry business. Podchlebnik remarried, a survivor of Auschwitz, and had two sons. In 1961, he testified at the Eichmann trial and again at the Bonn trial of Chełmno camp personnel in 1963. His experience in Chełmno, and particularly being forced to bury his first wife and children in the forest, weighed heavily on him for the remainder of his life, both emotionally and physically. Podchlebnik suffered for years with knee problems, resulting from his escape from the camp, and eventually developed heart problems. Michał Podchlebnik died of heart disease in September 1985, after making a brief appearance in Claude Lanzmann's film *Shoah*.[2]

Abram Rój returned to his hometown of Izbica Kujawska after being liberated by the Russians. While there, he registered with the local Jewish committee and learned that no one else in his family survived the war. He also met Taube Pakin (nee Froelich), whose family he had known before the war, who had likewise returned to Izbica in search of surviving family members. After learning that another survivor and childhood friend had just been murdered by local Poles, Abram and Taube decided to leave Poland. The two settled in the American sector of Berlin where they felt safe, and where they married on October 26, 1945. Over the next several years, Rój prospered financially as co-owner of a casino in the city.

Following a dispute with his business partner and concerns about possibly living under an oppressive communist regime (the couple had moved into the Soviet zone of the city, but by 1950 had returned to the American sector), Abram and Taube decided to emigrate to the United States. The couple sailed from Germany, arrived in New York on July 11, 1951, and settled in Hartford, Connecticut, adopting the anglicized last name Roy. Their initial years in the United States were difficult. Abram and Taube learned English by attending night classes. Abram returned to his pre-war profession, working for a custom tailoring establishment. Eventually he opened his own tailoring and dry cleaning business, while Taube worked in a box factory. The couple's only child, a daughter, was born in 1955. In 1964, the family bought a home and moved to the suburb of West Hartford. Abram Roy and his family lived the American dream, the culmination of which for him, and perhaps his proudest moment, was his daughter's acceptance to Harvard University in 1973. Abram endured kidney and lung problems throughout the postwar years. In 1967, he suffered the first in a series of heart attacks, to which he finally succumbed on June 10, 1975.[3]

Szymon Srebrnik was treated for his wounds by the Red Army initially in Dąbie, later in Koło, and then stayed at the Miszczak's home in Chełmno, recovering from his wounds. He subsequently returned to Łódź and eventually decided to leave Poland. In 1947, Srebrnik met his future wife, Hava, in a Jewish kibbutz in Milan, Italy, while awaiting travel to Israel. The couple was married in 1949, settled in Nes Ziona and had two daughters in the early 1950s. The young family man began working in construction and after 12 years was employed as an electrician in the defense industry, subsequently advancing into management. Srebrnik testified at the trial of Adolf Eichmann in 1961, and at the Bonn trial in 1963. In the mid-1970s, Srebrnik returned to Chełmno where his impressions were recorded as part of Claude Lanzmann's film *Shoah*. Following a long professional career, he retired in 1992. The last living survivor of the Chełmno death camp died of cancer on August 15, 2006. He is survived by his wife, two children, five grandchildren and three great-grand children.[4]

Yerachmiel Widawski was freed from his hiding place in Žilina, Slovakia, when the Red Army liberated the town on April 30, 1945. In 1947, Widawski settled in Berlin and the following year married Malke Tauber, a native of Oświęcim and a survivor of Auschwitz. The couple had three children during this period. The Widawskis did well as the owner of a liquor distillery (the family's pre-war business) and later a nylon stocking factory. In 1953, the businesses were sold to Americans and Russians and the Widawski's moved to Antwerp, Belgium, where another child was born. The family again prospered financially after entering the industrial diamond business.

Yerachmiel Widawski loved life and lived it to the fullest. He was a happy man with a great sense of humor. He never lost his faith and prayed every day to the memory of family members killed during the war. He was a pillar of the Antwerp Jewish community and a very charitable man. At the end of the 1950s, and the beginning of the 1960s, he worked to bring Jewish orphan children, saved from the Holocaust by Polish Christian families, to Belgium. Some were cared for in the Widawski home before new homes and families were found for them in Canada, the United States and Israel. He also financially supported devastated Israeli families following the Six-Day War in 1967. While visiting Israel in the 1960s, Widawski met with Meir Grünfeld, the man who hid him throughout most of the war. In 1972, while visiting Israel, he met with Naphtali Lau-Lavie, who helped save his life in Piotrków Trybunalski just after fleeing from Chełmno. Yerachmiel Widawski died at age 72 in April 1986 after suffering a heart attack. He never returned to Poland.[5]

Mieczysław Żurawski returned to Włocławek where he had lived before the war. Żurawski provided testimony to the Polish government's investigation of the Chełmno camp and was a witness at the trials of Arthur Greiser and Hermann Gielow. He emigrated to Israel in the early 1950s and eventually testified at the trial of Adolf Eichmann in 1961 and at the Bonn trial of Chełmno camp personnel in 1963. Mieczysław Żurawski died on March 5, 1989.[6]

The Perpetrators

Alfred Behm was believed to have been with Lange during the mobile gassing operations, but left Chełmno after a brief period as transport commander. At the end of the war, Behm was allegedly captured by the Russians. His ultimate fate is unknown.[7]

Hans Biebow was head of the Łódź Ghetto Administration. Biebow was arrested at his home in Bremen on May 17, 1945. The British army subsequently turned him over to Polish authorities as a war criminal. Biebow was tried in Łódź for crimes committed as head of the Gettoverwaltung and his participation in the murder of 300,000 Jews in Chełmno. Sentenced to death on all charges, Biebow was executed at half past five on the morning of June 23, 1947.[8]

Paul Blobel worked temporarily in Chełmno to devise a system of destroying the rotting corpses in the forest camp. His ultimate solution resulted in the construction of field furances, or crematoria, the method later employed throughout the Aktion Reinhard camps. Blobel was then assigned to head Sonderkommando 1005, charged with the task of destroying all evidence of the mass graves of the Einsatzgruppen in the east. After the war, Blobel was a defendant in the Einsatzgruppen trial, resulting in a death sentence in April 1948, and execution on June 8, 1951. The unrepentant Blobel's last moments were recorded as follows: "Shortly after midnight, four husky MPs led [Blobel] across the floodlit yard of Landsberg Prison. On the gallows platform, a US Army hangman was waiting for him. Blobel [...] got 90 seconds for his last words. Thrusting out his spade-bearded chin, he cried, 'I die in the faith of my people. May the German people be aware of its enemies!' 'Attention!' called Colonel Walter R. Graham, Landsberg's US commander. Blobel stiffened; the hangman and his assistants slipped a black hood over Blobel's head, adjusted the heavy noose. A priest intoned a prayer. The trap sprang open with a clatter."[9]

Walter Bock, a guard during the first period of the camp, was a defendant at the Chełmno trial, and was eventually acquitted.

Hans Bothmann, the second commandant of Chełmno, returned to Poznań after liquidating the camp in 1945. Accompanied by Walter Burmeister and Erwin Bürstinger, Bothmann drove to the area of Piła-Wałcz, north of Poznań, where he served in a liaison capacity between the security police and Himmler's office. As the Red Army advanced, they gradually made their way toward Berlin. Bothmann's final assignment at the end of the war was with the Sipo in Flensberg, near his hometown of Lohe. On April 4, 1946, Bothmann was arrested and imprisoned in Heide, Schleswig-Holstein, where he hanged himself in his cell that same day. Zofia Szacowna, the Bothmanns' maid, had alerted the British authorities that her employer was a Gestapo officer. Bothmann "transferred" Szacowna, a resident of Chełmno, to Poznań to work as a domestic for his wife and children. Mrs. Bothmann, during her evacuation from Poznań in 1945, took Szacowna with her to Lohe.[10]

Viktor Brack was the senior administrator of the Euthanasia Program in the Chancellery of the Führer. After the war he was a defendant in the Doctor's Trial at Nuremburg and was found guilty of war crimes, crimes against humanity and membership in a criminal organization. Brack was executed at Landsberg prison in Bavaria on June 2, 1948.[11]

Ernst Burmeister was head of the police guard during the camp's second period. After leaving Chełmno in July 1944, Burmeister and his police company participated in the suppression of the Warsaw uprising during which he was wounded and hospitalized in Łódź. As the Red Army approached the city, he was evacuated and eventually captured by the British. A defendant in the Chełmno trial, Ernst Burmeister originally received a sentence of three-and-a-half years in prison, but his case was later dropped due to the ill health of the then 71-year-old former police official.[12]

Walter Burmeister was Lange's and Bothmann's driver. Following the liquidation of the camp, Burmeister accompanied Bothmann and Bürstinger to Berlin. From there, he was transferred to a radio station in Wannsee, near Berlin, which later moved to Eutin. Burmeister was wounded on May 2, 1945, and taken to a field hospital in Flensburg Mürwik. After the war, he was interned as a member of the SS and released on October 1947. A defendant in the Chełmno trial, he received a sentence of 13 years in prison.[13]

Erwin Bürstinger, in charge of vehicles in Chełmno, went with Bothmann and Walter Burmeister to Berlin. In Berlin, he requested a transfer and was sent to Munich. His ultimate fate is unknown.[14]

Gustaw Fiedler was sergeant of the Polizeiwachtkommando. Fiedler did not return to Chełmno in 1944, but attended a training course and was subsequently transferred to Greece where he fought against partisans. Wounded in 1945, he was transferred to Copenhagen and fell into the hands of resistance fighters. Fiedler was arrested after the war for his membership in the SS and was released in 1948. His involvement with the death camp became known only years later for which he was tried in Kiel, West Germany. On November 26, 1965, Fiedler was sentenced to 13 months and two weeks in prison.[15]

Hermann Gielow, driver for the Sonderkommando, fought in the battle of Poznań where he was captured by the Russians on January 27, 1945. He was held in the Soviet Union for three years and then turned over to the Polish authorities on April 30, 1948, to stand trial for his activities in Chełmno. Legal proceedings against Gielow began on September 27, 1949, and ended with a death sentence on May 16, 1950. On March 16, 1951, the Supreme Court upheld the verdict and Gielow was executed in Poznań at 7:00 p.m. on June 6, 1951.[16]

Wilhelm Görlich, the camp administrator, fought in the battle of Poznań, was wounded and taken prisoner by the Red Army in February 1945. Görlich was sentenced to 25 years for belonging to a fascist organization in 1949, but was released in 1950.[17]

Arthur Greiser was the highest ranking government and party official of the Warthegau, and upon whose local authority and initiative the Chełmno camp was established. After the war, Greiser was arrested by American forces and turned over to the Polish authorities. During his trial in Poznań on a number of charges, he claimed to know nothing about the camp in Chełmno. Greiser was sentenced to death on July 9, 1946, and publicly hanged on July 21. His body was sent to the Anatomical Institute of the Medical Academy in Poznań and burned in a crematorium used by the Nazis to dispose of thousands of their Polish and Jewish victims.[18]

Alois Häfele, head of the Jewish labor squads, went from Chełmno to Poznań, and was ordered by Bothmann to deliver Gestapo files (perhaps Chełmno files) together with Laabs and Kretschmer, to an SD (Security Service) office near Berlin. Häfele and Kretschmer then reported to the main office of the Order Police in Berlin, where they were told to take a holiday. Häfele went to Karlsruhe and remained there throughout the war and after. A defendant in the Chełmno trial, Häfele received a sentence of 13 years in prison after appeals.[19]

Simon Haider, head of the police guard in the forest camp, died November 4, 1958.[20]

Karl Heinl headed police guards at the mansion and in the forest camp. A defendant in the Chełmno trial, Heinl received a sentence of seven years in prison.

Oskar Hering, gas van driver in the first period of the camp, is believed to have died in the Balkans in 1944.[21]

Wilhelm Heukelback, a guard during the first period of the camp, was a defendant at the Chełmno trial. He initially received a sentence of 13 months and two weeks in prison, but this was subsequently dropped as the court felt this minimum sentence was too severe.

Herbert Hiecke-Richter, the head of transports and later valuables, was captured in Poznań by the Red Army in February 1945, and was imprisoned there until at least May 1945. Walter Piller heard from a Poznań Gestapo photographer Willy Werd that Richter was taken to Berlin in connection with his activities in Chełmno. His ultimate fate is unknown.[22]

Rolf-Heinz Höppner, head of the SD (Security Service) office in Poznań, was sentenced to life imprisonment in Poland, but was granted amnesty and returned to West Germany in April 1956. In the 1970s, a Polish journalist found Höppner living in obscurity in Bad Godesberg, collecting memoirs of Nazi veterans for the Domus Publishing House.[23]

Gustaw Hüfing, head of the police guard during the first period, died on July 24, 1958.[24]

Fritz Ismer, in charge of valuables confiscated from the victims during the first period, remained in the Balkans when other members of Sonderkommando Kulmhof returned to Chełmno to reestablish the camp. He became ill in April 1944 and was hospitalized. He later served in the SS Division Frundsberg. In 1960, Ismer was questioned in connection with the investigation that eventually led to the Bonn trial but no charges were brought against him.[25]

Bruno Israel, a guard during the second period of the camp, was arrested by the Polish authorities on August 9, 1945. Israel was a key eyewitness in Judge Bednarz's investigation of Chełmno. Following his trial, Israel received the death sentence for his activities in connection with the camp, but the judgment was commuted to life imprisonment on September 3, 1946. After many requests, he was released on December 12, 1958, and died in Mindelheim, West Germany on April 17, 1968.[26]

Wilhelm Koppe was Higher SS and Police Leader (HSSPF) in Poznań until 1943. At the end of the war, Koppe assumed a new identity and became the director of a chocolate factory in Bonn, West Germany. The war criminal was recognized on the street and arrested in 1960. Trial proceedings were initiated in Bonn in 1964, but halted in 1966, due to the poor health of the then 70-year-old Koppe, who died in 1975.[27]

Rudolf Kramp, the Łódź ghetto administration official who transported people and goods to Chełmno, was arrested (with the gold teeth of Chełmno victims in his possession) and tried in Łódź, Poland after the war. Following his one-day trial, Kramp received the death sentence on December 18, 1945, and was executed by hanging on January 25, 1946.[28]

Erich Kretschmer was head of the police transport kommando, and, together with Häfele and Laabs, delivered Poznań Gestapo files (perhaps Chełmno files) to the Berlin area. Then he reported with Häfele to the main office of the Order Police in Berlin, where they were told to take a holiday. Like other members of the Sonderkommando, Kretschmer may simply have gone home. His hometown was Plauen. His ultimate fate is unknown.[29]

Gustav Laabs was a gas van driver during both periods of the camp's operation. On Bothmann's orders, together with Häfele and Kretschmer, he transported Poznań Gestapo files (perhaps Chełmno files) to an SD [Security Service] office, somewhere in Brandenburg province, near Berlin. Laabs was then attached to an SS regiment in Altenburg/Saxony and later captured by the Americans. He was interned until the end of 1946. A defendant in the Chełmno trial, Laabs received a sentence, after an appeal, of 13 years in prison.[30]

Harold (Harry) Lang was first commander, for a brief period of time, of the police guard in Chełmno. His ultimate fate is unknown.[31]

Herbert Lange, first commandant of the Chełmno camp, was transferred from there (officially from Poznań) in March 1942, to the Reich Security

Main Office (RSHA) in Berlin. Virtually nothing is known about Lange's post-Chełmno activity. In 1944, he was promoted to Sturmbannführer, at least in part for his faithful service in suppressing the anti-Hitler coup attempt of July 1944. Lange was killed in April 1945, in Niederbarim, while taking part in the defense of Berlin.[32]

Willi Lenz, supervisor of the forest camp, died in the early morning hours of January 18, 1945. After being overpowered in the granary, Lenz was hung by the last surviving group of Jewish workers.[33]

Friedrich Maderholz, a guard during the first period of the camp, was a defendant at the Chełmno trial, and was eventually acquitted.

Anton Mehring, a guard during the first period of the camp, was a defendant at the Chełmno trial, and was eventually acquitted.

Kurt Möbius was supervisor of arrivals at the mansion until August/September 1942. He returned to Łódź and served there until January 1945. Möbius was in Russian captivity until 1949, when he escaped to the west. A defendant in the Chełmno trial, Möbius received a sentence of eight years in prison.[34]

Friedrich Neumann was replaced by Görlich in April 1942, as the head of the administration office in Chełmno. His ultimate fate is unknown.[35]

Herbert Otto was assistant commandant for a brief period in Chełmno. Following his transfer back to Łódź, Otto was sent to Prague, Czechoslovakia, in August 1942, where he died on May 6, 1945.[36]

Walter Piller was deputy commandant during the second period of the camp's operation. Piller fought in the battle of Poznań, during which he was wounded in the hand and leg on February 15, 1945, and captured by the Russians on February 23. After interrogation in the Soviet Union, Piller was turned over to Polish authorities to stand trial for his activities in Chełmno. He received the death sentence on July 1, 1948, and was executed on January 19, 1949.[37]

Albert Plate was deputy commandant during most of the first period of the camp. Plate committed suicide on October 4, 1944, after being severely wounded in the Balkans.[38]

Johannes Runge, assistant to Lenz and builder of the crematoria, fought in the battle of Poznań, was wounded and taken prisoner by the Russians. Piller heard from friends that Runge had died.[39]

Erwin Schmidt, in charge of provisions for the Sonderkommando, was wounded and captured by the Russians in Poznań in February 1945. While in Russian captivity he gave testimony concerning Chełmno in February

1946, which was later presented at Piller's trial. Schmidt subsequently testified as a witness during the Bonn trial.[40]

Wilhelm Schulte, a guard during the first period of the camp's operation, was a defendant at the Chełmno trial, and eventually acquitted.

Max Sommer, Ismer's assistant, was in Berlin after the liquidation of the camp according to Piller. He is believed to have died prior to the trial in Bonn.[41]

Stefan Seidenglanz, a driver during the second period of the camp, transported the Jews from the church in Chełmno to the forest camp. In December 1944, he was transferred to Łódź. His further fate is unknown.[42]

Alexander Steinke, a guard during the first period of the camp, was a defendant at the Chełmno trial, and eventually acquitted.

Ernst Thiele, a driver during the second period of camp, transported the Jews from the church in Chełmno to the forest camp and supervised a Jewish labor kommando chopping wood in the forest. In fall 1944, he was released from the Sonderkommando due to illness. Thiele was later transferred to the Gestapo in Inowrocław as a driver. His further fate is unknown.[43]

The Polish Laborers

Lech Jaskólski returned to the Fort VII prison in Poznań after Chełmno was liquidated in 1943. Later that year he was employed by Legath's Wetterkommando until it too was disbanded in 1944. Jaskólski, together with the other three Poles who served in Legath's kommando, was transferred to the Żabikowo (Poggenberg) transit camp of the Poznań Gestapo. On June 23, 1944, Jaskólski was sent to Auschwitz. Two weeks later, he was transferred to the Mauthausen concentration camp (prisoner number 78253) and shortly thereafter to the newly-opened Linz III subcamp. He survived the war, was liberated by the Americans and went to southern France. In 1956, Jaskólski's family claimed not to know where he was, but the police were skeptical because the family was receiving packages from abroad. His further fate is unknown.[44]

Marian Libelt was accidentally trapped inside a gas van during the loading procedure and gassed on January 14, 1942. His body was taken back to the grounds of the mansion and buried there by the other Poles. It is believed Libelt's body was eventually exhumed and turned over to his family.[45]

Henryk Maliczak served with Jaskólski, Skrzypczyński and Mania in the Wetterkommando and was later an inmate in the Żabikowo transit camp near Poznań. From there, Maliczak was transferred to Auschwitz with his colleagues on June 23, 1944. On July 4, the group of four was transferred to Mauthausen (prisoner number 78435) and shortly thereafter to the newly-opened Linz III subcamp. American soldiers liberated the camp in May 1945. Maliczak returned to Poland after the war and settled in Piotrkowice. This key eyewitness and participant in the history of Sonderkommando Lange and the Chełmno death camp was interviewed in 1962 by a correspondent for Czechoslovakia's *Rudeho Prava* and questioned twice by Polish authorities, in 1964 and 1967. No charges were ever filed for his involvement with Sonderkommando Lange and Chełmno. Henryk Maliczak died on May 4, 1982.[46]

Henryk Mania served with Jaskólski, Maliczak and Skrzypczyński in the Wetterkommando. Afterwards, he was sent together with the other Chełmno veterans to the Żabikowo transit camp and subsequently to Auschwitz (prisoner number 189229), two weeks later to Mauthausen (78441) and then to the subcamp of Linz III, where he was liberated by American forces. After the war, Mania returned to Poland and his hometown of Wolsztyn, but was soon forced to leave. Locals whose loved ones died in Fort VII claimed Mania survived because he collaborated with the Germans. Mania left for Poznań, but eventually settled in Szczecin. Mania's legal problems began in 1949 following a case of mistaken identity. Polish authorities initiated a series of investigations over the following three decades looking into his wartime activities but no charges were filed. With the collapse of Communism in Poland, the Institute of National Remembrance re-examined the case and conducted its own investigation. Mania was arrested in November 2000, found guilty of complicity in genocide and sentenced to eight years in prison. Despite the conviction the elderly Mania was released and returned to society and obscurity.[47]

Franciszek Piekarski was returned to Fort VII following the liquidation of the Chełmno camp in 1943, and died there on July 29, 1943, allegedly from heart failure. According to Maliczak, Piekarski died in Fort VII of a blood clot. Mania stated he died a natural death in Fort VII.[48]

Stanisław Polubiński returned to Fort VII in 1943. Guards in Chełmno told the farmer Andrzej Miszczak that Polubiński had died. According to Henryk Mania, Polubiński died in Fort VII after being caught smuggling a letter within the prison.[49]

Kajetan Skrzypczyński served with the Wetterkommando and was held in the Żabikowo transit camp. Then he was transferred together with Jaskólski, Maliczak and Mania to Auschwitz on June 23, 1944, and two weeks later to Mauthausen (prisoner number 78722). After being liberated by the Americans in the Linz III subcamp, Skrzypczyński chose not to return to Poland and emigrated to Sydney, Australia in 1950. In 1962, Skrzypczyński's father told police that he hadn't been in contact with his son for two years. The last he had heard his son was severely ill with rheumatism and had been involved in two automobile accidents. Skrzypczyński lived another 30 years in obscurity and died of a heart attack on December 19, 1992 in Australia.[50]

Stanisław Szymański died in Chełmno at four o'clock in the afternoon on September 19, 1942, according to a notice received by his family. Szymański was killed due to his alleged involvement in a scheme to sell jewelry taken from the camp's victims.[51]

Notes

Introduction

1. The approximate English-language pronunciation of the name of the camp and village is "Helm-no." The small village, also known as Chełmno nad Nerem (Chełmno-on-Ner), should not be confused with the city of Chełmno, located in north central Poland.
2. Władysław Bednarz, *Obóz straceń w Chełmnie nad Nerem* (Warszawa: Państwowy Instytut Wydawniczy, 1946). Hereafter cited as *Bednarz*.
3. Edward Serwański, *Obóz zagłady w Chełmnie nad Nerem* (Poznań: Wydawnictwo Poznańskie, 1964). Hereafter cited as *Serwański*.
4. Janusz Gulczyński, *Obóz Śmierci w Chełmnie nad Nerem* (Konin: Wojewódzki Ośrodek Kultury w Koninie, 1991).
5. Manfred Struck, *Chełmno/Kulmhof Ein vergessener Ort des Holocaust?* (Bonn/Berlin: Gegen Vergessen-Für Demokratie e.V, 2001).
6. Shmuel Krakowski, *Das Todeslager Chełmno/Kulmhof - Der Beginn der Endlösung* (Jerusalem: Yad Vashem, 2007). This work was recently translated and published in English as: *Chełmno. A Small Village in Europe*, Jerusalem: Yad Vashem, 2009.
7. Following its postwar investigation of the camp, the Polish government determined that 360,000 people were murdered in Chełmno; this inflated number continues to be cited today.
8. Also in this regard, Polish place names are used throughout this work for purposes of consistency and simplicity. While terms such as Łódź ghetto and Poznań Gestapo are technically inaccurate, they have been adopted in the literature and contribute to a more reader-friendly text.
9. Ian Kershaw, *Hitler, the Germans, and the Final Solution* (Jerusalem: International Institute for Holocaust Research, Yad Vashem, and New Haven and London: Yale University Press, 2008): 89. Hereafter cited as *Kershaw*.

Chapter 1 Prologue

The Euthanasia Program

1. Michael Burleigh, *Death and Deliverance. "Euthanasia" in Germany 1900–1945* (Cambridge: Cambridge University Press, 1994): 55–56.
2. Eugen Kogon, Hermann Langbein, Adalbert Ruckerl, eds. *Nazi Mass Murder: A Documentary History of the Use of Poison Gas* (New Haven and London: Yale University Press, 1993): 14. Hereafter cited as *Nazi Mass Murder*.
3. Robert Jay Lifton, *The Nazi Doctors: Medical Killing and the Psychology of Genocide* (New York: Basic Books, 1986): 61–62.
4. *Nazi Mass Murder*: 16.
5. Henry Friedlander, *The Origins of Nazi Genocide. From Euthanasia to the Final Solution* (Chapel Hill and London: The University of North Carolina Press, 1995): 39. Hereafter cited as *Friedlander*.

6. Gita Sereny, *Into that Darkness*. (London: Pan Books, 1977): 54. The quoted individual is Franz Stangl, who later served as the commandant of the Sobibór and Treblinka death camps. Wirth later became inspector of the Aktion Reinhard camps.
7. Ibid. The quoted individual is Franz Suchomel, who later served in the Treblinka death camp.
8. *Nazi Mass Murder*: 20.
9. Ibid.: 26–27.
10. Friedlander: 209–10.
11. Procedure according to *Nazi Mass Murder*: 28.
12. Friedlander: 110.
13. NO-426, Viktor Brack, October 14, 1946.

Mobile Killing Operations

1. See Stanisław Batawia, 'Zagłada Chorych Psychicznie', *Biuletyn Głównej Komisji Badania Zbrodni Niemieckich w Polsce* III (1947): 93–106.
2. Marian Kaczmarek, 'Eutanazja w tzw. "Kraju Warty"', *Kronika Wielkopolska* 1/36 (1985): 73–74.
3. NO-2908, Koppe to Sporrenberg, October 18, 1940.
4. Zentrale Stelle der Landesjustizverwaltungen Ludwigsburg. 203 AR-Z 69/59, Bd. 1: 139, Wilhelm Koppe. Hereafter, Zentrale Stelle is the source of all documents cited with the 203 prefix.
5. 203 AR-Z 69/59, Bd. 5: 680, Alfred Trenker.
6. Friedlander: 87.
7. Berlin Document Center, personal file of Herbert Lange.
8. 203 AR-Z 69/59, Bd. 5: 678, Alfred Trenker.
9. SA Poznań 60: 54, Henryk Fink.
10. Ob 19: 241, Heinz May. Based on a conversation with the Poznań district forester Kranold.
11. 203 AR-Z 69/59, Bd. 6: 966, Walter Burmeister.
12. Friedlander: 138.
13. Marian Olszewski, *Fort VII w Poznaniu* (Poznań: Wydawnictwo Poznańskie, 1974): 22. Hereafter cited as *Olszewski*; and Marian Kaczmarek, *Organizacja Poznańskiego Gestapo 1939–1945* (Żabikowo: Muzeum Martyrologiczne w Żabikowie, 2003): 26. Numerous postwar testimonies by former inmates of Fort VII state that the commandant was Lange (or Langer, or Langner).
14. Olszewski: 19.
15. S. 8/01/Zn: 275, Henryk Mania. Hereafter cited as *Henryk Mania 1967*.
16. Christopher Browning, *The Origins of the Final Solution* (Lincoln: University of Nebraska Press and Jerusalem: Yad Vashem, 2004): 188.
17. Olszewski: 62–63.
18. AZIH. 301/1003. Zdzisław Jaroszewski. Los Szpitala Psychiatrycznego w Owińskach w Czasie Wojny.
19. Henryk Mania 1967: 271.
20. S. 8/01/Zn: 386, Zbigniew Grześkowiak.
21. In his testimony from April 1964, Maliczak states he was arrested in November, but mentions October in a subsequent interrogation three years later. In neither case does Maliczak state why he was arrested.
22. S. 8/01/Zn: 261, Henryk Maliczak. Hereafter cited as *Henryk Maliczak 1967*. Maliczak was confused in this testimony regarding the hospital from which

the patients originated. He mentions the Kościan facility, which was actually the second hospital visited by Lange. Henryk Mania specifically points out Maliczak's error in his own testimony.

23. Edmund Chróścielewski, Wiesław Celiński, 'Pseudoeutanazja w "Kraju Warty" podczas okupacji hitlerowskiej', Hereafter cited as *Przegląd Lekarski* 25/1 (1969): 45.

24. Zdzisław Jaroszewski, ed., *Zagłada chorych psychicznie w Polsce 1939–1945* (Warszawa: Wydawnictwo Naukowe PWN, 1993): 86. Hereafter cited as *Jaroszewski*.

25. NTN 38, tom 5: 837, Michał Woroch.

26. Henryk Maliczak 1967: 261. Maliczak is undoubtedly referring to Stanisław Szymański.

27. S. 8/01/Zn: 6–9; see also Chróścielewski S. 8/01/Zn: 934–36.

28. Jan Gallus, 'Dziekanka w latach 1939–1945 oraz jej udział i rola w wyniszczaniu umysłowo chorych Polaków', *Rocznik Psychiatryczny* 37/1 (1949): 78.

29. Volker Riess, *Die Anfänge der Vernichtung "lebensunwerten Lebens" in den Reichsgauen Danzig-Westpreussen und Wartheland 1939–40* (Frankfurt am Main and New York: Peter Lang Verlag, 1995): 306–307.

30. This is the first time witnesses report seeing the Kaiser's Kaffee van, suggesting that the logo was applied to the vehicle between the operations at the Gniezno and Kościan facilities.

31. *Przegląd Lekarski* 25/1: 44.

32. Ibid., and Zbiór 5 "Z" tom I: 2–14.

33. Henryk Mania 1967: 273–74.

34. Henryk Maliczak 1967, 262; see also Edward Serwański, *Wielkopolska w Cieniu Swastyki* (Warszawa: Instytut Wydawniczy PAX, 1970): 79.

35. These "false" graves along with actual graves on the grounds of the hospital were excavated in 2006; see: Alicja Muenzberg, 'To był duży cmentarz', *Gazeta Kościańska*, 21/2006 (May 24, 2006): 10.

36. *Przegląd Lekarski* 25/1: 45.

37. Anna Kulikowska, 'Okupacyjne wspomnienia ze Szpitala Psychiatrycznego w Gostyninie', *Przegląd Lekarski* 34/1 (1977): 213.

38. Henryk Maliczak 1967: 263.

39. Anna Kulikowska, 'Okupacyjne wspomnienia ze Szpitala Psychiatrycznego w Gostyninie', *Przegląd Lekarski* 34/1 (1977): 213–14.

40. Zbiór 5 "Z": 34; speculation on the identity of this person centers on Paul Budnik, assigned to the Poznań Gestapo.

41. Tadeusz Wierzbicki, 'Dzieje Państwowego Szpitala dla Nerwowo i Psychicznie Chorych im dra med. Józefa Babińskiego w Łodzi', *Archiwum Historii Medycyny* 25/1 (1962): 65–66. Hereafter cited as *Archiwum Historii Medycyny*.

42. OKBZN Łódź 35: 30, Wacław Berkowski.

43. Ibid.: 32–33, Antoni Buła.

44. Zbiór 5 "Z": 35, report by Judge Władysław Bednarz.

45. Henryk Mania 1967: 277–78.

46. Jaroszewski: 126.

47. Jan Milczarek, 'Wymordowanie chorych psychicznie w Warcie', *Przegląd Lekarski* 36, no. 1 (1979): 119; and Zbiór 5 "Z" tom IV: 2–7.

48. Ibid.: 115–17; and Zbiór 5 "Z": 26–29. The latter source originates from the Congress of Polish Psychiatrists held on November 1–3, 1945. It states that six civilians, not 13, accompanied the Sonderkommando.

49. Michael Burleigh, *Death and Deliverance. 'Euthanasia' in Germany 1900–1945* (Cambridge: Cambridge University Press, 1994): 132.
50. Friedlander: 141–42.
51. Henryk Mania 1967: 278–79.
52. Henryk Maliczak 1967: 264.
53. NO-2908, Koppe to Sporrenberg, October 18, 1940; NO-2911, Koppe to Wolff, February 22, 1941.
54. 203 AR-Z 69/59, Bd. 5: 679, Alfred Trenker. Each member of Sonderkommando Lange may well have received such a box. See Oberscharführer Wendelin Seith's letter of appreciation to Rediess in Christopher Browning, *Fateful Months. Essays on the Emergence of the Final Solution* (New York, London: Holmes and Meier Publishers, 1985): 3. Hereafter cited as *Fateful Months*.
55. Richard Breitman, *The Architect of Genocide. Himmler and the Final Solution* (New York: Alfred A. Knopf, 1991): 103. Hereafter cited as *Breitman*.
56. Jan Gallus, 'Dziekanka w latach 1939–1945 oraz jej udział i rola w wyniszczaniu umysłowo chorych Polaków', *Rocznik Psychiatryczny* 37/1 (1949): 80.
57. Zbiór 5 "Z" tom V: 4–5, Antoni Hołoga. Due to the fact that this may be the vehicle Henryk Mania referred to as a second gas van, the brief description of the vehicle (open to interpretation) is presented here in the original: "... ciągnik samochodowy z dużą, stalową, hermetycznie zamykaną przyczepką. Od ciągnika, przy którym znajdował się wielki basen, prawdopodobnie gazowy, prowadziły jakieś przewody do przyczepki."
58. *Archiwum Historia Medycyny*: 68.
59. OKBZN Łódź 35: 32, Antoni Buła.
60. Ibid.: 8, Sabina Raczyńska Pawłowska.
61. Henryk Mania 1967: 276.
62. Ld 139/5, tom 1: 23.
63. *Archiwum Historii Medycyny*: 66.
64. I. M. Lask, ed., *The Kalish Book* (Tel Aviv: Societies of Former Residents of Kalish and the Vicinity in Israel and the USA, 1967): 258–59. Hereafter cited as *Kalisz Book*. See also AZIH 301/567 testimony of Gedale Goldman; and Zbiór "Bd": 323.
65. Henryk Maliczak 1967: 263; Marian Kaczmarek, 'Eutanazja w tzw. "Kraju Warty"', *Kronika Wielkopolski*, 1/36 (1985): 79.
66. S. 8/01/Zn: 637, Henryk Mania.
67. 203 AR 609/61, Bd. 2: 23, Wilhelm Schmerse.

The Turning Point

1. Catherine Epstein, *Model Nazi. Arthur Greiser and the Occupation of Western Poland* (New York: Oxford University Press, 2010): 34–76. Hereafter cited as *Epstein*.
2. Epstein: 7.
3. The document is reproduced in: T. Berenstein, A. Eisenbach, A. Rutkowski, eds., *Eksterminacja Żydów na Ziemiach Polskich. Zbiór Dokumentów* (Warszawa: Żydowski Instytut Historyczny, 1957): 30–31.
4. Epstein: 166.
5. For a broader discussion of this topic see: Catherine Epstein, *Model Nazi: Arthur Greiser and the Occupation of Western Poland* (New York: Oxford University Press, 2010); 'Improvised Genocide? The Emergence of the "Final Solution" in the "Warthegau"', in Ian Kershaw, *Hitler, the Germans, and the Final Solution* (Jerusalem: International Institute for Holocaust Research, Yad Vashem,

and New Haven and London: Yale University Press, 2008); Phillip T. Rutherford, *Prelude to the Final Solution: The Nazi Program for Deporting Ethnic Poles, 1939-1941* (Lawrence: University Press of Kansas, 2007); and 'From "Ethnic Cleansing" to Genocide to the "Final Solution"', in Christopher Browning, *Nazi Policy, Jewish Workers, German Killers* (New York: Cambridge University Press, 2000).

6. D. Dąbrowska, 'Zagłada skupisk żydowskich w "Kraju Warty" w okresie okupacji hitlerowskiej', *Biuletyn Żydowskiego Instytutu Historycznego* 13–14 (1955): 122. Hereafter cited as *Dąbrowska*.

7. Ibid.: 126–27.

8. Lucjan Dobroszycki, ed., *The Chronicle of the Łódź Ghetto, 1941–1944* (New Haven and London: Yale University Press, 1984): xxxviii–xxxix. Hereafter cited as *Chronicle*.

9. NO-246, Greiser to Himmler, May 1, 1942.

10. NO-244, Himmler to Greiser, June 27, 1942.

11. NO-250, Blome to Greiser, November 18, 1942.

12. NO-249, Greiser to Himmler, November 21, 1942.

13. NO-247, Koppe to Brandt, May 3, 1942.

14. English language transcripts of the Adolf Eichmann Trial, Session 94. Hereafter cited as *Eichmann Trial*.

15. Artur Eisenbach, *Hitlerowska Polityka Zagłady Żydów* (Warszawa: Książka i Wiedza, 1961), 287. Hereafter cited as *Hitlerowska Polityka*. The letter is reproduced in A. Eisenbach, comp., *Dokumenty i materiały do dziejów okupacji niemieckiej w Polsce. Tom 3. Getto Łódzkie. Część 1* (Łódź: Wydawnictwo Centralnej Żydowskiej Komisji Historycznej, 1946): 187. Hereafter cited as *Dokumenty i materiały, tom 3*.

16. IPN Ld 139/23. Marian Kaczmarek, Hitlerowskie plany zagłady Żydów w Kraju Warty: 184.

17. Julian Leszczyński, 'Z Dziejów Zagłady Żydów w Kraju Warty', *Biuletyn Żydowskiego Instytutu Historycznego* 2/82, 1972: 67.

18. IPN Ld 139/23. Marian Kaczmarek, Hitlerowskie plany zagłady Żydów w Kraju Warty: 187–88.

19. S. 8/01/Zn: 8, police report based on an interview with Henryk Mania.

20. Ob 19: 241, Heinz May.

21. NTN 36: 161, 166; English quoted from *Documents of Destruction*: 87–88.

22. Kershaw: 105.

23. 203 AR-Z 69/59, Bd. 1: 139–40, Wilhelm Koppe; English quoted from *Nazi Mass Murder*: 74–5.

24. ASG 54: 23, 117.

25. Isaiah Trunk, *Lodz Ghetto. A History* (Bloomington and Indianapolis: Indiana University Press, 2006): 172–73; see also Anna Ziółkowska, 'Transporty powrotne (Rücktransporte). Eliminacja więźniów niezdolnych do pracy z obozów pracy przymusowej dla Żydów w Wielkopolsce': 37–44, *Ośrodek zagłady Żydów w Chełmnie nad Nerem w świetle najnowszych badań. Materiały z sesji naukowej*.

26. Piotr Rybczyński, 'Likwidacja Skupisk Ludności Żydowskiej w Powiecie Konińskim': 111, *Ośrodek Zagłady w Chełmnie nad Nerem i Jego Rola w Hitlerowskiej Polityce Eksterminacyjnej. Materiały z Sesji Naukowej* (Konin: Muzeum Okręgowe w Koninie, 1995). Hereafter cited as *Rybczyński*.

27. S. 2/83. Akta dot. śledztwa w sprawie zamordowania ok. 1,500 osób jesienią 1941 r. w lasach Niesłusz-Rudzica gm. Gosławice. These records contain a

number of accounts by Poles who provided shelter for the Jews who were deported to their villages.

28. Rybczyński: 112; and S. 2/83: 63, Jadwiga Rybarczyk.
29. S. 2/83: 7, Piotr Zalas (testimony from January 1983).
30. ASG 26: 90, Piotr Zalas (testimony from November 1945).
31. S. 2/83: 50, Józef Raczkowski.
32. Henryk Mania 1967: 280–81.
33. Ob 271, tom 3: 259, Józef Grabowski.
34. Kalish Book: 285, 288.
35. Ibid.: 258–59.
36. Ibid.: 259; see also Zbiór "Bd" 323: 62, testimony of Sala Heber and AZIH 301/567, testimony of Gedale Goldman.
37. Henryk Mania 1967: 279.
38. S. 2/83 tom II: 77, Kazimierz Bartczak.
39. ASG 26: 98–103, Mieczysław Sękiewicz.
40. Rybczyński: 113.
41. S. 8/01/Zn: 6, Henryk Mania.
42. *Fateful Months*: 30.
43. Christopher Browning, *The Origins of the Final Solution* (Lincoln: University of Nebraska Press and Jerusalem: Yad Vashem, 2004): 416.
44. Henryk Mania 1967: 281.

Chapter 2 Extermination: The First Period (1941–1943)

Establishing the Camp

1. AR-Z 69/59 Bd. 6: 967, Walter Burmeister. For the oath taken by members of the 'Aktion Reinhard' camps, Treblinka, Sobibór and Bełżec, see Józef Kermisz, comp., *Dokumenty i materiały do dziejów okupacji niemieckiej w Polsce. Tom 2. Akcje i Wysiedlenia. Część 1* (Łódź: Wydawnictwo Centralnej Żydowskiej Komisji Historycznej, 1946): 40–41. Hereafter cited as *Dokumenty i materiały, tom 2*.
2. Józef Stanisław Mujta, *Miasto Dąbie w XIX i XX Wieku* (Konin: Wydawnictwo Apeks, 1998): 146–56. A total of 55 victims were exhumed from three mass graves after the war during Judge Bednarz's government investigation of the Chełmno camp. See also Ds. III/9/71 Akta śledztwa w sprawie zbrodni na zakładnikach polskich w lesie Żuchowskim, and OKBZNwP 83. Sprawozdanie z ekshumacji zwłok. For the fate of a local doctor and social activist in Dąbie, see 'Egzekucja dr Czesława Zapędowskiego w Lasach Rzuchowskich', *Przegląd Lekarski* 37/1 (1980): 148–49.
3. ASG 54: 93, and Adam Grabowski interview.
4. In Polish and German, respectively, the words "pałac" and "Schloss" [palace] are used to describe the building. In English, the word "mansion" is more accurate, though still an exaggerated description of the building, and is used throughout this work.
5. Jacek Wojciechowski, *Dominium Sławsk* (Konin: Wydawnictwo BPB "Arkada" Jacek Wojciechowski, 2005): 124–25.
6. Klemens Rosiński and Helena Wojtczak interviews. Both of these individuals lived in the mansion.
7. Biblioteka Narodowa, Microfilm Collection, *Gazeta Kolska*, June 11, 1939.
8. Ibid., *Gazeta Kolska*, March 4, 1934, July 14, 1935, February 9, 1936.
9. 203 AR-Z 69/59, Bd. 7a: 1288–89, Konrad Schulz.

10. Ibid., and 203 AR-Z 69/59, Bd. 7a: 1266, Else Semmler.

11. Ob 271, tom 2: 191, Czesław Potyralski, and tom 3: 258, Leopold Chwiałkowski.

12. 203 AR-Z 69/59, Bd. 7a: 1290, Konrad Schulz.

13. Ibid., Bd. 7a: 1282, Erhard Michelsohn.

14. Testimony of Jan Bąberski: 2. I am grateful to Zdzisław Lorek for a copy of this document.

15. Henryk Mania 1967: 281.

16. 203 AR-Z 69/59, Bd. 6: 947–48, Karl Heinl.

17. S. 8/01/Zn: 639, Henryk Mania.

18. Stanisław Librowski, *Ofiary Zbrodni Niemieckiej spośród Duchowieństwa Diecezji Włocławskiej 1939–1945* (Włocławek: Księgarnia Powszechna i Drukarnia Diecezjalna, 1947): 104.

19. For the controversy surrounding the two gas van drivers see Appendix I: The Gas Vans.

20. Henryk Mania 1967: 281. Mania stated that personnel changes took place before the operation in Konin. Changes also occurred just after the arrival of the Sonderkommando in Chełmno as individuals, such as Fritz Ismer who was not attached to the mobile Sonderkommando and who arrived to Chełmno from Łódź remembered Otto and Behm.

21. 203 AR-Z 69/59, Bd. 6: 978, Walter Burmeister.

22. Ibid.: 890–91.

23. 203 AR-Z 69/59, Bd. 7a: 1283, Erhard Michelsohn; Bd. 7a: 1291, Konrad Schulz.

24. Schulz's participation in establishing the camp (the initial contacts with Lange and informing the local population by acting as intermediary) undoubtedly led to the term "Sonderkommando Schultze"; see Bednarz: 13. It is my contention that the locals cynically applied this term to Schulz. The Sonderkommando was never commanded by a person named Schulz.

25. 203 AR-Z 69/59, Bd. 7a: 1290–91, Konrad Schulz.

26. S. 8/01/Zn: 254a, on-site inspection, April 4, 1995; according to Henryk Mania.

27. 203 AR-Z 69/59, Bd. 4: 595–96, Alois Häfele.

28. Ibid., Bd. 7a: 1154, Wilhelm Heukelbach.

29. Ibid.

30. Ibid., Bd. 7a: 1219, Josef Islinger.

31. Ibid., Bd. 5: 824, Wilhelm Schulte.

32. Henryk Maliczak 1967: 264–65.

33. Henryk Mania 1967: 280.

34. IPN Po 04/2718/2: 20, Wanda Kropidłowska and ibid.: 16, Andrzej Miszczak.

35. S. 8/01/Zn: 643, Henryk Mania. Piekarski's efforts included getting the entire group registered as Volksdeutsche, thereby making them citizens of the Reich.

36. S. 8/01/Zn: 38, Henryk Mania, and S. 8/01/Zn: 32, Henryk Maliczak. Hereafter cited as respectively *Henryk Mania 1964* and *Henryk Maliczak 1964*. Why Maliczak would make such an incriminating statement is not known.

37. Ob 271, tom 3: 259, Józef Grabowski; tom 3: 292, Jan Krysiński. In November 2000, Henryk Mania told prosecutors that "I didn't think about escaping; maybe I was too stupid, I was afraid." S. 8/01/Zn: 643, Henryk Mania.

38. Henryk Maliczak 1964: 32.

39. Ob 271, tom 1: 80, Wiktoria Adamczyk, and AZIH. 301/5350, Andrzej Miszczak.

40. Henryk Maliczak 1964: 32, and S. 8/01/Zn: 601, Jan Szacowny.

41. Henryk Maliczak 1964: 32, and Henryk Mania 1964: 38, 39.

42. 203 AR-Z 69/59, Bd. 5: 883, Kurt Möbius.

43. Ibid., Bd. 6: 974, Walter Burmeister.

44. Unless otherwise indicated the source of all information concerning Abram Rój is his daughter, Sara Roy: Sara Roy correspondence.

45. Ob 271, tom 3: 203, Domicela Chaba, and S. 8/01/Zn: 502, Zofia Frątczak.

46. Henryk Maliczak 1967: 265.

47. Henryk Maliczak 1964: 30–31.

48. Ob 271, tom 1: 80, Wiktoria Adamczyk; tom 3: 259, Józef Grabowski; 203 AR-Z 69/59, Bd. 6: 969, 973, Walter Burmeister; Bd. 6: 1008, Friedrich Maderholz.

49. AZIH Ring I 394, Uszer Taube; N. Blumental, comp., *Dokumenty i materiały z czasów okupacji niemieckiej w Polsce. Tom 1. Obozy* (Łódź: Wydawnictwo Centralnej Żydowskiej Komisji Historycznej, 1946): 239. Hereafter cited as *Dokumenty i materiały, tom 1*.

50. 203 AR-Z 69/59, Bd. 5: 875–76.

51. Henryk Maliczak 1967: 265 and Henryk Mania 1967: 281.

52. AZIH Ring I 394, Uszer Taube.

53. C. F. Rüter, ed., *Justiz und NS-Verbrechen: Sammlung deutscher Strafurteile wegen Natioalsozialistischer Tötungsverbrechen 1945–1966* Bd. VII (Amsterdam: University Press, 1971): 217. Hereafter cited as *NS-Verbrechen Bd. VII*. See also Ob 271, tom 9: 830, police report.

54. Zbiór "Bd" 323: 66–67, testimony of Hersz Traube. This is one case in which two vehicles are mentioned. The witness could be mistaken, referring to the same vehicle making repeated trips. Other witnesses refer to a single van, e.g., AZIH 301/567, testimony of Gedale Goldman.

The Transports

1. *Dokumenty i materiały*, tom 3: 26–31.

2. Nachman Blumenthal, comp., *Słowa Niewinne* (Kraków, Łódź, Warszawa: Centralna Żydowska Komisja Historyczna w Polsce, 1947): 45.

3. 203 AR-Z 69/59, Bd. 6: 985, Walter Burmeister, and ibid., Bd. 4: 557, Fritz Ismer.

4. Ibid., Bd. 1: 116, Albert Meyer.

5. *Dokumenty i materiały*, tom 1: 239, Michał Podchlebnik.

6. Ob 271, tom 2: 191, Czesław Potyralski; tom 3: 259, Józef Grabowski; AZIH Ring I 394. Uszer Taube.

7. Adam Grabowski interview. Mr. Grabowski was a young boy at the time, but witnessed many events. His father, a carpenter, later built the shelving in the church that was used to store the articles of clothing brought from Chełmno.

8. AZIH 205/192. Korespondencja dotycząca przesiedlenia 20,000 Żydów.

9. Julian Baranowski, *Zigeunerlager in Litzmannstadt 1941–1942* (Łódź: Archiwum Państwowe w Łodzi & Bilbo, 2003): 16–40; see also *Chronicle*: 107–108.

10. Yad Vashem 03/2351: 13, Michał Podchlebnik.

11. AZIH 205/191. The protective clothing worn by the policemen is visible in photographs taken in Włocławek during the deportation operation and in Powiercie as a transport is disembarking and preparing to march to Zawadka.

12. 203 AR-Z 69/59, Bd. 4: 551–52, Fritz Ismer.

13. AZIH 205/9. Korespondencja dotycząca akcji specjalnych, wypłaty poborów uczestników akcji specjalnych, dodatki specjalne do poborów w akcjach specjalnych.

14. *Chronicle*: 96.

15. Ob 271, tom 3: 258, Leopold Chspecjalnychwiałkowski.
16. All figures concerning these Łódź transports from January through May are taken from the *Chronicle*: 125, 127, 132, 136, 143, 194. According to the *Chronicle*, the number of deportees from the first 40 transports was 44,056; see *Chronicle*: 143.
17. Isaiah Trunk, *Lodz Ghetto. A History* (Bloomington and Indianapolis: Indiana University Press, 2006): 231. Hereafter cited as *Trunk*.
18. AZIH 205/9. Korespondencja dotycząca akcji specjalnych, wypłaty poborów uczestników akcji specjalnych, dodatki specjalne do poborów w akcjach specjalnych.
19. Peter Witte, 'Two Decisions Concerning the "Final Solution"', *Holocaust and Genocide Studies* 9(3) Winter 1995: 335–36.
20. Trunk: 237.
21. Ob 271, tom 1: 77, Kazimierz Paterkowski.
22. Ibid., tom 1: 79, Helena Lange. The figure 1,000 was given by many witnesses to the postwar Polish investigation as the average number of daily arrivals.
23. Ibid., tom 1: 78, Edward Markiewicz.
24. Ob 19: 239–40, Heinz May.
25. Ob 271, tom 5: 420, August Piella.
26. Ibid., tom 2: 187, Zofia Szatkowska; tom 1: 79, Irena Lange.
27. 203 AR-Z 69/59, Bd. 5: 818–20, Wilhelm Schulte.
28. Ob 19: 240–1, Heinz May.
29. Ob 271, tom 3: 245, Kazimierz Grenda.
30. 203 AR-Z 69/59, Bd. 5: 823–24, Wilhelm Schulte.
31. Ob 271, tom 2: 116, Leopold Surgot.
32. Ibid.
33. 203 AR-Z 69/59, Bd. 5: 824–25, Wilhelm Schulte.
34. Ld 139/23: 110.
35. Ibid.
36. Ibid.: 101, 109.
37. Ob 271, tom 9: 827, Police Report.
38. Instytut Pamięci Narodowej. *Proces Hansa Biebowa* (Warszawa: Główna Komisja Badania Zbrodni Hitlerowskich w Polsce, 1987): 159. Hereafter cited as *Proces Biebowa*.
39. SO Łódź 5a: 214, Fanny Miller.
40. Ibid.: 224, Gedalie Fuks.

The Mansion: Arrival, Murder, Plunder

1. 203 AR-Z 69/59, Bd. 4: 553, Fritz Ismer, and S. 8/01/Zn: 639, Henryk Mania.
2. S. 8/01/Zn: 12, police report, based on interview with Henryk Maliczak.
3. Burmeister later said this was just a joke and he did not know why he did it. 203 AR-Z 69/59, Bd. 4: 632.
4. Ibid., Bd. 5: 877–78, 880–82, Kurt Möbius.
5. *Henryk Mania 1967*: 282, and S. 8/01/Zn: 639, Henryk Mania.
6. 203 AR-Z 69/59, Bd. 5: 822–23, Wilhelm Schulte.
7. Ibid., Bd. 7a: 1158–60, Wilhelm Heukelbach.
8. 203 AR-Z 69/59, Bd. 4: 525–29, Gustav Laabs.
9. Ob 271, tom 1: 10, Michał Podchlebnik.
10. 203 AR-Z 69/59, Bd. 4: 613–14, Alois Häfele.
11. Ibid., Bd. 4: 554, Fritz Ismer; Bd. 6: 1000, Walter Bock.

12. The original note is located at Yad Vashem, Jerusalem, Israel. The first publication of the note is believed to be in: Adam Rutkowski, *Męczeństwo, Walka, Zagłada Żydów w Polsce 1939–1945* (Warszawa: Wydawnictwo Ministerstwa Obrony Narodowej, 1960), photo numbers 309 and 310. For photographs of the original pages with accompanying English translation, see also Reuven Dafni and Yehudit Kleiman, *Final Letters: From Victims of the Holocaust* (New York: Paragon House, 1991): 119–20. Hereafter cited as *Final Letters*.

13. The original note is located at Muzeum Miasta Pabianic (Pabianice City Museum, Pabianice, Poland). See also *Final Letters*: 121–22.

14. 203 AR-Z 69/59, Bd. 4: 553, Fritz Ismer and Ob 271, tom 4: 362, Stanisław Śliwiński.

15. 203 AR-Z 69/59, Bd. 4: 554, Fritz Ismer.

16. Ibid., Bd. 6: 1031, Karl Heinl.

17. Jan Fijałek, Antoni Galiński, ed. *Getto w Łodzi 1940–1944* (Łódź: Okręgowa Komisja Badania Zbrodni Hitlerowskich w Łodzi, 1988): 93.

18. AZIH 205/307. Notatki dotyczące rozmowy Hansa Biebowa.

19. NTN 38: 856–57, Hans Biebow.

20. Ob 271, tom 2: 177, Rudolf Kramp.

21. 203 AR-Z 69/59, Bd. 1: 114–16, Albert Meyer.

22. *Dokumenty i materiały*, tom 3: 230–31.

23. 203 AR-Z 69/59, Bd. 4: 610, Alois Häfele.

24. *Chronicle*: 185.

25. *Dokumenty i materiały*, tom 3: 233–34.

26. 203 AR-Z 69/59, vol. 1: 118, Albert Meyer.

27. Copy in AZIH, 205/194.

28. J. Kermisz, comp., *Dokumenty i materiały do dziejów okupacji niemieckiej w Polsce. Tom 2. Akcje i Wysiedlenia. Część 1* (Łódź: Wydawnictwo Centralnej Żydowskiej Komisji Historycznej, 1946): 156–57, 166, 168–70, 177. Hereafter cited as *Dokumenty i materiały, tom 2*.

29. Sources concerning the "Commission" originate primarily from testimonies in the Bednarz investigation; see Ob 271, tom 1: 15, 50, 52, 57, 67, 80; tom 3: 268, 279; tom 5: 431, and others. See also The Polish Underground Movement (1939–1945), Study Trust. Aneks Nr. 26, and Jan Karski, *The Story of a Secret State* (Boston: Houghton Mifflin Company, 1944): 339–54.

30. AZIH. Pamiętniki. 302/220 NN. 'Piekło Chełmna.'

The Forest Camp

1. 203 AR-Z 69/59, Bd. 5: 856, Jacob Wildermuth.

2. Ibid., Bd. 5: 875, Kurt Möbius.

3. Ibid., Bd. 5: 856, Jacob Wildermuth.

4. Ob 271, tom 3: 210, Adam Milewski.

5. 203 AR-Z 69/59, Bd. 4: 555, Fritz Ismer.

6. Ibid., Bd. 7a: 1222–25, Josef Islinger.

7. Ob 19: 96.

8. Ibid.: 241–43, Heinz May.

9. Jochen Von Lang, ed., *Eichmann Interrogated*. (New York: Farrar, Straus and Giroux, 1983): 77–78.

10. Birth registration of Abram Rój: Urząd Stanu Cywilnego w Przedczu, Księga urodzeń ludności żydowskiej Przedcza za lata 1902–1916, U/18/1916. However, Rój may have actually been born in Zbijewo, a small village not far from

Przedecz. At the time of his birth, the family was living in Zbijewo and on at least one other document, Rój stated his place of birth was Zbijewo; see APPoK, AgIK, [1848] 1870–1954, sygn. 1150 (nowa)/ 1142 (stara), k.4-5. I am grateful to Przemysław Nowicki for bringing these documents to my attention.

11. US Immigration papers of Abram Roy (courtesy of Sara Roy), and APPoK, AgIK, sygn. 1392, k. 16-17, and sygn. 1291 z 1939, k. 498. The eighth name on the list is Albert Rój, born in 1916, and a resident of Izbica. As there was only one Rój family living in Izbica, the first name is undoubtedly a clerical error. I am grateful to Przemysław Nowicki for bringing this document to my attention.

12. According to Rój's Application for Immigration Visa and Alien Registration (courtesy of Sara Roy), he spent six weeks in Chełmno. This is obviously a mistake. If he spent about six days in Chełmno, he would have arrived with the second group from Izbica on January 9.

13. The identity of the person referred to as Szlamek (the diminutive form of Szlama) in the Chełmno literature has been a point of discussion for a number of years. He is often referred to as Jakub Grojnowski (and even Grojanowski), but this was the false identity he traveled under for purposes of safety following his escape from Chełmno. While in Warsaw, he presented a photograph of himself to Hersz and Bluma Wasser, signing the reverse side "Szlamek." After the war, two people who knew Szlamek referred to him as 'Winer' (Ob 271, tom 1: 10–12, Michał Podchlebnik, and tom 4: 314–15, Bajla Alszuld, a resident of Dąbie). This information and the registration of Szlamek's birth in Izbica Kujawska below should help end further speculation concerning the question of his true identity:

"On the fourteenth [Julian calendar] (twenty-seventh [Gregorian calendar]) of September, nineteen-eleven, at ten o'clock in the morning, Iccak Wolf Winer, a merchant residing in Izbica settlement, age thirty-five, having present with him the witnesses Yakov Winer, age forty-four, and Michał Sochaczewski, age fifty, both merchants residing in Izbica settlement, appeared before this office in Izbica settlement and presented a baby of the male gender, declaring that he was born in Izbica settlement on the tenth [Julian calendar] (twenty-third [Gregorian calendar]) of September of this year at five o'clock in the morning to his lawful wife, Srenca née Laskow, age thirty-six. This baby was named Szlama Ber. This act was read to the declarer and witnesses, and signed by this office and them.

[/-/] W. Winer, M. Sochaczewski, Ya. Winer."

Urząd Stanu Cywilnego w Izbicy Kujawskiej. Księgi Metrykalne Ludności Żydowskiej z lat 1905–1913, księga za 1911, nr aktu urodzenia 29 [Office of Public Records in Izbica Kujawska. Public Register of the Jewish Population for 1905–1913, register for 1911, birth registration number 29].

Winer's testimony is given in its entirety but has been divided into two sections. The second part, which concerns his escape, begins on page 131. The daily headings have been added for the convenience of the reader. For additional information concerning Szlama Winer, see: Przemysław Nowicki, 'Zanim "przybył z zaświatów," nazywał się Winer. Krąg rodzinny i konspiracyjny Szlamka, uciekiniera z ośrodka zagłady w Chełmnie nad Nerem,' Zagłada Żydów, No. 5, 2009.

14. This reference is to the Poles from Fort VII.

15. Days before while on the way to work in the forest, Chrząstkowski had thrown onto the road a letter he had written to his son. He had attached a watch and a ring as "postage" to ensure its delivery. Alexander Kamiński, a local forest worker, found the watch and the letter. He read the letter but did not deliver

it, because "in the meantime, the Jews from Kłodawa were deported." Ob 271 tom 3: 207, Alexander Kamiński.

16. Although it is not certain that this is the same event, a virtually identical scene was described by Abram Rój. For reasons known only to himself, he felt it especially important to bear witness to this horrific murder.

17. This was, in fact, one of the Polish workers, Marian Libelt. He became trapped inside the van as he was attempting to coax others into it. Libelt's body was returned to the grounds of the mansion and buried there. See Henryk Maliczak 1964: 31.

18. AZIH. Ring. I 412. This English language translation is from the Polish; see Ruta Sakowska, *Dwa Etapy. Hitlerowska polityka eksterminacji Żydów w oczach ofiar* (Wrocław: Ossolineum, 1986): 112–31.

19. Łucja Pawlicka–Nowak, 'Wyniki Badań Archeologicznych Przeprowadzonych w Latach 2003–2004 na terenie Cmentarzyska byłego Ośrodka Zagłady w Chełmnie n. Nerem (Las Rzuchowski)', *Przeszłość i Pamięć* Lipiec–Grudzień 2004: 84–85, 87.

20. Podchlebnik always referred to the Poles working in the camp as Ukrainians. Initially, this could have been caused by fear. While testifying to Polish authorities, he may not have wanted to implicate Poles in the operation of a Nazi death camp. His testimony at the Eichmann trial and his Yad Vashem testimony, taken in 1963, also refer to the Ukrainians. By this time, the Ukrainians may have simply become part of his story. Quotation marks around the word "Ukrainian" are in the original.

21. Ob 271 tom 1: 11, Michał Podchlebnik.

22. The graves mentioned by May are thought to be the graves dug by Winer and Podchlebnik, grave 1, and the so-called Włocławek Grave, where it appears machinery was used for the first time. See *Ośrodek zagłady Żydów w Chełmnie nad Nerem w świetle najnowszych badań. Materiały z sesji naukowej*: 21–22. Hereafter cited as *Ośrodek zagłady*. This book was also published in English as "The Extermination Center for Jews in Chełmno-on-Ner in the Light of the Latest Research." Symposium Proceedings, September 6–7, 2004.

23. Dąbrowska: 167.

24. Ob 19: 243, Heinz May. Bothmann was evidently "boasting" about the number of victims.

25. For more on the Einsatzgruppen, Aktion 1005, and Paul Blobel, see Yitzhak Arad, *The Holocaust in the Soviet Union* (Lincoln: University of Nebraska Press, 2009).

26. Ibid.: 244–45, Heinz May.

27. For this and additional archeological information concerning the crematoria, see *Ośrodek zagłady*: 17–20.

28. Ob 271, tom 3: 208, Czesław Urbaniak; tom 8: 767, Stanisław Rubach; 203 AR-Z 69/59, Bd. 3: 415, Theodor Malzmüller.

29. 203 AR-Z 69/59, Bd. 6: 1013, Friedrich Maderholz.

30. Ob 271, tom 2: 161, Rozalia Peham.

31. 203 AR-Z 69/59 Bd. 4: 555, Fritz Ismer.

32. Ob 271, tom 8: 767, Stanisław Rubach; 203 AR-Z 69/59, Bd. 6: 1002, Walter Bock.

33. Klee Ernst, Willi Dressen, Volker Riess, eds. *Schöne Zeiten* (Frankfurt am Main: S. Fischer Verlag, 1988): 201.

34. Ob 271, tom 1: 52, Helena Król; 203 AR-Z 69/59, Bd. 4: 561, Fritz Ismer; Bd. 6: 1013, Friedrich Maderholz.

35. *Dokumenty i materiały*, tom 3: 279. The inclusion of the final sentence begs the question of what the term "Sonderkommando Kulmhof" meant to Rumkowski.
36. Ibid.
37. 203 AR-Z 69/59, Bd. 6: 985, Walter Burmeister.
38. Ibid., Bd. 6: 1013, Friedrich Maderholz.
39. Ibid., Bd. 7a: 1164–65, Wilhelm Heukelbach.
40. Ob 19: 245–46, Heinz May. A photograph of a bone mill used in the Janowski camp in L'viv can be seen in Ernst Klee, Willi Dressen, Volker Riess, *'Gott mit uns.' Die deutsche Vernichtungskrieg im Osten 1939–1945* (Frankfurt am Main: S. Fischer Verlag, 1989): 225. While it is not known if the bone mill used in Chełmno was identical to this one, it fits the general description and provides a visual image of just what a bone mill looked like.
41. Ob 271, tom 1: 70, Aleksander Woźniak.
42. Bednarz: 20–21.
43. 203 AR-Z 69/59, Bd. 5: 858, Jacob Wildermuth. See also the statement of Walter Piller on page 165.
44. Ob 271, tom 1: 82, Janina Małolepsza; tom 1: 52, Helena Król. These figures appear inflated and may reflect the number of Jewish prisoners and German policemen.

Resumption of Transports

1. SO Łódź 5a: 219, Aron Jakubowicz.
2. Dr. Yaakov Lemberg was the head of the Judenrat in the ghetto of Zduńska Wola.
3. Ld 139/23: 64–75, Rafał Lewkowicz.
4. Ob 19: 247, Heinz May.
5. *Proces Biebowa*: 172–73, Rafał Lewkowicz.
6. Ibid.: 155–56, Sasza Lewiatin.
7. Ld pf 1/135–156 tom 2: 3–6.
8. Trunk: 239.
9. Ibid.: 240.
10. *Chronicle*: 248–50.
11. An English-language translation of the speech is printed in Trunk: 272–75.
12. For a more detailed description of this deportation, see *Chronicle*: 248–50, as well as Yitzhak Arad, Yisrael Gutman, Abraham Margaliot, eds., *Documents on the Holocaust: Selected Sources on the Destruction of the Jews of Germany and Austria, Poland, and the Soviet Union* (New York: Ktav Publishing House in association with Yad Vashem and Pergamon Press, 1981): 283–84. Hereafter cited as *Documents on the Holocaust*.
13. *Chronicle*: 294.
14. 203 AR-Z 69/59, Bd. 6: 1014, Friedrich Maderholz.
15. Ibid., Bd. 3: 412–13, Theodor Malzmüller.
16. Ibid., Bd. 3: 446, Rudolf Otto.
17. Ibid., Bd. 4: 531, Gustav Laabs.
18. *Chronicle*: 331–32.
19. Ob 271, tom 8: 768, Stanisław Rubach.
20. Ibid., tom 2: 115, Józef Czupryński.
21. *Dokumenty i materiały*, tom 1: 237–38.
22. Ob 271, tom 2: 136, Józef Przybylski.
23. Henryk Mania 1967: 282, and Henryk Maliczak 1967: 266.
24. 203 AR-Z 69/59, Bd. 3: 454, Kurt Meier.

25. Ob 271, tom 1: 69, Marianna Woźniak.
26. Ibid., tom 1: 80, Wiktoria Adamczyk.
27. Ibid., tom 7: 631–34, 647.
28. Ibid., tom 1: 107, Zygmunt Szkobel.
29. Ibid., tom 1: 36, Zygmunt Antecki.
30. See also supporting testimonies in Ob 271, tom 1: 52, 69, 80; tom 4: 322.
31. Ibid., tom 3: 292, Jan Krysiński.
32. Ibid., tom 3: 259, Józef Grabowski.
33. Ibid., tom 2: 121, Michał Radoszewski.
34. Ibid., tom 2: 115, Józef Czupryński.
35. The figures vary concerning the children from Lidice; see Jochen von Lang, *Eichmann Interrogated* (New York: Farrar, Straus and Giroux, 1983): 188–92, and Joseph Wechsberg, "A Reporter at Large, The Children of Lidice", *The New Yorker*, May 1 (1948): 36, 38. Wechsberg spoke with three of the children who were selected for Germanization. A memorial to the murdered children of Lidice was erected on the grounds of the former forest camp after the war.
36. Ob 271, tom 1: 82, Janina Małolepsza.
37. Ibid., tom 1: 81, Wiktoria Adamczyk.
38. S. 8/01/Zn: 501, Zofia Frątczak.
39. Ibid.: 936, Marie Kocikova.
40. 203 AR 609/61, Bd. 2: 95, Wilhelm Orlowski.
41. 203 AR-Z 69/59, Bd. 4: 554, Fritz Ismer.
42. *Chronicle*: 226.

Escapes

1. Ruta Sakowska, comp.; *Archiwum Ringelbluma. Tom 1. Listy o Zagładzie* (Warszawa: Wydawnictwo Naukowe PWN, 1997): 35. Hereafter cited as *Listy o Zagładzie*. In a second letter written the same day, Róża Kapłan states the man was from Kłodawa. Winer, who escaped from Chełmno on January 19, never mentioned this escape in his report. There are no accounts of an escape later that day, the following day, or even the subsequent day (January 21) when Kapłan met with the escapee. One possible explanation is Rój told Róża Kapłan that he had been in Kłodawa before reaching Krośniewice and she assumed he was from the town. For this second letter, see Adam Puławski, *W Obliczu Zagłady. Rząd RP na Uchodźstwie, Delegatura Rządu RP na Kraj, ZWZ-AK wobec deportacji Żydów do obozów zagłady (1941–1942)*. (Lublin: Instytut Pamięci Narodowej, 2009): 67.
2. Yad Vashem, 03/2351: 12–13, Michał Podchlebnik.
3. Ob 271, tom 1: 11, Michał Podchlebnik.
4. Ibid., tom 2: 120, Michał Radoszewski.
5. Ibid., tom 4: 360, Stanisława Testkowska.
6. Ibid., tom 3: 287, Władysława Bielińska.
7. Yad Vashem, 03/2351: 15–17, Michał Podchlebnik.
8. Rabbi Aronson's writings are self-published in his book *Alei Merorot: Yomanim, Shut, Hagut ba-Shoah* (Bnei Brak, 1996). Hereafter cited as *Aronson*.
9. Aronson: 128. I am grateful to Yudith Nave and the Hebrew Institute of Boston, Inc. for translating the relevant text.
10. For additional information see Esther Farbstein, *Hidden in Thunder: Perspectives on Faith, Halachah and Leadership during the Holocaust* (Jerusalem: Mossad Harav Kook, 2007): 20–22, 28–32. Hereafter cited as *Farbstein*.

11. AZIH, Ring, I, 412.
12. *Chronicle*: xxi. The original postcard is lost.
13. AZIH, Ring, I, 549. English translation from Farbstein: 35. For a Polish translation and photograph of this letter see *Listy o Zagładzie*: 3–6.
14. Yad Vashem, MIE 215/90, Testimony of Fiszel Brejtsztajn. Fiszel Brejtsztajn has been incorrectly reported as an escapee from Chełmno; see Farbstein: 24. His own testimony makes clear he escaped before the transport reached the camp. Brejtsztajn probably learned details of Chełmno from Rabbi Szulman. After leaving Grabów, according to Solomon Uberbaum, an employee of the Łódź ghetto Judenrat and a man who knew Rumkowski before the war, Brejtsztajn brought a letter from Rabbi Szulman into the ghetto. See Shmuel Huppert, "King of the Ghetto. Mordecai Haim Rumkowski, the Elder of Lodz Ghetto", *Yad Vashem Studies* 15 (1983): 125–57.
15. *Listy o Zagładzie*: 7–9 (AZIH, Ring, I, 549).
16. Ibid.: 10–11 (AZIH. Ring. I 549).
17. Eichmann Trial, Session 65, Michał Podchlebnik.
18. See testimony of Uszer Taube. AZIH, Ring I, 394. Taube states that Winer, Rój, and Podchlebnik arrived in Grabów separately on January 18 and 19. Only Rój could have arrived on the 18th, Winer did arrive on the 19th, and Podchlebnik arrived on the 21st. However, neither Winer nor Podchlebnik mention seeing Rój in Grabów or hearing that he had been there. Nor does Rabbi Szulman inform Winer, or Podchlebnik for that matter, that he has already spoken to an escapee. Taube does not state that he was in Grabów at the time or that he actually saw all three escapees. He may be repeating second-hand information received at a later date, perhaps while in the Warsaw ghetto.
19. Evidence that Rój may have been in Grabów at some point originates from the postcard he later wrote to Winer in which he states he received a postcard from Grabów. This information must have meant something to Winer and someone in Grabów must have known Rój's travel plans in order to correspond with him.
20. AZIH, Ring, I, 412/2.
21. Ob 271, tom 4: 314, Bajla Alszuld. Alszuld went on to say that Winer wrote her a letter from Zamość explaining that what was happening in Chełmno was also happening there.
22. Lau-Lavie, Naphtali. *Balaam's Prophecy: Eyewitness to History, 1939–1989* (Cranbury, NJ: Cornwall Books, 1998): 65–66.
23. AZIH, Ring, I, 596/3.
24. Stanisław Mączka, *Żydzi polscy w KL Auschwitz. Wykazy imienne*, (Warszawa: Żydowski Instytut Historyczny, 2004): 359, 369; and US Immigration papers of Abram Roy (courtesy of Sara Roy). While Rój's name does not appear on the list, Rój's tattooed Auschwitz number falls within the registration sequencing of prisoner numbers for the Starachowice transport of July 1944.
25. See Ruta Sakowska, "Szlojme, der antlofener fun Chełmno", *Bleter far Geshikhte* 23, (1985): 218.
26. For pre-war background information on Winer and Rój, see respectively Przemysław Nowicki, 'Wokół Szlamka. Szkic do portretu rodzin Łaskich i Winerów z Izbicy Kujawskiej', *Zapiski Kujawsko-Dobrzyńskie* 22 (2007): 153–60, and Przemysław Nowicki, 'O Abramie Roju, pierwszym uciekinierze z obozu zagłady na polskich terenach wcielonych do Rzeszy', *Zapiski Kujawsko-Dobrzyńskie* 23 (2008): 185–200.
27. Ob 271, tom 4: 367, Natalia M.
28. Ibid., tom 4: 366, Lidia M.

29. Szymon Datner, *Ucieczki z niewoli niemieckiej 1939–1945* (Warszawa: Książka i Wiedza, 1966): 234–35.
30. Henryk Mania 1964: 38.
31. Bednarz: 55.
32. Quoted from Shmuel Krakowski, *Chełmno. A Small Village in Europe* (Jerusalem: Yad Vashem, 2009): 79.
33. Netty Kalman interview.
34. In his account of their escape, Naphtali Lau-Lavie mistakenly names one of the escapees Chaim Yerachmiel Widawski. According to information provided by the Widawski family to the author, the man's name was Yerachmiel Israel Widawski. It is Lau-Lavie's "impression" that the men spent about two weeks in the camp. Another area of contention surrounding these events is the date they occurred. Lau-Lavie states in his book, and maintains to this day, that the escapees arrived in Piotrków just before the holiday of Purim (March 2) 1942. However, the Widawski family is just as adamant that the escape occurred in September 1942, which is supported by the fact that, as related in the account, the Jewish community of Sieradz was deported to Chełmno at the end of August 1942. Lau-Lavie may have confused around which holiday the event occurred, choosing Purim rather than Rosh Hashanah, which fell on September 12 of that year.
35. The following account is from the Polish edition of Lau-Lavie's autobiography, *Zraniony Lew* (1997). The English-language edition of the book, *Balaam's Prophecy* (1998), lacks some details concerning events in Chełmno, but includes minor details omitted in the Polish edition. Those details are included in brackets and therefore this account is a compilation of the two similar versions.
36. Naphtali Lau-Lavie, *Zraniony Lew. Autobiografia.* (Kraków: Wydawnictwo Znak, 1997): 92–94. and Naphtali Lau-Lavie, *Balaam's Prophecy: Eyewitness to History, 1939–1989* (Cranbury, NJ: Cornwall Books, 1998): 66–67.
37. Naphtali Lau-Lavie interview.
38. Rudolf Vrba and Alfred Wetzler, who escaped from Auschwitz in 1944 and informed the Allies with a detailed 32-page report about the mass murder that was taking place there, also found shelter in Žilina.
39. Netty Kalman, Chava Stern, and Chaim Grünfeld interviews.
40. Farbstein: 40.
41. See http://www.whosyerdad-e.com/families-g/individual.php?pid=I2127& ged=14022 007bb.ged&tab=0, accessed June 1, 2010.
42. The account is published in Barbara Gańczyk, *Dzieci Hioba* (Kłodawa: Drukarnia Braci Wielińskich, 2000): 28–37.

First Liquidation of the Camp

1. NO-246, Greiser to Himmler, May 1, 1942; NO-247, Koppe to Brandt, May 3, 1942; NO-250, Blome to Greiser, November 18, 1942; NO-251, Himmler to Greiser, December 3, 1942.
2. *Hitlerowska Polityka*: 447.
3. Ob 271, tom 8: 769, 771, Stanisław Rubach.
4. 203 AR-Z 69/59, Bd. 6: 985, Walter Burmeister.
5. Ibid., Bd. 6: 987, Walter Burmeister.
6. Ob 271, tom 3: 223, 225, 249, 254.
7. 203 AR-Z 69/59, Bd. 7a: 1284, Erhard Michelsohn.
8. Ibid., Bd. 4: 641, Walter Burmeister.

9. Ibid., Bd. 6: 1002, Walter Bock; Bd. 3: 418, Theodor Malzmüller. A copy of the restaurant's bill for the party is in the photo section of *Hitlerowska Polityka*.

10. Berlin Document Center, personal file of Hans Bothmann.

11. Ob 19: 247, Heinz May.

12. 203 AR-Z 69/59, Bd. 4: 556, Fritz Ismer.

13. Henryk Maliczak 1964: 32.

14. S. 8/01/Zn: 644, Henryk Mania.

15. Ibid.: 582, Zdzisław Lorek.

16. Ob 271, tom 3: 259, Józef Grabowski.

17. IPN Po 04/2718/2, Waleriana Wawrzyniak and Jan Skorupski.

18. 203 AR-Z 69/59, Bd. 6: 986, Walter Burmeister.

19. Ibid., Bd. 4: 532, Gustav Laabs.

20. Ibid., Bd. 6: 985, Walter Burmeister.

21. Herkner was also the district organizing leader of the Nazi party. 203 AR-Z 69/59, Bd. 7a: 1270, Herbert Wauer.

22. Ob 271, tom 1: 13–14, Henryk Kruszczyński; tom 2: 143–44, Michał Sokolnicki; tom 2: 185, Stanisław Brodnowski; tom 3: 245, Kazimierz Grenda.

23. Ibid., tom 1: 52–53, Helena Król; tom 1: 80–81, Wiktoria Adamczyk; tom 2: 137, Mikołaj Kazimierski; tom 2: 138, Helena Kazimierczak.

24. Ibid., tom 3: 259–60, Józef Grabowski.

25. Ibid., tom 2: 134; tom 8: 772, Stanisław Rubach.

26. 203 AR-Z 69/59, Bd. 6: 958, Karl Heinl.

27. T. Berenstein, A. Eisenbach, A. Rutkowski, eds., *Eksterminacja Żydów na ziemiach polskich w okresie okupacji hitlerowskiej* (Warszawa: Żydowski Instytut Historyczny, 1957): 326.

28. 203 AR-Z 69/59, Bd. 5: 829, Wilhelm Schulte; Bd. 6: 958, Karl Heinl.

29. Ibid.; 203 AR-Z 69a/59, Bd. 3: 476–77, Wilhelm Görlich.

30. 203 AR 609/61, Bd. 2: 17, Johannes Legath; ibid., Bd. 1: 16, Letter.

31. Henryk Mania 1967: 284. See also 203 AR 609/61, Bd. 1: 63–64, Walter Piller.

32. 203 AR 609/61, Bd. 1: 65, Walter Piller.

33. Henryk Maliczak 1964: 33. Mania stated that the Jews were taken to the Żabikowo camp and shot there; see also Henryk Mania 1967: 286.

34. Henryk Mania 1967: 286.

35. 203 AR-Z 69/59, Bd. 4: 601, Alois Häfele.

Chapter 3 Extermination: The Second Period (1944–1945)

Re-Establishing the Camp

1. Letter quoted from *Chronicle*, lxii.

2. 203 AR-Z 69/59, Bd. 4: 541, Gustav Laabs.

3. Marian Kaczmarek, *Organizacja Poznańskiego Gestapo 1939–1945* (Żabikowo: Muzeum Martyrologiczne w Żabikowie, 2003): 30.

4. Ob 271, tom 8: 772, Stanisław Rubach.

5. Fritz Ismer, in charge of valuables during the first period, did not return to Chełmno, but remained in Yugoslavia.

6. 203 AR-Z 69/59, Bd. 2: 236.

7. 203 AR 609/61, Bd. 1: 65–66, Walter Piller.

8. Ibid.: 70, Walter Piller. Bruno Israel, a guard, stated that the policemen received RM 13 per day; see Bednarz: 69.

9. Ob 271, tom 2: 176–77, Rudolf Kramp.
10. Szymon Srebrnik interview. Hereafter cited as *Srebrnik interview*. Bruno Israel testified that the portion of the fence "on the village side" was wooden; see SAP 67: 159.
11. Bednarz: 73, Bruno Israel; 203 AR 609/61, Bd. 1: 80, Walter Piller.
12. Srebrnik interview.
13. 203 AR 609/61, Bd. 1: 78, Walter Piller.
14. Srebrnik interview. Bruno Israel places the hole for burning the personal items as "at the end of the park where there are three apple trees", Bednarz: 73.
15. SAP 66: 18, Herman Gielow.
16. Srebrnik interview. The precise location of the barracks has not been established. Srebrnik and Bruno Israel stated they were located on the same field as the crematoria; Israel adding that they were close to the entrance. The museum in Chełmno places them at the southern end of Plot III, containing the so-called Włocławska grave. Both locations are in close proximity to each other. Based on an aerial photograph taken by the Luftwaffe in January 1945, as well as testimonies of people being led through the forest from the barracks to the crematoria, I tentatively place the two structures at the site of the first grave.
17. 2 Ks 2/65, Bd. 8: 227, Gustav Laabs.
18. Oskar Hering was not in Chełmno during the second period and is believed to have died in Yugoslavia in 1944. See C. F. Rüter, ed., *Justiz und NS-Verbrechen: Sammlung deutscher Strafurteile wegen Natioalsozialistischer Tötungsverbrechen 1945–1966* Bd. XXI (Amsterdam: University Press, 1979): 234. Hereafter cited as *Justiz und NS-Verbrechen Bd. XXI*.
19. 203 AR-Z 69/59, Bd. 4: 541–2, Gustav Laabs.
20. Ob 271, tom 2: 163, Szymon Srebrnik.
21. Eichmann Trial, Session 66, Szymon Srebrnik.
22. Srebrnik interview.
23. This scene was reenacted in Claude Lanzmann's film *Shoah*.
24. Łucja Pawlicka-Nowak, 'Chełmno n. Nerem - Relacja Ocalałego z Zagłady', *Przeszłość i Pamięć* 1/2 (Styczeń-Czerwiec 2001): 102–103.
25. Ob 271, tom 8: 772, Stanislaw Rubach.
26. 203 AR 609/61, Bd. 1: 70, Walter Piller.
27. Ibid.: 77, Walter Piller.
28. 203 AR 609/61, Bd. 1: 78, Walter Piller; Ob 271, tom 4: 396, Bruno Israel.
29. Eichmann Trial, Session 66, Szymon Srebrnik.
30. Ibid., Session 65, Mordechai Żurawski.
31. Entries in the *Chronicle* for May 2, 17, and 18 report on people taken for "work outside the ghetto."
32. Ob 271, tom 2: 163, Szymon Srebrnik; Srebrnik interview.
33. 203 AR-Z 69/59, Bd. 6: 904–05, Ernst Burmeister.

A New Killing Procedure

1. *Chronicle*: 506–507.
2. Ibid.: 513.
3. *Proces Biebowa*: 159, Perec Wołkowicz.
4. 203 AR-Z 69/59, Bd. 6: 905–906, Ernst Burmeister.
5. Ob 271, tom 2: 163, Szymon Srebrnik.
6. Srebrnik interview. The question arises if this could be one of the unaccounted-for escapees from the first period; see pages 136–37.

7. Eichmann Trial, Session 65, Mordechai Żurawski.
8. Bednarz: 74, Bruno Israel.
9. Simon drowned in the Ner River while bathing sometime before the liquidation of the camp.
10. SAP 67: 143, Herman Gielow.
11. 203 AR 609/61, Bd. 1: 75–76, Walter Piller.
12. Ibid.
13. Ob 19: 248, Heinz May.
14. 203 AR-Z 69/59, Bd. 6: 906–07, Ernst Burmeister.
15. 203 AR 609/61, Bd. 1: 93, Hermann Gielow.
16. Srebrnik interview.
17. SAP 66: 24, Mordechai Żurawski; 19, Hermann Gielow; Bednarz: 72, Bruno Israel.
18. Ob 271, tom 2: 164, Szymon Srebrnik.
19. 203 AR 609/61, Bd. 1: 76–77, Walter Piller.
20. *Proces Biebowa*: 138, Szlama Uberbaum.
21. *Chronicle*: 534.
22. 203 AR 609/61, Bd. 1: 77, Walter Piller.
23. Ob 271, tom 4: 343, Mordechai Żurawski.
24. The guard Bruno Israel personally witnessed these atrocities; see Bednarz: 68.
25. Ob 271, tom 4: 343, Mordechai Żurawski.
26. SAP 66: 24, Mordechai Żurawski; SAP 67: 143, Mordechai Żurawski; Ob 271, tom 2: 163, Szymon Srebrnik.
27. 203 AR 609/61, Bd. 1: 77, Walter Piller.
28. Bednarz: 70, Bruno Israel.
29. Ob 271, tom 1: 13, Henryk Kruszczyński; tom 2: 143, Michał Sokolnicki; tom 2: 179, police statement.
30. Ob 271, tom 2: 109, Franciszek Kazmierski; see also tom 1: 14 and tom 2: 114.
31. SO Łódź 29: 41, Walter Piller.
32. 203 AR 609/61, Bd. 1: 79, Walter Piller; Bednarz: 72, Bruno Israel.
33. All entries from the *Chronicle* are taken from the respective date excluding the entry for Wednesday, July 5; see Ob 271, tom 4, folder in back, card from the Statistical Department of the Eldest of the Jews, Litzmannstadt Ghetto.
34. Srebrnik interview.
35. Ob 271, tom 2: 136, Józef Przybylski.
36. SAP 66: 25, Mordechai Żurawski.
37. Ob 271, tom 2: 165, Szymon Srebrnik; Bednarz: 72, Bruno Israel.
38. Ob 271, tom 4: 351, Roman T.
39. Eichmann Trial, Session 66, Szymon Srebrnik.
40. Ibid.

Final Liquidation of the Camp

1. *Chronicle*: 535.
2. Bednarz: 72, Bruno Israel; NTN 38: 742, Mieczysław Żurawski.
3. Ob 271, tom 1: 14, Henryk Kruszczyński; tom 1: 48, Andrzej Miszczak; tom 1: 71, Aleksander Woźniak. The bricks could still be seen over sixty years later on the grounds of the former estate.
4. Srebrnik interview.
5. SO Łódź 29: 42, Walter Piller.
6. 203 AR 609/61: 79, Walter Piller; Srebrnik interview.

7. 203 AR-Z 69/59, Bd. 4: 544, Gustav Laabs; Bednarz: 72, Bruno Israel. These vans have never been located.
8. Aharon Weiss, ed. *Yad Vashem Studies*, XXI. "The Testament of the Last Prisoners of the Chełmno Death Camp", Introduction by Shmuel Krakowski and Ilya Altman (Jerusalem: Daf Noy Press, 1991): 122. Hereafter cited as *Yad Vashem Studies XXI*. See also AZIH 301/3080, Icchek Tryter.
9. Helene J. Sinnreich, 'The Rape of Jewish Women during the Holocaust', in Sonja M. Hedgepeth and Rochelle G. Saidel, eds. *Sexual Violence against Jewish Women during the Holocaust* (Waltham, MA: Brandeis University Press, 2010): 113–14.
10. 203 AR 609/61, Bd. 1: 90, Walter Piller.
11. *Yad Vashem Studies* XXI: 110–11.
12. SSKW-Ł 1145: 7, Roman Orłowski, 10 Adam Rapaport.
13. Ob 271, tom 5: 442. After the war, Żurawski recovered the note and turned it over to the Bednarz investigation. Portions of this note appear today on the monument located on the grounds of the former forest camp. According to Żurawski, Izaak Sigelman wrote the note. (Żurawski may have been referring to Israel Zygelman.) However, the signature at the bottom does not appear to be that of Izaak Sigelman or variations thereof.
14. Srebrnik interview. Srebrnik was able to slip his feet out of the shackles and so was able to undress.
15. Eichmann Trial, Session 66, Szymon Srebrnik.
16. 203 AR 609/61, Bd. 1: 81, Walter Piller.
17. Srebrnik interview.
18. 203 AR 609/61, Bd. 1: 82, Walter Piller.

Chapter 4 Epilogue

Chełmno: 1945 to the Present

1. 203 AR 609/61, Bd. 1: 82, Walter Piller.
2. AZIH. Pamiętniki. 302/220 NN. *'Piekło Chełmna.'*
3. For a copy of the report, see 203 AR 609/61, Bd. 1: 46–48. A more detailed report was to have been submitted later.
4. The circumstances surrounding his death are unclear. One version of Waldman's death states he committed suicide (Gilbert: 816). A second version states he was killed by members of the Polish underground who suspected Waldman was working for the Soviet security services (Lorek interview, information based on conversations with local residents).
5. Ob 271, tom 6: 502. The photograph collection of IPN Warsaw includes three pages from the notebook, but the notebook itself appears to be lost.
6. For the list of catalogued items contained in 183 envelopes, see OKBZNwŁ 46.
7. Ob 271, tom 4: 380–82, 388–89; tom 9: 901–02. Letter to the author from Izydor Rekść, vice president of the district court of Łódź, February 26, 1992. As of this writing, the further fate of the objects themselves has not been determined.
8. Bednarz: 16–17.
9. Ob 271, tom 6: 504–17. Report of the Examination of the Synagogue, Jewish Committee Building and Ritual Baths in Koło, June 10, 1945.
10. Ob 271, tom 2: 164, Szymon Srebrnik; tom 4: 345, Mordechai Żurawski; Bednarz: 72, Bruno Israel.
11. 203 AR 609/61, Bd. 1: 79, Walter Piller.

12. OKBZNwW 46: 72.
13. Adalbert Rückerl, *The Investigation of Nazi Crimes 1945–1978: A Documentation* (Hamden, CT: Archon Books, 1980): 48, 52.
14. 203 AR-Z 69/59 Sammelakte Nr. 128. Urteil des Schwurgericht vom 30 III 1963.
15. *Justiz und NS-Verbrechen Bd. XXI*: 228.
16. 203 AR-Z 69/59 Sammelakte Nr. 128, Bd. 1. Urteil des Schwurgericht vom 30 III 1963.
17. For sentence reductions and reasons, see *Justiz und NS-Verbrechen Bd. XXI*: 262–64. Concerning Ernst Burmeister, see 203 AR-Z 69/59 Sammelakte Nr. 128, Bd. 2, Beschluss des Landgericht Bonn 8 Ks3/62 vom 15 IV 70.
18. S. L. Shneiderman, "Attention: The Bundestag in Bonn", *Congress Bi-Weekly* (February 15, 1965): 7–9.
19. The list is a composite drawn from: Ring. I 412; 301/376; Ob 271 tom 1: 11, 80; tom 2: 163, 165; tom 4: 344; S. 8/01/Zn: 236; *Yad Vashem Studies* XXI: 105–23 and Srebrnik interview. Note that the list includes the name of one woman, Hela Kowalska. This is the only mention that a woman worked in the camp. The source of the name is Żurawski.

The Number of Victims

1. 203 AR 609/61, Bd. 1: 46–47.
2. Bednarz: 29. In August 1945, the police (MO) in Koło was still reporting more than 1 million victims killed in Chełmno. See OKBZNwP 83. Sprawozdanie z ekshumacji zwłok: 9.
3. Dąbrowska: 126–27.
4. For an English language translation of the relevant portion of the document, see *Documents on the Holocaust*: 332–34.
5. See Appendix, The Gas Vans, note 38.
6. Dąbrowska: 122–84.
7. Martin Gilbert, *The Holocaust. The Jewish Tragedy: A History of the Jews of Europe during the Second World War* (New York: Henry Holt and Company, 1987): 241. Hereafter cited as *Gilbert*.
8. *Encyclopaedia Judaica* (Jerusalem: Keter Publishing House Ltd., 1972), vol. 10: 1305. Hereafter cited as *EJ*.
9. *Chronicle*: 143.
10. Ob 271, tom 9: 827.
11. See http://www.zchor.org/gombin/ghetto.htm, accessed May 25, 2010. Another source offers May 12, 1942, as the date when some 1,800 Jews were deported to Chełmno; see Guy Miron, ed. *The Yad Vashem Encyclopedia of the Ghettos during the Holocaust* (Jerusalem: The Holocaust Martyrs' and Heroes' Remembrance Authority, 2009): 203–04. Hereafter cited as *Encyclopedia of the Ghettos*.
12. *Encyclopedia of the Ghettos*: 79, cites a deportation date of mid-May, 1942.
13. *EJ*, vol. 4: 1427.
14. Ibid., vol. 4: 1430.
15. Isaiah Trunk, *Judenrat. The Jewish Councils in Eastern Europe under Nazi Occupation* (New York: Macmillan Publishing Company, 1972): 443. This is the source for both the date and the figure. *Encyclopedia of the Ghettos*: 567–8 cites a figure of approximately 2,000 deportees to Chełmno.
16. Ob 271, tom 9: 832.
17. Israel Gutman, ed. *Encyclopedia of the Holocaust* (New York: Macmillan Publishing Company, 1990): 159.

18. Ob 271, tom 9: 833.
19. *EJ*, vol. 16: 497.
20. Ld 139/23: 75.
21. *Chronicle*: 294.
22. *Encyclopedia of the Ghettos*: 977–78.
23. Ob 271, tom 9: 833.
24. Farbstein: 299.
25. Julian Baranowski, 'Zagłada Żydów z Kraju Warty i z Europy Zachodniej w Chełmnie nad Nerem': 19–25, and Janusz Gulczyński, 'Ośrodek zagłady w Chełmnie nad Nerem': 29–42, in *Ośrodek zagłady w Chełmnie nad Nerem i jego rola w hitlerowskiej polityce eksterminacyjnej. Materiały z sesji naukowej* (Konin: Muzeum Okręgowe w Koninie, 1995).

Conclusion and Reflection

1. 203 AR 609/61, Bd. 1: 65, Walter Piller; IPN Po 04/2718/1: 18, 21, 22–23; IPN Po 04/2718/2: 7, 49, 74; IPN Po 04/2718/3: 3, 6–7; S. 8/01/Zn: 34–39, 44–46, 253, 269–86, 966–70; KL Mauthausen Haftlings-Personal-Karten.

Appendices

Appendix I: The Gas Vans

1. Henryk Maliczak 1967: 261.
2. Henryk Mania 1967: 275.
3. For an account of this event, see Breitman: 194–96.
4. *Fateful Months*: 59–60.
5. Mathias Beer, 'Die Entwicklung der Gaswagen beim Mord an den Juden', *Vierteljahrshefte für Zeitgeschichte* 35/3 (1987): 409. Hereafter cited as *Mathias Beer*.
6. *Nazi Mass Murder*: 53–54.
7. *Fateful Months*: 62, and Mathias Beer: 414.
8. The bill is reproduced in Adam Rutkowski's *Męczeństwo, Walka, Zagłada Żydów w Polsce 1939–1945*.
9. 203 AR-Z 69/59, Bd. 4: 535, Gustav Laabs.
10. Ibid., Bd. 4: 613, Alois Häfele.
11. Ibid., Bd. 6: 968, Walter Burmeister.
12. 2 Ks 2/65, Bd. 9: 193, Fritz Ismer.
13. 203 AR-Z 69/59, Bd. 7a: 1227, Josef Islinger.
14. S. 8/01/Zn: 500, Zofia Frątczak.
15. Winer testimony, see page 98.
16. Podchlebnik testimony, see page 113.
17. Henryk Maliczak 1967: 261.
18. Henryk Mania 1967: 274.
19. Ibid.: 281.
20. Ibid.: 282, Henryk Maliczak 1967: 265, and S. 8/01/Zn: 8, police report based on interview with Mania.
21. 203 AR-Z 69/59, Bd. 6: 1031, Karl Heinl. Heinl stated the new vans arrived some two months later, an exaggerated period of time as these vans were seen by the gravediggers Winer and Podchlebnik in early January.
22. Ob 19: 246–47, Heinz May.

23. Ob 271, tom 1: 11, Michał Podchlebnik.

24. 203 AR-Z 69/59, Bd. 5: 875–76, Kurt Möbius.

25. There is an alternative history of the two smaller vans. According to this theory, these vans operated in the same manner as the original van, using cylinders of carbon monoxide. The theory is supported by the testimony of Szlama Winer, reporting his observations of these gas vans in the forest concerning the manipulation made by the driver (pushing a button on a "gas apparatus" in the cab of the van to begin the gassing). Winer makes it clear that the victims were gassed in the forest; he could hear the screaming begin following the driver's manipulations in the cab. Moreover, Winer never mentions the driver getting out of the cab and sliding under the van to connect the section of exhaust pipe to channel the gas into the van. This theory discounts the testimony of Podchlebnik, given in June 1945, when "everyone knew" the victims were killed with exhaust gas. The theory is also supported by the testimony of Henryk Maliczak, who clearly stated that these vans functioned just as the furniture van did, but were later converted to kill the victims using exhaust gas [Henryk Maliczak 1967: 265].

This alternative scenario is not supported by any documentation and specifically RSHA documents concerning the gas vans. Wentritt did not produce vehicles of this type. Therefore, Lange would have had to initiate their production, but again there is no documentation or testimony concerning their origin. Moreover, among the postwar testimonies from individuals who worked for companies that supplied the Sonderkommando with various types of provisions, there is no mention that cylinders of any kind were received [Ob 271: 31, 36, 41, 431, 716]. However, this does not rule out the possibility that the Sonderkommando procured the cylinders directly from Berlin, bypassing any intermediaries, as it did during the mobile killing operations. Nevertheless, Winer's compelling testimony and Maliczak's unequivocal assertion indicate the gap in knowledge concerning the original gas vans employed in Chełmno may be wider than previously thought.

26. 203 AR-Z 69/59, Bd. 6: 968, Walter Burmeister.

27. Ibid., Bd. 4: 523, Gustav Laabs.

28. Ibid., Bd. 6: 974, Walter Burmeister.

29. Ob 271, tom 1: 80, Wiktoria Adamczyk; tom 2: 108, Zygmunt Szkobel; tom 2: 141, Stanisław Śliwiński; tom 3: 206, Józef Dzięgielewski; tom 1: 70, Alexander Woźniak; as well as tom 3: 285, Kazimierz Gibaszek.

30. AZIH Ring I/394, Uszer Taube. Taube was a resident of Kłodawa who received this information from messengers sent to the village of Chełmno, in the December–January 1942 timeframe, and who questioned Chełmno residents to learn to fate of those deported there.

31. Ob 271, tom 1: 62, Józef Klonowski.

32. Ibid., tom 3: 285, Kazimierz Gibaszek.

33. Ibid., tom 3: 261, Bolesław Antkiewicz.

34. Ibid., tom 1: 69, Marianna Woźniak.

35. Ibid., tom 2: 113, Józef Budynek.

36. 203 AR-Z 69/59, Bd. 6: 968, Walter Burmeister.

37. 2Ks 2/65, Bd. 5: 209, Anton Sukkel.

38. For an English language translation of a portion of the report, as well as a photocopy of the original in German, see *Nazi Mass Murder*: 228–30.

39. Ob 271, tom 1: 17, Józef Piaskowski.

40. Ibid., tom 1: 28, Bronisław Falborski.

41. Ibid., tom 1: 43, Zenon Rossa. Rossa stated that this was in 1943, an obvious error.
42. Ibid., tom 2: 189, Michał Lewandowski.
43. Ibid., tom 1: 30, Bronisław Mańkowski.
44. Ibid., tom 3: 221, Jerzy Fojcik.
45. Ibid., tom 1: 42, Adam Swiętek. See also tom 1: 31, Wacław Nowacki.
46. Ibid., tom 1: 36, Zygmunt Antecki.
47. Ibid., tom 5: 431, Stanisław Bosiński.
48. Ibid., tom 8: 716, Jerzy Markiewicz.
49. Ibid., tom 3: 279, Józef Grabowski.
50. Ibid., tom 1: 17, Josef Piaskowski.
51. Ibid., tom 1: 30, Bronisław Mańkowski.
52. Ibid., tom 2: 119, Jan Grudziński.
53. Ibid., tom 3: 221, Jerzy Fojcik.
54. Bednarz: 72.
55. 203 AR-Z 69/59, Bd. 4: 544, Gustav Laabs; Bednarz: 72, Bruno Israel.
56. On April 24, 1950, the president of the Board of the Koło branch of the Union of Fighters for Freedom and Democracy (Związek Bojowników o Wolność i Demokrację – ZBoWiD) wrote a letter to Prof. Ludwik Rajewski with the Museums and Monuments of Struggle and Martyrdom to the Polish Nation in the Ministry of Culture and Art in Warsaw, informing him that a large vehicle used by the Nazis to gas people was located in Koło and, in his opinion, the vehicle should be secured and transported to the museum in Majdanek or Oświęcim (Auschwitz). About a month later, Prof. Rajewski raised the issue in a letter to the Main Commission for the Investigation of Nazi Crimes in Poland. In July 1950, the Main Commission informed the Museums and Monuments of Struggle and Martyrdom to the Polish Nation that, based on the results of the Bednarz investigation, the vehicle under consideration was used to disinfect clothing and not gas people [Ob 19: 102, 103, 105]. The van was forgotten and, exposed to the elements, the condition of the vehicle deteriorated and was finally hauled away and scrapped.

Appendix II: The Kaszyński Affair

1. SAP 67: 139, Andrzej Miszczak.
2. Janusz Gulczyński, 'Stanisław Kaszyński i próby ratowania Żydów z obozu zagłady w Chełmnie nad Nerem', *Kronika Wielkopolski* 1/97 (2001): 56.
3. Ob 271, tom 5: 434, Jan Oliskiewicz.
4. Oliskiewicz could not deny his involvement in the affair but, for political reasons, did all that he could with Polish investigators to minimize it.
5. Dorota Siepracka, 'Stanisław Kaczyński wobec eksterminacji Żydów w obozie zagłady w Chełmnie nad Nerem', in Alexandra Namysło, ed. *"Kto w Takich Czasach Żydów Przechowuje?..." Polacy Niosący Pomoc Ludności Żydowskiej w Okresie Okupacji Niemieckiej.* (Warszawa: Instytut Pamięci Narodowej, 2009): 234. Hereafter cited as *Siepracka*.
6. Zygmunt Walter Janke, 'Na Wywiadowczym Froncie', in Władysław Kazaczuk, ed. *Życie na krawędzi. Wspomnienia żołnierzy antyhitlerowskiego wywiadu.* (Warszawa: Czytelnik, 1980): 72.
7. Maria Tyszkowa, 'Eksterminacja Żydów w Latach 1941–1943', *Biuletyn Żydowskiego Instytutu Historycznego* 2–3 (162–163) (1992): 47–48.
8. Permission to publish the name of this person was not obtained.

9. Siepracka: 234.

10. Piotr Litka, Michał Olszewski. 'Żółte', *Tygodnik Powszechny* 3/3210, January 16, 2011: 5.

11. Zdzisław Lorek interview based on information collected from local residents.

12. Janusz Gulczyński, 'Stanisław Kaszyński i próby ratowania Żydów z obozu zagłady w Chełmnie nad Nerem', *Kronika Wielkopolski* 1/97 (2001): 57.

Appendix III: Fates of Key Figures

1. Naphtali Lau-Lavie interview, Henech Widawski correspondence.

2. Jacob Peled correspondence.

3. AZIH CKZP R 13763 [Karta Informacyjna nr 13763 o osobach ocalałych, Centralny Komitet Żydów Polskich – Wydział Ewidencji i Statystyki. Ocaleni rejestrowali się w oddziałach Centralnego Komitetu Żydów Polskich (CKZP)], Sara Roy correspondence.

4. Srebrnik interview, Hava Srebrnik correspondence.

5. Henech Widawski correspondence; Netty Kalman interview; Chava Stern interview; Chaim Grunfeld interview.

6. Srebrnik interview.

7. Mania 1967: 15; 203 AR 609/61, Bd. 1: 96, Hermann Gielow.

8. SO Łódź 5a: 188, 191; Ld pf 1/18–20: 38, 41.

9. *Time* magazine, June 18, 1951: 24.

10. 203 AR-Z 69/59, Bd. 4: 641–42, Walter Burmeister; ibid., Bd. 1: 73, Bothmann's death; Ob 271, tom 2: 199, Zofia Szacowna.

11. *Trials of War Criminals before the Nuremberg Military Tribunals under Control Council Law No. 10*. Nuremberg, October 1946–April 1949. Washington D.C.: U.S. G.P.O, 1949–1953.

12. 203 AR-Z 69/59, Bd. 6: 909–10, Ernst Burmeister, 203 AR-Z 69/59 Sammelakte Nr. 128, Bd. 2, Beschluss des Landgericht Bonn 8 Ks3/62 vom 15 IV 70.

13. 203 AR-Z 69/59, Bd. 4: 642, Walter Burmeister; ibid. Bd. 6: 967, Walter Burmeister.

14. 203 AR-Z 69/59, Bd. 4: 642, Walter Burmeister.

15. *Justiz und NS Verbrechen*, Bd. 22: 415–18.

16. SAP 67: 91, 135, 208, 212, Hermann Gielow.

17. 203 AR-Z 69a/59, Bd. 3: 477, Wilhelm Görlich.

18. Epstein: 326, 335. See also NTN 34–38, Janusz Gumkowski, *Zbrodniarze Hitlerowscy Przed NTN*: 78.

19. 203 AR-Z 69/59, Bd. 4: 602, Alois Häfele.

20. 203 AR 609/61, Bd. 2: 57, list of Sonderkommando members.

21. *Justiz und NS Verbrechen*, Bd. 21: 288.

22. SO Łódź 29: 45, Walter Piller; 203 AR 609/69, Bd. 1: 69, Hermann Gielow; SAP 60: 52, Heinrich Fink.

23. Epstein: 338; http://pl.wikipedia.org/wiki/Co_u_pana_s%C5%82ycha%C4%87%3F, accessed November 22, 2010.

24. 203 AR 609/61, Bd. 2: 58.

25. 203 AR-Z 69/59, Bd. 4: 556, Fritz Ismer.

26. SSKW-Ł 1237: 2, 37, 45, 84, Bruno Israel; 203 AR-Z 69/59, Bd. 9: 1704, death of Israel.

27. IPN Po 3/503; Adelbert Rückerl, *Nationalsozialistische Vernichtungslager*: 251.

28. SSKW-Ł 1146: 44–46, 61, Ld pf 2/1688: 1, 26.

29. 203 AR-Z 69/59, Bd. 4: 602, Alois Häfele; 203 AR-Z 69/59, Bd. 4: 558, Fritz Ismer.

30. 203 AR-Z 69/59, Bd. 4: 544, Gustav Laabs.
31. Adelbert Rückerl, *Nationalsozialistische Vernichtungslager*: 262.
32. Berlin Document Center, personal file of Herbert Lange; 203 AR-Z 69/59, Bd. 5: 703, death of Lange.
33. Ob 271, testimonies of Szymon Srebrnik, Mordechai Żurawski, Bruno Israel and Andrzej Miszczak.
34. 203 AR-Z 69/59, Bd. 5: 873, Kurt Möbius.
35. Ibid., Bd. 4: 559: Fritz Ismer.
36. Wacław Szulc, *Hitlerowski aparat wysiedleńczy w Polsce. Sylwetki głównych jego "Działaczy"*: 36.; Adelbert Rückerl, *Nationalsozialistische Vernichtungslager*: 248.
37. SO Łódź 29: 20, 152, Walter Piller; *Proces Biebowa*: 38.
38. 203 AR-Z 69/59, Bd. 2: 236, death of Plate; 203 AR-Z 69/59, Bd. 6: 1002, Walter Bock.
39. 203 AR-Z 609/61, Bd. 1: 96, Hermann Gielow; 203 AR-Z 609/61, Bd. 1: 53, Walter Piller.
40. SO Łódź 29: 60, 62, Erwin Schmidt.
41. 203 AR-Z 609/61, Bd. 1: 53, Walter Piller; 203 AR 609/61, Bd. 2: 69, list of Sonderkommando members.
42. SO Łódź 29: 45, Walter Piller.
43. SO Łódź 29: 45, Walter Piller.
44. 203 AR 609/61, Bd. 1: 65, Walter Piller; Ob 271, tom 4: 331; IPN Po 04/2718/2: 72; KL Mauthausen Häftlings-Personal-Karten.
45. 203 AR-Z 69/59, Bd. 6: 972, Walter Burmeister; S. 8/01/Zn: 31, Henryk Maliczak.
46. 203 AR 609/61, Bd. 1: 65, Walter Piller; IPN Po 04/2718/1: 22; S. 8/01/Zn: 30–33, 85, 260–68; KL Mauthausen Häftlings-Personal-Karten.
47. 203 AR 609/61, Bd. 1: 65, Walter Piller; IPN Po 04/2718/1: 18, 21, 22–23; IPN Po 04/2718/2: 7, 49, 74; IPN Po 04/2718/3: 3, 6–7; S. 8/01/Zn: 34–39, 44–46, 253, 269–86, 966–70; KL Mauthausen Häftlings-Personal-Karten.
48. Olszewski, Appendix; S. 8/01/Zn: 33, Henryk Maliczak; S. 8/01/Zn: 283, Henryk Mania.
49. Ob 271, tom 1: 50, Andrzej Miszczak; S. 8/01/Zn: 283, Henryk Mania.
50. Ob 271, tom 4: 335; S. 8/01/zn: 267, Henryk Maliczak; IPN Po 04/2718/1: 21; S. 8/01/Zn: 378; KL Mauthausen Häftlings-Personal-Karten.
51. Ob 271, tom 3: 259, Józef Grabowski; tom 4: 338, police report; S. 8/01/Zn: 582, Zdzisław Lorek.

Bibliography

I. Documents

Auschwitz–Birkenau State Museum [Państwowe Muzeum Auschwitz–Birkenau w Oświęcimiu]. Oświęcim, Poland.

   KL Mauthausen Häftlings-Personal-Karten.

Berlin Document Center. Berlin, Germany.
1. SS Personnel File: Hans Bothmann.
2. SS Personnel File: Herbert Lange.
3. SS Personnel File: Fritz Ismer.

Central Office of the State Justice Administration for the Investigation of National Socialist Crimes [Zentrale Stelle der Landesjustizverwaltungen zur Aufklärung Nationalsozialistischer Verbrechen]. Ludwigsburg, Germany.
1. 203 AR-Z 69/59.
2. 203 AR-Z 69/59 Sammelakte Nr. 128.
3. 203 AR-Z 69a/59.
4. 203 AR 609/61.

District Museum [Muzeum Okręgowe w Koninie]. Konin, Poland.
1. Ośrodek zagłady w Chełmnie nad Nerem i jego rola w hilterowskiej polityce eksterminacyjnej. Materiały z sesji naukowej, 24 kwietnia 1995.
2. Mówią Świadkowie Chełmna, 2004.

Harvard Law School Library. Nuremberg Trials Project. Online: nuremberg.law.harvard.edu
1. NO-244: Letter, Himmler to Greiser, June 27, 1942.
2. NO-246: Letter, Greiser to Himmler, May 1, 1942.
3. NO-247: Letter, Koppe to Brandt, May 3, 1942.
4. NO-249: Letter, Greiser to Himmler, November 21, 1942.
5. NO-250: Letter, Blome to Greiser, November 18, 1942.
6. NO-251: Letter, Himmler to Greiser, December 3, 1942.
7. NO-426: Deposition, Viktor Brack, October 14, 1946.
8. NO-2908: Letter, Koppe to Sporrenberg, October 18, 1940.
9. NO-2909: Letter, Rediess to Wolff, November 7, 1940.
10. NO-2911: Letter, Koppe to Wolff, February 22, 1941.

Holocaust Martyrs' and Heroes' Remembrance Authority (Yad Vashem). Jerusalem, Israel.
1. 03/2351. Testimony of Michał Podchlebnik (July 1963).
2. MIE 215/90. Testimony of Fiszel Brejtsztajn.

Institute of National Remembrance [Instytut Pamięci Narodowej]. Warsaw, Poland.

1. ASG 26. Kwestionariusz o egzekucjach masowych i grobach masowych.
2. ASG 54. Kwestionariusz o obozach i ghettach.
3. Najwyższy Trybunał Narodowy (NTN) 34–38. Akta w sprawie karnej Artura Greisera.
4. Ob 19. "The Great Lie. National Socialism as the German People Do Not Know It. A Report based on Experience," by H. May ["Die grosse Lüge: Chełmno, der Nationalsozialismus, wie ihn das deutsche Volk nicht kennt: Ein Erlebnisbericht," von H. May.]
5. Ob 271. Akta Śledztwa obozu straceń w Chełmnie.
6. OKBZN Łódź 35. Zakład dla umysłowo chorych w Kochanówku.
7. OKBZHwŁ 46. Chełmno nad Nerem – protokoły sądowych oględzin dokumentów wykopanych na terenie obozu.
8. OKBZHwW 144. Chełmno nad Nerem – obóz zagłady opracowanie dot. obozu.
9. OKBZNwP 83. Sprawozdanie z ekshumacji zwłok. Korespondencje.
10. SAP 60. Erich Adolf Stielau.
11. SAP 66, 67. Hermann Gielow.
12. SOŁódź 3-5a. Hans Biebow.
13. SOŁódź 29, 29a. Walter Piller.
14. SSKW-ł 1145, 1146. Rudolf Kramp.
15. SSKW-ł 1237. Bruno Izrael.
16. Zbiór 5 "Z." Eksterminacja umysłowo chorych.
17. Zbiór "Bd" 323. Ferdinand Göhler.

Institute of National Remembrance. Łódź, Poland.

1. Ld 139/5 t1-4. Łódź 1939–1945 Hitlerowska Polityka Eksterminacji.
2. Ld 139/23. Referaty i komunikaty na sesję naukową w Zduńskiej Woli w 45. rocznicę zagłady skupisk żydowskich w Kraju Warty.
3. Ld 139/46. Sesja naukowa Delegatura Powiatowa dla powiatu Łódzkiego.
4. Ld pf 1/18-20. (Fate of Hans Biebow.)
5. Ld pf 1/135-136 t1-2. (Fate of Stanisław Kapica.)
6. Ld pf 2/1688. (Fate of Rudolf Kramp.)

Institute of National Remembrance. Poznań, Poland.

1. Ds. III/9/71. Akta śledztwa w sprawie zbrodni na zakładnikach polskich w lesie rzuchowskim.
2. IPN Po 3/503. Zbrodnicza działalność Wilhelma Koppe'go.
3. IPN Po 04/2718/1, 04/2718/2, 04/2718/3. Akta kontrolne sprawy dochodzeniowej dot. zbrodniczej działalności na terenie obozu śmierci w Chełmnie.
4. OKP III S. 19/68. Akta dot. masowej eksterminacji Żydów w lesie koło Kazimierza Biskupiego.
5. S. 2/83. Akta dot. śledztwa w sprawie zamordowania ok. 1,500 osób jesienią 1941r. w lasach Niesłusz-Rudzica gm. Gosławice.
6. S. 3/00/Zn. Akta śledztwa w sprawie zagłady przez hitlerowsów pacjentów Szpitali Psychiatrycznych na terenie Kraju Warty w latach 1939–1945.
7. S. 8/01/Zn. Akta śledztwa w sprawie udziału Polaków – więźniów Gestapo w zbrodniach ludobójstwa dokonanych przez hitlerowskich zbrodniarzy w l. 1941–1945 w obozie zagłady w Chełmnie nad Nerem.

Jewish Historical Institute [Żydowski Instytut Historyczny]. Warsaw, Poland.

1. Centralny Komitet Żydów Polskich – Wydział Ewidencji i Statystyki [Central Committee of Polish Jews – Department of Records and Statistics].

   AZIH CKZP R 13763 [Karta Informacyjna nr 13763 o osobach ocalałych, Centralny Komitet Żydów Polskich – Wydział Ewidencji i Statystyki. Ocaleni rejestrowali się w oddziałach Centralnego Komitetu Żydów Polskich (CKZP)].

2. Getto Łódź [Łódź Ghetto]

   205/9. Korespondencja dotycząca akcji specjalnych, wypłaty poborów uczestników akcji specjalnych, dodatki specjalne do poborów w akcjach specjalnych.
   205/189. Korespondencja administracji getta z przedstawicielem Rzeszy w Kraju Warty.
   205/191. Korespondencja dotycząca wykonania ubrań ochronnych dla Chełmna nad Nerem.
   205/192. Korespondencja dotycząca przesiedlenia 20,000 Żydów.
   205/194. Korespondencja administracji getta.
   205/204. Korespondencja z DWHW.
   205/307. Notatki dotycząca rozmowy Hansa Biebowa.

3. Archiwum Ringelbluma [Ringelblum Archive]

   Ringelblum I, 394. Testimony of Uszer Taube.
   Ringelblum I, 412. Testimony of Jakub Grojnowski.
   Ringelblum I, 412/2. Registration Certificate of Jakub Grojnowski.
   Ringelblum I, 549/1. Postcard from A. Zontag.
   Ringelblum I, 549/2. Postcard from Mira Jachimiak.
   Ringelblum I, 596. "Winer Correspondence."

4. Relacje [Testimonies]

   301/153. Testimony of Jakub Waldman.
   301/265. Testimony of Andrzej Miszczak.
   301/269. Testimony of Wilczerah.
   301/370. Testimony of Andrzej Miszczak.
   301/371. Testimony of Andrzej Miszczak.
   301/376. Testimony of Mieczysław Żurawski.
   301/567. Testimony of Gedale Goldman.
   301/1002. Testimony of E. Herman. O Okrucieństwach Niemieckich w Stosunku do Umysłowo Chorych w Szpitalu w Kochanówce.
   301/1003. Testimony of Zdzisław Jaroszewski. Los Szpitala Psychiatrycznego w Owińskach w Czasie Wojny.
   301/1008. Testimony of Eugeniusz Wilczkowski. Los chorych psychicznie w szpitalu dla psychicznie i nerwowo chorych w Gostyninie w latach okupacji niemieckiej.
   301/1009. Testimony of Jan Gallus. Dziekanka w latach 1939–45 oraz jej udział w wyniszczeniu umysłowo chorych Polaków.
   301/3080. Testimony of Icchek Tryter.
   301/5349. Testimony of Miszczak.
   301/5350. Testimony of Miszczak, Srebrnik, Kaszyński.
   301/5354. Testimony of Domzal.

5. Pamiętniki [Memoirs]

302/220 NN. "Piekło Chełmna."

Mauthausen Memorial Archives [KZ-Gedenkstätte Mauthausen]. Vienna, Austria.

Entry Registers Y/36, Y/43, Y/44.

National Library [Biblioteka Narodowa]. Warsaw, Poland.

Microfilm Collection: *Gazeta Kolska*, 1934 (Mf. 57144), 1935 (Mf. 57145), 1936 (Mf. 57146), 1937 (Mf. 57147), 1939 (Mf. 57149).

Polish Underground Movement (1939–1945) Study Trust [Studium Polski Podziemnej]. London, England.

1. Aneks. Nr. 26 February 16–28, 1942. File 3.1.1.2.
2. Aneks. Nr. 28 March 16–21, 1942. File 3.1.1.2.

Public Prosecutor's Office Hannover [Staatsanwaltschaft Hannover]. Hannover, Germany.

2 Ks 2/65, Strafverfahren gegen Pradel und Wentritt.

Public Records Office [Urząd Stanu Cywilnego]. Izbica Kujawska, Poland.

Księgi Metrykalne Ludności Żydowskiej z lat 1905–1913, księga za 1911.

Public Records Office [Urząd Stanu Cywilnego]. Przedecz, Poland.

Księga urodzeń ludności żydowskiej Przedcza za lata 1902–1916.

State Archives in Poznań, Konin Branch [Archiwum Państwowe w Poznaniu Oddział w Koninie – APPoK]. Konin, Poland.

1. Akta Gminy Izbica Kujawska, sygn. 1291. Wykaz doręczonych kart powołania do odbycia służby czynnej wojskowej, poborowym zamieszkałym na terenie gminy Izbicy Kuj. Pow. Kolskiego.
2. Akta Gminy Izbica Kujawska [1848] 1870–1954, sygn. 1392. Rejestr poborowych rocznika 1916-go Gminy Izbica Kuj. Pow. Kolskiego 1934–1937.
3. Akta Gminy Izbica Kujawska [1848] 1870–1954, sygn. 1150 [nowa]/1142 [stara]. Wykaz absolwentów zatrudnionych w przemyśle i rzemiośle w os. i gminie Izbica Kuj. Pow. Kolskiego.

YIVO Institute for Jewish Research. New York, New York.

1. Adolf Eichmann Trial Transcripts, Sessions 65, 66, 94.
2. 3/22766A. Register of Jewish Survivors II.

II. Published Sources

Adelson, Alan, and Lapides, Robert, eds. *The Łódź Ghetto. Inside a Community under Siege*. New York: Viking Press, 1989.

Apenszlak, Jacob, ed. *The Black Book of Polish Jewry: An Account of the Martyrdom of Polish Jewry under Nazi Occupation*. New York: Howard Fertig, 1982.

Arad, Yitzhak. *The Holocaust in the Soviet Union*. Lincoln: University of Nebraska Press, 2009.

————. *Belzec, Sobibor, Treblinka. The Operation Reinhard Death Camps*. Bloomington and Indianapolis: Indiana University Press, 1987.

Arad, Yitzhak; Gutman, Yisrael; and Margaliot, Abraham, eds. *Documents on the Holocaust: Selected Sources on the Destruction of the Jews of Germany and Austria, Poland, and the Soviet Union*. New York: Ktav Publishing House in association with Yad Vashem and Pergamon Press, 1981.

Aronson, Yehoshua Moshe. *Alei Merorot: Yomanim, Shut, Hagut ba-Shoah* [Leaves of Bitterness: Diaries, Responsa, and Theology in the Holocaust]. Bnei Brak, 1996.

Baranowski, Julian. *Zigeunerlager in Litzmannstadt 1941–1942*. Łódź: Archiwum Państwowe w Łodzi & Bilbo, 2003.

Batawia, Stanisław. 'Zagłada Chorych Psychicznie.' *Biuletyn Głównej Komisji Badania Zbrodni Niemieckich w Polsce* III (1947): 93–106.

Bednarz, Władysław. *Obóz straceń w Chełmnie nad Nerem*. Warszawa: Państwowy Instytut Wydawniczy, 1946.

————. 'Obóz zagłady Chełmno.' *Biuletyn Głównej Komisji Badania Zbrodni Niemieckich w Polsce* I (1946): 147–61.

Beer, Mathias. 'Die Entwicklung der Gaswagen beim Mord an den Juden.' *Vierteljahrshefte für Zeitgeschichte* 35/3 (1987): 403–17.

Berenstein, T.; Eisenbach, A.; and Rutkowski, A., eds. *Eksterminacja Żydów na ziemiach polskich w okresie okupacji hitlerowskiej. Zbiór Dokumentów*. Warszawa: Żydowski Instytut Historyczny, 1957.

Binder, Jerzy. 'Śmierć czaiła się nad Nerem,' *Dziennik Łódzki*, 239/5340 (October 6–7, 1963): 3.

Blumental, N. *Słowa niewinne*. Kraków: Centralna Żydowska Komisja Historyczna, 1946.

————, comp. *Dokumenty i materiały z czasów okupacji niemieckiej w Polsce. Tom 1. Obozy*. Łódź: Wydawnictwo Centralnej Żydowskiej Komisji Historycznej, 1946.

Breitman, Richard. *The Architect of Genocide: Himmler and the Final Solution*. New York: Alfred A. Knopf, 1991.

Browning, Christopher. *Fateful Months: Essays on the Emergence of the Final Solution*. New York: Holmes and Meier, 1985.

————. *Nazi Policy, Jewish Workers, German Killers*. New York: Cambridge University Press, 2000.

————. *The Origins of the Final Solution: The Evolution of Nazi Jewish Policy, September 1939–March 1942*. Lincoln: University of Nebraska Press, and Jerusalem: Yad Vashem, 2004.

Burleigh, Michael. *Death and Deliverance: "Euthanasia" in Germany 1900–1945*. Cambridge: Cambridge University Press, 1994.

Chróścielewski, Edmund, and Celiński, Wiesław. 'Pseudoeutanazja w "Kraju Warty" podczas okupacji hitlerowskiej.' *Przegląd Lekarski* 25/1 (1969): 42–47.

Dąbrowska, D. 'Zagłada skupisk Żydowskich w "Kraju Warty" w okresie okupacji hitlerowskiej.' *Biuletyn Żydowskiego Instytutu Historycznego* 13–14 (1955): 22–84.

Dafni, Reuven, and Kleiman, Yehudit. *Final Letters: From the Victims of the Holocaust.* New York: Paragon House, 1991.

Datner, Szymon. *Ucieczki z niewoli niemieckiej 1939–1945.* Warszawa: Książka i Wiedza, 1966.

Datner, Szymon; Gumkowski, Janusz; and Leszczyński, Kazimierz. *Genocide, 1939–1945.* Poznań: Wydawnictwo Zachodnie, 1962.

Dawidowitz, Lucy S. *The War Against the Jews, 1933–1945.* New York: Holt, Rinehart and Winston, 1975.

Dobroszycki, Lucjan, ed. *The Chronicle of the Łódź Ghetto, 1941–1944.* New Haven and London: Yale University Press, 1984.

Eisenbach, Artur. "Operation Reinhard. Mass Extermination of the Jewish Population in Poland." *Polish Western Affairs.* Vol. 3, No. 1 (1962): 80–124.

———. *Hitlerowska polityka zagłady Żydów.* Warszawa: Książka i Wiedza, 1961.

———, comp. *Dokumenty i materiały do dziejów okupacji niemieckiej w Polsce. Tom 3. Getto łódzkie. Część 1.* Łódź: Wydawnictwo Centralnej Żydowskiej Komisji Historycznej, 1946.

Encyclopedia Judaica. Jerusalem: Keter Publishing House, 1972.

Epstein, Catherine. *Model Nazi: Arthur Greiser and the Occupation of Western Poland.* New York: Oxford University Press, 2010.

Farbstein, Esther. *Hidden in Thunder: Perspectives on Faith, Halachah and Leadership during the Holocaust.* Jerusalem: Mossad Harav Kook, 2007.

Fieg, Konnilyn G. *Hitler's Death Camps: The Sanity of Madness.* New York: Holmes and Meier, 1979.

Fijałek, Jan and Galiński, Antoni, eds. *Getto w Łodzi 1940–1944.* Łódź: Okręgowa Komisja Badania Zbrodni Hitlerowskich w Łodzi, 1988.

Fleming, Gerald. *Hitler and the Final Solution.* London: Hamish Hamilton, 1985.

Friedlander, Henry. *The Origins of Nazi Genocide: From Euthanasia to the Final Solution.* Chapel Hill and London: University of North Carolina Press, 1995.

Friedman, Philip. *Roads to Extinction: Essays on the Holocaust.* New York and Philadelphia: Jewish Publication Society of America and the Conference on Jewish Social Studies, 1980.

Gallus, Jan. 'Dziekanka w latach 1939–1945 oraz jej udział i rola w wyniszczaniu umysłowo chorych Polaków.' *Rocznik Psychiatryczny* 37/1 (1949): 75–91.

Gańczyk, Barbara. *Dzieci Hioba.* Kłodawa: Drukarnia Braci Wielińskich, 2000.

Gilbert, Martin. *The Holocaust: a History of the Jews of Europe during the Second World War.* New York: Henry Holt and Company, 1987.

Gorczyca, Krzysztof and Kapustka, Józef. 'Chełmno n/ Nerem, gm. Dąbie, woj. konińskie.' *Informator Archeologiczny* (1987): 213–14.

———. 'Chełmno n/ Nerem, gm. Dąbie, woj. konińskie.' *Informator Archeologiczny* (1988): 218.

Gulczyński, Janusz. *Obóz Śmierci w Chełmnie nad Nerem.* Konin: Wojewódzki Ośrodek Kultury w Koninie, 1991.

———. 'Stanisław Kaszyński i próby ratowania Żydów z obozu zagłady w Chełmnie nad Nerem.' *Kronika Wielkopolski,* 1/97 (2001): 54–58.

Gumkowski, Janusz and Kułakowski, Tadeusz. *Zbrodniarze Hitlerowscy Przed Najwyższym Trybunałem Narodowym.* Warszawa: Wydawnictwo Prawnicze, 1961.

Gutman, Israel, ed. *Encyclopedia of the Holocaust.* New York: Macmillan Publishing Company, 1990.

Hedgepeth, Sonja M. and Saidel, Rochelle G., ed. *Sexual Violence against Jewish Women during the Holocaust.* Waltham, MA: Brandeis University Press, 2010.

Hilberg, Raul. *The Destruction of the European Jews.* Revised and definitive edition. New York: Holmes and Meier, 1985.

———, ed. *Documents of Destruction: Germany and Jewry 1933–1945.* London: W. H. Allen, 1972.

Höhne, Heinz. *The Order of the Death's Head: The Story of Hitler's SS.* New York: Coward-McCann, 1970.

Horwitz, Gordon J. *Ghettostadt: Łódź and the Making of a Nazi City.* Cambridge, MA: The Belknap Press of Harvard University Press, 2008.

Huppert, Shmuel. "King of the Ghetto. Mordecai Haim Rumkowski, the Elder of Lodz Ghetto." *Yad Vashem Studies* 15 (1983): 125–57.

Instytut Pamięci Narodowej. *Proces Hansa Biebowa. Zagłada Getta Łódzkiego.* Informacja Wewnętrzna 91. Warszawa: Główna Komisja Badania Zbrodni Hitlerowskich w Polsce, 1987.

———. *Getto w Łodzi 1940–1944.* Łódź: Okręgowa Komisja Badania Zbrodni Hitlerowskich w Łodzi, 1988.

Jaroszewski, Zdzisław, ed. *Zagłada chorych psychicznie w Polsce 1939–1945.* Warszawa: Wydawnictwo Naukowe PWN, 1993.

Kaczmarek, Marian. 'Eutanazja w tzw. "Kraju Warty"', *Kronika Wielkopolski,* Nr 1/36 (1985): 69–81.

———. *Organizacja Poznańskiego Gestapo 1939–1945.* Żabikowo: Muzeum Martyrologiczne w Żabikowie, 2003.

Karski, Jan. *Story of a Secret State.* Boston: Houghton Mifflin Company, 1944.

Kazaczuk, Władysław, ed. *Życie na krawędzi. Wspomnienia żołnierzy antyhitlerowskiego wywiadu.* Warszawa: Czytelnik, 1980.

Kermisz, Józef, comp. *Dokumenty i materiały do dziejów okupacji niemieckiej w Polsce. Tom 2. Akcje i Wysiedlenia. Część 1.* Łódź: Wydawnictwo Centralnej Żydowskiej Komisji Historycznej, 1946.

Kershaw, Ian. *Hitler, the Germans, and the Final Solution.* Jerusalem, International Institute for Holocaust Research, Yad Vashem. New Haven and London: Yale University Press, 2008.

Klee, Ernst. *'Euthanasie' im NS-STAAT. Die 'Vernichtung lebensunwerten Lebens.'* Frankfurt: Fischer Taschenbuch Verlag, 1986.

Klee, Ernst and Dressen, Willi. *Got mit uns. Die deutsche Vernichtungskrieg im Osten 1939–1945.* Frankfurt: S. Fischer Verlag, 1989.

Klee, Ernst, Dressen, Willi, and Riess, Volker. *Schöne Zeiten. Judenmord aus der Sicht der Tater und Gaffer.* Frankfurt: S. Fischer Verlag, 1988.

Kłodziński, Stanisław. 'Egzekucja dr Czesława Zapędowskiego w Lasach Rzuchowskich.' *Przegląd Lekarski* 37, No. 1 (1980): 148–49.

Kogon, Eugen; Langbein, Hermann; and Rückerl, Adelbert, eds. *Nazi Mass Murder. A Documentary History of the Use of Poison Gas.* New Haven and London: Yale University Press, 1993.

Krakowski, Shmuel. *Chełmno: A Small Village in Europe.* Jerusalem: Yad Vashem, 2009.

Kulikowska, Anna. 'Okupacyjne wspomnienia ze Szpitala Psychiatrycznego w Gostyninie.' *Przegląd Lekarski* 34/1 (1977): 211–15.

Lang, Jochen von, ed. *Eichmann Interrogated: Transcripts from the Archives of the Israeli Police.* New York: Farrar, Straus & Giroux, 1983.

Lanzmann, Claude. *Shoah: An Oral History of the Holocaust.* New York: Pantheon Books, 1985.

Laqueur, Walter. *The Terrible Secret: Suppression of the Truth about Hitler's "Final Solution."* Boston: Little, Brown and Company, 1980.

Lask, I. M., ed. *The Kalish Book.* Tel Aviv: The Societies of Former Residents of Kalish and the Vicinity in Israel and the USA, 1968.

Lau-Lavie, Naphtali. *Balaam's Prophecy: Eyewitness to History, 1939–1989.* Cranbury, NJ: Cornwall Books, 1998.

———. *Zraniony Lew. Autobiografia.* Kraków: Wydawnictwo Znak, 1997.

Leszczyński, Julian. 'Z Dziejów Zagłady Żydów w Kraju Warty,' *Biuletyn Żydowskiego Instytutu Historycznego* 2/82, 1972: 57–71.

Lewin, Nora. *The Holocaust: The Destruction of European Jewry 1933–1945.* New York: Schocken Books, 1973.

Librowski, Stanisław. *Ofiary Zbrodni Niemieckiej spośród Duchowieństwa Diecezji Włocławskiej 1939–1945.* Włocławek: Księgarnia Powszechna i Drukarnia Diecezjalna, 1947.

Lifton, Robert Jay. *The Nazi Doctors. Medical Killing and the Psychology of Genocide.* New York: Basic Books, 1986.

Litka, Piotr, and Olszewski, Michał. 'Żółte,' *Tygodnik Powszechny* 3/3210 (January 16, 2011): 3–5.

Mączka, Stanisław. *Żydzi polscy w KL Auschwitz. Wykazy imienne.* Warszawa: Żydowski Instytut Historyczny, 2004.

Milczarek, Jan. 'Wymordowanie chorych psychicznie w Warcie,' *Przegląd Lekarski* 36/1 (1979): 115–19.

Miron, Guy, ed. *The Yad Vashem Encyclopedia of the Ghettos during the Holocaust.* Jerusalem: The Holocaust Martyrs' and Heroes' Remembrance Authority, 2009.

Muenzberg, Alicja. 'To był duży cmentarz,' *Gazeta Kościańska*, 21/2006 (May 24, 2006): 10.

Mujta, Józef Stanisław. *Miasto Dąbie w XIX i XX Wieku.* Konin: Wydawnictwo Apeks, 1998.

Muszkat, Marian. *Polish Charges against German War Criminals.* Warszawa: Główna Komisja Badania Niemieckich Zbrodni Wojennych w Polsce, 1948.

Nałkowska, Zofia. *Medaliony.* Warszawa: Czytelnik, 1961.

Namysło, Aleksandra, ed. *Zagłada Żydów na Polskich Terenach Wcielonych do Rzeszy.* Warszawa: Instytut Pamięci Narodowej, 2008.

———. "Kto w Takich Czasach Żydów Przechowuje?..." *Polacy Niosący Pomoc Ludności Żydowskiej w Okresie Okupacji Niemieckiej.* Warszawa: Instytut Pamięci Narodowej, 2009.

Nowicki, Przemysław. 'Zanim "przybył z zaświatów," nazywał się Winer. Krąg rodzinny i konspiracyjny Szlamka, uciekiniera z ośrodka zagłady w Chełmnie nad Nerem,' *Zagłada Żydów. Studia i Materiały* 5 (2009): 163–92.

———. 'O Abramie Roju, pierwszym uciekinierze z obozu zagłady na polskich terenach wcielonych do Rzeszy,' *Zapiski Kujawsko-Dobrzyńskie*, vol. 23 (2008): 185–200.

———. 'Wokół Szlamka. Szkic do portretu rodzin Łaskich i Winerów z Izbicy Kujawskiej,' *Zapiski Kujawsko-Dobrzyńskie*, vol. 22 (2007): 153–60.

Olszewski, Marian. *Fort VII w Poznaniu.* Poznań: Wydawnictwo Poznańskie, 1974.

Pawlicka-Nowak, Łucja. 'Wyniki Badań Archeologicznych Przeprowadzonych w Latach 2003–2004 na terenie Cmentarzyska byłego Ośrodka Zagłady w Chełmnie n. Nerem (Las Rzuchowski),' *Przeszłość i Pamięć* (Lipiec–Grudzień 2004): 84–87.

———. 'Chełmno n. Nerem – Relacja Ocalałego z Zagłady.' *Przeszłość i Pamięć* (Styczeń-Czerwiec 2001): 102–104.

Polish Ministry of Information. *The Black Book of Poland.* New York: G. P. Putnam's Sons, 1942.

Puławski, Adam. *W Obliczu Zagłady. Rząd RP na Uchodźstwie, Delegatura Rządu RP na Kraj, ZWZ-AK wobec deportacji Żydów do obozów zagłady (1941–1942).* Lublin: Instytut Pamięci Narodowej, 2009.

Rada Ochrony Pomników Walki i Męczeństwa. *Chełmno nad Nerem.* Warszawa: Wydawnictwo "Sport i Turystyka," 1969.

————. *Scenes of Martyrdom and Fighting of Jews on the Polish Lands 1939–1945.* Warszawa: Sport i Turystyka, 1978.

Reitlinger, Gerald. *The Final Solution.* London: Sphere Books, 1971.

Riess, Volker. *Die Anfänge der Vernichtung "lebensunwerten Lebens" in den Reichsgauen Danzig-Westpreussen und Wartheland 1939–45.* Frankfurt am Main: Peter Lange GmbH, 1995.

Rückerl, Adelbert. *The Investigation of Nazi Crimes, 1945–1978. A Documentation.* Hamden, CT: Archon Books, 1980.

————. *Nationalsozialistische Vernichtungslager im Spiegel deutschen Strafprozesse. Belzec, Sobibor, Treblinka, Chełmno.* München: Deutscher Taschenbuch Verlag, 1977.

Rüter, C. F., ed. *Justiz und NS Verbrechen. Sammlung deutscher Strafurteile wegen Nationlsozialistischer Tötungsverbrecher 1946–1966*, Bd. 7. Amsterdam: University Press, 1971.

————. *Justiz und NS Verbrechen. Sammlung deutscher Strafurteile wegen Nationlsozialistischer Tötungsverbrecher 1946–1966*, Bd. 21. Amsterdam: University Press, 1979.

————. *Justiz und NS Verbrechen. Sammlung deutscher Strafurteile wegen Nationlsozialistischer Tötungsverbrecher 1946–1966*, Bd. 22. Amsterdam: University Press, 1981.

Rutherford, Phillip T. *Prelude to the Final Solution: The Nazi Program for Deporting Ethnic Poles, 1939–1941.* Lawrence: University Press of Kansas, 2007.

Rutkowski, Adam. *Męczeństwo, Walka, Zagłada Żydów w Polsce 1939–1945.* Warszawa: Wydawnictwo Ministerstwa Obrony Narodowej, 1960.

Sakowska, Ruta. *Dwa Etapy. Hitlerowska polityka eksterminacji Żydów w oczach ofiar.* Wrocław: Ossolineum, 1986.

————. "Szlojme: der antlofener fun Chelmno." *Bleter far Geshikhte* 23 (1985): 215–18.

————, comp. *Archiwum Ringelbluma. Tom 1. Listy o Zagładzie.* Warszawa: Wydawnictwo Naukowe PWN, 1997.

Sereny, Gita. *Into that Darkness.* London: Pan Books, 1977.

Serwański, Edward. *Wielkopolska w cieniu swastyki.* Warszawa: Instytut Wydawniczy Pax, 1970.

————. *Obóz zagłady w Chełmnie nad Nerem 1941–1945.* Poznań: Wydawnictwo Poznańskie, 1964.

Sheiderman, S. L. "Attention: Bundestag in Bonn," *Congress Bi-weekly* (February 15, 1965): 7–9.

Szulc, Wacław. *Hitlerowski aparat wysiedleńczy w Polsce. Sylwetki głównych jego "Działaczy,"* (Informacja Wewnętrzna 26). Warszawa: Ministerstwo Sprawiedliwości, Główna Komisja Badania Zbrodni Hitlerowskich w Polsce, 1973.

Trials of War Criminals before the Nuremberg Military Tribunals under Control Council Law, No. 10. Nuremberg, October 1946–April 1949. Washington D.C.: U.S. Government Printing Office, 1949–1953.

Trunk, Isaiah. *Łódź Ghetto: A History.* Bloomington and Indianapolis: Indiana University Press, 2006.

———. *Judenrat. The Jewish Councils in Eastern Europe under Nazi Occupation.* New York: Macmillan Publishing Company, 1972.

Tyszkowa, Maria. 'Eksterminacja Żydów w Latach 1941–1943,' *Biuletyn Żydowskiego Instytutu Historycznego* 2–3, 1992: 47–48.

Wechsberg, Joseph. 'A Reporter At Large. The Children of Lidice.' *The New Yorker* (May 1, 1948): 34–51.

Weiss, Aharon, ed. Yad Vashem Studies XXI. *The Testament of the Last Prisoners of the Chelmno Death Camp,* introduction by Shmuel Krakowski and Ilya Altman. Jerusalem: Daf Noy Press, 1991: 105–24.

Wierzbicki, Tadeusz. 'Dzieje Państwowego Szpitala dla Nerwowo i Psychicznie Chorych im dra med. Józefa Babińskiego w Łodźi.' *Archiwum Historii Medycyny* 25/1 (1962): 27–70.

Witte, Peter. 'Two Decisions Concerning the "Final Solution to the Jewish Question": Deportations to Lodz and Mass Murder in Chelmno.' *Holocaust and Genocide Studies* 9/3, Winter 1995: 318–45.

Wojciechowski, Jacek. *Dominium Sławsk.* Konin: Wydawnictwo BPB "Arkada" Jacek Wojciechowski, 2005.

Yahil, Leni. *The Holocaust. The Fate of European Jewry.* New York: Oxford University Press, 1991.

III. Interviews and Correspondence

Klemens Rosiński. Chełmno, Poland. April 22, 1990.
Szymon and Hava Srebrnik. Nes Ziona, Israel. July 24, 1990; July 27, 1990.
Helena Wojtczak. Chełmno, Poland. April 22, 1990; May 16, 1991.
Adam Grabowski. Dąbie, Poland. September 13, 2006.
Zdzisław Lorek. Chełmno, Poland. September–October 2006.
Jacob Peled. Tel Aviv, Israel. April 4, 2008.
Hava Srebrnik. Nes Ziona, Israel. April 6, 2008; May 2, 2008.
Sara Roy. Boston, USA. January 2008–August 2009.
Henech Widawski. Antwerp, Belgium. June 25–26, 2009.
Naphtali Lau-Lavie. Jerusalem, Israel. July 29, 2009; January 10, 2010.
Netty Kalman. Tel Aviv, Israel. July 30, 2009; September 1, 2009.
Chava Stern. Tel Aviv, Israel. September 1, 2009.
Chaim Grunfeld. Tel Aviv, Israel. September 22, 2009.

IV. Photographs

AGO – Art Gallery of Ontario (Toronto, Canada)
BA – Bundesarchiv (Berlin, Germany)

BDC – Berlin Document Center (Berlin, Federal Republic of Germany)
FORUM – FORUM Polskiej Agencji Fotografów (Warsaw, Poland)
GPO – Government Press Office (Jerusalem, Israel)
HW – Henech Widawski (Antwerp, Belgium)
IPN – Instytut Pamięci Narodowej (Warsaw, Poland)
ŁPN – Łucja Pawlicka-Nowak (Konin, Poland)
PM – Patrick Montague (Warsaw, Poland)
SR – Sara Roy (Boston, USA)
YV – Yad Vashem (Jerusalem, Israel)
ŻIH – Żydowski Instytut Historyczny (Warsaw, Poland)
ZL – Zdzisław Lorek (Chełmno, Poland)

Index